Cultures of Abortion in Weimar Germany

Monographs in German History

Volume 1
Osthandel and Ostpolitik: German
Foreign Trade Policies in Eastern
Europe from Bismarck to Adenauer
Mark Spaulding

Volume 2
A Question of Priorities: Democratic
Reform and Economic Recovery in
Postwar Germany
Rebecca Boehling

Volume 3
From Recovery to Catastrophe:
Municipal Stabilization and Political
Crisis in Weimar Germany
Ben Lieberman

Volume 4
Nazism in Central Germany: The
Brownshirts in 'Red' Saxony
Christian W. Szejnmann

Volume 5
Citizens and Aliens: Foreigners and
the Law in Britain and the German
States 1789–1870
Andreas Fahrmeir

Volume 6
Poems in Steel: National Socialism
and the Politics of Inventing from
Weimar to Bonn
Kees Gispen

Volume 7
"Aryanization" in Hamburg:
Frank Bajohr

Volume 8
The Politics of Education: Teachers
and School Reform in Weimar
Germany
Marjorie Lamberti

Volume 9
The Ambivalent Alliance: Konrad
Adenauer, the CDU/CSU, and the
West, 1949–1966
Ronald J. Granieri

Volume 10
The Price of Exclusion:
Ethnicity, National Identity, and the Decline of
German Liberalism, 1898–1933
Eric Kurlander

Volume 11
Recasting West German Elites:
Higher Civil Servants, Business Leaders and
Physicians in Hesse between Nazism and
Democracy, 1945–1955
Michael R. Hayse

Volume 12
The Creation of the Modern
German Army: General Walther
Reinhardt and the Weimar Republic,
1914–1930
William Mulligan

Volume 13
The Crisis of the German Left: The
PDS, Stalinism and the Global
Economy
Peter Thompson

Volume 14
The 'Conservative Revolutionaries':
The Protestant and Catholic
Churches in Germany after Radical
Political Change in the 1990s
Barbara Thériault

Volume 15
Modernising Bavaria: The Politics of Franz Josef
Strauss and the CSU, 1949–1969
Mark Milosch

Volume 16
Sex, Thugs and Rock 'n' Roll: Teenage Rebels in
Cold-War East Germany,
1949-1957
Mark Fenemore

Volume 17
Cultures of Abortion in Weimar Germany
Cornelie Usborne

Volume 18
Selling the Economic Miracle:
Economic Reconstruction and Politics in West
Germany, 1949–1957
Mark E. Spicka

Volume 19
Between Tradition and Modernity:
Aby Warburg and the Public Purposes of Art in
Hamburg
Mark A. Russell

Volume 20
A Single Communal Faith?
The German Right from Conservatism to
National Socialism
Thomas Rohkrämer

Cultures of Abortion in Weimar Germany

Cornelie Usborne

Berghahn Books
New York • Oxford

First published in 2007 by
Berghahn Books
www.berghahnbooks.com

©2007 Cornelie Usborne

All rights reserved. Except for the quotation of short passages for the purposes of criticism and review, no part of this book may be reproduced in any form or by any means, electronic or mechanical, including photocopying, recording, or any information storage and retrieval system now known or to be invented, without written permission of the publisher.

Library of Congress Cataloging-in-Publication Data

Usborne, Cornelie, 1942-
 Cultures of abortion in Weimar Germany : the strategy of tension and the politics of nonreconciliation / Cornelie Usborne.
   p. cm. -- (Monographs in German history ; v 17)
 Includes bibliographical references and index.
 ISBN 978-1-84545-389-3 (hardback : alk. paper)
 1. Abortion--Germany--History. 2. Abortion--Social aspects--Germany. I. Title.

HQ767.5.G3U83 2007
363.460943--dc22

2007044787

British Library Cataloguing in Publication Data
A catalogue record for this book is available from the British Library

Printed in the United States on acid-free paper.

ISBN: 978-1-84545-389-3 (hardback)

Contents

List of Plates	vii
Preface	ix

1 **Towards a Cultural History of Abortion**   1
   Historical perspectives   8
   Cultures of abortion in Weimar Germany   19

2 **Cultural Representation: Abortion on Stage, Screen and in Fiction**   26
   Abortion in the movies   31
   The novel *Gilgi* and the female reader and spectator   40
   Socialist plays and novels   42
   Abortion pathologized   53

3 **Medical Termination of Pregnancy: Theory and Practice**   64
   The case of Dr Hartmann   67
   Abortion in the medical discourse   70
   Divided opinion within the medical profession   71
   Medical blunders and legal practice   76
   The case of Dr Hope Bridges Adams Lehmann   79
   Financial considerations   85
   Medical attitude and medical power   87
   Women's experience   90

4 **Abortion in the Marketplace: Lay Practitioners and Doctors Compete**   94
   The anti-quackery campaign   94
   Self-induced abortions   99
   Lay abortionists   102
   Gender and the abortionist   105
   The careers of 'wise women'   111
   The safety record of quack abortionists   114

	Methods and money	123
	Class differences and shared culture	125
5	**Women's Own Voices: Female Perceptions of Abortion**	127
	The construction of the criminal in abortion trials	130
	The experience of abortion	136
	'Blocked menses' (*Blutstockung*) as a popular lay concept	148
	Advertising abortifacients	151
	Women's sensory perceptions	154
6	**Abortion as an Everyday Experience in Village Life: A Case Study from Hesse**	163
	Rural communities in decline	167
	Female communication networks	174
	Reproductive *Eigensinn*	179
	Rebellious women and men	181
	Relations between the sexes	186
	The career of a successful abortionist	192
	Denunciation	195
	Conclusions	199
7	**Abortion in Early Twentieth-century Germany: Continuity and Change**	201
	Gender roles and gender relations	203
	The blurring of boundaries	209
	Continuity and change	214
	Abortion in Nazi Germany	216
	Continuity with Imperial Germany	223

Abbreviations	227
Notes	228
Bibliography	260
Index	279

List of Plates

1. Demonstration by communist *Rotfrontkämpferbund*, 19 August 1928, Leipzig (Bildarchiv Preussischer Kulturbesitz) — 2
2. Anja Zimowa as the modern wife, Maly Delschaft as the young teacher in *Kreuzzug des Weibes*, directed by Martin Berger, 1926 (ASDKB). — 32
3. Maly Delschaft as the young teacher, rape scene, *Kreuzzug des Weibes*, directed by Martin Berger, 1926 (Deutsches Filminstitut Frankfurt). — 32
4. Renée Stobrawa as Hete in Friedrich Wolf's play *Cyankali. §218*, Berlin, 1929 (Ullstein). — 43
5. Film poster, *Cyankali. §218*, directed by Hans Tintner (1930), Grete Mosheim as Hete, 'Madame Heye', the abortionist in the background. (Deutsches Filminstitut Frankfurt) — 46
6. Programme for Carl Credé's play *§218. Gequälte Menschen*, directed by Erwin Piscator, illustration by Käthe Kollwitz, 'At the Doctor's'. (Author's own copy) — 48
7. Poster for mass demonstration against §218, March 1922, Hackerkeller, Munich. It lists Dr Klauber and Wendelin Thomas, member of the Reichstag, but Dr Hartmann also spoke (BAB). — 73
8. Hope Bridges Adams Lehmann, September 1914 (Monacensia Literaturarchiv, Munich). — 79
9. *Mutterspritzen* and other douches, from mail-order catalogue *Medico*, Nurnberg, n.d. (SAM, Pol. Dir. 7250). — 100
10. Article about 'sexology, enforced procreation and mass misery', *Arbeiter Illustrierte Zeitung*, no. 30, 1928. — 106
11. Artificial miscarriage, guidelines for doctors by Professor Dr Georg Winter, 'Strittige Punkte in der Behandlung des fieberlosen Abortes', *Medizinische Welt*, vol. 1, 27 August 1927. — 123
12. Map of some of the seventeen Hesse villages. From top clockwise: Niederbrechen, Oberbrechen, Dauborn, Kirberg, Neesbach, Nauheim, Werschau. Limburg is to the north west along the railway. (Helmuth Gensicke, *750 Jahre 12350-1985 Werschau*, Limburg, 1985). — 168
13. Timbered buildings in Nauheim as it is today. (Photo: C. Usborne) — 169
14. Oberbrechen seen from a field above the village (Josef Kramm, *Brechen stellt sich vor*, 1974). — 169

List of Plates

15. Werschau seen with a donkey in the foreground (Josef Kramm,   171
    Brechen stellt sich vor, 1974).
16. Oxcart in Dauborn, 1936 (K.H.W. Schmidt, *Dabornaha.*   173
    Die Geschichte eines Dorfes und seiner Landschaft, Dauborn, 1984).

Preface

Abortion has been legalized in many Western countries in the last three decades or so and yet it remains controversial and a subject which is never far away from the news.[1] In March 2006 the American state of Dakota passed the most sweeping ban on abortion in more than thirty years and provoked what one newspaper report called an 'epic confrontation' by 'activists on either side of the abortion divide – the great faultline of American politics'.[2] Hardly a year goes by without a private member's bill in the British parliament to reverse the liberal abortion law reform of 1967.[3] As I write, a referendum has been won in Portugal on a proposal for abortion on demand which would end 'one of Europe's harshest abortion laws'.[4] In May 1991 the disagreements over the abortion law threatened to split the German coalition government and in January 1998 German Catholic theologians called for a campaign of disobedience against a papal edict on abortion counselling.[5] The new German Pope Benedict continues to wrestle with the dilemma.[6] Abortion remains newsworthy because women of all classes, creeds and ethnicity continue to terminate their unwanted pregnancies in spite of laws criminalizing abortion and religious dogma condemning it, just as they have always done. It reveals women's agency in exercising control over their lives and destinies, which is why abortion remains controversial to this day in societies that are still essentially patriarchal. In Weimar Germany abortion was practised not just as a back-up to other contraceptive methods but often as the first choice of family limitation; in the great majority of cases women were able to terminate unwanted pregnancies successfully and without harm to themselves. What is more, hundreds of thousands did so and influenced the law, public policies and official attitudes to women's social role.

I originally set out, many years ago for my doctoral thesis, to study women's reproductive behaviour in Weimar Germany; as my archival research progressed, however, and I found file after bulging file containing evidence of abortion reform campaigns and the reaction to this in official circles, another story began to emerge, more amenable to historical study. This was the evolution from an anti-abortion society to one in which it was increasingly condoned. At the beginning of the Weimar Republic abortions rose sharply but were officially condemned and heavily penalized; during the Depression it was estimated that the abortion rate exceeded the birth rate and the authorities of state, law and even the Protestant – though not the Roman Catholic Church – were increasingly accommodating the changing demographic behaviour. The result of this research was my monograph, *Politics of the Body in Weimar*

Germany: Women's Reproductive Rights and Duties (1992) which provides the sociopolitical context for this book. It explores how abortion features in popular culture but focuses mainly on women: how abortion affected their relations with husbands or lovers and how they experienced it, whether it was performed by family members or friends, professional abortionists or doctors.

Court records proved an invaluable source for my investigation but there were some anxious moments when it looked as if the German law on personal data protection would bar me from studying them. I was familiar with and had respected this law in my previous publications; but so worried were some archivists about letting me loose on what they regarded as delicate and compromising personal data that only protracted negotiations secured my access. Photocopies of records would have to be made anonymous by blanking out all proper names. I argued that this made it impossible to establish sexual, family and work relationships, understand their material circumstances or indeed recognize when individuals were accused a second or third time of criminal abortion. In one instance I was told to swear on the Bible to uphold the law and protect the secrets of my historical subjects. I accepted – but not before securing a better site than outside the gents' lavatories for this ceremony. The table with the Bible was moved, my oath was sworn and access was granted to what turned out to be very rich material indeed. In deference to the data protection law all proper names of suspects, accused or defendants in criminal abortion trials have been changed in this book but care has been taken to choose new names with an appropriate regional flavour. Only personalities well known at the time have retained their real names, either because they were familiar to the public from their political or professional role or because they gained notoriety through their involvement in a sensational court case which was covered extensively in the contemporary press.

Registered medical practitioners attempted to gain a professional monopoly by marginalizing or even outlawing lay practitioners whom they called 'quacks'. In the interest of legibility the words quacks or quackery will be used without quotation marks, which does not, however, indicate that I share contemporary doctors' prejudices against their competitors in the medical market.

During its long gestation, the embryonic project has been nourished by the support and advice of many colleagues and friends: different parts of my research were discussed in London by the Modern German History Seminar and the Women's History Seminar (both at the Institute of Historical Research), the Wellcome Institute for the History of Medicine and the History Workshop Seminar; in History seminars at the universities of Cambridge, Manchester, Roehampton, Southampton, Surrey and Sussex; in Germany at the universities of Hanover and Magdeburg; and at conferences in Britain, Germany, Ireland, Italy, the Netherlands and the U.S.A. I am grateful for the many valuable comments I received. There is not the space to thank everyone by name or convey the extent of my indebtedness but I owe a special debt to Lynn Abrams,

Preface

Meg Arnot, Anna Bergmann, Richard Bessel, Kelly Boyd, Barbara Brookes, Kathleen Canning, Gabie Czarnowski, Anna Davin, Ross Dickinson, Barbara Duden, Isa van Eeghen, Richard Evans, Karin Friedrich, Johanna Geyer-Kordesch, Marijke Gijswijt-Hofstra, Karin Hagemann, Anne Hardy, Liz Harvey, Karin Hausen, Robert Jütte, Annette Kuhn, Eva Labouvie, Machteld Löwensteyn, Angus McLaren, Elisabeth Meyer-Renschhausen, Jinty Nelson, the late Roy Porter, Lyndal Roper, Mark Roseman, Adelheid von Saldern, Lutz Sauerteig, Jürgen Schlumbohm, Reinhard Spree, Nick Stargardt, Pat Thane, Richard Wetzell and John Woodward. Many scholars helped me with advice and finding material of early films: Heide Schlüpmann, Ursula von Keitz, Reinhard Kämpf and Malte Hagener. Several people read earlier versions or portions of the manuscript, and I thank them for their encouragement and criticism: Willem de Blécourt, Kathleen Canning, Liz Harvey, Matthew Jefferies, Sabine Kienitz, Dorothy Rowe, Katharina Rowold and Susan Tegel. My research trips in Germany were made more enjoyable by the generous hospitality offered on numerous occasions by my friends Steffi Gäbler, Gudrun von Rimscha and Katja Schwalb, my brother Werner Tücking and his wife Marliese, my niece Eva Tücking, my cousin Ursula Hornack (who selflessly drove us round the many villages in Hesse which feature in Chapter 6) and Peter and Gudrun Tücking. In Berlin I was always welcomed by Anna Bergmann, Gabie Czarnowski, Elisabeth Meyer-Renschhausen, Carola Sachse and Karen Schönwälder.

An unusual number of midwives finally delivered me from the burden of my labour: the five other members of my brilliant writing group, Lucy Bland, Clare Midgley, Alison Oram, Krisztina Robert and Katharina Rowold did some exacting close reading of several chapters and gave wonderful advice for how to improve them. Jenny Willis was, as always, invaluable for polishing my English. This book would not have been conceived or completed without the support of my husband, Willem de Blécourt, who was not only a constant source of inspiration and comfort but also acted as a daily reminder of how much still needed doing, spurring me on to bring this project to fruition. My children, Nicola and Martin, managed to divert my attention in a most delightful manner and my grandsons Jesse and Caspar, very much wanted children, set the perfect counterpoint to the sombre theme of this book.

Last but not least I owe a debt of gratitude to the many (now anonymous) women I found in the archives and on whose stories I base much of my book. I have come to admire their strength of character in the face of adversity and their determination to fight their corner in the male-dominated world of law and medicine.

For their financial support I am grateful to the Wellcome Trust and the Leverhulme Trust for Research Leave Awards, and to the British Academy, The Wellcome Trust, the Scouloudi Foundation and The German Academic Exchange Service for research travel grants.

Previous versions of the following chapters appeared in articles in journals and edited volumes and are used here, substantially reworked and extended, by kind permission of the publishers or editors. 'Rebellious Girls and Pitiable Women: Abortion Narratives in Weimar Popular Culture', *German History*, special issue on 'Sexuality in Modern German History', 23(3) (2005), 321-38. 'Heilanspruch und medizinische Kunstfehler. Abtreibungen durch Ärzte in der Weimarer Republik: offizielle Beurteilung und weibliche Erfahrung', *Medizin, Gesellschaft und Geschichte*, 19 (2000), 95-122 (Wiesbaden, Franz Steiner). 'Wise Women, Wise Men and Abortion in the Weimar Republic – Gender, Class and Medicine', in Lynn Abrams, Elizabeth Harvey (eds), *Gender Relations in German History – Power, Agency and Experience from the Sixteenth to the Twentieth Century* (London, 1996), 143-175. 'Abortion for Sale! The Competition between Quacks and Doctors in Weimar Germany', in Marijke Gijswijt-Hofstra, Hilary Marland and Hans de Waardt (eds), *Illness and Healing Alternatives in Western Europe* (London and New York, 1997), 183-204. '"Gestocktes Blut" oder "verfallen"? Widersprüchliche Redeweisen über unerwünschte Schwangerschaften und deren Abbruch zur Zeit der Weimarer Republik', in Barbara Duden, Jürgen Schlumbohm and Patrice Veit (eds), *Geschichte des Ungeborenen. Zur Erfahrungs- und Wissenschaftsgeschichte der Schwangerschaft, 17.-20. Jahrhundert* (Göttingen, 2002), 293-326. 'Female Voices in Male Courtrooms – Abortion Trials in Weimar Germany', in John Woodward and Robert Jütte (eds), *Coping with Sickness. Medicine, Law and Human Rights – Historical Perspectives* (Sheffield, 2000), 91-106.

London
February 2007

◈ Chapter 1 ◈

TOWARDS A CULTURAL HISTORY OF ABORTION

In July 1918, when the First World War was in its final throes, a large delegation from the German women's movement assembled in front of the Reichstag to protest against the Imperial government's bill to ban contraception and tighten the surveillance of abortion. Using the language of civil rights, these women demanded the bill be scrapped as an 'insupportable interference into the free right of women's self-determination'.[1] In February 1919, only three months after the Revolution in November 1918, which granted women the vote, and a month after the January election of a Constituent Assembly of the new Weimar Republic which was committed to political equality for men and women, the issue of abortion mobilized women again. This time a group of self-declared ordinary women in Berlin sent a resolution to the Constituent Assembly demanding the repeal of part of the abortion law, §218 of the penal code,[2] in respect of married women with three children and single women 'who can prove that they are victims of seduction or of their own irresistible passion', presumably a reference to women's sexual freedom fostered by wartime conditions, the discourse of sex reform and revolutionary concessions to gender equality.[3] Such forthright action was followed by a number of other determined efforts by women from the grass roots to gain access to abortion. In June 1919 a petition arrived at the Prussian Ministry of Justice from Erfurt in Thuringia with the following text:

> Many women are urgently requesting the revision of §218 and §219. The abortion law should have been repealed a long time ago. For wealthy childless women have the means and way to do this and a poor woman is branded a criminal and punished with penal servitude. This, too, should be remedied. Every woman should do with her body as she wishes.

It was simply signed: 'Many women.'[4]

1. Demonstration by communist *Rotfrontkämpferbund*, 19 August 1928, Leipzig

Astonishingly, such ideas of women's biological rights had been voiced even earlier by feminists in Germany: for example, in 1904 by Countess Gisela von Streitberg (alias Gertrud Countess von Bülow Dennewitz) and, two years later, by Dr Helene Stöcker, the founder in 1905 of the radical sex reform organization, *Bund für Mutterschutz* (League for the Protection of Motherhood).[5] In 1908 the Federation of German Women's Organizations (*Bund deutscher Frauenvereine*), the huge bourgeois arm of the German women's movement, demanded a repeal of the abortion clause in order for every woman to be '*Herrin ihres Körpers*' (master of her body).[6] The important difference between Imperial (1871-1918) and Weimar Germany (1918-33) in this respect was that before the First World War such strongly feminist demands were voiced exclusively by women of the educated elite, whereas after it, the campaigns against §218 involved ordinary women, especially lower-class women who participated regularly, passionately and on a very large scale. As newly enfranchised citizens, their views directly influenced parliamentary debates, political programmes, legal reform, health policy and the attitudes of the Churches.[7] Popular protest rallies reached a peak in 1931 during the height of the Depression when many thousands of women were mobilized under the communist slogan *Dein Körper gehört Dir!* (Your body belongs to you!). This veritable people's storm against §218 consisted of 'ordinary' women, socialists, liberals and sex reformers. It was sparked off by two events: the publication on New Year's Eve 1930 of the Papal Encyclical *Casti Connubii* (On Christian Marriage) and the arrest, in February 1931, of two left-wing doctors in Stuttgart on suspicion of procuring illegal abortions.[8] Such public protest and a mass violation of the law, estimated at over one million illegal abortions in 1931, was an important sign of women exercising their citizenship rights but also ensured that the issue of abortion was catapulted to a central position in public policy on health and welfare, sexual morality and judicial reform. The private decisions of women and their partners had become the focus of high politics.

This public protest and the ensuing political debates and policies are, however, not the focus, merely the dramatic context to the abortion narratives explored in this book. My aim is rather to shed light on a much more neglected area of reproductive history, namely the circumstances and perceptions of women terminating their unwanted pregnancies, the reactions by third parties and the law enforcement agencies as well as the detailed narratives of women experiencing the various practices. My study thus forms the companion volume of my earlier *The Politics of the Body in Weimar Germany*, which explored the public discourse about birth control; this volume aims to explore the history from below, to make visible the more hidden practices and private encounters between predominantly lower-class women and their helpers. This book employs a cultural approach to the past, on the one hand, in that it seeks to make visible the web of meanings attached to terminations of unwanted pregnancies in everyday life, but, on the other, it also analyses the representation of abortion in Weimar feature films, plays and novels. How much agency did women have who sought to rid themselves of an unwanted pregnancy? Did they share the attitudes expressed by pro- or anti-abortion reformers in the public discourse or did they have an altogether different agenda? How important for women and their partners was the commercial sector of lay abortionists and pedlars of menstruation pills and potions? How did women and men find an abortionist? Were lay operators as dangerous and ruthless as claimed by the medical profession? What role did husbands or boyfriends play in the planning and the execution of an abortion? What shaped women's own perceptions of pregnancy and its termination? Did feature films and novels convey dominant ideas of women's roles and reproductive choice or did they subvert these? Finally, how were perceptions and actions shaped by gender, class, denomination, age and location?

In this introductory chapter I will discuss, first, the pivotal position of abortion and its regulation in the sociopolitical history of modern Germany and subsequently comment critically on the historiography of abortion relating to Germany and beyond, the 1920s but also to earlier and later periods. This is followed by pointing out the major theoretical and methodological approaches used in my study. Finally I elucidate, chapter by chapter, the narrative thread and the structure of the argument of the study which follows.

The history of Germany in the twentieth century can be read against the background of §218. Each regime's regulation of abortion was informed by and reflected the contested and changing relationship between private and public, family and state, personal procreative strategies and population policy, health professionals and individual women, and last but not least men and women. In Wilhelmine and Weimar Germany abortion proved an explosive issue because it concerned the least acceptable aspect of fertility control at a time of a rapidly declining birth rate and changing gender roles.[9] As Carroll Smith-Rosenberg has argued, abortion functions like 'a sexual language through which divergent gender, economic, regional and religious groups discuss issues of social change and social conflict far broader than the fate of fetuses or even the sexual rights of adult women.'[10] Between the first German unification in 1871 and the reunification of the Federal Republic of Germany (FRG) and the German Democratic Republic (GDR) in 1990 the changes to the abortion law constituted a fine barometer of the social status of women, official family policy and views on sexual mores. It can be said that time and again women's bodies were used as battle flags of the political agenda of various governments.

§§218–220 of the penal code of the newly unified Reich reflected and reinforced patriarchal, authoritarian and pronatalist notions. For the first time in legal history abortion was punishable at any time of gestation and enshrined the medical principle of the animation of the embryo at conception.[11] According to the legal historian Eduard Seidler, the 1871 penal code did not explicitly define the embryo as a human being and retained the moment of birth as the beginning of life; this meant that in the new law of 1871 abortion was not deemed as destruction of independent life but only of the conditions which made subsequent life possible.[12] Nevertheless, in the new criminal code the abortion clauses featured under the rubric of 'crimes against life' and prescribed draconian penalties.

In the more liberal climate of the Weimar Republic this law was derided by the political left, left-leaning doctors, the radical women's movement as well as by many novelists, poets, playwrights, artists, filmmakers and, last but not least, many thousands of women from all walks of life. The law was amended in 1926, liberalizing it for aborting women, i.e. women who had terminated their own unwanted pregnancies or had done so with the help of others. This was achieved despite the volatility of the political situation, the Catholic Centre Party, an important partner within the Weimar coalition, hindering radical social reforms, and the reluctance of jurists to anticipate the planned overhaul of the entire penal code. The new law consolidated the three clauses into a single clause, §218, and declared simple abortion, i.e. a woman's action to terminate her unwanted pregnancy, a misdemeanour of the pregnant woman and her accomplice, rather than a crime against life; it also reduced the maximum penalty for a woman from penal servitude to ordinary imprisonment, although the penalty for commercial abortion or abortion without consent was increased.[13] Moreover, in 1927 a decree of the Supreme Court permitted therapeutic abortion, making the German regulation of abortion one of the most liberal in the world.[14]

This permissive legislation was quickly reversed by a number of repressive measures and laws during the Third Reich (1933–45), whose attempt to control women's reproductive capacity is unparalleled in recent history. The Nazi dictatorship tightened state surveillance and increased the penalties for commercial abortionists dramatically from November 1933; during the Second World War the death penalty was introduced and aborting women, too, were treated more harshly. Moreover, as Gabriele Czarnowski has shown, in the new racial state the entire approach to abortion had fundamentally altered: instead of a crime against life it became a crime against the *Volk*, the race and the 'genetic heritage' (*Erbgut*) 'by urging or coercing abortion for "hereditarily diseased" women and those of "alien races" while simultaneously restricting, prosecuting and increasing the penalties for abortion on women of the preferred "race" of "valuable" or "flawless hereditary stock"'. This, according to Czarnowski, ensured that the state assumed for the first time the unlimited 'right to dispose of the embryo' as it saw fit.[15]

After the Second World War the two new German states, wishing to shake off their Nazi heritage, repealed the laws stipulating the death penalty and compulsory abortion on eugenic grounds; they also legalized abortion after rape and reintroduced the permissibility of abortion on grounds of ill health.

In the 1970s both the GDR and the FRG introduced bills to liberalize the abortion law further, though with different results. In 1972 the GDR legalized abortion on demand within the first three months of pregnancy, thereby realizing the dream of radical reform by Social Democrats in the Weimar Republic.[16] Two years later a similar West German abortion bill, passed by both houses of parliament, was declared illegal by the Supreme Court. In 1976 a revised law enacted by the ruling Social Democratic-Liberal coalition replaced the so-called time-limit model – that is, permitting a termination of pregnancy within a certain period of gestation – with a more restricted 'indication model', that is, permitting abortion on medical, genetic, social and criminological grounds but making the aborting woman subject to tight medical control.[17] These two legal approaches to abortion in the GDR and FRG provoked a protracted political conflict in the reunited Germany after the 'turning point' of 1989/90. Although East German female critics contended that the GDR law was motivated less by women's right to self-determination than the state's interest in the female labour force, and despite suggestions in the West, that East German women lacked an ethical approach, the GDR negotiators refused to relinquish their own law and adopt the West German abortion law. The issue was sufficiently contentious to be taken out of the newly adopted criminal code for the united Germany and the abortion regulation remained unresolved until December 1992, with the existing laws of the 'old' and 'new' *Länder* remaining in force. After a tortuous debate in the Bundestag, no less than seven draft bills were tabled, reflecting the different stances between and within the various parties, with an additional cross-bench proposal initiated by a cross-party coalition of women members of the Bundestag. This latter bill, called *Law on Aid for Pregnant Women and for Families*, was adopted in June 1992 with the majority votes of all parties. The new law prescribes counselling instead of punishment, prevention instead of repression; however, it fails to grant women the final word on whether to terminate a pregnancy or not. The imposition of compulsory registration of every abortion, the counselling procedure and the ban on financing a termination through sickness funds, all laid down by the Constitutional Court, presupposes the clear underlying premise that 'unborn life' needs protection and a termination should only be allowed 'under exceptional circumstances'. East German women forfeited their right to better access to safe terminations, and for West German women, too, the new law was far more interventionist than the previous regulations. Moreover, as Czarnowski has pointed out, the law constituted an important departure from previous laws: 'for the first time in legal history, the foetus was accorded an independent right to life' which has 'far-reaching consequences for all pregnant women, not just those who decide to have an abortion'.[18]

The new 1992 law was decisively shaped by both the Protestant and Catholic churches, whose views on unborn life had traditionally influenced state policies and in turn were influenced by medical science. The Christian churches' perceptions of pregnancy had been predicated since antiquity on the imagined stages of development of the embryo and quickening, the sensory onset of movement. Before the nineteenth century, canon law had adopted Aristotelian and Augustine theories that the foetus was not ensouled until forty or eighty days after conception, depending on whether it was male or female. A premature expulsion of the 'fruit' (*Frucht*) was then acceptable as it was viewed as inanimate; after this period it was considered as murder.[19] At the beginning of the nineteenth century new findings of embryology, however, made these notions untenable. Human-like forms of the foetus detected by microscope had brought about the new claim that the embryo was ensouled at conception.[20] This persuaded church circles to adopt a different language; they now talked about *keimendes Leben* (literally 'germinating life') or even of a 'child' in the womb at every stage of pregnancy. In one aspect canon law remained constant, at least in the Roman Catholic church, namely in the condemnation of every 'direct abortion', that is, any intervention which aimed to kill the foetus, even if it constituted the only chance to save the life of the mother. This dogma stemmed from the teaching of the eighteenth-century moral theologian Alfons von Ligori, who distinguished between direct and indirect abortion. The former referred to an operation which consciously aimed to destroy the foetus; the latter referred to the unintentional side effect of a medical intervention to save a mother's life and it was tolerated only if doctors were convinced that the operation or treatment was absolutely necessary to save not only the mother but also the embryo. Ligori's teaching remained influential for at least two centuries and by the time of the Weimar Republic it was apparent in canon and secular law and accepted in wider religious, official, and medical circles.[21]

I have discussed the influence of Christian dogma and its adapting to changed scientific paradigms elsewhere[22] and this is not the place to rehearse it again in detail. The insistence by both Christian churches on the dogma that life begins with conception was nevertheless extremely important, the more so since it was voiced by Christian men and women in all walks of life. This was despite the fact that the Protestant Church, since its disestablishment after the Revolution of 1918, had more difficulty in projecting a unified stance on issues of sexual morality, and individual pastors, Protestant doctors or politicians were more ready to compromise dogma under social pressure. One Catholic doctor put it like this: 'The medical termination of pregnancy with the intention to kill the child is a sin, a grievous, outrageous sin.'[23] Spokesmen of the Protestant church conveyed a similar message. While a medical termination was permitted on strictest health grounds and after rape, they agreed with Catholics that the *werdende Kind* (the nascent child) was not 'part of the mother's body which one has the right to dispose of'.[24] Friedrich Lönne, director of a maternity hospital in the Rhineland and therefore likely to have been a Catholic himself or at least respectful of Catholic sentiments, and a much quoted authority in government circles, expressed the opinion of the medical profession in his book *Das Problem der Fruchtabtreibung* (The Problem of Abortion), published in 1924 with a preface by the *Oberreichsanwalt* (chief public prosecutor) Ludwig Ebermayer. Lönne declared that 'the vitality of the foetus begins with the union of ovum and semen'.[25] Another Catholic doctor asserted that 'once pregnancy has occurred ... a living being exists which has the right to live'.[26] This led many conservative medical men to refer to abortion as an 'artificial intervention in foetal life' (*künstlicher Eingriff in das keimende Leben*), as 'destruction' (*Beseitigung*) or 'killing of an embryo' (*Abtötung einer Leibesfrucht*) or even the murder of 'a child in the womb'. Even pronounced champions of an extensive reform of §218 like Alfred Dührssen, the left-wing professor of gynaecology in Berlin, spoke about 'nascent life'[27] which he felt called upon to protect. But all doctors were keen to distinguish permissible therapeutic terminations of pregnancy performed by them from criminal quack abortions, not only to win support for their claim to a monopoly in this field, as we will see in Chapter 3, but also to overcome the strictures of the Hippocratic oath which, at least in the context of that time, rendered every artificial miscarriage problematical. Medical terminations were to be executed quite differently from quack abortion, the former relying on specific training and knowledge.[28] Georg Winter, the doyen of German gynaecologists during the Weimar Republic, called a termination of pregnancy 'without parallel in that it could both constitute a crime punishable by penal servitude and also be supremely valued as a life-saving operation'. He and most other doctors pleaded therefore that the 'two meanings should not be confused in contemporary language'.[29] A 'quack abortion' or 'criminal expulsion of the fruit' (*kriminelle Fruchtabtreibung*) should be linguistically clearly distinguished from a legitimate 'termination of pregnancy', also referred to as 'induced miscarriage' (*künstliche Frühgeburt* or *Abort*) rather than *Abtreibung* (abortion).[30]

Historical Perspectives

For a long time abortion received little attention from historians. Angus McLaren, one of the most prolific authors on sexuality, has suggested that this was because abortion was not considered a 'respectable' subject of research. He was one of the first to make amends in the late 1970s, albeit only in a single chapter in a study of nineteenth-century birth control in England focusing mainly on contraception.[31] There are many reasons why abortion as a topic of historical research was avoided. In the modern period public commentators tended to associate abortion with sexual immorality. Before the First World War, aborting women tended to be either unmarried or widowed and were perceived as seeking to destroy the fruits of illicit love. Abortion also represented the visceral aspects of reproduction and proved distasteful to many men; many women were also disturbed by what Smith-Rosenberg termed 'fetal life, violence to a woman's reproductive organs, the retention or expulsion of a foreign body suddenly found within one's own'.[32] The history of abortion as an uncomfortable subject revealed rebellious women who strove to be in charge of their own physical destiny, refusing to conform to socially ascribed roles of maternity, ignoring medical advice and apparently undaunted by legal sanctions and police investigations. As McLaren has put it, abortion 'was a female form of birth control and historians are reluctant to accept the notion that women would play an active part in determining family size'.[33]

Many historians writing in the past forty years or so seem to have shared such perceptions that the subject was not fit for study rather than countering them by historicizing past attempts to terminate unwanted pregnancies and contextualizing them with reference to pertaining cultural attitudes and socioeconomic circumstances. As a result a thorough discussion of abortion as an important means of birth control has been strikingly absent from many a classic text on fertility control: Norman Himes's 1936 medical history of contraception, reissued unrevised in 1963, is one example; another is J.A. Banks's 1954 study of family planning among the Victorian middle classes.[34] When abortion was emerging as a subject in post-Second World War historiography, church historians were amongst the earliest authors and naturally they concentrated on the moral dimension,[35] followed by statistical studies in which abortion featured as the unacceptable face of fertility control.[36] Abortion was less open to the quantitative analysis so central in these projects since its illegality ensured that no reliable statistics of its occurrence existed. Moreover, the phenomenon of abortion could only be adequately explained by searching for ideological, political and cultural reasons for demographic change, and these were usually outside the remit of such studies. Demographers usually adopted modernization theories and explained lower fertility by a mixture of socioeconomic changes. In these accounts the arrival of smaller families featured as a beneficial development and one which was achieved through a vertical diffusion of contraceptive knowledge from the upper to the lower classes.[37]

It is no coincidence that abortion emerged as a historical subject in its own right in the form of the campaigning literature during the political struggle in the early 1970s to decriminalize abortion in West Germany. This political analysis of abortion was often written by journalists rather than historians and it emerged in Germany earlier than in other Western European countries or the United States. The two best-known German publications by Luc Jochimsen (1971) and Petra Schneider (1975) extolled the left-wing campaign for abortion law reform during the Weimar Republic.[38] Jochimsen's and Schneider's books grew out of the resurgence of the post-Second World War feminist movement in West Germany, which had taken its cue from the widespread protest by women in the Weimar Republic against the anti-abortion clause 218 of the 1871 penal code. Thus, the two books reveal a direct nexus between historical research and political commitment: it was a socialist journalist and a historian disillusioned with the demands and tactics of the 1970s West German campaigns who sought information and inspiration from those who fought fifty years earlier. Both authors argued that during the Weimar Republic abortion was the last resort for desperate women of the lower classes who needed to limit their family size out of economic hardship. As a result of social inequality, according to these authors, poor women suffered appalling injuries or even death through unprofessional operations while rich women could buy the cooperation of doctors and circumvent the law. These two books had an electrifying effect on the 'autonomous' German women's movement and (despite a number of factual errors and some very selective source material) have much influenced subsequent research both in empirical data and underlying assumptions. They initiated a spate of literature celebrating the radical reformers who had fought for better access to safe, effective and affordable termination of pregnancy at a time when illegal abortions were estimated at an annual rate of between 250,000 to one million and thus reclaimed a movement that had disappeared into relative oblivion through systematic repression in the Nazi period. This type of campaigning literature was also a refreshing departure from the more traditional clerical and demographic interpretations of fertility control from above, whose inadequacy at explaining the intensity of passions about the abortion issue was thereby revealed. Such was the impact of these campaigning writers that the approach to birth control as a political history of women's rights has remained dominant among women historians in Germany to this day.[39] Feminist scholars started to associate the regulation of abortion with patriarchy and chart women's campaigns to reform the law as a struggle for reproductive freedom and women's biological self-determination. This in turn influenced the social history of medicine and history of the body to arrive at a much more nuanced interpretation of the meaning of abortion in modern Germany and elsewhere.[40]

Anglo-American feminist research on this subject emerged in the mid-1970s in the form of a pathbreaking political history by two socialist feminists, Linda Gordon in the U.S.A. and Sheila Rowbotham in Britain.[41] They, too, focused not only on sex reform and especially radical women reformers in the early twentieth century but also offered a vision forward in the struggle for reproductive rights. More importantly, they set the agenda for future research by establishing the vital link between the history of sexuality, class struggle and the power relation between men and women. As Gordon put it, 'there is a complex, mutual causal relationship between birth control and women's overall power. Birth control was as much a symptom as a cause of larger social changes in the relations between the sexes.'[42] Gordon established a careful definition of birth control to encompass all efforts to improve women's control over reproduction including contraception, abortion and infanticide or child abandonment. This was very different from the technical definitions adopted by demographers and a huge step forward from the often undifferentiated approach by historians who used terms such as 'birth control', 'contraception' and 'population control' as if they were interchangeable.[43] Rowbotham's book anticipated many later studies by revealing an early English history of radical feminist campaign for women's reproductive control in the shape of Stella Browne. Gordon's and Rowbotham's studies were of crucial importance for future feminist analyses in Europe and America, as is evident in the important work of McLaren, Smith-Rosenberg, Rosalind Pollack Petchesky and Barbara Brookes, all exemplary for an exploration of the question from the angle of women's reproductive choice.[44]

One of the great values of the feminist analysis developed in these books is that it has argued convincingly that women's reproductive behaviour is not biologically but rather historically determined; in other words, that there is a close connection between women's choice to reproduce or not to reproduce and their social, political and cultural situation. Abortion is not a timeless phenomenon but one that differed greatly according to gender, age, class, occupational and educational background, geographical area and period. In Petchesky's words, a sociocultural approach helps 'to free us and our theory from the oppressive persistence of the "body eternal"'.[45] The insistence on investigating the social relations of reproduction implies a double challenge: firstly, to contextualize the abortion experience in order to make it fully comprehensible and, secondly, to use this knowledge to enrich our understanding of the society at the time. Abortion is a fundamental issue for women and for the distribution of power within the gendered society, or as Petchesky put it, 'abortion is the fulcrum of a much broader ideological struggle in which the very meanings of the family, the state, motherhood, and young women's sexuality are contested. How else to explain the intensity and ferocity of these attacks?'[46] It was indeed an important consideration for social historians of England,[47] but especially historians of early twentieth-century Germany who set out to tackle the subject within a wider framework of welfarism and women's social and biological role. As far as Weimar Germany is concerned, we cannot make sense of the mass rallies clamouring for a repeal of §218 or the passionate debate about the New Woman and the alleged destruction of the family, or indeed the bitter tensions between the sexes and the generations without providing an insight into abortion reform within the wider debates at the time about socioeconomic and cultural change.[48]

In contrast, other historical accounts discussed the practice of abortion as if it were a timeless and biologically rooted process because they situated it inadequately in specific circumstances at specific times when particular decisions of fertility control were taken. Edward Shorter's *History of Women's Bodies* is one such example. He displayed considerable disrespect for the historical context of evidence in the way he quite uncritically produced figures from different regions and periods to support his central argument: women were traditionally less healthy than men and were only released from the terrible historic burden of their own physical weakness by doctors whose advances in medical science overcame most women's diseases and who offered women relatively safe abortions and thereby control over their fertility. Women's reproductive capacity, according to Shorter, was intrinsically a source of danger and only transformed into a life-giving force through the use of birth control.[49]

This approach is typical of other accounts based on the assumption that fertility control is a product of modernization, that a declining birth rate was the consequence of modern techniques or methods invented by the medical profession and distributed commercially under the control of doctors. This kind of determinism is based on the erroneous belief that it was technology rather than social structures or cultural communications which persuaded Western societies to limit the size of their families. As feminist historians have argued forcefully, abortion and contraceptive practices, like demographic change, have more to do with changes in the social relations of reproduction, than with technology. For example, in societies in which women have considerable political and economic power, whether this is derived from educational opportunities, employment patterns, inheritance law or strong networks among female kin, work colleagues or neighbours, there will normally be good access to effective fertility control. Where these conditions do not exist and where motherhood is women's only or most significant source of power, access to fertility control will be significantly limited.[50] Shorter's disciple, James Woycke, is another example of the positivist school of birth control.[51] Although he denies 'technological determinism', much of his analysis is founded on just such a belief. He admits that 'there is no agreement on the ultimate cause of the [German] fertility decline' but he nevertheless asserts that 'modern birth control techniques [lie] behind the fertility decline of the late nineteenth century'. This argument is advanced despite the evidence (acknowledged by Woycke elsewhere in his book) that the most common form of birth control continued to be coitus interruptus closely followed by abortion, as had been the case in preindustrial societies. Abortion, Woycke claimed, was made possible 'on a large scale' in Germany by the 'new products and new medical procedures' which had become available in Germany since the turn of the century, and these ensured that women 'increasingly sought out doctors' rather than quacks.[52] This emphasis on methods rather than social circumstances ignores the fact that abortion is historically and culturally constructed. As Carroll Smith-Rosenberg has put it, although abortion was practised at all times and in all cultures 'social responses to women's and men's desires to terminate specific pregnancies have differed sharply between and within cultures'.[53] The decisions by so many hundreds of thousands of German women to rid themselves of unwanted pregnancies were based on changes in their social conditions and altered attitudes to their role in society as well as on personal hopes and wishes.

Woycke's uncritical use of countless medical journals and unpublished medical dissertations to buttress his main argument ensures an uncritical reproduction of the inherent biases of medical and official beliefs. Such sources offer insights into official reactions to the declining birth rate, but they are unsatisfactory or indeed misleading about popular ideas and behaviour, and thus present a skewed view of history as a whole.[54] The social historian of medicine Paul Weindling also bemoaned the fact that Woycke had omitted 'to probe the biases of official, professional and political interest groups' and to attempt to utilize published medical commentaries to explain popular reproductive behaviour.[55] Unfortunately, Weindling's own vast survey of health policies in modern Germany also does not satisfactorily engage with the problem of abortion: a mere five pages are devoted to the subject and much of it is based on secondary research and situated only within eugenics during the Depression.[56] It took women scholars, such as Anna Bergmann, Atina Grossmann, Elisabeth Domansky and Ute Planert to offer a gendered critique of German population policy.[57] For example, Anna Bergmann, in her nuanced reinterpretation of the population debate in imperial Germany, subverted medical positivism through a critical reading of government and parliamentary papers, legal and medical journals; she went as far as describing late nineteenth- and early twentieth-century contraceptive and abortion technology as 'a risky gamble with death' and symbolic of a male medical 'negation of and aggression towards female fertility'.[58]

Legal historians like James Mohr for the U.S.A. and Günter Jerouscheck for Germany have explored historical developments of the criminalization of abortion and the legal changes thereafter. Jerouscheck argues that legalization of abortion in German history was tightened in the Enlightenment due to populationist concerns, especially to preserve the life of children born out of wedlock.[59] Mohr's book stressed the role of physicians in this process which served their own crusade to secure the professionalization of medicine and enlist the state's help to employ sanctions against their competitors.[60] In such legal histories the aborting woman appears either not at all or merely as a target of the law.

This is in stark contrast to socialist–feminist historians such as Gordon and Rowbotham, who insisted that women's adoption of birth control was a realm of activity that not only structured their lives but was consciously shaped by them. This approach to women as subjects, not objects of history was indeed of crucial importance to subsequent feminist theorists such as Michele Barrett, Mary O'Brien and Rosalind Petchesky.[61] Shorter's *History of Women's Bodies* is remarkable in that it hardly deals with the female body (it is in fact about female genitalia) nor women in charge of their own bodies or indeed their lives; this was precluded by false assumptions and a myopic selection of sources, none of which offer any insight into how women themselves viewed birth control.

In Germany, as elsewhere, the history of abortion has mostly been a history written from above which focused on the politics of reproduction control and elite discourse and thus marginalizes or even ignores grassroots attitudes altogether.[62] This is not surprising since the historian has relatively easy access to the pronouncements of those who dominated the public debate: in Weimar Germany there is an abundance of sources about attitudes to §218, be it in the form of parliamentary papers, medical journals, ecclesiastical sources, campaigning literature or newspaper reports of demonstrations of the vociferous reform movements. In contrast, it is much more difficult to discover how abortion was actually practised. After all, few women or men left incriminating written sources about their involvement in illegal abortions. It was far too risky. The law did not just prescribe penalties for the aborting woman but also particularly harsh penalties for professional abortionists, whether regular doctors or lay operators. Moreover, accomplices of aborting women – husbands, family members or friends who knew, encouraged or supported a woman's quest for a termination of her unwanted pregnancy – were all punishable under §218. Paradoxically, however, the same circumstances which muffled the free speech of aborting women and their helpers also created vital source material for the historian: the judicial files of criminal abortion cases. The fact that these have not been exploited fully is probably partly due to the problem of access because of the stringent application of the German rules protecting personal data, and partly due to a reluctance to engage with sources that are difficult to evaluate. In addition to such criminal records, we have some rare surveys by a Berlin doctor on women's and men's attitudes towards the practice of abortion, made possible because of the special trust he was able to establish with his patients, who seem to have candidly answered his questions about very intimate matters.[63]

If we are to avoid the pitfalls of studying abortion exclusively from above we need to consult such sources and go beyond government, parliament and medical circles. In consulting a broader range of sources in my own book I have drawn inspiration from Angus McLaren's 1978 study of birth control in nineteenth-century England.[64] In order to trace the opinions and behaviour of the consumers of birth control he evaluated popular tracts, quack literature, pornographic tracts, Grub Street journalism and literary works such as Defoe's *Moll Flanders* as well as newspaper advertisements. Moreover, as a result of consulting judicial files of criminal abortionists McLaren suggests that abortion was not as dangerous as opponents claimed. Only unsuccessful abortion cases came to light and the very fact that certain drugs were recommended from generation to generation suggests that they were not dangerous and probably effective. McLaren was also in a position to reject the 'cultural diffusion' theory, i.e. the belief that birth control knowledge percolated down the social scale, though he was less able to provide evidence for his thesis that birth control knowledge was shared amongst women of the working-classes. For his book *Reproductive Rituals* which examined early modern and modern England, McLaren had to rely on an even broader source base ranging from almanacs, folk-songs, proverbs, to court reports and literary accounts.[65]

Until recently most feminist investigations did not contain first-hand accounts of women's views. Petchesky, for example, vows to portray women 'as conscious agents of reproductive processes' but relies in practice predominantly on a very imaginative and astute assessment of secondary sources which do not allow her to explore the female point of view. Petchesky freely admits that 'because of insufficient evidence' definite judgements about various aspects of popular practice cannot be made.[66] Until recently most other authors seem to have relied mainly on medical and official sources,[67] although Hera Cook has shown how to illuminate women's situation and attitude by a feminist reading of such sources.[68]

A breakthrough occurred with the work of Patricia Knight and Mary Chamberlain and later Kate Fisher, who gave us an insight into popular perceptions and practices in the realm of reproduction control by uncovering sources written by women themselves and through oral history.[69] Barbara Brookes, too, in her study of abortion in twentieth-century England, set out to discover the 'realm of intimate personal experience' and 'explore the female subculture where women shared information on abortion, and to look at the intersection between women's culture, medicine, law and public policy'. Brookes certainly went some way towards this task with the help of criminal depositions, a crucial source for reconstructing the organisation and experience of abortion from below. As a result we learn much about why women decided to undergo the operation, about different methods, different prices charged and different policing, conviction rates and penalties for doctors and non-doctors. Yet, because only those cases came to light which had resulted in medical complications or death, and the fact that the aborting women were generally reluctant to give evidence so as not to implicate themselves, the picture had to remain incomplete. Moreover, there is in Brooke's analysis a subtle bias against nonmedical abortions, evident not only in the references to 'amateur operators', 'amateurs', 'sharks' 'women without medical expertise' but also in an underlying assumption that only operations by qualified doctors were desirable, reliable and risk-free.[70] The demonization of the 'back-street abortionist', however, was a useful strategy by doctors of the time in their campaign to medicalize birth control and abortion. In reality, as I will argue below, the picture was far more complex. If we are to reconstruct it we need to challenge the hegemony of academic medical thinking and the positivist heritage we have internalized for so long. Only if we approach the history of abortion from below and try and discover the practice by and the voice of individual women and men can we begin to understand how they viewed an event which was part of their daily life because they themselves had terminated a pregnancy or knew this from friends, relatives or neighbours.

Janet Farrell Brodie's 1993 study of birth control in nineteenth-century America also uses a new kind of primary source to chart the diffusion of knowledge of reliable contraceptive methods and devices as well as abortifacients: chemists' catalogues, patent records, advertisements, business papers, gynaecological advice literature and morality leagues' publications. While it is very good on the manufacturing and retailing of contraceptives and abortifacients, the organization and experience of abortion plays a very secondary role. The book also makes much of the New York abortionist Madame Restell, the one case which has already received ample historical treatment.[71] The film historian Ursula von Keitz, in a masterful study of abortion and reproduction as represented in the feature film of the Weimar Republic, is able to illuminate not only how elite discourses influenced film but how this new mass culture reacted to the dramatic changes in reproductive behaviour.[72] Another study of abortion in nineteenth- and twentieth-century America by Leslie Reagan corrects the image of the victimized aborting woman by showing that she often had much more choice and agency, even with doctors, than is usually admitted. Reagan demonstrated the power of female patients to influence medical practice, which suggests that doctors were more involved in abortion than their frequent public hostility would suggest. As well as drawing on medical literature she has consulted some legal records from lower-level court and criminal trial records, and coroners' inquests which recorded the statements of dying women about the abortionists who had caused their fatal injuries or illnesses; this enables her to present a very subtle picture of women's perceptions and their ability and or lack of it to voice their concerns.[73]

Most historians of reproductive policies in Weimar Germany, women historians included, adopted the pattern of the dominant discourse about abortion law reform at the time which was divided into two camps: those, usually on the political left, who wanted the law liberalized or even repealed, and those, usually on the political right, who wanted the existing law upheld but better policed.[74] To take, for example, Kristine von Soden's fine study of the movement for sexual advice centres in Weimar Germany: here working-class women are portrayed as innocent targets of the 'draconian abortion law' which was constructed and administered by bourgeois society. She assumes the vantage point of the contemporary political left, especially the communist women's organizations as well as the medical profession in whose eyes underprivileged aborting women were victims of unscrupulous back-street abortionists and of lethal attempts at self-help.[75] Yet the perpetuation in recent studies of this division in Weimar Germany into reformers and upholders of the abortion legislation obscures a different division of equal significance, that between official disdain for abortion per se and popular acceptance of it as a legitimate method of birth control. In this last constellation of official versus popular views we find the old adversaries united against common foes, the 'deviant woman' neglecting her duty to procreate and the 'quack abortionist' leading her astray and ruining her health because of greed. But unlike the drama between abortion reformers and their opponents, which was played out before the public in parliament, street demonstrations, party political rallies, newspapers, on stage and in film, this second drama was never enacted in the open. Instead, it appeared in the public discourse only obliquely because the main protagonists were in agreement: the medical profession, politicians, churchmen and -women, even sex reformers and feminist leaders all regarded the voluntary termination of a pregnancy, especially by a layman or -woman, as unacceptable. Even for those on the left who sought to legalize it, abortion remained a necessary evil needing the strictest regulation and medical control. Abortion, it was implied, would become superfluous in a society in which inequality was abolished, everyone had proper access to social welfare, and medical problems endangering the health of a pregnant woman would be overcome through medical progress. The assumptions behind this judgement were rarely questioned.

Atina Grossmann's study of the German sex reform movement at the end of the Weimar Republic concurs with my own findings that it was in the interest of abortion reformers in the medical profession to exaggerate the possible dangers resulting from illegal abortion. Grossmann rightly dismisses the suggestion that abortion was necessarily dangerous: 'in fact, many women did not bleed to death or commit suicide but survived reasonably safe abortion performed by doctors or competent "quacks"'.[76] As we have seen, the popular and political representation of the aborting woman as a victim of the harsh anti-abortion law also proved useful to the political left. My task in this book is to provide the necessary counter-image: to show that abortion was not necessarily deadly, that women had real agency, and that their view of abortion was often in opposition to the dominant discourse, although there is no doubt that most women were well versed in medical terminology and familiar with scientific concepts.

This book has drawn inspiration not only from the feminist historians mentioned above but also from *Alltagsgeschichte*, the history of everyday life, microhistory, cultural anthropology and body history. *Alltagsgeschichte* is important in the way in which it explores experience and the formation of identity in the home, the community and at work, often questioning the conventional boundaries between them.[77] Microhistory means a reduction in scale to the level of the individual and the singular case study; moreover it dictates, as Giovanni Levi has put it, that the historian is 'not simply concerned with the interpretation of meanings but rather with defining the ambiguities of the symbolic world, the plurality of possible interpretations of it and the struggle which takes place over symbolic as much as over material resources'.[78] Microhistory, or as Peter Burke defined it, '"fieldwork" among the dead', developed out of cultural anthropology, which taught historians to ask different questions and use different concepts to 'compensate for certain deficiencies in traditional history' although, as Willem de Blécourt has warned, there can arise real difficulties when historians stray into neighbouring disciplines without concerning themselves with solving fundamental problems like 'ethnographic authority' or the 'contexts of the production of knowledge'.[79] Since much of the information of women's attitudes are culled from police interviews or trial depositions and therefore extracted in an atmosphere of fear and mediated through male officials, this point is particularly relevant. The use of anthropological questions and methods to explore emotional, ritual and cultural aspects of events has paved the way for a history of reproduction from below, a history of multiple practices and one in which popular and official views, folk as well as academic medicine is represented. The major impetus still tends to come from historians of earlier periods[80] but there have recently been many important forays into the modern period.[81]

As far as German history of crime is concerned, excellent examples include Richard J. Evans' *Tales from the German Underworld* (1998) or Regina Schulte's *The Village in Court* (1994). Like these books, my study uses criminal records not so much to establish how authorities dealt with particular crimes but rather as a medium of historical anthropology, or as Schulte puts it, as a 'probe to acquire a deeper insight' into a particular segment of society. Indeed, the value of criminal records for history has often less to do with what they can tell us about specific crimes than with what insights they can provide the historian into very private problems usually hidden from the researcher.[82] Criminal abortion files can indeed afford glimpses into the most intimate sphere of women and their relationships with their husbands/lovers, family members, friends and their abortionists. They can also reveal the attitudes to abortion by the historical actors: women who terminated their pregnancies, their helpers and those who assisted them professionally. Regina Schulte's study of nineteenth-century crime in Bavarian village life is an excellent example of how one can interpret not just what was 'objectively' recorded in criminal trials but also find '"other texts" in the layers of reality' contained in those records, such as 'the hidden, unconscious, latent rule systems of the village itself'. Schulte managed to ferret out such other evidence by paying attention to '"what" people said about their actions' and also '"how" they spoke of them, what imagery they used'; she did the latter by carefully reconstructing the social context in which symbolism, gestures and images arose.[83] The anthropologist Emily Martin in her seminal 'cultural analysis of reproduction', based on interviews among American women of the 1980s, has been concerned with the social production of knowledge. She was surprised to find that her respondents' views of their bodies 'reflected no more than "actual scientific fact"'; only when she acknowledged her own 'acceptance of scientific, medical statements as truth' did she recognize apparent 'facts' as 'cultural organizations of experience' and began to recognize 'evidence of women's consciousness of their situation and for a wide variety of forms of objections or resistance'.[84]

Similarly, the historian of the body, Barbara Duden, pointed out how present-day attitudes hinder our study of those in the past. 'We now cannot differentiate', she claims, 'between what we experience and what has been ascribed by science'. For example, she argues, we have internalized the modern scientific concept of foetal development to such an extent that we cannot understand the way women viewed pregnancy in the past centuries. So familiar are we with the image of the growing embryo from medical scans and television, that most women today believe they are pregnant as soon as and only when a test has verified fertilization. But, Duden claims, 200 years ago women only thought of themselves as pregnant when they felt the first movement of the unborn child. We need to accept that our own concept of pregnancy and abortion is a product of modernity and not necessarily more 'true' than earlier concepts.[85] Duden's 'body as experience' in the last decade or so has been somewhat marginalized in gender history, which is dominated by researching the 'discursive body', that is the body defined and constructed by elite discourses such as the medical profession, state agencies and the Church. Kathleen Canning has criticized what she called 'the largely unexplicated and undertheorized concept' of the body in recent history. She pleads for using it in a 'more conceptually conscious and historically grounded' way instead of merely invoking it or allowing it to 'serve as a more fashionable surrogate for sexuality, reproduction, or gender without referring to anything specifically identifiable as body, bodily, or embodied'. She suggests that the 'notion of embodiment may be the most promising' approach and she defines 'embodied practices' as always 'contextual, inflected with class, ethnic, racial, gender, and generational location, with "place, time, physiology and culture"'.[86]

Cultures of abortion in Weimar Germany

This book examines the years of the Weimar Republic, the period in which abortion was sensationalized in popular culture, sparked controversy in politics, health policy, and among religious circles and became an everyday experience for millions of women: on the one hand, women seemed to practise abortion on an unprecedented scale and voiced radical demands for reproductive self-determination with varying support from left-wing and progressive factions; it became a popular topic in bestselling novels, plays and movies. On the other hand the medical profession fought to eradicate lay and self-abortion and the subject attracted heavy censure from the moral right. The subject needs precise situating in its wider social and cultural context and the Weimar Republic, with its distinct political, economic and social developments, provides just such a framework.

'Culture' in the title refers here to two disparate and yet related issues. Firstly, it refers to popular culture: the way abortion was portrayed in the new mass culture of Weimar Germany, in bestselling and serialized novels, workers' theatre and mainstream movies which conveyed mixed messages about women's reproductive rights, the role of the state and the medical profession. Secondly, the use of 'culture' in the title signals a willingness to perceive past events through the utterances and behaviour patterns of ordinary people. Statements in police interviews, depositions in criminal court cases, private letters, advertisements and newspaper reports were all used to this end. Such a cultural approach means interpreting a complex web of meanings, sifting through contradictory, opaque and ambiguous sources of evidence to patch together what might have gone on in the minds of women and men or what happened in their lives. To uncover the experience of abortion as an everyday event, or what Brookes called 'the private decision-making that collectively determined the wider history of reproduction', requires careful attention to different languages used. Official discourse in medicine, law or religion is always a man-made language and aborting women and their – often – female helpers, expressed themselves quite differently from this; women's language was usually marginalized in the elite discourse. The latter had also been adopted by populationists, feminists and sex reformers. In the main, aborting women also used the medical/legal vocabulary but they mixed in concepts derived from an older tradition; this could also be found in the commercial language of businessmen and -women who sold 'feminine hygiene' articles directly to the public. These different discourses were not autonomous but were closely interrelated whenever the diverse points of view touched on each other, for example at court, at the doctor's or in the medical marketplace.

Yet, the meaning of private reproductive decisions cannot be regarded in isolation. Aborting women rarely took the decision to terminate their unwanted pregnancies alone, nor were they necessarily alone during the operation itself. The role of spouses, lovers, family, friends and neighbours was often crucial in the initial deliberations, the search for an abortionist and the eventual outcome; yet, with the exception of Kate Fisher, an exploration of these agents has been sorely missing in existing historiography.[87] Shorter, for example, dismisses men as insignificant in just four pages. Mohr, it is true, makes some interesting remarks about America but displays a middle-class bias. Diana Gittings, who examined reproductive behaviour in early twentieth-century England, suggests that husbands and partners were not necessarily uninvolved or against abortion but she has unfortunately few sources to corroborate these assertions.[88] Evidence of cooperation between men and women does not mean, however, that attitudes did not differ according to gender; there is much evidence of serious altercations between aborting women and their male partners.[89]

Of course, attitudes to and the experience of abortion varied crucially according to class, occupation and geographical area. I have found that the great majority of the aborting women in the judicial files and newspaper reports belonged to the lower classes. This is probably due to their demographic preponderance but also to the way their actions were criminalized. There is a curious gap in the source material consulted: there is hardly any evidence of religious differences in attitudes or customs, although the official stance of the Roman Catholic clergy differed markedly from their Protestant counterparts. The first was characterized by a determination to maintain strict support for the unborn life, even when the life or health of a woman was endangered by her pregnancy: the only solution was to attempt to save both mother and child.[90] The latter was more amenable to compromise.

The research for this book is based on a number of popular culture sources, such as silent feature films, novels, plays and poetry, to show the representation of attitudes to and the effects of abortion in the Republic. The analysis of the practice and experience of abortion is based on a rich variety of court cases, many of them very full documents containing police interviews, trial depositions and reports by social workers and medical experts; some even include correspondence between the aborting woman and her sweetheart. The judicial records derive from both Local Courts (*Amtsgerichte*) and Regional Courts (*Landgerichte*). Since Germany is based on a federal system and has a very diverse culture it is notoriously difficult to achieve some measure of representativeness. This was attempted here by consulting archives in four different *Länder*, two Protestant (Prussia and Saxony) and two Catholic (Bavaria and the Prussian Rhineland). Similarly, there is a mix of urban and rural material from northern, southern, western and eastern regions. Some judicial cases refer to the early years of the Republic, when it suffered from extreme political, social and economic instability and when a different law applied; others derived from the middle period when there was some measure of stability, or from the final years during the Depression when campaigns for abortion law reform peaked and the severity of the economic recession often rendered procreation untenable. Records relating to Dresden are significant for alternative medicine as the Saxon capital was the centre for naturopathy; those relating to Munich are particularly able to shed light on the traffic with contraceptives and abortifacients since the Munich headquarters of police, together with those in Berlin, were chiefly responsible for controlling offences of §184.3 of the penal code, which regulated pornography and advertisements of objects 'intended for indecent use', which referred to both contraceptives and abortifacients. Court records are supplemented with contemporary newspaper reports, doctors' casebooks, diaries and women's reminiscences (some of which appear within the trial files).

My sources are interpreted according to the principles of *Alltagsgeschichte* and cultural history rather than the tradition of social-science history with its emphasis on analysing 'big structures, large processes, huge comparisons'.[91] A cultural history of abortion demands investigating popular responses and subjective experiences. As Alf Lüdtke put it, it means a 'systematic decentralization of analysis and interpretation' through painstakingly composing a picture made up of 'miniatures'.[92] The resulting patchwork of different practices and attitudes by aborting women and their helpers reflects the complexity of often ambiguous and contradictory ways ordinary people led their lives. As we shall see in later chapters the various experiences of aborting women and the different ways they talked about it was influenced in varying degree by discourses of ideological projects such as pronatalism, eugenics, the professionalization of medicine, positivism, welfarism and maternalism. Aborting women in the archives rarely talk to us directly. There are only a few letters preserved in which they write about what they went through; otherwise their views or experiences are mediated by others: doctors in their casebooks, abortionists in their testimonies, and police and court clerks in legal documents. It falls to the historian to unravel how reality is socially constructed and to ascertain how abortion has been historically constructed as a crime in order to deconstruct it appropriately; this will help to reveal women's own voices and expose the major disjuncture between official penal prescription and popular perceptions and practices.

Weimar Germany, and the capital Berlin in particular, is usually portrayed as the byword for modernity[93] and by the end of the 1920s many young women, including those from the working classes, were perceived to lead a thoroughly rationalized lifestyle.[94] But, maybe surprisingly, many women in the files consulted talked about their bodies in ways which evoke prescientific medical notions; they also consulted fortune-tellers when seeking help with ill health, relationship problems or unwanted pregnancies and they referred to this as if it was nothing out of the ordinary.[95] Reading cards and sympathetic magic – that is, the use of personal items such as underwear, which contained the aura of its owner – to 'conjure back' a missing sweetheart or husband fits uneasily into a picture of sobriety, rationalization and modernity. When I stumbled across pieces of evidence revealing this 'exotic' custom among the working classes it felt as if my research into twentieth-century legal documents concerning abortion and reproductive strategies would not only yield dry and prosaic documents. I understood that, rather than perpetuating the received opinion of the Weimar Republic as a symbol for modernity, I should appreciate the cultural diversity in daily life and the coexistence of science and superstition.

My story will unfold gradually from the representation of abortion on stage, screen and in literature, via courtroom dramas probing into medical practices to the more secretive encounters with wise women and wise men and the sometimes subservient but often defiant statements of women in the dock whose language could serve as an instrument of independence and identity. When women did not ape the expressions of the medico-legal establishment they produced oppositional terms whose meanings were deeply encoded and multilayered, requiring careful unravelling. Finally, we encounter women in discreet or even open conversation with friends and neighbours, or in intimate scenes within families, when the popular ethic revealed itself as markedly different from that expressed in law or medical guidelines. With the help of numerous case studies we will learn about the practice of abortion ranging from the apparently more rational procedure of academic medicine to the apparently more irrational world of lay practitioners, including healers and fortune tellers, and to women's own tales hidden beneath the various layers of meaning expressed in the judicial records. A detailed case study encompassing seventeen villages in Hesse, involving a carpenter's wife and her husband and no fewer than 93 co-defendants, will illustrate many of these aspects and enrich our understanding of cultures of abortion in a modern industrialized society in which the medicalization process had neither displaced a marketplace for abortions nor traditional perceptions of women's bodies. This study shows that abortion was frequently not regarded as crime or tragedy but as an everyday experience and a useful remedy for unwanted pregnancies.

The multiple and contradictory ways in which the topic of abortion was represented in popular culture are discussed critically in Chapter 2. Many Weimar artists and writers regarded the female body as an icon of modernity, representing women's new sexual freedom and self-determinism. Others represented it as an expression of class and gender inequality, as in the popular depiction of destitute mothers overburdened with children they could not feed. Socialist writers and artists, in particular, constructed the image of the dejected proletarian woman who risked gaol, injury or even death to free herself from an unwanted pregnancy through a back-street operation. Examples include Käthe Kollwitz's drawings and etchings; novels like Franz Krey's *Maria und der Paragraph* (Maria and the law); plays like *Cyankali. §218* (Potassium cyanide. *§218*) by the socialist doctor Friedrich Wolf, which caused a sensation when it was premiered in 1929 in Berlin and on its subsequent tour through Germany; films like *Kuhle Wampe oder Wem gehört die Welt?* (Kuhle Wampe or whom does the world belong to?), based on the script by Bertolt Brecht; and poetry like Erich Weinert's *§218*. Less politically committed filmmakers exploited the high profile of the issue in such long-lost but once very prominent feature films as *Kreuzzug des Weibes* (Women's crusade, 1926), and women writers like Irmgard Keun in her 1931 best-selling *Gilgi, eine von uns* (Gilgi, one of us) managed to offer an alternative, sometimes subversive interpretation of the abortion problem by portraying a New Woman who had the courage and conviction to challenge dominant beliefs.

Chapter 3 looks at the role of doctors and their encounter with aborting women. It concentrates on two case studies from Bavaria; the first concerns a young general practitioner from a provincial town in Upper Bavaria who spoke publicly against §218 and was investigated for illegal abortion as well as serious medical negligence; the second relates to a well-known woman gynaecologist practising in Munich who was indicted for illegal abortion performed on seventy-five women. These two court cases are analysed in the context of national policies, medical discourse and with reference to other similar judicial cases. They reveal a serious gap between theory and practice, i.e. between official standards of medical ethics and obstetric training, on the one hand, and the actual behaviour of individual doctors, on the other. Doctors were generally shielded from public criticism or legal prosecution on account of their high social standing, partly achieved during the gradual process of professionalization and medicalization begun during the nineteenth century, and partly through advising first the Imperial and later the Weimar governments on population policy and public health. Furthermore, doctors generally received preferential treatment by the judiciary when the profession closed ranks and colleagues acted as expert witnesses or when doctors were, as they usually were, tried before a medical tribunal quite independently of the state judicial system. There was also a striking contradiction between doctors' professed public aims and their private views. Many doctors who decried abortion publicly nevertheless obliged their patients in private. And despite campaigning to gain a monopoly of therapeutic abortions, many doctors regarded the operation with disdain. This is revealed in the rich symbolism contained in their language and their insistence on using specific instruments and procedures.

Chapter 4 examines the power relationship between academic and lay medicine in the medical campaign against *Kurierfreiheit*, the right for everyone to practise healing quite independent of training or state registration which was enshrined in the trade laws of 1871. The chapter compares the careers and practices of lay abortionists and members of the medical profession. The conventional division adhered to by Weimar as well as present-day commentators, between the 'good' doctor and the 'bad' quack, as well as the apparently clear boundary between academic medicine and quackery, will be questioned. It is argued that the notorious image of the back-street abortionist was to a significant extent a construction of the medical discourse which also fed the representation in the press and popular culture. This negative image reflected wider fears about women's emancipation and national decline. In their fight to monopolize the lucrative area of reproductive health, it was in doctors' professional interests to denigrate 'quack abortionists'. Yet, contrary to their negative image, many women preferred lay abortionists, especially midwives or 'wise women', for a number of reasons, such as cost, safety record, methods employed and, probably most importantly of all, a common cultural approach rooted in class and gender similarities.

Chapter 5 analyses women's perceptions of abortion and compares their own language with advertising copy by entrepreneurs of abortion products as well as with the official discourse that was heavily influenced by the medical profession. It also explores the dichotomy between public perception and private experience of abortion. The official discourse normally presented abortion as a tragedy which should be avoided, but in female working-class culture it widely featured as a fairly routine event. What is more, in the world characterized both by economic insecurity and by increasing awareness of women's new social roles, an unwanted pregnancy was thought of as an intolerable burden which needed to be terminated to secure a women's and her family's well-being. To find out how women attempted to control their fertility and interpreted their own bodily changes (often quite untouched by scientific notions), women's own voices need to be tracked down and sensitively interpreted. They emerge as baffling and contradictory, often speaking in two quite different languages. In the 1920s and early 1930s most women were well informed about reproduction and gynaecology and adopted medicalized terms, though not necessarily meaning the same as doctors; but other women, or sometimes the same women on a different occasion, used an oppositional language in keeping with older notions of female reproduction. The result was that the police and the courts dismissed women's talk generally as a tactic to dodge punishment or simply as ignorance. Here I try to reconstruct the personal experience of abortion through seeking insights into women's own perceptions, fears and strategies.

Chapter 6 discusses the outstandingly successful and very large abortion practice of a carpenter's wife and her husband in a Hesse village. For more than five years they performed a peripatetic service for the inhabitants of seventeen villages near Limburg, offering help with unwanted pregnancies, but in 1924 they finally stood trial after having been indicted for illegal abortion for 'commercial gain' in seventy-one cases. In contrast to the views, expressed in court and reflected in the very harsh sentence, that this husband-and-wife team were dangerous criminals, ninety-three co-defendants, including aborting women and those who aided them, expressed their gratitude towards the abortionists. They never caused a serious injury and worked conscientiously and discreetly, complementing the work of midwives and helping to restore the fragile economic equilibrium of a farming community in decline at a time of social dislocation, political unrest, occupation and rising inflation. By carefully tracing the movements of abortionists and their various clients to their homes and their places of employment, and during the daily routine of fetching water, tending vegetables and animals as well as making visits to relatives and friends, this case study reveals a close cooperation between villagers of different classes and occupations, within families and between men and women: husbands or lovers not only supported their wives or sweethearts in the decision to terminate unwanted pregnancies but also actively assisted during the operation itself.

The book's final chapter contains an exploration of the radical changes as well as surprising continuities in abortion policy from Imperial to Weimar Germany and from Weimar to Nazi Germany; it summarizes how a cultural approach to the abortion question throws light on the social history of Weimar Germany and sets out prospective desiderata for future research.

◈ Chapter 2 ◈

CULTURAL REPRESENTATION: ABORTION ON STAGE, SCREEN AND IN FICTION

> Don't be stupid, woman! Don't go, woman, where you will be given potassium cyanide or syringed with carbolic soap or infected by dirty instruments and you will be sure to die in the convulsions of puerperal fever, don't go there! I warn you!

With these words a doctor pleads with a young proletarian woman, Hete, to stay away from a back-street abortionist. She had asked him to terminate her unwanted pregnancy, which he declined, although he had just arranged this for the previous patient, a middle-class woman. The scene is taken from Friedrich Wolf's play *Cyankali. §218* (Potassium cyanide. *§218*) which caused a sensation when it was premiered in 1929 in Berlin and on its subsequent tour through Germany. Hete's journey of pain and humiliation takes her from the cynical doctor and a pathetic attempt at self-help into the clutches of a so-called wise woman, Madame Heye. Just as the doctor predicted, Madame Heye poisons Hete with potassium cyanide and she dies in agony in her mother's arms.[1]

Wolf, a member of the KPD (German Communist Party), as well as a doctor who got into trouble with the abortion law barely two years later for referring women for medical terminations, wrote his play as a rallying cry against an unjust law. It presents abortion as a tragedy for the working classes and the proletarian aborting woman as a victim of the bourgeois state. How typical was this portrait of other cultural presentations and of the experience of the hundreds of thousands of women who underwent an abortion during the Weimar Republic? This chapter will explore the way events surrounding abortion were portrayed in Weimar popular culture and compare it with the meaning women themselves attached to the operation. It seems that there was a remarkable disparity between women's perceptions (as we will see in Chapters 5 and 6 below) and the way abortion featured in most cultural productions at the time, and the question is why this was the case. Did scriptwriters, directors, playwrights and authors pay little heed to women's own views? Or was it the case that while films, plays and novels may have entertained their female spectators or readers, they did not influence their opinion?

While the passionate debate about §218 and the extraordinary mass street demonstrations of the later Weimar years has received due attention by historians in recent years, the full significance of cultural representations of abortion has, apart from the occasional brief reference, been largely neglected by historians, leaving it a subject almost exclusive to literary, art and film studies.[2] Yet, popular culture contributed to the social construction of abortion in the Weimar years and must be taken seriously. Scott Spector made a similar point in an essay on the importance of feature film for the study of Nazi Germany. He bemoans the fact that few historians use the work of their colleagues in literature and film departments. Even when historians do use popular culture as a primary source they tend to concentrate on plot and factual information, paying little attention to artistic style, production and consumption, or, in the case of film, to how visual representation is 'cinematically produced and experienced'. Film and literary studies, he argues, enrich historical interpretation by complicating our understanding of important concepts: in addition to analysing plot they also interpret extranarrative aspects of films by addressing 'the semiotic complexity of images and of sound, the sequencing of images and the establishment of visual tropes, and, not least importantly, the referentiality of aspects of the film to things outside the frame'.[3]

Key to interpreting popular culture properly is to situate it in its historical context and analyse it with reference to literary or film scholars; nevertheless I will, throughout this book, also want to go beyond the discussion of film and literary studies by exploring the interrelationship of multiple voices in the abortion discourse: from gendered 'official' prescriptions via the opinions of various pressure groups to grassroots views by ordinary people and finally to the attitudes implied in cultural representations. Thus, in the following I will analyse examples of popular representation of abortion as a social and individual issue in films, plays, novels and poems. Popular culture as a source of attitudes to §218 of the penal code in Weimar Germany is especially significant for two reasons. Firstly, the proliferation of cultural products in which abortion featured as the main or a subsidiary topic; secondly, the 'classical modernity' of the Weimar Republic with a shorter working day, reasonably high wages and women's increased participation in public life led to the emergence of a mass culture which often catered particularly for a female audience.[4]

The term 'popular culture' signals that this discussion is not confined to 'high art', indeed there will be little high art considered here; instead the focus will be on working-class culture, especially linked to the parties of the left, the SPD and the KPD, as well as on mass culture disseminated through popular theatre and the new media of high-circulation journals and especially of silent film. Dismantling the strict distinction between 'high' and 'low' culture, as propounded by contemporary bourgeois critics, was indeed the self-confessed aim of many avant-garde and socialist artists, writers and producers at the time who strove to make their products accessible to a wider audience, particularly of the poorer social strata. But their aim went further: to overcome not just class demarcations, but also those between different artistic disciplines and between culture and other areas of public life. Culture was to be inclusive and it was interrelated with the various areas of private and public life. In Weimar Germany, as the literary and film historian, Anton Kaes remarked, culture, society and political life criss-crossed and intersected and did so usually by complex routes.[5] Ernst Toller was not alone in spanning a career both as one of the most successful playwrights of his time and as a political activist. He took part in the Bavarian revolution of 1919, was briefly Minister of the Interior of the Soviet Republic of Bavaria and, once imprisoned for high treason for this, he set about writing a play about his experiences.[6] Other literati straddled two professions, too: medical practitioners such as Friedrich Wolf, Carl Credé and Alfred Döblin who were also successful playwrights, with Döblin also writing one the most original novels of the Republic, *Berlin Alexanderplatz* (1929). The playwright Bertolt Brecht and the theatre director Erwin Piscator, both inspired by communist ideals, set out to activate spectators by breaking down the barriers between the classes and also between the performer and the audience. Plays were made relevant to contemporary politics and specific dramaturgic devices were meant to awaken the audience's rebellious spirit. One of the purposes of Brecht's theories of epic theatre and his use of *Verfremdungseffekt* (alienation effect) was to prevent spectators from simply identifying uncritically with the characters on the play. This meant a reversal of the tradition of late nineteenth-century realism which asked for the suspension of disbelief and emotional empathy with the drama unfolding on stage. In an early statement Brecht wrote that the 'essential point of the epic theatre is perhaps that it appeals less to the feelings than to the spectator's reason. Instead of sharing an experience the spectator must come to grips with things.'[7]

Abortion and the reform of §218 of the penal code were apt subjects to engage the public with. It was, as we have seen, one of the discursive obsessions of the time. It had been at the centre of debates on national and gender identity since the end of the First World War. Not surprisingly, it attracted many well-known writers and filmmakers and others who made their name by portraying the problem on stage, in novels, poems and on screen. For example, Klabund, Walter Mehring, Brecht, Erich Weinert, Kurt Tucholsky and Erich Kästner all wrote poems about abortion, many of them published in working-class or popular journals. Stage plays like *Der Frauenarzt* (The gynaecologist) by Hans Rehfisch and *Die Verbrecher* (The criminals) by Ferdinand Bruckner (1928) reached a wider public; but the play with by far the biggest impact was *Cyankali.§218* by Wolf (1929). Wolf was the most successful communist playwright at the time and it was directed by Erwin Piscator, the most famous of the young generation of left-wing directors.

Carl Credé, a socialist doctor who was imprisoned for illegal terminations, authored the play *§218. Gequälte Menschen* (§218. Tortured people), which Piscator also staged in 1929. In 1932 Döblin's play, *Die Ehe* (The marriage) appeared. Then there were proletarian *Zeitromane*, or more pejoratively, *Tendenzromane*, describing the pernicious effects of §218 on the working classes, such as Rudolf Braune's *Das Mädchen an der Orga Privat* (The girl at her Orga Private typewriter, 1925), Franz Krey's *Maria und der Paragraph* (Maria and the law) and Willi Bredel's *Rosenhofstraße* (both 1931). Finally, there were the best-selling serialized entertainment novels by women authors, such as Vicki Baum's *stud.chem. Helene Willfüer* (1928), serialized in a mass-marketed illustrated journal, and Irmgard Keun's *Gilgi – eine von uns* (Gilgi, one of us, 1931), later made into a film with the same name, which featured abortion as an important issue in their protagonists' development.

Novels by male writers who thematized women's reproductive problems were Arthur Schnitzler's *Therese. Chronik eines Frauenlebens* (Therese. A chronicle of a woman's life, 1928), Arnold Zweig's *Junge Frau von 1914* (Young woman of 1914, 1931) and Hans Fallada's *Kleiner Mann, was nun?* (Little man, what now?, 1932). A further sign of the intense artistic engagement with this question is the fact that in 1931 the Committee of Self-incrimination against §218 (encouraging well-known people to admit to an abortion or having aided one) included a whole array of celebrities, e.g. the writers Lion Feuchtwanger, Thea von Harbou, Ernst Toller, the poet Else Lasker-Schüler and the scientist Albert Einstein.[8]

Last but by no means least, there were a surprising number of silent feature films dedicated to the subject which captivated contemporary audiences; many are lost or had slipped from our sight and are only gradually being rediscovered. By the mid-1920s the cinema had become one of the most influential mass media, attracting both intelligentsia and the general public alike. Conservative estimates put the number of daily spectators at that time at one million; by the end of the 1920s the domestic film industry produced more films than the rest of Europe put together and had become, according to one historian, already by 1920 the third largest branch of industry.[9] But the stabilization of the German currency in 1923 was also the beginning of a much-debated German 'film crisis', as the production companies lost the advantage of cheap prices on the international market and had to fear artistic competition from imports particularly from the U.S.A. The need to ensure an audience meant that directors were increasingly looking for 'realistic' high-profile themes. §218 fitted the bill well.

To understand how abortion was constructed in the Weimar Republic we need to tease out the interrelations between the official discourse (e.g. among doctors, lawyers, government officials, churchmen), women's own testimony gleaned from, amongst other sources, depositions in criminal court cases, and the way abortion was represented in popular culture. As to the latter, the different cinematic and literary narratives have to be carefully situated, revealing their specific historical influences and the existing aesthetic and literary conventions. But this does not, of course, mean that cultural representation should be reduced to a passive reflection of the 'real' world. As has often been pointed out, reflection theory, so powerfully expressed in the works of film critics Siegfried Kracauer and Lotte Eisner,[10] is misleading as it assumes a simplistic pattern of cause and effect according to which an artistic production is judged as a more-or-less truthful reflection of an already existing social reality, or, even more complicated, by the way it is meant to fit historical interpretations.[11] Cultural products do not simply convey official ideology; they are not a neutral vehicle which 'expresses' social meaning. Rather, cultural representations function to transform and mediate the world through their own specific codes and the institutions of which they are a part. Thus, to study the social construction of abortion the relationship between artistic representations, dominant and popular discourses need to be understood as an interactive process.

With the help of some examples from the screen, stage and fiction I want to explore whether they subscribed to dominant views, whether they subverted them and whether they diverged from views of ordinary women and men. I will argue that the different cultural representations provided a vital link mediating between the frequently opposing views of the official discourse and attitudes held by ordinary women and men. These films, plays etc. also demonstrate the extent to which the issue of abortion had moved from being a medico-moral and political concern to a popular cultural one. This was accompanied by a shift in gender and class: away from academic and professional men to women, particularly of the lower classes, which changed the means of communication and the language used. Women were the new consumers of popular theatre, film and print culture, especially the illustrated journals.

At any rate, all journals, including the communist and social democratic press, certainly profited from addressing the concerns of contemporary women. The modern novel, the *Zeitroman*, invariably made a reference to women's sexuality and reproduction control and it reached millions of women readers in cheap editions and serialized form. No doubt the attraction of abortion as subject matter was also due to a decisive change in the artistic climate from about the mid-1920s when Expressionism in the arts gradually gave way to *Neue Sachlichkeit*, only imperfectly rendered in English as New Sobriety or New Objectivity. While Expressionism, with its stress on the struggle of the individual – always represented as a type rather than personalized – against the forces of evil, suited the extreme experiences of a society in shock after the dislocation of a lost world war, *Neue Sachlichkeit* was characterized by a cooler and more sober rendering of social drama rooted in recognizable issues of the day. Indeed most important abortion narratives originated in the second half of the Weimar Republic, presented in a *neusachlich* style, or even in the last few years, during the Depression after 1929, when agitprop (agitation propaganda) was characteristic of left-wing proletarian art. In this cultural climate writers and filmmakers were inspired by the spectacular mass demonstrations against §218 and by the tangible hardship experienced by many hundred of thousands of women who sought to free themselves from the burden of an unwanted pregnancy.

Abortion in the movies

As early as September 1918, that is, in the last few weeks of Imperial Germany, the film *Sündige Mütter (Strafgesetz §218)* (Sinful mothers, §218 of the penal code) was premiered in Dusseldorf, the fourth part of a tetralogy, *Es werde Licht!* (And there was light) of sexual enlightenment films, all directed by Richard Oswald and with the active cooperation of sexologists. Magnus Hirschfeld acted as scientific consultant for *Sündige Mütter*, which portrayed the negative implications of quack abortions and the illegal status of children born out of wedlock, and echoed the official line of Wilhelmine abortion policy.[12] October of the same year saw the premiere of another sexual enlightenment film, *Keimendes Leben* (Nascent life), directed by Georg Jacoby, which was the last part of a trilogy; despite its suggestive title, it only dealt with abortion in passing. A third film to be produced in 1918, Walter Creutz's *Arme kleine Eva* (Poor little Eva) dealt with the seduction of an innocent young woman who was subsequently tricked into undergoing an abortion performed by a quack, with the result that she faced a trial and imprisonment, had she not been pardoned in the last minute.[13]

In Weimar Germany the first serious cinematic critique of §218 and its impact on women, however, was Martin Berger's 1926 silent film *Kreuzzug des Weibes* (Women's crusade).[14] As a young socialist Berger had previously produced feature films for the SPD's *Volksfilmbühne* (People's Cinema); in 1925, with the help of the trade union and the Reichsbanner, he filmed *Freies Volk* (Free people) 'the first major republican film', which proved, however, a financial fiasco.[15] In *Kreuzzug* Berger portrays the abortion law as dysgenic and class discriminatory. With the help of no less than four big stars – Maly Delschaft, Conrad Veidt, Werner Krauß and Harry Liedtke – the film was a considerable popular success.

The narrative interweaves the starkly contrasting stories of three women from different social backgrounds, all depicted as types and without names: firstly, the tragedy of a proletarian mother of four who is refused a

2. Anja Zimowa as the modern wife, Maly Delschaft as the young teacher in *Kreuzzug des Weibes*, directed by Martin Berger, 1926

3. Maly Delschaft as the young teacher, rape scene, *Kreuzzug des Weibes*, directed by Martin Berger, 1926

termination of her fifth pregnancy by a young doctor (Harry Liedtke). Even though he expects her child to be 'sickly', he says he cannot 'help' because the law permits a termination of pregnancy only on strict medical grounds and her pregnancy does not endanger her life. He warns her against a quack or self-induced abortion. But the woman turns to the concierge who encourages her to do just that, probably offering her the necessary means to do it. As a result the woman falls mortally ill. The incident is brought to the attention of the public prosecutor (Conrad Veidt) who issues an arrest warrant for her and her husband. When the police officer arrives at their lodging the woman has already died. Nevertheless he apprehends the widower, thus depriving his four children of their only parent.

The second story is about a 'modern wife' who seeks a termination purely for vanity. She tells her husband, 'Why would I want to ruin my figure just so that you can enjoy fatherhood?' Nevertheless, she easily secures an abortion from her family doctor on fabricated medical grounds which were permissible if not in law then in practice.[16] This case has also come to the notice of the (same) public prosecutor (it is hinted that the angry maid had denounced her former mistress) but on this occasion he is unable to press charges.

The third story concerns the chief protagonist of the film, the prosecutor's fiancée (Maly Delschaft). She lives in the elegant front apartment block and has just received her certificate as a teacher in a state high school for girls. She has heard about the death of the proletarian woman, who lived in the rear building, witnessed the husband's arrest and pleads with her fiancé on behalf of the husband. When she fails, her relationship with the prosecutor undergoes a crisis. The dramatic climax of the film occurs when she is raped by the caretaker's 'mentally handicapped' son (Werner Krauß) and finds herself pregnant. Her life now seems in ruins: she knows that as an unmarried mother she will lose her job and probably her fiancé, too. In desperation she turns to the young doctor (Harry Liedtke). Shaken by the death of the proletarian woman, for which he feels responsible, he is now determined to save the teacher's life from a 'back-street abortion'. He offers his 'help' (we then assume he also performs the abortion) and then honourably gives himself up to the police and the prosecutor. When the latter learns that the case concerns his own fiancée he suffers a nightmarish vision: he perceives first the silhouette of his fiancée in a white nightdress and then those of women walking in an eerie procession over a bridge against the backdrop of ringing church bells. They are the ghosts of abortion victims and the scene represents the woman's crusade of the title. This hallucination signifies the prosecutor's change of heart: instead of morally condemning his fiancée and bringing charges against her, he resigns his position as a civil servant because he cannot work for a state whose laws he no longer supports. His inner development makes reconciliation with his fiancée possible.

The release of this film was brilliantly stage managed for maximum impact. It was premiered on 1 October 1926 in two large cinemas simultaneously, the

Alhambra on the Kurfürstendamm and the Primus Palast.[17] It also benefited from a number of well-staged events: the high-profile campaigns, in the previous year, by sex reformers, the political left and women's groups to liberalize the abortion law. In the same year the conservative German Medical Association had dedicated its annual conference to the issue; there had been a number of motions in the Reichstag to legalize abortion; and the commission set up to revise the entire penal code published their own proposal to liberalize the abortion clauses. Indeed, in May 1926, just three months before filming of *Kreuzzug* started,[18] the abortion clause was revised. All this guaranteed high-profile publicity for an issue which juxtaposed aspects of health, morality, women's rights, class discrimination, culture and gender in a complex set of relationships. Not surprisingly then, the focus on §218 and its class-specific effects on women secured *Kreuzzug* immediate public attention – obviously hoped for by the film's publicity material, which pointed to the 'hotly disputed subject' and 'the many tragedies which are caused by it. Must a woman become a mother? Or may a hardpressed woman ... ?'[19] Indeed, according to the influential journal *Film-Kurier*, *Kreuzzug* was the eighth most popular film of the 1926/7 season.[20] Contemporary reviews were generally positive. One review praised the film for its 'extraordinarily subdued and refined' style and the 'love and care' with which the notion of 'compulsory motherhood' had been 'formed into a great work of art'. Another commended the seriousness with which the film portrayed 'the sanctity of motherhood' and a third especially liked the director, Martin Bergers' 'sparse, restrained and dispassionate' approach which 'broke with all cinematic convention. No car passes by, no cigarette is being smoked, there are no love scenes ... ' This was 'a film of hard facts, narrated with intentional matter-of-factness and through it especially impressive'. The film proved a huge success for its main actors and Maly Delschaft's fame as a first-rate actress was secured.

On the other hand, none of the reviews failed to mention the commercial appeal of the subject matter, predicting 'good business'.[21]

Berger's film was a sufficient hit in Germany to secure U.S. distribution and to usher in a veritable flood of other abortion films, most of them in favour of liberalizing the law.[22] But it would be wrong to dismiss films like *Kreuzzug* purely as a clever commercial exploitation of a controversial subject as, for example, Siegfried Kracauer did. Writing in 1947, he took topical films to task because he felt they deflected from revolutionary issues of the day as they merely 'pretended to tackle the social problem by harping on the sufferings of the proletariat ... '. He thought filmmakers tried to neutralize pent-up indignation of social critics by directing it against what he regarded as evils of small importance, such as stigmatizing the 'rigors of the penal code'. Since these films, moreover, 'emphasized sex matters, they were bound to arouse a mixture of indignation and sexuality which could not but increase their value as safety valves.'[23]

Certainly, Berger's message in *Kreuzzug* was reformist rather than revolutionary, resolving the moral crisis with a personal conciliation between two middle-class professionals rather than class solidarity to institute change. Nevertheless *Kreuzzug*, or bestselling novels like Irmgard Keun's *Gilgi – eine von uns* and a selection of other abortion narratives were important means of communication about women's everyday experience of modernity in Weimar Germany. Whereas abortion is the central topic in *Kreuzzug*, Keun's novel affords a useful comparison because abortion features only as a marginal issue in it. Nevertheless both touch on other fashionable subject matters. *Kreuzzug* places abortion within the context of contemporary views on eugenics, population policy, medicine versus quackery and, last but not least, the phenomenon of the New Woman. *Gilgi* explored amongst other topics the new rationalized working woman, consumption, single motherhood and adoption. It is this interrelationship between fiction and the debates of the day that makes these works especially relevant for analysis.

What is immediately striking is how uncritically *Kreuzzug*, and many other films and novels, too, adopted medical opinions. Doctors are always depicted as male despite the large and increasing number of women in the profession – which itself throws an interesting light on the adherence to stereotypical gender roles; they feature as sole arbiters and reliable executors of abortion. The tacit assumption is that the aborting woman is always safe in medical hands and that there would be no 'abortion crisis' if doctors were allowed to help the deserving woman. This is certainly the underlying idea in the resolution of the young teacher's dilemma: once the young doctor agrees to 'help' her, her life and her career are saved. As will be shown below in Chapters 3 and 4, the notion of medical infallibility was, however, not borne out in practice.

But the film does not just condone medical claims; it positively celebrates the profession by presenting a young doctor as the hero of the plot and by casting the heart-throb Harry Liedtke for the role. Thus the physician in the film was not only young and glamorous but his character undergoes an impressive development from the professional blinkered by conventions and class bias to the humane and courageous individual who takes on the law and saves the female lead. His former and future self in fact neatly mirrored the two camps within the medical profession during the Weimar Republic fighting each other over the abortion question: on the one hand, the traditionalists who resisted law reform or, at best, tolerated abortion on strict health grounds; on the other hand, the progressives, mostly on the left, who advocated medical, social and/or eugenic abortion.[24]

While *Kreuzzug* pleads the case for the social indication – the proletarian woman's plight is clearly caused by her material hardship – it aligns itself even more strongly with those who campaigned for eugenic abortion to prevent 'degenerate' offspring. After all, the central drama concerns the young teacher's rape and subsequent pregnancy. Significantly the perpetrator is the 'mentally deficient' son of the caretaker and by implication his unborn child would in all probability have inherited his 'dysgenic' traits. Sex crimes perpetrated by the mentally ill were a favourite topic in the contemporary medical literature. It usually evoked the danger to the *Volkskörper* in the darkest tones emanating from the allegedly growing number of 'degenerates' who were considered to be especially fecund.[25] The eugenic argument is also explicitly and rather didactically put in the fourth act of the film when the young doctor and the prosecutor argue over the merits of a quantitative versus a qualitative population policy. In future women, like the sick proletarian woman he was not permitted to help, should be permitted to terminate unwanted pregnancies, declares the young doctor: 'the removal of a sick foetus serves the good of the *Volk* and is no murder'. Eugenic danger is also implied cinematically when the camera focuses on her son at the very moment when the concierge encourages the proletarian couple to procure an abortion without medical help. Surely the spectator is meant to conclude that had the concierge practised what she preached ('if the doctor does not want to help, why not do it yourselves?'. 'Rubbish, dangerous? If you knew how many do it!')[26] she would have been spared a son with learning difficulties and the teacher her rape? Finally, as von Keitz points out, in Werner Krauß's acting the 'mental debility' of the caretaker's son translates physically into a 'total lack of control over his own body'. He behaves exactly as no child of respectable parents was allowed: he eats with his fingers like a savage and reveals an unchecked oral and sexual appetite; as soon as he sets eyes on something, he wants to touch and possess it. Aided by an appropriately infantile hairstyle and ghostlike facial expression Krauß gives an exuberant performance of 'mental deficiency' in close-up shots. Interestingly, the heinous deed of rape is only punished physically when the public prosecutor pushes Krauß's character down the stairs; significantly, he desists from pursuing proper legal sanctions against the culprit. Von Keitz suggests that this reveals a belief that the 'feeble-minded' were without a sense of guilt or remorse.[27]

The second example of medicalized thinking concerns the way the film accepts that abortion should be a prerogative of doctors and that back-street abortionists were a bad thing. While the medical press vilified quack abortionists openly, *Kreuzzug* condemns them more indirectly: it is left ambiguous whether the caretaker – in court case narratives indeed frequently the abortionist – merely encourages the proletarian couple to induce their own abortion or actually provides the necessary instruments for it. At any rate, her persona is unmistakably associated cinematically with darkness through her physical surroundings, with 'degeneration' through her son and finally with murder through the death of the proletarian woman who follows her advice.

Irmgard Keun's novel *Gilgi* does not criticize lay abortionists outright but damns them by omitting any reference to them. The pregnant Gilgi does not turn to a 'wise woman' but instead goes straight to the next doctor and even when he rejects her request she still does not consider 'help' from a quack. Even more surprisingly, Hertha, the pregnant wife of Gilgi's destitute friend Hans, also only refers to medical help. When Gilgi exclaims in horror: 'Hertha, my God, how can you think of having this child!', she replies resignedly: 'What else can I do, Gilgi? Or do you really think I could go along to the local health insurance fund?', a reference to the well-known fact that sick funds usually paid for a termination induced by a doctor on health grounds.[28]

When criminal abortion did feature in films and fiction the road to it was shown as a stony one. For example, the young unemployed Hete in the film of Wolf's play *Cyankali* has to suffer not only an attempted sexual assault by the caretaker in return for an abortifacient but also a degrading consultation with a general practitioner. He furnishes a rich woman with the necessary medical certificate for a termination on dubious therapeutic grounds but rebuffs the poor young woman, Hete. Wise women (or, more rarely, 'wise men') appear invariably as negative characters (see Chapter 4). The former were usually called 'Madame' like a procuress and were given the appearance of the unacceptable or exotic 'other'. For example, Madame Heye in the film *Cyankali* is the undisputed villain of the plot; long before Hete meets her, the uncooperative medical practitioner warns her not to go where she will meet certain death, associating lay abortion with death and preparing the spectator precisely for Hete's actual end. Despite Madame Heye's superficially respectable appearance (neatly dressed in a white blouse and dark skirt and wearing a homely apron) she soon reveals her coarseness by her rude and abrupt gestures, ungrammatical speech and the merciless way she strikes a hard bargain: extracting a large sum of money (30 Marks in instalments) from a distraught Hete, who can ill afford it; in return Heye offers an operation (with dirty instruments) and poison (the potassium cyanide of the title) for Hete to take home, eventually causing her agonising death.

Madame Lu in Franz Hofer's 1929 film *Madame Lu, die Frau für diskrete Beratung* (Madame Lu, the woman for discreet advice), however, seems to be a departure from the rule: she is well dressed and well spoken, conscientious and painstakingly hygienic. Yet, her counterpart in the film, a dark, gypsy-like woman of the demi-world conforms to the stereotype of the sluttish abortionist. Only at the denouement do we learn that Madame Lu is not really a wise woman at all but a philanthropist who works closely with social welfare and uses her guise to attract desperate women whom she then saves from the clutches of the real back-street operators. Her mission is fuelled by her own daughter's tragic death after a bungled quack abortion. I have yet to find an example in film or fiction which offers a neutral, let alone positive, image of commercial abortionists.[29] This is in line with academic medicine, which aimed to 'stamp out' a practice which it blamed officially for the rise of maternal morbidity and mortality. Yet, as we shall see in Chapter 4, women's own stories and judicial investigations often offer a more complex picture: while there are of course numerous examples of lay abortionists having exploited their position of power and having caused injuries and even deaths, there is also a surprising wealth of evidence that a good many operators possessed considerable skills and medical knowledge and helped women efficiently. Consequently, they were often regarded by their clients with gratitude rather than disdain.

Although the *Film-Kurier* in its review of *Kreuzzug* emphasized the lack of 'party political interventions',[30] like the play and film *Cyankali* and a number of novels (e.g. Keun's *Gilgi*, Franz Krey's *Maria und der Paragraph* and Willi Bredel's *Rosenhofstraße*) *Kreuzzug* stressed the social inequality of access to medical abortion. This was very much in tune with the campaign by the political left.[31] We have seen how *Kreuzzug* (and *Cyankali*, too) compares the deserving yet unsuccessful case of the proletarian woman with the undeserving, but successful abortion case of the society lady. Left-wing advocates of abortion law reform repeatedly argued that the existing law favoured the rich who could afford to 'buy' safe surgical terminations, while it drove the poor to risky self-help or to dangerous back-street abortionists. This is precisely the line of the film; yet it goes further. It also portrays the law enforcement agencies as class discriminatory: a public prosecutor does not hesitate to have the proletarian couple arrested, thereby ruining an entire family, while he dismisses the case against the wealthy woman. Only at the close of the film have the representatives of bourgeois mores and civil service freed themselves from their restrictive roles: the doctor performs an illegal abortion on the teacher, and the public prosecutor refrains from pressing a charge. As von Keitz points out, at the very end the grip of the out-of-date law dissolves literally, because none of the civil servants respect it: 'the doctor aborts, the prosecutor stops prosecuting, the teacher teaching sitting at home instead and the written law becomes superfluous when the prosecutor quite literally leaves it behind and quits his job'.[32]

The film also decries class differences cinematically by its use of space and lighting: the public areas of the middle-class professionals like the prosecutor's office, which is reminiscent of a 'mediaeval' hall complete with an exaggeratedly high gothic chair, emphasize the supreme importance of the law while rendering the figure of the prosecutor curiously fragile. The doctor's surgery is also relatively large and very brightly lit; so are the staircase of the teacher's apartment block and the living area of the 'modern' couple. In contrast, the spaces of the poor are narrow and gloomy. For example, the working-class drama unfolds on the dark stairwell of the tenement block at the back, in the caretaker's tiny office and the cramped family room where the woman dies.[33]

Paradoxically, however, the narrative structure and characterization in the film reinforces the very class inequality it seeks to criticize: it focuses on the story of the middle-class teacher and marginalizes the proletarian tragedy as a sideshow. It also perpetuates the stereotype of the proletarian woman as victim, an image well known from the graphic art of Käthe Kollwitz, the most successful woman artist of the Weimar years. It depicted the hopeless and helpless mother, a symbol of capitalist exploitation, and was made available to a wider public through being reprinted in popular journals, in pamphlets and on posters. The working-class family in *Kreuzzug* is almost a caricature of suffering writ large on their worn faces, unfashionable clothes and their children's general beseeching look. The unspoken judgement that this proletarian family is marked with 'degeneration' is thus established entirely through cinematic means.

Kreuzzug anticipated many other tragic abortion narratives in working-class circles. In *Cyankali* Hete's helplessness in the face of a class-ridden society is magnified by her inability to prevent the sexual attacks of the caretaker or overcome the reluctance of the two-faced doctor. More subtly, Hete's mother, who looks old and worn out despite being only fifty,[34] serves as a warning example of wasted proletarian womanhood. In Keun's *Gilgi*, the protagonist's old friend Hans and his wife Hertha have similarly given up hope. During the Depression Hans has slipped down the social ladder and finds himself amongst the down-and-outs facing imprisonment unless he can repay his debts; Hertha has resigned herself to a third child despite being destitute. She admires Hans and professes to be prepared 'to die for him' but 'illness, tiredness and the constant fear of a child' has made sex for her 'torture, a terrible torture' and she is tempted to give Hans enough money for a prostitute.[35] When Gilgi fails to deliver the money she has obtained for them, Hans and Hertha end in the most pathetic way possible: they gas themselves and their children. Their lack of resolve provides a poignant backdrop to Gilgi's own fate: while her friends have sunk into apathy, the reader cannot but admire the heroine who fights on. Instead of muddling through with her charming but irresponsible layabout boyfriend she leaves him and bravely faces the future as an unwed mother in the capital. Berlin, of course, was associated with modernity and sexual reform. Gilgi thus signals her determination to retain agency and break the stereotypical fate of young women as victims of seduction and abandonment; as the literary scholar Barbara Kosta has remarked, it is also a powerful 'affront to notions of family and dominant culture'.[36]

Finally, both *Gilgi* and *Kreuzzug* can be accused of anti-working-class prejudice in their characterization. Whereas the protagonists, both middle class or, in the case of Gilgi, lower middle-class, are drawn as more rounded personalities, the lower classes, in true Expressionistic style, remain one-dimensional types. In the case of *Kreuzzug* this is despite the fact that the main characters, too, have no names and are not rounded but primarily represent professional roles, thereby elevating the drama into an almost abstract argument, a strategy particularly applauded in a contemporary review.[37]

The novel *Gilgi* and the female reader and spectator

We know from contemporary studies that women comprised a large number – if not the majority – of the cinema-going public and the same was true of the serialized novel. Patrice Petro has convincingly argued that if we look at different textual practices we can deduce that 'a female spectatorship was indeed assumed and addressed' by the cinema and the illustrated press, and that it 'is the existence of a female spectator and the function of representation for mobilizing her desires and unconscious fantasies, that analyses of the Weimar cinema have repressed'.[38] It may be reasonable to assume that the portrayal of upwardly mobile lower middle-class or middle-class heroines attracted both the proletarian and the bourgeois woman spectator and was therefore eagerly pursued by film distributors as well as publishers. The young teacher in *Kreuzzug* fitted the new model of the emancipated Weimar woman whose higher education afforded her a profession, enough self-confidence and economic independence to control her own fate (until she found she had little control over her own body). New Woman narratives were extremely popular. The fortune of the illustrated press was much boosted by printing in instalments a novel which conformed to the new vision of women's modernity. The serialization of Vicki Baum's *stud. chem. Helene Willfüer* (1928) reputedly increased the circulation of the *Berliner Illustrirte Zeitung* by no less than 200,000 to reach more than two million copies.[39] Baum's protagonist was also the epitome of the New Woman: a middle-class chemistry student, a single mother (after failing to obtain an abortion), a successful scientist working on the fashionable process of rejuvenation, all the rage at that time.[40]

Keun's bestseller *Gilgi* was also serialized, no doubt riding on the wave of the huge public protests against the arrest in early 1931 of the two doctors Else Kienle and Friedrich Wolf for illegal terminations, which took place in the same year. Keun dealt deftly with one of the key conflicts of the New Woman: to overcome the apparent incompatibility of work, love and motherhood, exacerbated in the slump. Interestingly, *Gilgi* was not serialized in the illustrated press but in the SPD organ, *Vorwärts*. In 1932 it was filmed by the German Paramount film company as *Eine von uns*, directed by Johannes Meyer. Despite the first-class cast, with Brigitte Helm in the title role and Ernst Busch as the musician Pit, however, it proved a disappointment.[41] But it was a popular and critical success both as book and serial. Within a year of publication the book was reprinted five times, having sold no less than 30, 000 copies for the 26-year-old first-time author (who claimed to be only 21).[42] Tucholsky praised her as a 'woman with humour', others like Hans Fallada and Kadidja Wedekind followed suit. Conservative critics liked the protagonist's courage but might well have been shocked by Keun's tough description of the scene at the abortion doctor's.[43]

Gilgi, the white-collar heroine, strives to advance through a tough regime of self-improvement, body culture and work discipline and a fashionably sober attitude to life and love at the beginning of the book. It must have spoken to thousands of other young women with similar worldly aspirations. Gilgi's modernity was perfectly conveyed in Keun's idiosyncratic style. As Kosta has formulated it, 'both Gilgi's tempo and time schedule, punctuated by Keun's rapid scene changes, fragmented writing and abrupt sentences replicate the pulse of the city' of the 1920s.[44] Sentimentality in sexual relations is spurned by Gilgi from the outset and she criticizes her own unexpected feelings for Martin, her *bon-vivant* lover as a *Betriebsstörung* (operational difficulties).[45] This was very much in keeping with the atmosphere of sexual cynicism among the younger generation and the notion of rationalized sexuality discussed by sex reformers and population strategists alike.[46] Bemoaning the 'increasingly hard, cold, masculine tone' of contemporary literature, Max Brod, writing in 1929, explained that 'it is unacceptable either to sing or to speak of love' since it was 'incompatible with "objectivity", the supreme postulate of the present.'[47] Gilgi was surely the perfect role model for all aspiring New Women. She is well aware of her youth, her slim build, her tight muscles and her taut face. In fact she insists on being called Gilgi rather than Gisela, her real name, because 'a name with two i's fits slender legs and prepubescent hips, a tiny fashion cap which balances mysteriously on the outer edge of the head'.[48] She is the very image of that phenomenon, the confident white-collar worker, maligned by Kracauer in his 'The Little Shop Girls Go to the Cinema' and the 'typists who fashion themselves according to their ideals on the screen'.[49] Gilgi fits this stereotype well: she is a stenotypist with huge social ambitions, intensely aware of advertising and consumer values, who names brand names effortlessly and seemingly unaware ('Kaloderma soap, Pebeco toothpaste'), and is able to hum current pop songs ('Reich mir zum Abschied noch einmal die Hände – good nighit, good nighit … ').[50]

In contrast to the working-class victims Hans and Hertha, Gilgi is proud of getting on under her own steam. She is successful despite not being especially talented: ' I am pretty average and I'm not letting that get me down. But I'll make what I can of myself … '. She has no time for melancholy thoughts: 'You know, if you are healthy and not hungry you have simply no right to be unhappy.'[51] Yet, her supreme self-confidence is shattered later in the book when she falls in love in an old-fashioned romantic way, loses her self-control and her job, gets into debt and finally finds herself pregnant. In an effort to regain control of her life and her body she seeks an abortion from a general practitioner, but in vain. Thus the book illustrates very powerfully the problematic experience of modernity by Weimar's young women, who bravely strove to challenge conventions and create a new social role for themselves. Kosta suggests that the 'narrative resolution holds the tenuous promise of a new family structure in a modern, secular society that does not bind marriage with maternity. Perhaps she alludes to the possibility of re-imagining the maternal.'[52]

Both book and protagonist met with strong criticism from the political left. In 1932 when the novel appeared in daily instalments in *Vorwärts*, the editor, evoking Keun's title, asked readers: 'Is Gilgi one of us?' and apparently received a sackful of letters. Judging from the selection printed in the paper, the response on the whole was more critical than positive. Readers took Keun's character Gilgi to task for her 'contempt' and her 'lack of empathy'. One woman journalist even wrote an invective in the KPD journal *Weg der Frau*, accusing Keun's heroine of fascist tendencies. The real Gilgis, she argued, had more important worries than a love affair; they needed work and bread; what was needed was not 'social climbing but a struggle of all Gilgis against the existing economic circumstances ... '. She called on 'all Gilgis of the real world – to defend themselves!'[53] This is reminiscent of Kracauer's critique of the 'false consciousness' of the white-collar workers whose comprehension of the real world of work, social position and class adherence was, he suggested, diverted by the illusions created by entertainment film and advertising.[54] His tendency to accuse the female spectator, especially the young female spectator, of passivity and gullibility has for some time been challenged by a number of feminist scholars.[55] It is of course especially unconvincing to accuse women watching films like *Kreuzzug* of merely wanting an easy escape from reality when what they were watching was precisely the very real problems they encountered in everyday life. But, as we know, Kracauer was not the only one who viewed the rise of mass culture with alarm, as is shown in the widespread debates about *Kitsch*, *Trivialliteratur* and *Schund und Schmutz* throughout the 1920s and the various articles by Walter Benjamin and Georg Simmel before him.[56]

Socialist plays and novels

Only left-wing film and fiction dared to put the plight of the working-class heroine centre stage. The best-known examples are two agitprop plays, Friedrich Wolf's *Cyankali*. §218 (1929) and Carl Credé's '§218. Gequälte Menschen (Tortured people) of the same year. The protagonist in *Cyankali* is 20-year-old Hete who lives with her widowed mother. Hete started off as a manual worker but has recently become a white-collar worker in an office. Her boyfriend Paul is a boiler man in a steel factory. When Hete finds herself pregnant she looks forward to the child; but this changes when Paul loses his job in a lock-out and is subsequently imprisoned for stealing from the works canteen (to prevent starvation). When Hete's mother accuses her of bringing shame on them she runs away to seek a termination at all cost. She consults a doctor who, like the family doctor in *Kreuzzug*, hides behind the law ('the law ties the hands of us doctors ... ') which he quotes verbatim to the bewildered Hete and then tells her about abortion and mortality statistics issued by the Annual Conference of the German Medical Association, for good measure.[57] Even more than in the film, the play spells out all the mortal dangers of wise women: cyanide or 'syringing with carbolic soap', 'infection from dirty instruments' leading to death 'in convulsions of puerperal fever'.[58] Like the working-class mother in *Kreuzzug*, Hete seeks a lay abortion and dies like her. Her road to perdition has the usual stops along the way: the attempted self-abortion (here in the back of a newspaper kiosk) after Hete had obtained a syringe from the male caretaker, who wanted to be paid for it 'in kind'; the quack abortionist Madame Heye, found through a small ad in the papers, and finally the death in her mother's arms. It is in fact her mother who is tricked into administering the deadly poison and thereby becomes the murderess of her only daughter.

The play was written as a 'docudrama' interspersing fiction with documentary material of statistics and newspaper cuttings to make it seem like a dramatized reportage and help to mobilize the audience into political action, in the belief that 'Kunst ist Waffe' (Art is a weapon).[59] *Cyankali* was premiered on 5 September 1929 in Berlin's Lessing Theatre, the so-called second Piscator stage. Wolf's aspirations became real when the socialist collective of the unemployed *Gruppe junger Schauspieler* (group of young actors), who in 1930 took it on tour throughout Germany and Switzerland, created a sensation: they faced theatre scandals and right-wing attacks, as well as left-wing

4. Renée Stobrawa as Hete in Friedrich Wolf's play *Cyankali*. § 218, Berlin, 1929

support.[60] Critics praised and mocked it in equal measure. For example, the *Hamburger 8 Uhr Abendblatt* praised the young actors as being

> of our generation. They are inhabited by *zeitgeist*. They do not only identify with the characters, but also with the playwright, the social will of the drama comes alive in them ... This is the first strong impetus to a national theatre of the present.[61]

Although the SPD press, probably motivated by Wolf having joined their arch rival, the KPD, could be critical at times – one paper described Wolf's drama as 'a reflex of petty-bourgeois ideology'[62] – left-wing writers and journals generally praised Wolf's commitment to the cause of class equality but recognized the artistic limits of his writing. The novelist Erich Kästner thought the play a 'simple work' but an 'exemplary thesis play'. He described how at the end of the performance he attended, a voice rang out from the balcony with 'Down with §218!' followed by a tumultuous chorus of female and male voices: 'Down with it! Down! Down!' Kästner predicted, rightly, that the play would stimulate discussion in the Reichstag, in newspapers, among doctors and the legal commissions in parliament. A Stuttgart left-leaning newspaper praised it as a 'powerful indictment of bourgeois society' but criticized what it regarded as Wolf's 'failure to tread the path of the proletarian class struggle' by omitting to offer a solution for social problems and show the importance of solidarity amongst the striking workers.[63]

The bourgeois press was naturally more hostile and stressed the incendiary message which led to uproar. One critic, Ludwig Marcuse, called *Cyankali* 'hurried and coarsely constructed' and predicted that 'once the law is discarded so Wolf's play will be'. There were reports of protests in several towns such as that by Catholic associations, which issued a complaint in Frankfurt am Main.[64] A serious factual critique was printed in November 1929 in the influential *Frankfurter Zeitung*. A Dr Kögel, a high-ranking lawyer, accused the play of misinformation and Wolf of 'not even knowing the current penal provisions relating to abortion'. Kögel made three important points. Firstly, the law was misrepresented when at the start of the play, §218 and other texts were projected on a screen, presumably to underline the actuality of the topic.[65] But the text of §218 used (and repeated in publicity material for the play) was that of 1871 despite the fact that the law had been reformed in May 1926.[66] In addition, the play misrepresented legal practice. In Frankfurt where he was public prosecutor, Hete's case would have led to only one week (suspended) imprisonment or a fine of 20 to 30 Marks for the aborting woman. Moreover, the final scene of Hete's mother's arrest was quite implausible, as was the harsh attitude to Hete herself. Secondly, Paul's imprisonment was off the mark. In Kögel's own experience Paul's theft of food would have been condoned as petty theft in times of genuine hardship. Thirdly, no doctor was legally obliged to inform the authorities of a criminal abortion about which he had heard in his professional capacity.[67]

Why this slip on Wolf's part? Despite a rather feeble attempt in the same newspaper by a woman lawyer to exonerate Wolf and a more spirited response by the author himself, the accusation was never properly refuted. Ignoring the issue of misquoting §218, Wolf simply stated that every year 'many women and girls' had to defend themselves in court, that they were thus branded and lost earnings and that the reform of §218 had not brought relief.

> 10,000 German women would rather go to a quack and a back-street abortionist than to a doctor who is not permitted to help, they would rather endure a bad operation than have none at all, rather suffer puerperal fever and gynaecological problems than enforced motherhood and shame: This is where the problem is, Sir![68]

This amounted to Wolf's tacit admission of his error. Why did this come about? It is inconceivable that he was ignorant of the 1926 legal reform; after all, he wrote the play a full three years later and he was a prominent and outspoken law reformer. Indeed he had practised what he preached and had referred patients for termination on social grounds, which led to his arrest in February 1931. It seems more probable that Wolf used artistic 'licence' in reproducing the outdated 1871 law to strengthen his dramatic message: that thousands of poor women were victims of an unjust and murderous law. The same motivation was probably behind the other inaccuracies. But they sit uneasily with the claim of *Cyankali* as a *Zeitstück*, rooted in the social realities of the day and fulfilling the characteristics of the new political theatre supported by Piscator as functional, authentic and devoid of symbolism.[69] Furthermore, more errors were committed: Wolf asserted implicitly in the play and explicitly in his newspaper retort above, that doctors were not permitted to perform terminations. However, in 1927 the Supreme Court had decreed the permissibility of termination on medical grounds. Finally, Madame Heye's prescription of cyanide is unrealistic; not a single one of the many judicial abortion files examined for this book mention this method of lay abortion.

The success of the play secured Wolf lucrative offers from many film companies, amongst others Prometheus, close to the KPD and part of the International Workers' Aid. In spite of Wolf having joined the KPD in 1928 he rejected Prometheus in favour of Atlantis-Film, the German subsidiary of the U.S. Fox Film Company. Wolf was apparently anxious to prevent the film from being sentimentalized but, as the correspondence between Wolf and the film's director, Hans Tintner, testifies, artistic cooperation soon proved problematic and Wolf distanced himself from the end result, dismissing it as 'kitsch'.[70] Wolf's own disaffection and the endless problems of censorship notwithstanding, it proved to be one of the most successful of all so-called sexual enlightenment films and was considered *the* 'classic' *Thesenfilm* against §218. It was premiered on 23 May 1930 not on the Kurfürstendamm, but in the Babylon in the working-class east of Berlin (with 120 seats, one of

5. Film poster, *Cyankali*. §218, directed by Hans Tintner (1930), Grete Mosheim as Hete, 'Madame Heye', the abortionist, in the background

Germany's smaller cinemas).[71] The film was soon shown all over Germany and was used by both SPD and KPD in their election campaigns, as indeed was Berger's *Kreuzzug* and Eduard Tissé's *Frauennot – Frauenglück* (Women's misery and women's happiness) in 1928.[72]

Cyankali certainly contained all the stereotypical ingredients of vintage abortion drama: the young lower-class Hete is vulnerable to capitalist economic vagaries and finally falls victim to the bourgeois abortion law; Madame Heye, in the guise of the grim and greedy quack whose potion proves lethal, functions as the archetypal villain. Reminiscent of the uncontrolled sensual appetite of the caretaker's son in *Kreuzzug*, Heye's thirst for money is expressed in several ways: we first see her eating greedily and at the same time 'devouring' the downmarket *8 Uhr Abendblatt*. Her gestures are rude; she beckons Hete with a mere movement of her head and also uses street slang: 'What about dough?'. Her boasting of her attention to hygiene ('everything with antisepsis and sterilization [sic!] you see, because of puerperal fever!') only serves to draw attention to her negligence of asepsis and antisepsis in the following sequence. She takes out of an old chest of drawers instruments loosely wrapped in cloth and offends the most basic rule of hygiene by not rendering them sterile or washing her hands. Instead she wipes them on her grubby apron. Commerce rules, as when Heye signals the value of her time by pointing to her watch at the beginning of the encounter with her client. Heye drives a hard bargain, thereby reducing the gravely ill Hete into little more than a commodity: 'Do you really believe that I'd risk this for a lousy 10 Marks – and in your state!' (In the play she demanded 30 Marks). Finally the abortionist rids herself of an uncomfortable customer by selling her potassium cyanide which would not only kill the foetus but also Hete herself. The director uses a paradoxical voyeuristic strategy: showing the operation in silhouette behind an opaque glass wall impeded the spectators' gaze of gynaecological details but stimulated their imagination.[73]

In fact, as we will see in Chapter 4, this must be rated as a highly partisan portrait of a lay operator. Abortionists worth their salt would have declined such a risky case: the presence of a temperature and abdominal pain pointed to an infection by a previous bungled operation. This posed a significant legal risk, since medical complications or death almost always led to police investigation and prosecution of both aborting woman and her accomplice. Hete's sickly looks do indeed arouse Heye's suspicion ('Been at the doctor – or tried it yourself? You look so seedy!') at the outset; once it is established that Hete has fever (here the German word 'FIEBER' is written in distorted letters all over the screen) and we see her writhing with stomach pain, these suspicions are confirmed. In Wolf's play Heye does not risk an operation; in the film she does. Both play and film imply that Hete pays with her life as a result of Madame Heye's intervention. This is, however, wilfully misleading; since Hete had attempted self-abortion her final death cannot be blamed

GASTSPIEL DER PISCATOR BÜHNE / BERLIN

CARL CREDÉ

§ 218 Gequälte Menschen

Das Titelbild von Käthe Kollwitz mit Genehmigung des Reißverlages Dresden dem Buche „Volk in Not" entnommen.

6. Programme for Carl Credé's play *§218. Gequälte Menschen*, directed by Erwin Piscator, illustration by Käthe Kollwitz, 'At the Doctor's'.

only, or even mainly, on the intervention or administrations of this abortionist. What is more, the film also commits an extraordinary medical blunder: Heye dramatically pronounces a fever not after she has used a thermometer but after she has taken Hete's pulse!

Immediately in the wake of *Cyankali* a second abortion play, '§218'. *Gequälte Menschen* (Tortured people), swept Germany by storm. There are many striking parallels between the two plays. The author of '§218', Carl Credé, was also a left-wing doctor and he, too, got into trouble with the law. In 1927 he had published a polemic written while in prison for illegally terminating pregnancies. It was illustrated with several drawings by Käthe Kollwitz, who herself had leftist sympathies and whose husband was a socialist doctor working in a working-class district of Berlin. One, *Beim Arzt* (At the doctor's) showed an emaciated proletarian woman with a swollen belly knocking on the door of a doctor with a mixture of resignation and quiet determination.[74] The play was based on a 'reportage', *Frauen in Not*. '§218' (Suffering women) for abortion law reform which was serialized in the Communist Party paper *Die Rote Fahne* and which also inspired, in October 1931, a touring exhibition with the same name and organized by the communist journal *Weg der Frau*.[75] The play '§218', also directed by Piscator, was premiered in Leipzig in November 1929 and was, like *Cyankali* a *Kampfstück*, a campaigning drama for the liberalization of the abortion law, an aim made very explicit in the theatre programme: Credé called for a referendum on §218 and Piscator wrote a eulogy on the institution of the theatre, which he regarded as one of the few media to instil a sense of outrage. People, he said, were usually passive, 'for lack of imagination ... [and] do not fully experience their own life, let alone their world. Otherwise reading a single newspaper page would suffice to stir humanity to uproar.' '§218' (*Gequälte Menschen*) and *Cyankali* were perfect examples of the kind of agitprop drama in which Piscator believed: 'Theatre today has to be linked to the needs, demands and pain of the mass for better or worse, if it is not to remain a pretentious institution for the upper five hundred.' Abortion was just such a topic which had politicized the masses in the 'post-revolutionary state'.[76]

Like *Cyankali*, the programme quoted §218 in the 1871 rather than the 1926 version, again no doubt an artistic licence which ran, however, counter to a claim of authenticity sought by quoting details of actual abortion trials in 1929 in Berlin and Swabia. The misquoted law also sat uncomfortably with a eulogy by Herbert Ihring, a fellow left-wing director. He praised Piscator as 'the greatest director of contemporary material that Germany possesses', as a director who deals in 'actual events' rather than in 'fables and fiction'. The author's misleading background information notwithstanding, one reviewer, the legal adviser to the General Medical Council, found the message of the play so convincing that he urged his colleagues to go and see it to better engage with the central issue of abortion law reform.[77]

Like *Cyankali* and the film *Kreuzzug*, Credé's play thematized the supposed class inequality of the law and the judiciary. The first act showed the death of a proletarian mother of eight malnourished children at the hands of a quack abortionist. A well-meaning doctor, previously consulted, felt obliged to turn down her request for a qualified medical termination. The third act was set in a poor housing estate. It was the second act, however, which proved the dramatic climax: against the background of an examining magistrate investigating the case of a well-to-do childless couple accused of a 'convenience abortion' by a colluding doctor, the pros and cons of the abortion law were debated by the couple, a medical officer of health, a curate and a progressive doctor. To increase the dramatic impact of this discussion Piscator placed all but the magistrate amidst the audience, from where they voiced their opinions with increasing passion and anger. Financed by the Free Trade Unions, the play toured throughout Germany cities. It was frequently staged not in central theatres but cinemas, community centres or suburban theatres because of censorship invoked by municipal authorities.[78] Critics were divided roughly along political lines: those on the right deplored it and those on the left enthused about it. A Bremen critic praised Credé for pointing 'his finger relentlessly at a wound of the social body of modern humanity which has caused the most excruciating pain: ... the question of the justification of termination of pregnancy.'[79] The *Barmer Stadtanzeiger* went as far as calling the play:

> true, great theatre of the kind we see rarely. Like Greek theatre ... , like *Die Räuber* [by Friedrich Schiller] [it] dismantles the boundary between stage and spectator ... between art and life. This is an evening which tears apart and rages through souls ... .This evening is unforgettable.[80]

But the most feared critic of his time, Alfred Kerr, characteristically rubbished its artistic content: 'there is no author; he is called Credé'. According to Kerr the play had 'no artistic merit', it was a mere *Nutzwerk, ein Zweckwerk, ein Zeitwerk, ein Massenwerk* ... (a mere utility drama, a functional drama, a topical drama, a mass drama).[81] Other reviewers concurred albeit in a less hostile language; one wrote that the play was an 'unpoetic version' of Wolf's play but 'for the less gifted'.[82]

Nevertheless, most agreed about the originality of Piscator's direction, aimed at the active involvement of a thinking audience.[83] Reviews applauded an 'enchanting playing on the blurred boundaries between illusion ... and reality which is invigorating' and they liked the way the play was staged like a tribunal, in which the audience found themselves in the dock since they tolerated a law 'which spawns misery and crime'.[84] The popular success of the play seems undisputed and most newspapers reported an enthusiastic reception everywhere. In Mannheim where the play was staged in Germany's oldest theatre, the slow and painful death of the proletarian woman apparently made such a strong impression that it caused several members of the audience to faint, by no means only women.[85] At the end of the opening night a straw poll was taken among the audience for or against a repeal of §218 which resulted in unanimous support for a repeal. But given the likelihood of leftist spectators this was not really surprising. The *Rheinische Zeitung* described how 'people left the theatre only slowly, and they could not calm down'. In some cities like in Worms in December 1929, however, the performance was hijacked by Nazi thugs who beat up communists.[86]

Another example of a left-wing treatment of abortion was the novel *Maria und der Paragraph* (Maria and the law) by the young communist Franz Krey.[87] Adorned with a preface by Friedrich Wolf, it was published in 1931 in the KPD's Red-One-Mark-Series and clearly rode the wave of popularity of the left-wing abortion dramas inaugurated by *Cyankali*. But despite Wolf's praise for the young working-class author and despite the fact that Krey based his fiction on actual judicial case material, it suffers from a turgid style, an improbable storyline and a relentless agglomeration of clichés which are only tenuously held together by a crude political message: only a KPD-led class struggle can overturn the 'shameful law' and save the proletariat in their daily fight for survival. Interestingly, in this novel the heroine of the title is not a blue- but a white-collar worker but because of her allegiance to organized labour she figures as an honorary proletarian. Maria is a typist in a small town who has undergone a back-street abortion and now needs to endure the taunts and blackmail of an office cleaner who had found her out. When Maria can no longer endure this she assaults and finally murders the cleaning woman. Her eventual trial is the dramatic climax of the novel: the court case is transformed into a proletarian mass demonstration against §218 of the kind which had taken place in real life that same year. It ends with a melodramatic letter by a young doctor who has lost his position because of his active support for abortion law reform. He writes that he is prepared to sacrifice his existence, although he is in danger, 'already has one foot in prison', for the sake of working women: 'these women don't just have one foot in prison, but also in the grave'.[88] Despite its doubtful literary qualities the topic was obviously compelling enough for the novel to be serialized in the communist *Arbeiter Illustrierte Zeitung*.[89]

Abortion as a topic also attracted poets. For example, the political revolutionary writer and member of the KPD Erich Weinert wrote two polemical poems about the abortion clause: in 1929 a poem with the title '§218', published in *Mahnruf*, a working-class monthly journal, and in 1931 'Was sagt Ihr nun zu §218?' (What do you now say about §218?) in which he argued that only a socialist revolution could abolish a law which harms the working class.[90] In this poem, the abortion clause is personified and accused of being a destructive 'monster' in the first stanza:

§218

In the dark of the Church and the chill of the Law
Is the monster of old yet lurking,
With a priggish attorney's cadaverous claw
To crawl on Love's dream, still smirking?

A good woman serves with confidence
Morality, yes, and the Nation.
Her support is paid for by Providence:
That's enough for the genuine Christian.

Here's a moral precept that still survives,
Meant first for the humblest, maybe:
A true German woman has no other drives,
She's always having a baby.

Our human stocks are our vital resource,
For employers and (one day) for battle;
And all women have their duty of course,
Which is unremittingly natal.

We see it afresh every single day,
Moral rot in the lower divisions:
The superior elements, come what may,
Stay strictly within the provisions.

So trust in the Lord, lowly workers and clerks,
And breed like the mice in your houses.
Think of Crown briefs, stewed in their rectitude:
Take after their stainless spouses.

Erich Weinert, 1929.[91]

Couched in sardonic irony, this poem attacks the antiquated powers of the clergy ('the dark of the Church'), the cruel and lethal power of the law ('chill of the law' with its 'cadaverous claw') and pious but inhuman public prosecutors ('priggish attorney'). The central message conforms to the standard opinion articulated by the KPD in that it decries §218 as a class law and links it to the misguided, but by then largely outdated, pronatalism ('our human stocks are our vital resources for employers and (one day) for battle') of the ruling classes. Certainly, in Imperial Germany the state, in tandem with economists and the medical profession, exhorted the poor to procreate ('breed like mice in your houses') and to imitate the wives of the professional classes ('the stainless spouses' of the 'crown briefs, stewed in their rectitude'), although this should be understood as irony, since the latter were actually producing far fewer children. It echoes the demands of socialists to repeal §218 and instead introduce proper maternity and child welfare because the state could not impose a *Gebärpflicht* (obligation to reproduce) without accepting a *Nährpflicht* (obligation to feed its children).[92]

Two years later, Kurt Tucholsky, a social critic and a satirist with communist leanings, published an abortion poem. He was a leading contributor to the most important radical cultural/political journal, *Die Weltbühne*, where he earned himself the nickname, the 'heckling voice in the gallery'.[93] He was also a prime representative of the cool style of *Neue Sachlichkeit*, apparent in this poem:

An Embryo Speaks

They all take care of me: the church, the state, the physicians, the judges.
I'm supposed to grow and to thrive: I'm supposed to slumber for nine months, to take it easy
– they wish me well. They protect me and watch over me. Heaven help my parents if they do me any harm; then they all come running. Anyone who touches me is punished; my mother would land in jail, so would my father; the doctor who'd do it would have to stop being a doctor; the midwife who'd assist would be locked up. You see, I'm something precious.
Yes, they take care of me: the church, the state, the physicians, the judges.
For nine months.
But once these nine months are past, I am on my own.
TB? There's no doctor to help me. Nothing to eat? No milk? There's no help from the state. Torment and mental anguish? The church consoles me but does not fill my stomach. And I haven't a thing to eat, so I go out and steal; immediately there's a judge who locks me up.
For fifty years of my life no one will look after me, not a soul. I'll have to shift for myself.
For nine months they kill one another if someone wants to kill me.
Now I ask you: Isn't that a strange welfare system?

Kurt Tucholsky, 1931.[94]

With typical irreverence and wit Tucholsky sends up the sanctimonious official system which cared more for a foetus than for a living child. The poem also pokes fun at all those who ignored the hot debates about the beginning of life and the permissibility of a termination at what precise stage of gestation. The disembodied voice of the 'embryo' works well as a dramatic device in this satire of bourgeois and religious attitudes (where abortion was regarded as the killing of an unborn child) and it makes light of the stance of feminists and left-wing pro-abortionists, namely that a termination up to three months of pregnancy was not the killing of nascent life. As we will see in Chapter 5, many women concurred with these latter convictions.

Abortion pathologized

All the directors, writers and artists examined have not only insisted on a stereotypical unsympathetic portrait of the lay abortionist but have also depicted abortion, often even pregnancy, as a negative experience. Maybe it is not surprising that popular culture, driven as it was by commercial considerations, sensationalized both events and tragedy to render plots more dramatic. As we have seen, in the play (as well as the film) *Cyankali*, pregnancy and its termination is associated with disaster and death. As soon as Hete reveals she is expecting, she is told that feckless breeding leads to suicide. 'This house is not a rabbit warren [proclaims the caretaker]. Every week another woman opens the gas tap or jumps into the water', thereby foretelling the subsequent suicide of Hete's neighbour. Hete's attempt to rid herself of her pregnancy exposes her to the caretaker's sexual advances, then to the doctor's warning that both quack abortion and cyanide will mean that she will die 'of puerperal fever in convulsions'![95] At the wise woman's Hete invokes death herself ('I do not want to die, you! I am still young, you') and so does the police inspector who questions Hete's mother ('we have to find the person who has ... lethally damaged your daughter'). Lay abortion is linked to death most explicitly at the beginning (in the montage of newspaper cuttings) and at the very end of *Cyankali* the pros and cons of §218 are debated: 10,000 deaths annually from back-street abortion is alleged, repeated in Hete's last words: '10,000, 10,000 must die. Does nobody help us?'.[96]

Similar associations occur in *Gilgi* (Hans and his wife's suicide), in Krey's novel *Maria und der Paragraph*, and the film *Kreuzzug* (death of the working-class mother).[97] *Kreuzzug*, of course, also thematizes the death nexus in the ghost scene at the end of the film depicting the souls of dead abortion victims. Similarly, the huge cross at the centre of Alice Lex-Nerlinger's 1931 poster, *Paragraph 218*, conjures up the image of death very emphatically.

Interestingly, the gender of the writer or director/producer does not seem to have made much difference here. As we have seen, in Irmgard Keun's and Vicki Baum's books *Gilgi* and *Helene Willfüer* abortion was portrayed as unobtainable and the quest for it so humiliating and frustrating so that the heroines actually prefer to cope with unwed motherhood. As far as I know only two women wrote films about §218: Jane Beß, the most prolific of all female scriptwriters in the Weimar Republic[98] and Marie Louise Droop. Both offer striking examples of intertextuality and they seemed to have stuck firmly to the conventions, probably not surprising given the film industry in which men dominated and women scriptwriters were very unusual. Beß wrote *Frauenarzt Dr. Schäfer* (1929) which also boasted a female distributor, Marie-Luise Fleck, who, with her husband Jakob, acted as a team. Any expectation of a subversive, possibly even feminist, angle by these women is dashed. In this film a woman's reproductive and moral dilemma is not resolved and it was indeed derided by most critics for its simplistic and superficial treatment of a complex topic.

Two strands of the plot end in sentimentality. In the first, the daughter of a respected medical authority is raped and consults Dr Schäfer, her former fiancé. He rejects her and her father's urgent request for a termination but instead asks to marry her and thereby, so we are meant to believe, he preserves her honour. The other strand concerned the intergenerational debate within the local medical society in which the representative of the older generation, the heroine's father and Dr Schäfer's former professor, rejects abortion on any ground and the young gynaecologist, Dr Schäfer, campaigns for abortion law reform in order to guarantee 'fewer but fitter children for the state'. The villain of the piece is the young and ambitious Dr Greber, the new protegé of the professor, who is found responsible for a botched abortion on the heroine's friend, who dies. When the heroine detects his misdeed, Dr Greber revenges himself by raping her. If spectators thought that this film took a critical stance of the medical profession and its renegade doctors, they were mistaken. At the final denouement Dr Greber is revealed to have faked his medical certificate.[99] Thus, the villain of the film is conveniently revealed as a quack and the honour of the medical profession has been exonerated. The woman scriptwriter and her female distributor had not, after all, rocked the boat.

Marie Louise Droop, who scripted *Der Sittenrichter. §218. Eine wahre Begebenheit* (The moral censor. §218. A true incident), (1929), proved no more challenging. Her story concerned the tragedy of Susi, a police constable's daughter, who is seduced by her married boss and subsequently finds herself pregnant. She has an abortion by a 'woman with a dark trade', acted by the exotic-looking Maria Forescu. When the latter is arrested Susi is also summoned to court on suspicion of having offended against §218. Rather than face public humiliation and her father's certain wrath, Susi commits suicide.[100] Thus, this script, too, conforms to the stereotypical notion of abortionists as untrustworthy outsiders, women as victims and abortion as tragedy.

Such cultural portrayal of the events surrounding abortion is strikingly different, however, from women's own views as we glimpse them in transcripts of police interviews, letters and gossip within the neighbourhood (see Chapters 5 and 6 below). Why then this disparity between so many women's actual experience and its fictional representation? An important reason was surely the success of the medicalization process of German society, which meant that the middle classes had absorbed the arguments of doctors and passed them on as their own, at least in such public arenas as the theatre, the screen and fiction. Most medical men considered abortion as an exceptional event and one which they avoided (see Chapter 3). The profession as a whole also denounced quack abortionists supposedly in the interest of public health, in reality also in pursuit of their own professional interests (see Chapter 4).

But what about censorship? Could one not argue that even if writers had wanted to cast abortion and lay abortionists in a positive light, they had to reckon with censorship, especially on screen and stage. The Council of People's Representatives had abolished censorship immediately after the First World War, but after there had been a proliferation of so-called sexual enlightenment films, often thinly veiled pornography, censorship was re-introduced on 12 May 1920. The *Reichslichtspielgesetz* set up two censorship boards in Munich and Berlin to vet scripts and films.[101] It seems that abortion films were generally prohibited from referring openly to medical misdemeanours, from portraying law enforcement as unreasonable and from downplaying the dangers of lay abortionists, although, as we have seen, they seem to have got away with misquoting the abortion law. Literature and stage plays continued to be ruled by the pornography law, §184 of the penal code; furthermore the 1926 law 'to protect young people from *Schund und Schmutz* (trash and smut) instituted censorship panels in Berlin and Munich to scrutinize and, if necessary, ban offending publications or plays.[102]

In 1930 the film *Cyankali* is a good case in point. It was examined and then approved four times by the Berlin *Film Prüfstelle* (Board of film censors).[103] In August of the same year the *Film Oberprüfstelle* (Supreme board of film censors) in Berlin banned the film after a successful application by Bavaria, Baden and Württemberg. They had argued that the depiction of the law and its enforcement officers as immoral and unjust had a demoralizing effect on the audience and could endanger public order. The three *Länder* also asserted that the stark portrayal of Hete's physical suffering, her screams of agony at Madame Heye's and on her deathbed scene were 'brutalizing', especially since it occurred in the brief soundtrack at the end of an otherwise silent movie. In September the film was approved once more, but it was banned for young people and suffered several cuts: e.g. the caretaker's sexual harassment of Hete (presumably because it was deemed too coarse); the neighbour's suicide (Bavaria found this scene one of 'exaggeration and distortion'); the partisan preference of an elegant lady in the doctor's surgery over the proletarian Hete (Bavaria thought this brought the medical profession into disrepute); originally the entire scene at Madame Heye's was to be cut – it was only rescued by the filmmakers' ingenious idea of referring to the danger of cyanide through the insertion of newspaper cuttings and by illustrating the uncouth nature of Madame Heye's practice by adorning her with a dirty apron on which to wipe first her hands and than the gynaecological instruments. When the Berlin board of film censors wrote to the Supreme Board justifying the readmittance of the film in its changed format they added ironically that the new version 'seems to imply the possibility that a spectator regards the wise woman as carrying out her work in an especially hygienic manner'. Bavaria's renewed protest in November 1930 was finally rejected in December of the same year, but not before further cuts were demanded.[104]

Kreuzzug, too, encountered problems with censorship. The subtitles referring to §218 as a 'class law' had to be substituted with a blander version which diminished the class character of the film. Even after the approval by the Berlin board of film censorship Bavaria demanded a further censorship review. Although this was rejected the production company sought to preempt future problems by cutting four sequences in the third and fourth acts, all to do with the rape scene. As von Keitz points out, these damaged the portrayal of the central story as without them it was difficult to understand the motivation for the rape and, more importantly, its devastating effect on the young teacher.[105] Similarly and predictably, in the film *Frauenarzt Dr. Schäfer*, the rape scene had to go in its entirety, too.[106]

Yet, censorship alone cannot account for the striking consensus in a one-sided portrayal of abortion in general and lay abortionists in particular. By linking the aborting woman and her helper with death, destitution and criminality these narratives also implied such associations with female sexuality and thereby conjured up similarities with the topic of *Lustmord* (sexual murder) and prostitution, both frequent themes in popular culture. The disturbing images of mutilated female corpses as well as of prostitutes' bodies ravaged by age and destitution in the work of celebrated artists like Otto Dix, George Grosz and Rudolf Schlichter have been discussed by feminist scholars as examples of sexual cynicism and deep misogyny in modernist Weimar art.[107] I suggest that misogyny is also at work in the various forms of representation of abortion and, by implication, women's sexuality which was linked to male fears and fantasies. While much of popular culture privileged the image of the 'downtrodden' working-class woman seeking a termination after multiple pregnancies, abortion was also an option for middle-class New Women like Gilgi or Vicky Baum's Helene Willfüer and, as we shall see in Chapter 5, for married women who regarded it as a means of family planning. Birth control, that is contraception and abortion, had long been associated with extramarital sex and many contemporary commentators feared women's access to it as an encouragement to female sexual libertinage.[108] Aborting women appeared doubly threatening as they seemed to be in control of their fertility without having to depend on men's cooperation (as with coitus interruptus or the use of a condom) and sometimes also without their husbands' or lovers' knowledge.[109]

The contemporary unease with women's new public role and their increasing confidence to claim the same right of sexual experience and independence traditionally reserved for men must surely account for the way aborting women were portrayed. In part it was male anxieties about destabilized gender identities which conjured up visions of a destructive female sexuality. As Patrice Petro has argued with reference to such 'street films' as Pabst's *Joyless Street*, Weimar popular culture did not just convey male regression, or the story of 'male subjectivity in crisis' but a tragedy of women, who expressed their desire within a still largely patriarchal order.[110] Women were blamed, in large measure, for threatening the very fabric of society which depended on female acquiescence and subservience.

In part there was also a generational divide amongst women themselves at work: while younger women seemed to enjoy their new freedoms, older feminists and reformers were concerned about what they regarded as young women's irresponsible erotic behaviour, and attempted to channel it into socially more acceptable institutions like the new concept of a trial marriage or the old institution of marriage made more palatable to women once doctors helped husbands to fulfil their wives' erotic desires.[111] And of course opinions were shaped by attitudes to class, politics and culture, too.

Although the New Woman was also projected as a classless phenomenon, as we have seen above, the behaviour and the looks of New Women were more often regarded as a middle-class privilege while the stereotypical image of the proletarian woman remained steadfastly maternal, ageless and unerotic. Such ambiguous reactions to Weimar's modernity in general and women's aspirations in particular explains the striking dichotomy between the emancipatory vocabulary of sex reformers and radical feminists celebrating female desire and insisting on women's right of erotic satisfaction and the trend to pathologize women's sexuality in so many cultural products at the time. Thus abortion served also as a rhetorical device in the construction of female sexuality as deviant and dangerous.

Only those authors/directors of films, plays and novels which merely touched on the subject of abortion in passing and did not have to fear the censor on this account actually managed to convey the idea that the termination of an unwanted pregnancy was often an 'ordinary' and not particularly threatening event. Slatan Dudow's *Kuhle Wampe oder Wem gehört die Welt?* (Kuhle Wampe or who does the world belong to?) (1932), is a good example. It was sponsored by the KPD and was the only film during the Weimar Republic in which Brecht had a hand (he co-wrote the script with the young Bulgarian director). The film was originally produced by Prometheus-Film, founded in 1926 as an anti-capitalist and anti-bourgeois production company. But when it went into liquidation in January 1932 the film was taken on by Präsens-Film.[112] Independent of the commercial cinema, *Kuhle Wampe* could be artistically innovative and textually subversive. It refers to abortion according to the KPD party line: as a right for the working woman who cannot combine her economic role as producer with her biological function as reproducer in an uncaring capitalist system.[113] The story is about the Bönikes, a lower middle-class family who have fallen on hard times during the Depression. When young Anni (Hertha Thiele), who works in an electrical goods factory and is very much a New Woman, finds herself pregnant by her boyfriend, the taxi driver Fritz (Ernst Busch), Anni becomes the focus of attention. Brecht wrote: 'We see her struggling not for the right of her offspring to live, but for her own right to destroy it.'[114] Fritz suggests an abortion. When Anni's father is indignant, however, Fritz conforms and offers to marry Anni. But after an ill-fated engagement party, a true Brechtian farce of petty bourgeois pretensions and meant as a dig against the SPD, accused of being insufficiently revolutionary, Anni decides to call the engagement off. She moves in with a 'politicized' girl friend, has an abortion, joins a communist sports club and develops a sense of workers' solidarity. Fritz and Anni are reconciled when he, too, has developed a sense of political responsibility and together with their comrades they sing the song of solidarity.[115] Although abortion in this film is only implied, it is nevertheless a pivotal event in the narrative. It means liberation for the heroine from a degrading 'enforced' engagement and from the petty bourgeois conventions of her parents' generation. Anni is thus free to realize her own potential in the world of work, politics and leisure and to form a more equal and meaningful relationship with her boyfriend Fritz. And of course witnessing that Anni had not sustained any ill effects from her, presumably, lay operation, was in itself a powerful oppositional message about the value of an operation which was officially so maligned.

But despite the failure of so many of these abortion films to develop an independent view from the dominant medical discourse and the tendency of some to exploit commercially rather than explore seriously the theme of abortion, it would be wrong to belittle the impact of these abortion narratives. Most films pleaded for sex and abortion reform. And the very fact that women's biological fate was portrayed so publicly was undermining the traditional power relationship between the genders and the classes. The exposure of the abortion issue in literary and cinematic representations probably did more to raise awareness of women's reproductive problems and thereby of female sexuality than debates in the Reichstag or amongst doctors had ever managed to do. What is more, the subject was often also explored from the woman's point of view even if an explicit feminist line was rare. This was less surprising with novels like *Gilgi* and *Helene Willfüer*, written as they were by authors who were New Women themselves and naturally put their heroines' plight centre stage. The narrative voice in *Gilgi* is not the protagonist's but hers are the only thoughts and feelings we are told about, so we necessarily see things with her own eyes, especially when we are let it on Gilgi's secret thoughts and emotions, often rendered in a stream of consciousness, that is, Gilgi's unreflected and unordered ideas. This is, of course, the strength of the novel as a genre: it is able to make visible, invisible things like inner thoughts. Baum's treatment of *Helene* is less immediate; nevertheless the book's narrator also seems to inhabit the protagonist's thoughts.

Even male film directors such as Martin Berger in *Kreuzzug*, who argued for eugenic rather than women's rights, could not but elicit his spectators' sympathy for his women protagonists by revealing such an extraordinary keyhole view of their intimate fears and desires.[116] Berger's film, it is true, features three male stars and only one female but he managed to boost the part of Maly Delschaft as the young teacher through the narrative structure, the use of montage and by thoughtful intertitles. It is she who acts as the mediator between the different social classes and between the state (in the guise of the doctor and the public prosecutor) and ordinary women. Although her rape emphasizes her vulnerability, she alone possesses the moral authority to change the inhumane stance of the representatives of medicine and law. When she has extracted the promise of a termination she appears to redeem the tragic death of the proletarian mother and has reasserted her role as a professional woman and gained at least some measure of reproductive self-determination. Finally, at the very beginning of the film, Berger contrasts the young teacher's sensual desire with the prosecutor's timidity through montage: the camera switches from the tête-à-tête between the prosecutor and his fiancée in his office to the first signs of the impending storm outside, a tactic which prepares the spectator for the coming sexual crisis.[117] And in the course of the film, Berger provides his heroine with sufficient room for personal development and endows her with agency and strength which is grounded in an awareness of her body and her sexuality.

Of course, the full extent of the emancipatory or subversive message is sometimes not immediately understood. In silent films it has to be sought in the visual image rather than overt text (i.e. in sub- or intertitles) and it is of course significant that most films were silent and therefore the image was particularly important and could be instilled with potent meanings. As Anton Kaes puts it, the visual image 'was not only quicker and easier to decipher than a written text, but also guaranteed ... stronger identification than any description, no matter how detailed'.[118] As Heide Schlüpmann has argued, in *Madame Lu*, for example, the poetic world of adolescent female love is contrasted to the cold male world of public strictures. This is conveyed only to a certain extent in the narrative but much more powerfully through cinematography. The opening scene, for example, is a close-up of the backs of two teenage girls' heads studying the small ad of 'Madame Lu, the woman for discreet help' in a newspaper. As Schlüpmann notes, the way the camera seems to caress the soft outlines of the adolescent napes framed by bobbed hair and then cuts abruptly to a gathering of older men in dark suits and high collars (politicians, doctors, lawyers) suggests that the film is about the fragility of female sexuality exposed to the bluntness of male authority. The girls have a problem and look for a way out; when the camera swings suddenly to the representatives of state authority who look disapprovingly at the same ad, we know that the young heroines cannot expect to receive support from this quarter.[119] The visual images also reveal a clash between female and male adolescent sexuality not touched on by the sub- and intertitles. They outline the overt story about two women social workers who set out to save a pregnant teenager from the clutches of a quack abortionist. As Schlüpmann has shown, it is the cinematography of the film which conveys an altogether more interesting story: the unfolding of female desire, the transmutation from adolescent to a woman's body set against the encroaching male lust and patriarchal violence.

Similarly, the tone of a passage in fiction could twist the meaning in subtle and subversive ways. In Keun's *Gilgi* the boundaries of acceptable female behaviour are frequently transgressed even if the impact is muted by the use of irony and the distancing effect of inner monologue. For example, the description of Gilgi's visit to the doctor, to have her pregnancy confirmed and to obtain a termination, is a bravura piece of blunt criticism of official medicine and of §218. The vehemence of Gilgi's attack is unparalleled. It probably proved acceptable to publish because it was rendered not as speech but as inner monologue by a very young rebel who was also in dire straits. In this highly subversive encounter Keun reverses the usual doctor-patient power relationship. Gilgi takes the moral high ground, thinking it immoral to have a child whom she cannot look after. She has her come-uppance by the sheer force of her anger and her quick wit but the ambiguity of her role is still present: on the one hand, she is the outraged customer and her behaviour is appropriately abrasive; on the other hand, she is also vulnerable because her biological fate seems to depend on the goodwill of a professional man. Dressed androgynously with a tie tightly knotted round her neck, she orders the doctor to come to the point and tell her straight – and without recourse to Latin – whether she is pregnant or not. Taken aback by her verbal onslaught, the doctor tells her condescendingly that the 'little miss' is 'sound as a bell' and possesses 'a wonderful pelvis'. She explodes; the reader is privy to her thoughts:

> One needs a strong shot of street urchin to protect oneself. No fear of words, no fear of concepts – German to be spoken. She has a bad and unfair anger about the harmless little doctor. Stop being so pompous, you miserable Mickey Mouse dipped in carbolic acid, you ... what do you mean by a splendid pelvis! I don't want a child![120]

When the doctor refuses to 'help', Gilgi switches tack and relies on the well-known trick of playing the little woman: 'Oh, please help doctor! I have such confidence in you!' She tells herself (and us) that 'every doctor likes hearing this' and continues all abashed, 'I don't know, what – I think – I ... ' before she dismisses this play acting: 'Rubbish, this is stupid, I cannot do it.' Whereupon the doctor reacts quite authentically with a very oblique hint that she should return in three weeks since sometimes these things 'put themselves to rights – and yes, – in that case one could possibly help it along'.[121] This is a splendid example of the kind of unsatisfactory medical encounter which many women in trial records had actually experienced; but it also gives voice to the gutsy New Woman-speak using a *Neue Sachlichkeit* style of sort, sharp, ironic sentences.

The matter-of-factness of the style notwithstanding, *Gilgi* and the abortion films discussed above employed the medium of melodrama to address women spectators or readers and to challenge dominant ideology by conveying women's own, often alternative viewpoints. Melodrama has been so much maligned by cultural commentators but recently rescued from our disdain for them as a banal art form. Inspired by Peter Brooks's text, *The Melodramatic Imagination*, Patrice Petro has argued that melodramatic narratives should be reevaluated for their ability to render everyday events in a new light, or, quoting Brooks, 'to exploit the dramatics and excitement discoverable within the real, to heighten in dramatic gesture the moral crises and peripeties of life'.[122] As Petro put it, in melodrama there is the inherent 'desire to say all, to stage and utter the unspeakable'. Melodrama uses abstraction by creating character types and intimate situations which were immediately recognizable and therefore particularly useful for silent films. It was a genre which has recently been associated by film historians and literary scholars with a 'feminine' emotional expression.[123] It suited the female spectator and reader, in that it addressed the drama of the real, the ordinary and the private life, mediating women's own experiences of the everyday in a post-First World War society.

At the beginning of this chapter I posited that popular culture which engaged with the problem of §218 contributed to the social construction of abortion and sexuality in Weimar Germany. Judging from the examples discussed above (and a number of others which could not be analysed here)[124] there is no doubt that they reinforced the dominant ideology of abortion as a bleak and dangerous experience and the role of the lay abortionist as wholly negative. In part this was due to medicalization of middle-class professionals who made up the writers, directors and actors; in part these ideas were upheld through censorship. But, as I have argued above, the tragic portrayal of termination was also a warning that unchecked female sexuality was marked for doom and destruction. This was part of the fear of modernity in general and women's emancipation in particular. The hidden message in many of the films and plays, especially those by male writers and directors, is that the New Woman's much-vaunted sexual freedom must be contained in tested social structures such as marriage, family and community. Yet, women writers and artists, though not scriptwriters and film producers, have furnished us with an alternative vision: combining public life with reproduction is shown to be difficult for young women but not necessarily impossible, thanks to the albeit often illegal access to birth control and abortion.

But how to explain the dichotomy between the official view of abortion and the wise woman displayed in the abortion narratives in films and plays, and ordinary women's own testimony in court cases when they stood accused of having violated §218? Were these women not influenced by what they saw on the screen or stage and read in popular novels? It is of course impossible to know for sure whether the audience of mass culture and the women, who feature in the judiciary files I consulted actually overlapped, although feminist film scholars like Hansen, Schlüpmann and Petro agree with the 1914 analysis of Emilie Altenloh that German women of all classes were 'addicted' to the cinema, particularly when it concerned romances and social dramas. Given the extraordinary sales of women's fiction quoted above and the popular successes of realist drama about §218, it seems reasonable to suggest that we can include in this interpretation the other genres of popular culture, fiction and plays, too. But these feminist scholars have disputed the charge by Kracauer and others that women's addiction and therefore distraction from important political participation was a consequence solely of successful strategies of mass cultural domination; rather they have argued that women's eager involvement was due to gender inequalities, i.e. women's relative deprivation within the economy and society of the time. For women, it is argued, the cinema (and other forms of popular culture) provided the chance, in Altenloh's words, 'to live in another world, a world of luxury and extravagance which makes them forget the monotony of the everyday'.[125]

Even if it was the case, as Altenloh suggested, that women sought a distraction from the greyness of daily life, we cannot simply assume that female spectators or readers concurred with the message inscribed within the text, or were manipulated into certain views. Given the often very sophisticated responses from ordinary women to their interrogators in the police station or in court which we will witness in Chapter 5, it might indeed be safer to assume that even women from relatively deprived educational and social backgrounds were well able to immerse themselves in a work of art, even identify with fictional stories and characters, while holding on to their own quite different experiences. In other words, they applied quite naturally the demands of Brecht's epic theatre without knowing it, not really forgetting that what they say on screen or stage or what they read in novels was mere fiction. The balancing act so many women were able to perform in the presence of a policeman or judge, conforming to the dominant discourse without losing a sense of their own everyday reality, rather points in this direction. The ability of works like *Kreuzzug* or *Gilgi* to convey a thrillingly rebellious meaning hidden in images and between the lines no doubt reinforced the sense of independence of female consumers of popular culture to appropriate texts, or aspects of them, for their own use.

∽ Chapter 3 ∾

MEDICAL TERMINATION OF PREGNANCY: THEORY AND PRACTICE

Abortion narratives in popular novels, plays and films conveyed powerful messages about the bleakness, even tragedy, of the event, though this was at odds with most women's own perceptions. The negative images were largely informed by the medical discourse which had also shaped legal theory and judicial practice, the political debate, as well as population and health policies. In the dominant positivist culture which believed in the inevitability of progress in general and the advances of medical science in particular, physicians' advances in epidemiology and insights into hygiene (as well as social hygiene) were central to public health policies.[1] Similarly, their views on public health dominated the public debate on abortion. The influence of the profession on opinion makers in this area was not new; it had gradually become more powerful since the first decade of the twentieth century, when the panic over the declining birth rate led the authorities to consult doctors, often in preference to churchmen or economists, to explain the causes of and remedies for the startling demographic change. This was not surprising since enterprising doctors had begun very early on to conduct their own surveys on sexual and birth control practices; hospital consultants and district medical officials collected and interpreted statistics of illegal miscarriages and many medics came up with practical programmes to reverse the fertility trend.[2] But soon government officials and other opinion formers also began to adopt medical terminology in their policy statements. For example, the trend towards smaller families was expressed in organicist terms and pathologized: the nation became the *Volkskörper*, the social body, and it was presented as afflicted by the disease of the declining birth rate, also called an 'ethical degeneration'.[3]

Moreover, discussion of class-specific reproduction trends was permeated with an inegalitarian eugenic ideology and frequently informed by suspect 'scientific' concepts of congenital degeneracy. Talking about corporal images and diseases rather than population size and demographic trends rendered an abstract subject more tangible and promoted apocalyptic visions of imminent national decline which captured the public imagination, especially as they coincided with the arms race hysteria in the decade before the First World War.[4] The outbreak of the war paved the way for a coercive pronatalism tinged with eugenic antinatalism; both pronatalists and eugenists were united in their rejection of individual 'arbitrary' birth control, preaching instead that the common good was to be put before individual interests. The formulation of a national population policy culminated in three far-reaching government bills, one of which was designed to tighten the regulation of abortion of 1871. While conservative doctors postured as custodians of national fertility, many enterprising doctors were busily patenting and marketing an array of contraceptive gadgets and techniques and quite a few also built up large abortion practices; finally, a minority of doctors, mostly on the political left or from the new breed of women doctors, became outspoken opponents of the Wilhelmine government's repressive policies and called for a liberalization of the abortion clauses.[5]

The new status of academic medicine in government and other influential circles notwithstanding, there remained considerable uncertainty about a doctor's legal right to terminate a pregnancy. The law of 1871 did not distinguish between lay and medically trained abortionists, although in practice law courts usually handed down much more lenient sentences, or, as we shall see below, even acquitted doctors with impunity. Doctors could invoke §54 of the penal code, the so-called 'emergency clause' (*Notstandsparagraph*), which permitted termination of a pregnancy so as to avert imminent danger to the health or life of the pregnant woman, but, as explained by the *Oberreichsanwalt* (the supreme public prosecutor), under this law doctors were only permitted to intervene if the pregnant woman was a relative and in all other cases there was no guarantee of medical impunity.[6] During the First World War the Prussian Ministry of the Interior and the Reich Health Office published guidelines to clarify the legal position for doctors: that 'state registered physicians' were permitted to induce 'artificial miscarriages' if a pregnancy 'endangered the life or health of a woman and if this could not be averted in any other way'.[7] But, not satisfied with this temporary measure, doctors would not rest until this principle was encoded in law. On the surface the campaign by left-leaning doctors against the abortion law derived from the fact that §218 was class discriminatory: while better-off women could avail themselves of professional and (as it was implied) safe, intervention by doctors, women of the poorer classes had to depend on quacks and therefore ran serious health risks.[8]

The aim was therefore to secure for doctors, and only doctors, the right to perform terminations on grounds which only they could judge. While there was no agreement about the permissible grounds for such operations, the legalization of medical abortions was in fact the single issue which united the disparate campaigners for the liberalization of the abortion law. Their professed aim was to save women's lives by limiting and possibly eradicating quack abortions. Reform of §§218-220 must have seemed hopeful at a time when the entire penal code was under review, from the second decade of the last century onwards. Yet, none of the new drafts between 1911 and 1927, nor the government bill of 1918 mentioned above, contained the exclusive right of doctors to terminate a pregnancy on medical grounds. Not even the reform of the abortion clauses in 1926 offered any hope.[9] A breakthrough of sorts occurred only in 1927, when therapeutic abortion was permitted by a Supreme Court decree. Although this again failed to bestow a medical monopoly on doctors explicitly, it was nevertheless considered an important step towards it.[10] This was because it was relatively easy for qualified medical practitioners to convince the authorities that a termination had been indicated on health grounds, especially when a second medical opinion had been obtained, something which proved all but impossible for lay operators.[11] But the case for a medical monopoly rested on the doctors' claim that not only were they alone qualified to diagnose correctly the necessity of a termination but that they alone were qualified to perform the operation safely. They generally succeeded in convincing the educated middle – though not necessarily the working – classes and official circles of both; this was evidence of the high standing of the profession and their successful public relations campaign as well as of the gullibility of contemporary bourgeois society.

More surprisingly, this alleged medical superiority has seldom been questioned in recent historiography.[12] This chapter will show, however, that medical abortion practice was not always unproblematic; that the supposedly clear boundary between medical and lay operations was a construct of medical propaganda, judicial bias and political ideology. With the help of micro-history – a detailed reconstruction of court cases involving a male and a female doctor from South Germany – I will discuss possible pitfalls of medical abortions, the different reactions by colleagues, law enforcement agencies and finally the views of women patients and witnesses.

Retracing the story of individual doctors and their patients has the advantage over more quantitative approaches of social or crime history in that it offers explanations that often elude large-scale studies. Such glimpses into particular incidents help us to question received opinions of contemporary authorities or interpretations of historians. The examples of medical blunders discussed below are not necessarily representative of the general medical abortion practice of the time since they came to the attention of the authorities precisely because something had gone badly wrong. Many other medical terminations were uneventful enough to have avoided scrutiny by the police and, by implication, by the historian's gaze. Yet, medical complications were almost certainly fairly frequent, as was tacitly admitted by leading gynaecologists who acted as expert witnesses in investigations or trials of aborting doctors. Moreover, the cases cited here suggest that it was by no means unusual for magistrates' investigations of doctors' criminal abortions malpractice or negligence to be quashed. Some cases were not investigated by the law enforcement authorities but by doctors in internal medical disciplinary hearings.[13] Furthermore, the cases selected below reveal the typical attitudes displayed by doctors, the police and the courts both to medical abortionists and to the aborting woman. As long as we contextualize these individual events and connect them to the collective they raise a number of important questions about the nature of medical training and skill, the process of quality control of medical practice or lack of it, the bias of the police and the judiciary and, last but not least, the hidden political agenda behind the profession's campaign to 'medicalize' abortion.

The case of Dr Hartmann

Shortly after the First World War a case of medical abortion malpractice made newspaper headlines. It concerned Dr Karl Hartmann, a 24-year-old medical practitioner in Rosenheim, a district town in Upper Bavaria. With its approximately 30,000 inhabitants Rosenheim was situated on the river Inn and close to the undulating slopes of the Alpine foothills; it was typical of Upper Bavaria in that it combined small-scale industry with tourism as a well-known saline spa. Hartmann was suspected of having terminated the pregnancy of one of his patients, the 25-year-old shop assistant Maria Leicht. At Christmas 1920 she had started an affair with her employer, the owner of a patisserie. In February or March of the following year she had anxiously waited for her monthly period in vain and therefore feared pregnancy. What happened subsequently is difficult to reconstruct from a series of contradictory statements made by Leicht and Hartmann to the committee of enquiry. Leicht claimed she had had an accident in the shop and had fallen down the cellar steps' resulting in a miscarriage. But she conceded that shortly afterwards, at the end of May 1921, she had consulted Hartmann, who was generally regarded as a good gynaecologist in Rosenheim. She had gone to him because she was bleeding and wanted to be on the safe side. Without examining her, Hartmann had allegedly told her, that he needed to 'scrape out her blocked blood' and that she should return that same evening. She did and he asked her into his private quarters where he inserted a laminaria (*Laminarstift*). A few days later he also carried out a curettage, this time in his practice room. Maria Leicht could remember an injection in her arm for the anaesthetic but had then become unconscious. When she came to she found herself travelling in a car with Hartmann at the steering wheel; at the sight of the tramways she recognized that they were in

Munich. She also remembered being carried into an operating theatre before she lost consciousness again.[14]

Only much later did she learn that Hartmann was not a gynaecologist but only a general practitioner and that he had inflicted on her very serious injuries. So grave were these that Dr Zwicknagel, the forensic pathologist at the *Landgericht* (Regional Court) Traunstein, where the case was investigated, concluded that Hartmann was guilty of medical malpractice; he had perforated Maria Leicht's uterus and small intestine with his probe. Zwicknagel was also very critical of Hartmann's procedure: instead of using a specialist he had asked a dentist friend to administer the anaesthetic and Hartmann had also operated without the necessary assistance. Furthermore, Zwicknagel accused Hartmann of medical negligence since he had failed to arrange appropriate emergency transport to take his by then dangerously ill patient to the nearest hospital. It was implied that in the interest of secrecy Hartmann had driven the unconscious Leicht in his own 'inadequately covered' car the distance of c. 50 km to Munich where one of his friends performed the life-saving operation in a private clinic.[15]

Unusually, it was not Maria Leicht's injuries which alerted the authorities to examine Hartmann, but the intervention of other doctors in Rosenheim. Shortly after the incident described above, Hartmann was denounced directly to the public prosecutor by three of his local colleagues for suspected criminal abortion. As a result, a judicial enquiry into his actions was initiated in 1922 at the *Landgericht* Traunstein which covered a series of alleged crimes, such as criminal abortion for commercial gain on five counts; aiding and abetting criminal abortions; grievous bodily harm caused by negligence; and finally, serious professional misconduct on two counts, of which one had proved fatal (this latter case concerned another woman, not Leicht).[16] Here, then, the personal freedom and career of a young doctor was at stake. But the enquiry did not only throw light on the personal and professional fate of one individual doctor; it also revealed a contradictory interpretation of the medical and legal meaning of abortion performed by doctors in general.

The enquiry had an immediate and devastating effect on Hartmann. The public prosecutor, fearing his attempted flight and the risk of collusion, ordered Hartmann to be remanded in prison. Zwicknagel, the forensic pathologist at the *Landgericht*, examined the case and his verdict was unusually harsh, as we have seen above. He called Dr Hartmann 'wholly unscrupulous' and found that his medical conduct called for 'strong criticism'. He accused Hartmann of three things: first, of having 'procured illegal abortions ... to an extent never witnessed with a newcomer in the medical profession, especially if one considers that a large number of other doctors practise in Rosenheim'; second, of having acted 'improperly and without due regard to medical rules and skills'; and finally, of having committed professional fraud.[17] Zwicknagel requested an expert opinion from the medical committee of Munich University. This committee duly met and their report seemed to support Zwicknagel's own judgement. The Munich professors concluded that in the case of Maria Leicht, Hartmann was to be charged with grievous bodily harm of a kind not commensurate with 'such operations'.[18] Despite this conclusion, Dr Hartmann was released from remand in prison at the end of August. Shortly afterwards, at the beginning of September, Hartmann took over his practice again and two months later the criminal court at the *Landgericht* Traunstein ruled out a formal prosecution of Hartmann.[19]

This extraordinary decision can only be understood if we consider Hartmann's case in all its complexities against the backdrop of the medicalization of society and the professionalization of abortion, which contrasted with the glaring lack of skills in abortion techniques displayed by not only general practitioners but also eminent gynaecologists. Hartmann's own role as a provincial doctor was also ambivalent rather than straightforwardly objectionable: on the one hand, he seems to have been popular, especially with his working-class patients; on the other, many other patients and his medical colleagues were very critical of him. Similarly, Hartmann's 'reputation as a good gynaecologist', as some Rosenheim newspapers would have it, was contradicted by his gross medical ineptitude and serious professional misconduct in the treatment of Maria Leicht and other women, something that was admitted by all experts who examined this case. And finally, the verdict by the various medical authorities was contradicted by Hartmann's acquittal from criminal prosecution.

Hartmann escaped indictment as a direct consequence of the ambivalent verdict of the medical committee, made up of four leading professors of the medical faculty at Munich University, and the influence it had on the Traunstein *Landgericht*. Although the Munich professors admitted that Hartmann had caused Maria Leicht grievous bodily harm, they offered the investigating magistrates a get-out clause by choosing to describe Hartmann's operation on Leicht as a 'misfortune' rather than 'medical malpractice'. This implied that the injuries incurred by her were caused by bad luck rather than by a lack of professional skills or ethics. What is even more significant for our purpose is that the professors declared that such injuries 'occurred not infrequently' as a result of a termination and must therefore be tolerated. Implicit in their verdict was the assumption that a termination by a medical practitioner could not necessarily be considered a safe procedure. Such a tacit admission had obvious ramifications for the campaign to reform §§218–220 to permit access to 'safe' medical terminations in general and doctors' exclusive rights over this operation in particular. How risky, then, were medical abortions in the 1920s and how significant was the discrepancy between medical claims and medical ability in practice? How well were doctors trained in medical schools and during their practical years and did their academic study and their state registration always guarantees conscientious and responsible practice?

Abortion in the medical discourse

To pose such questions is particularly relevant against the background of the medical discourse at the time which centred on doctors' claim to a monopoly of treatment in the whole area of reproduction and most especially of birth control and induced miscarriages. Although there were deep rifts within the profession about how best to reform the abortion law, there was a closing of ranks when it came to singling out 'quacks' as the source of all evil in the abortion business, i.e. driving up the numbers of criminal terminations and causing mounting maternal morbidity and mortality.[20] There were of course certain rogue colleagues in their midst, contemptuously referred to as *Auskratzer* (scrapers), who indulged in illegal termination operations purely for profit, but it was always the medical lay operators who earned the collective wrath of the profession. They were accused of bungling and botching because of their ignorance of gynaecology or hygiene and because greed was, so it was alleged, their only motive. Both supporters and opponents of a liberalized law in the medical profession agreed on the danger of quack abortions. Conservative doctors who wanted the existing law upheld (with more rights for doctors) thought that every attempt to terminate a pregnancy contained certain risks, but these were far more serious in the hands of a quack. Reforming doctors, to be found mostly on the political left, argued that a termination was safe as long as it was performed by a qualified doctor. That is why they wanted medical terminations legalized but quack abortions outlawed.[21]

Alfred Dührssen, Professor of Gynaecology at the University of Berlin, supported a radical law reform to prevent the 'death of thousands of young people ... due to quack abortions' every year. He claimed that 'the majority of abortions' were 'procured by midwives or by paramedics or by lay people – mostly in an inappropriate manner and at extreme risk to the pregnant women's life'. He asserted that this affected first and foremost proletarian women 'since they lacked the necessary funds'; they had become 'victims of "wise women" or of their own daring'.[22] The well-known Berlin communist doctor and abortion reformer, Leo Klauber, went so far as to declare that every year 20,000 German lives were squandered and 100,000 cases of morbidity occurred because of self- and quack abortions.[23]

Naturally such powerful claims served to strengthen the case for granting to doctors alone the right to terminate pregnancies. I contend, however, that doctors were also vilifying lay abortionists in the hope of excluding them permanently from this operation and of revoking, at least in this field, the medical law of 1871 which declared medicine a trade open to all. By obtaining a monopoly on terminations doctors hoped to gain the loyalty of women of the lower classes. Women, and above all proletarian women, had proved that they were a force to be reckoned with in the new republic, as the demonstrations against the abortion law and petitions to reform it had shown. Since the 1918 Revolution had bestowed on women full civil rights, including the vote, their public role was considerably enhanced and they had become worthwhile allies. Moreover, women had entered the medical profession itself in increasing numbers and their voices were being heard in this respect, generally defending professional interests.[24] But reforming doctors had something else in mind, too: women were traditionally considered as guardians of family health and any means of winning their trust might usefully gain doctors entry to the lucrative role of family practitioners and prise women out of the clutches of quacks whose popularity was rising despite greatly increased access to doctors working for sick funds.[25]

Divided opinion within the medical profession

Doctors were the decisive element in Hartmann's judicial enquiry. It was doctors who had brought him to the attention of the authorities in the first place and it was also doctors who finally came to his rescue and ensured that he was acquitted. The judicial enquiry against Hartmann opened after three of his colleagues in Rosenheim alleged that he was 'a public danger'.[26] This resulted, as we have seen, in the damning expert opinion of Dr Zwicknagel, the forensic pathologist at the Traunstein Landgericht. Hartmann's hostile local colleagues had also accused him of professional fraud for calling himself a gynaecologist on his practice sign. When this accusation proved to be true, Hartmann lost his sick fund practice. Although, as we saw above, it was restored to him only a few weeks later, he was not to know this at the time and his suspension was no doubt a tough blow – as it would have been a tough blow for any doctor, but for a young doctor at the beginning of his career it was potentially disastrous.

But how should we interpret the denunciations by Hartmann's detractors? Were they a legitimate attempt to defend professional standards or rather a self-serving strategy to exclude a newcomer who had poached their patients? We cannot dismiss a genuine concern to defend moral and professional standards on the part of the three doctors; they were, after all, likely to have been Catholics and therefore were almost certainly objecting to abortion on religious grounds. But they might also have pursued tactical aims. Even if, as many other doctors did, they had helped one or other patient privately to rid herself of an unwanted pregnancy, they would have been ill advised to defend abortion publicly. As members of the professional middle classes and working in a provincial town in Upper Bavaria they needed to be seen to be defending traditional sexual and ethical mores. Moreover, it was probably expedient to shore up their own reputation by repudiating a colleague who performed a suspiciously high number of curettages. They might also have been shocked at the way the novice was blatantly flouting both the Hippocratic oath and the law of the land to build up his abortion business. But even if we give Hartmann's colleagues the benefit of the doubt we cannot rule out the probability that they were also motivated by commercial considerations. Hartmann himself was certainly convinced that the 'smear campaign' against him was fuelled by 'professional jealousy', because he had 'repeatedly strayed into their patch'.[27] The *Rosenheimer Volkszeitung* came to a similar conclusion and called the complaints against Hartmann 'utterly base libellous allegiations cunningly constructed by a corrupt clique of competitiors'.[28] Even Zwicknagel's damning report gave support to such an interpretation. He thought Hartmann had been concerned 'solely with catching more patients' and had performed 'operations ... for easy monetary gain'.[29] Professional envy as a motive for the denunciation should certainly not be discounted, especially at a time of a serious oversupply of doctors.[30]

Furthermore, Hartmann seems to have been genuinely popular with the poorer inhabitants of Rosenheim; a petition by forty-eight members of the assembly of the works council of a local firm went as far as calling him a 'real philanthropist'. This petition pleaded for his release from remand imprisonment, because he had

> treated the family members [i.e. wives and children of the insured workers] in the most conscientious way like no other doctor in and around Rosenheim. Moreover, workers are prepared to stand witness as they believe they can prove that similar cases as those which Dr Hartmann has been accused of can also be found among persons from better circles and other doctors.[31]

The suggestion was that abortion was practised among bourgeois circles with the collusion of local doctors, something which may well have been more widespread than was officially accepted. Moral support for Hartmann also came from a group of disabled war veterans who regarded it the 'bounden duty' of the working population of Rosenheim ... on whose behalf he undoubtedly suffered this wrong, to express their confidence in him'.[32] An editorial in the *Rosenheimer Volkszeitung*, too, campaigned on Hartmann's behalf. It praised his 'medical competence, personal integrity, and exemplary humanity'. It also demanded that he be paid damages and readmitted as a health insurance doctor.[33]

There is further evidence of Hartmann's honourable and idealistic stance. He did not just carry out terminations in private, he also had the courage to speak out in public in favour of abortion reform. In the spring of 1922, a few weeks before the judicial enquiry into his case began, he appeared as one of two public speakers at a Munich mass rally that had the slogan 'Women who do not want to be mothers'. It was organized by the KPD and took place in the Hackerkelle, near the Theresienwiese, the site of the annual beer festival, the *Oktoberfest*. Like the other speakers, the communist doctor Leo Klauber and the KPD Reichstag delegate Wendelin Thomas, Hartmann called for the decriminalization of abortion. This was no small feat given that he was doing it in one of Munich's famous beer halls in Munich.[34] This may well have provided ammunition for the denunciation by Hartmann's colleagues. Another indication that Hartmann was likely to have been serious rather than opportunistic in his attitude to medicine and patients is that he was born into the medical establishment of which he then became such a controversial member. He followed in the footsteps of his parents who were both doctors, and his younger brother joined the profession, too. It would therefore be wrong to accept too easily the view of the forensic pathologist at the *Landgericht* that Hartmann had acted 'unscrupulously' as a doctor or that he constituted 'a public danger', as his hostile colleagues would have us believe.

Neverthless, it would equally be wrong to accept unconditionally the glowing praise of Hartmann's supporters. Hartmann's case is a good example of the complexity of medical abortion practice at a time when the legal position was at best uncertain and at worst untenable. The judicial enquiry into Hartmann's activity shows how differently such a practice could be viewed by different members of the medical and the legal professions and the aborting women. Even if, as I assume, Hartmann acted with the best intentions, how do I judge his serious surgical blunders and the evidence of his lack of care? Dr Zwicknagel, the forensic pathologist, criticized his medical procedure, suggesting that he had 'bungled' operations and

Massen-
Protest-Kundgebung

wirksam unterstützen, damit diese nur für das Proletariat geltenden u. ihren Zweck verfehlenden Gesetze zu Fall gebracht werden.

Arbeiter, Angestellte, Beamte, Frauen u. Männer erscheint in Massen zu d. öffentl. Versammlung

im Hackerkeller - Theresienhöhe
am Samstag, den 11. März 1922 abends 7 Uhr

Referenten: Gen. Dr. Klauber-Berlin und Reichstagsabg. Wendelin Thomas-Augsburg

=== Freie Aussprache! ===

Zur Deckung der Unkosten: Mitglieder Mk. 1.50 Nichtmitglieder Mk. 2.- / Kassa-Eröffnung 6 Uhr

K. P. D., Bezirk Westend i. A. Mehltretter
Druck von A. Waldbaur, München, Sendlingerstr. 57

7. Poster for mass demonstration against §218, March 1922, Hackerkeller, Munich. It lists Dr Klauber and Wendelin Thomas, member of the Reichstag, but Dr Hartmann also spoke.

contravened 'the rules of medical science' by causing 'injury' and even the death of at least one of his abortion patients through 'negligence'.[35] But Dr Zwicknagel may well not have been entirely objective. Certainly, he made much of the unusual circumstances of Hartmann's medical education and associated these cleverly with his later medical malpractice. Zwicknagel suggested that Hartmann's medical training had been inadequate. Hartmann had admitted himself that he had fought at the front from 1915 to 1918 and had therefore had to interrupt his medical studies for four years. He was granted his licence to practise in 1920 but had, according to Zwicknagel, 'no specialist training whatsoever and otherwise only a deficient training, as was rather typical during the war'.[36] If Hartmann's speedy dispatch onto the medical market was indeed typical it sheds light on possible reasons for the oversupply of doctors in the early postwar years.

At that time medical students normally received specialist obstetric and gynaecological training and often gained practical experience performing an 'artificial miscarriage', a curettage or other such operations. But Hartmann's gynaecological training had by all accounts been comparatively short, sporadic and incomplete, amounting to just one year in the surgical clinic of Professor Sauerbruch, the famous Munich gynaecologist, two semesters merely as 'a guest' in the gynaecological clinic of another professor and little more than a semester in that of Professor Döderlein, another of Munich's well-known specialists, where Hartmann worked mostly nights.[37] Hartmann admitted that he had no right to call himself 'specialist in gynaecology' because this title would have presupposed a one- to two-year continuous specialist training. He gambled on not being found out and put 'medical practitioner and gynaecologist' on his practice sign, probably to attract lucrative women patients who desired a termination of pregnancy and were willing to make his assistance worth his while; or, as the forensic pathologist put it, Hartmann used the elevated title to 'lure patients'. After his colleagues and the professional medical organization complained, he was forced to remove the offending sign and henceforth called himself simply 'obstetrician'.[38] The fact that he did not attempt to operate on the seriously injured Maria Leicht but instead risked a long car journey to Munich to put her in the hands of a doctor of his acquaintance, thereby also involving an eyewitness, suggests not only that he tried to conceal his own intervention and the injuries he had inflicted on Leicht, but, more importantly in this context, that he did not trust his own surgical skills to save her.

One possible mitigating factor in favour of Dr Hartmann was that he had committed these medical blunders at the very beginning of his career, only two years after he had received his registration, when he was still only twenty-seven years of age and relatively inexperienced, even though he had managed to gain the trust of a group of loyal patients from the lower classes. Hartmann was not alone in this. Many other recently trained medics with little or no experience had to defend themselves in court against accusations of criminal abortion after bungled operations leading to injury or death had alerted the police.[39]

Hartmann's circumstances notwithstanding, the decision by the public prosecutor not to open formal proceedings against him appears strange in view of the gravity of the medical damage he had inflicted and is at odds with the extremely critical report by Dr Zwicknagel. Why did Hartmann's case not come to court? The answer may be found in the role of the Munich medical comittee. They acted as medical experts and effectively shielded Hartmann from prosecution. The four renowned professors of medicine, Miller, Sauerbruch, Borst and Döderlein, pronounced that in the case of Maria Leicht there could not be any doubt 'that the perforation of the womb had been a direct consequence of inserting the laminaria'; this injury was 'not uncommon with this kind of operation but which cannot lead one to the accusation of injury through negligence'. These medical experts also did not reproach Hartmann for 'the rupture of the mesentery and the multiple perforation of the small intestines'. They concluded that the latter probably pointed to the fact that

> Dr Hartmann had worked with forceps-like instruments for the purpose of extirpating the uterus. But this, too, does not allow us to conclude the crime of bodily injury through negligence [*fahrlässige Körperverletzung*] even though this should normally not occur with such operations.

Furthermore, not only was Hartmann not rebuked, he was praised for having immediately transported in his own car the 'anaethetized patient [Maria Leicht] wrapped in blankets, thereby enabling the operation on the abdominal cavity which alone saved her life'. Even more astonishingly, the professors also concluded that Hartmann should not be blamed for the death of another patient, a 26-year-old married woman, who had succumbed to an infection after Hartmann had performed a curettage of her uterus to terminate her unwanted pregnancy. These expert findings were adopted unanimously and signed by all four medical men.[40]

The alternative interpretation of such heavyweight university professors overruled the opinion of a 'mere' *Landgerichtsarzt*, Dr Zwicknagel, the forensic pathologist attached to a regional court, although his judgement should have been given preference. It showed that doctors who clearly had got into trouble with the law as well as with medical ethics and standards could be saved by influential patrons who acted as experts for the judiciary. Hartmann had the good fortune to have such patronage since he had been a student of both Döderlein and Sauerbruch, who were obviously prepared to defend one of their protegés. Nevertheless, their defence was predicated on a public admission that the expertise to terminate pregnancies was not a skill medical practitioners could be automatically assumed to possess; if individual doctors could not be held responsible for serious injuries as a result of a medically induced miscarriage it followed that such operations could not necessarily be regarded as safe in the hands of a doctor. What then differentiated academically trained practitioners from their lay counterparts in this respect?

Medical blunders and legal practice

This throws an important light on the claim of the medical profession to a medical monopoly and especially their desired disassociation from lay abortionists. The campaign by a vociferous minority of the profession to legalize termination of pregnancy or 'artificial miscarriage', as abortion was called if performed by a state-registered doctor on justified grounds, was misleading in as far as it presented medical intervention as relatively risk-free.[41] Even if we concede that judicial records give a distorted picture because they overrepresent problem cases, the source material provides ample evidence that Dr Hartmann's record of injuries was by no means untypical even among gynaecologists in specialist hospitals but especially when operations were undertaken in secret in private practice. Serious injuries and fatalities were by no means rare. This was hardly extraordinary since medical students were not necessarily routinely instructed in abortion techniques and had to obtain their knowledge and skill through hands-on experience, almost certainly also learning from tragic mistakes they had made.[42]

Indeed many prominent gynaecologists were so concerned about the lack of knowledge of abortion technology among medical practitioners that they recommended all terminations be procured by specialists in hospitals only. Naturally, their concern for the welfare of mothers was mixed with their professional concern to emphasize their own status and reinforce proper boundaries between general medical practice and specialism. Ernst Bumm, the doyen of Berlin gynaecologists, asserted that courts of law were inundated with cases brought against family doctors for medical errors and negligence.[43] His assertion was proved right when a collection of forensic medical judgements from the Weimar Republic was published, documenting sensational cases of medical blunders and malpractice, especially in gynaecology and obstetrics. The editors commented that their material revealed 'alarming examples of medical ignorance, inadequate medical knowledge and serious negligence'.[44] The leading gynaecologist, Friedrich Lönne, reporting to the Prussian Medical Committee, had such a low opinion of the gynaecological and obstetric training and skills of many practitioners that he demanded an extension of the compulsory clinical education in obstetrics for all medical students.[45] But family doctors defended their profession and maintained that serious errors with terminations occurred even among the most experienced gynaecologists.[46] This had been pointed out as early as 1921 in an anonymous publication, of a collection of case studies from university maternity hospitals; it claimed that even the most prestigious gynaecologists were responsible for the deaths of many hundreds of women because they had terminated pregnancies either far too late or without the necessary professional care and expertise.[47]

In the context of the general medical abortion knowledge and skill of the time it should not surprise us that even the most serious errors such as Hartmann's were condoned by medical councils and the judiciary. In fact Hartmann's case is typical of the way in which medical practitioners and gynaecologists, suspected of criminal operations and medical blunders, were investigated officially. They were usually acquitted on the grounds that a medically induced miscarriage necessarily carried certain risks. Another example is the trial of the 30-year-old Berlin doctor Kurt Metall, who performed a termination on a 17-year-old dancer. He inserted a laminaria tent before he rushed off on his honeymoon and left a colleague to do the curettage. The dancer died of severe injuries, a perforated cervix and a lacerated uterus, inflicted, as it was later confirmed, by both doctors. Neither doctor was convicted for manslaughter because the medical expert stated that 'the incidence of such injuries ... was well within the accepted level of surgical errors' and that there was no reason to assume the doctors had acted negligently'.[48] When doctors *were* tried (and many more investigations of doctors' abortion practice were quashed) they were often acquitted even when they had shown incompetence or negligence as well as malpractice. Even in cases when they were found guilty of criminal abortion in general their sentences tended to be far milder than those of lay abortionists.[49] In one case, the former director of a maternity hospital in the Rhineland, Dr Bauer, stood trial for seven cases of illegal abortion performed for commercial gain, two of which ended in death. The three medical experts could not agree whether the gynaecologist had performed the abortions in question on permissive grounds or not and whether he should be held responsible for the two fatalities. One of the medical experts, Professor Ernst Bumm from Berlin, more or less relied on Dr Bauer's own assertions, another expert was privately paid by Dr Bauer and came to his defence. But the third medical expert, the director of another women's hospital in the Rhineland, made an impassioned plea on behalf of the two women who had died and accused the gynaecologist of medical misconduct and gross negligence: among other things, he had failed to disinfect properly. He also suggested that the severe internal injuries which the autopsies had revealed were almost certainly caused by Dr Bauer's 'impatient' surgery.[50] Furthermore, Dr Bauer was found to have been given a previous warning by the local medical council who had long suspected him of criminal abortions. Other evidence was the testimony of five women patients who confessed to having had abortions procured by Dr Bauer and who made clear that he was well known in the area 'to do it for money'. The judge dismissed the evidence by the five women as unreliable and, judging from the verdict, preferred the two positive expert opinions to the critical third one. The result was the acquittal of the defendant 'on the grounds of insufficient evidence'.[51]

Sometimes judges treated accused doctors extraordinarily leniently of their own accord. In one particular trial of 1929, a family doctor from Hamborn, in the district of Duisburg, was convicted of criminal abortion and manslaughter in two instances but his punishment consisted of a mere two months' imprisonment. This outcome was not the consequence of mitigating circumstances but was proclaimed despite the fact that the injuries caused were, at least in one case, in the words of the medical expert, truly 'terrible and one could not imagine any worse'. The Hamborn doctor had, rather like Dr Hartmann, sent the fatally ill patient by ambulance to the nearest hospital without, however, taking the trouble to 'notify them [the hospital staff] in a satisfactory manner'; as a result, an operation which might have saved the patient was delayed and the patient had perished. Although an appeal was heard by the public prosecutor and the sentence revised, it was only increased to three months' inprisonment, which was still very lenient considering that officially the law prescribed a maximum sentence of fifteen years' penal servitude and that lay abortionists were generally punished more harshly.[52] This demonstrates the extent to which the judiciary favoured the medical profession and the extraordinary influence that medical experts wielded in the courts reinforced this bias since medical experts usually tended to protect their beleagered colleagues.

Of course, Hartmann's surgical blunders could only be condoned if the termination of the pregnancies had been indicated on strict health grounds. There was considerable evidence to the contrary. For a start, Hartmann's hostile colleagues from Rosenheim denounced him specifically for 'illegal abortions', a view shared by Dr Zwicknagel. He wrote that he 'had not the slightest doubt that he [Hartmann] repeatedly performed illegal abortions'.[53] A midwife who attended several of Hartmann's operations agreed; in her deposition she also suggested that Hartmann was so keen to perform terminations that he had, on at least one occasion, performed an abortion even though the patient had assured him that she had already miscarried the foetus. The midwife's statement was later corroborated by the woman in question.[54] The Munich medical commission, however, paid little heed to the midwife's testimony and dismissed Dr Zwicknagel's suggestion that Hartmann's operation might not be legally defensible. The main author of the commission's report, Professor Döderlein, also refused to take seriously the testimonies of the various women patients or any other references to illegal interventions and declared that there was no evidence of his protegé's guilt. In this respect, too, the case of Hartmann was representative of many other doctors' trials.

Judges presiding over abortion trials of doctors tended to overlook improper indications for termination because medical practice differed substantially from legal theory. Although therapeutic abortion was not officially permitted until the 1927 Supreme Court decree, it had been practised widely before and justified with reference to the 1917 guidelines by the Reich Health Council; as mentioned, these prescribed that medical practitioners only were permitted to terminate a pregnancy on the strictest health grounds as long as two doctors had certified this. In Hartmann's case, however, even these most basic rules had been ignored; there was no evidence that Hartmann had ever sought or obtained a second medical opinion.[55] Such judicial bias towards doctors was even more noticeable in the aquittal of the former director of the maternity hospital in the Rhineland mentioned above. He had not only caused the death of two aborting women but there was also no doubt that he had procured abortions on other than medical grounds because five of his women patients admitted to these.[56]

The case of Dr Hope Bridges Adams Lehmann

There was an important precedent to judges defending members of the medical profession against serious accusation. The trial in 1915 of the well-known Munich gynaecologist Hope Bridges Adams Lehmann, for criminal abortion on at least twenty-seven counts, is probably the most famous abortion case involving a doctor which Germany witnessed at this time and

8. Hope Bridges Adams Lehmann, September 1914

it, too, had ended in aquittal. The case caused a sensation because it revealed that this prominent woman doctor had maintained a very extensive abortion practice for at least twelve years, not in the relative privacy of her own consulting rooms but openly in the operating theatre of a large municipal hospital, under the aegis of the Red Cross, located at a busy intersection, the Rotkreuzplatz, in Munich's west end. In 1913 she had terminated as many 127 pregnancies, out of a total of 259 operations performed, which meant that every other surgical case of hers was an abortion case. In the first five months of 1914 alone, out of a total of seventy-six operations, twenty-seven proved to be terminations.[57] It is interesting that Dr Adams Lehmann was acquitted before the guidelines for aborting doctors were drawn up in 1917 and at a time when the law dictated that abortion on any grounds was considered as murder, although in practice doctors felt they had more leeway with therapeutic miscarriages as long as they had the indication confirmed by a second doctor. Indeed, the 1917 guidelines were in large measure drawn up as a result of Adams Lehmann's trial, especially her acquittal. The Reich government was dismayed at this and sought to tighten the control of 'medically induced miscarriages'. But the trial of Adams Lehmann also became famous – or notorious, depending on one's point of view – for a number of other reasons.

There can be little doubt that Adams Lehmann had attracted a judicial investigation into her abortion practice because she was a prominent woman doctor with an unusual life story, career and uncomfortable views.[58] She had been one of the female pioneers in German medicine and the first woman doctor in Munich. Born near London, she had moved to Germany when she was eighteen to study, first, German and assorted other topics as a guest student in Dresden; later, medicine in Leipzig; finally in Berne, Switzerland where she received her doctorate. All her adult life she was an active member of the SPD and her political views translated into helping the less privileged in her private life and in her medical practice.[59] At the same time she was a fearless feminist who dedicated her work to caring for women, especially mothers from the lower classes. In 1896 she had published her best-known book, the two-volume *A Women's Book. A Medical Handbook for the Woman in the Family and for Gynaecological Problems*, aimed at imparting a basic knowledge of the body and its functions (vol. 1) and women's specific health problems (vol. 2) to the gender who was central to guarding the health of the whole family. This book proved a runaway bestseller with 40,000 copies sold in only a few years. In this publication she revealed her radical feminist ideas by advocating easier access to both birth control and abortion as a woman's right. With her first husband she ran a tuberculosis sanatorium in Baden. In 1896 she moved to Munich with her second husband to work in general medicine and gynaecology. Here, in the capital of Roman Catholic Bavaria, she practised what she had long preached, helping women to control their fertility and terminate their unwanted pregnancies – and she did so candidly. What is more, almost all these operations were performed for the minimum health insurance contribution of 30 Marks; often she reduced her fees because most of her patients were working class and poor, and frequently physically worn out.

Adams Lehmann was also notable for the high regard in which she was held by her many women patients and for of her brilliant surgical skills; indeed there is no hint of any mishap or ill effect as a result of her many terminations. She entered all her operations conscientiously in her medical diary and scrupulously sought the necessary second opinion from a colleague before each one. Unlike most of the other doctors whose abortion practice came to the notice of the authorities after medical complications had arisen, or dissatisfied patients – or, as we saw with Dr Hartmann, discontented colleagues – had lodged complaints, Adams Lehmann was denounced by a midwife, Frau Rahnstein. This Munich midwife was seeking to defend herself but was also looking for revenge. In March 1914 she was summoned to the police station on suspicion of having performed illegal abortions ('curettage') in her home. When she was interrogated she tried to divert attention away from herself to the Red Cross Hospital in West Munich. She named a number of doctors there, especially Adams Lehmann who, as the midwife alleged, 'brought about regular miscarriages and premature births as well as tubal ligations' (*Unterbindung des Eierstocks*).[60] Frau Rahnstein almost certainly resented the doctor because of Adams Lehmann's long-standing campaign against the state of German midwifery which had aroused the hostility of many midwives, who accused her of undermining their professional status and threatening their economic security. This view of Adams Lehmann was certainly corroborated by some of her activities, such as her role as vice president of the *Verein Frauenheim*, an association formed for the purpose of fundraising and building a new maternity hospital to the most modern standards of hygiene and design, and her high-profile campaign to replace home births (usually attended by midwives) by hospital deliveries (attended by gynaecologists/obstetricians).[61] This provoked hostility especially from midwives but also from directors of maternity hospitals who might well have feared the competition. Munich's main journal of midwifery quoted several passages of Adams Lehmann's *Women's Book* in which she attacked the institution of midwifery while seeking to defend individual practioners. It was wrong, she had written, to hold the midwife morally responsible for 'the infection which she had helped to spread' because 'the midwife errs out of ignorance'. Midwives, she suggested, did not possess the necessary 'medical or general education which alone could guarantee the proper administration of disinfection'. Adams Lehmann thought that 'only social circumstances' prevented the phasing out of the midwife, while 'her inadequacy has long been recognized by science and we will see the day when she will disappear together with the barber-surgeon'.[62] She herself suspected that midwives associated their economic misery with the increase of abortions. Indeed, midwives did not think kindly of Adams Lehmann who, they felt, was contributing to this trend and therefore to their hardship.[63]

There is no doubt that Adams Lehmann was genuinely dedicated to improving the life and health of women, especially of the lower classes. She was by all accounts also extremely popular with her many health insurance patients; one of her female patients testified that Adams Lehmann was never too tired to help, even at a very late hour. Long after surgery hours, the witness reported, there was usually a queue stretching all the way up the stairs to see her. A colleague reported that her patients had told him that they sometimes had to wait from three in the afternoon to eleven at night and that Adams Lehmann continued her surgery hours despite visible signs of exhaustion. Apparently she never gave priority to wealthy over poor health insurance patients and saw everyone in strict order of arrival, which drove away many of her better-off clientele. Her patients' care did not stop at medical advice but extended to financial and practical help, such as trying to find them work, assisting with welfare support and even paying for operations in hospital. She was also highly regarded as an experienced and conscientious gynaecologist by her colleagues at the Red Cross Hospital.[64] The court order stated that she 'had terminated for money pregnancies which were not justified from a scientific/medical point of view' but there was 'no evidence that she violated the law and scientific/medical views knowingly'.[65] Although this was almost certainly a fudge to get her off the hook, nevertheless it appears that Adams Lehmann terminated pregnancies in good faith and on medical grounds, even if these must have easily merged into social grounds which were not admissible in practice. She had after all always obtained a second medical opinion; when her indications were examined by the medical commission they were always found to have been correctly diagnosed. Sometimes Adams Lehmann even went to the trouble of sending her patients to the gynaecological clinic of Professor Döderlein in Munich – a mistake, as it turned out later.[66] Several doctors, among them some who had originally expressed doubts about the acceptability of Adams Lehmann's extensive termination practice, later testified on her behalf. Dr Anton Hengge, who assisted her during operations and who also often countersigned her indications for abortion, agreed that the number of her abortion patients had indeed increased extraordinarily but suggested this was explained by the socio-economic background of her patients, who were 'members of the poor, nay poorest social strata'; for many of them, he wrote, 'childbirth meant risk to life'. He stated that many other doctors, too, were often convinced of the necessity of a termination but they 'do not dare to take this step for fear of trouble, gossip, and prosecution'.[67] In her testimony Adams Lehmann asserted her belief that

> every woman should be granted the right to determine freely the fate of her foetus until the end of the fifth month of pregnancy. I cannot recognize the inner moral justification of the legal ruling which declares abortion punishable, even criminal.

But, she wrote, despite this belief, she had naturally acted strictly according to the current law.[68] The investigating magistrate seemed determined to make an example of Adams Lehmann in order to deter other doctors, and Döderlein, the head of the medical commission examining the case (as he was again to be eight years later in Hartmann's investigation), seemed to be her chief critic. But in the end not even Döderlein was in favour of indicting her.

A careful scrutiny of the details under investigation reveals one extraordinary aspect of Adams Lehmann's practice which seems unacceptable judged by the medical ethical standards of today but which, strangely, was not mentioned by the judge when he quashed the investigation in September 1915; it is also curiously downplayed by her recent biographer.[69] This is Adams Lehmann's habit of performing sterilizations. There was no reference to this significant detail in the court order, despite the fact that the expert testimony by Professor Döderlein had not only called her abortion practice 'an enormous error' but had also criticized her tendency to sterilize her abortion patients. He was emphatic that the 'Porro operation, that is the supravaginal amputation of the uterus which makes any further conception impossible, contravenes the rules of medical treatment'.[70] How then do we judge Adams Lehmann's role vis-à-vis her patients? Why did this celebrated feminist and friend of the poor not confine herself to inducing miscarriages but also took the opportunity of a general anaesthetic to sterilize many of her patients into the bargain? Between January and June 1914, according to her own deposition, nineteen of the twenty-seven patients who underwent terminations (that is, more than half) were also sterilized.[71] Adams Lehmann herself never denied her procedures. Her meticulous medical diary showed many entries of *'Porro'*, a reference to the nineteenth-century Italian gynaecologist, the first to carry out a hysterectomy, the operation to remove a woman's womb by a caesarian section. Adams Lehmann also explicitly mentioned this operation in her letter to the chair of the Medical Association of the Munich district.[72]

Today we would judge her behaviour as grave malpractice on two counts: firstly, frequently, she did not choose the relatively minor operation of sterilization such as laparotomy or tubal ligation, which was widely practised at the time and which she herself employed occasionally,[73] but tended to use the much more risky and intrusive hysterectomy, that is the removal of the entire upper womb. Secondly, the police interviews of many of her patients reveal that Adams Lehmann failed to seek the informed consent before the operation and on occasion omitted to alert her patients to their operation even after the event. Thus, many women remained in ignorance and some returned to Adams Lehmann asking her to insert a 'Schüsserl', a little dish (that is a diaphragm), as a contraceptive.[74] Adams Lehmann insisted that she had acted solely in the interest of her patients and that they had all completely recovered. She wrote to the Munich Medical Association to whom she appealed for support, that she had performed Porro operations even though 'with its simple technique it was not an operation with which one could shine' but that 'the positive impact on women patients is astonishing'. Moreover, she was convinced of the actual healing power of Porro, claiming that it could arrest 'tuberculosis in the second stage' and 'serious anaemia will be relieved or cured, a hopeless nutritional condition will be alleviated'. She believed there were profound psychological benefits, too, since the operation liberated women from 'the worry of getting pregnant' and therefore also improved women's psychological health.[75] Yet, looking at her own list of her nineteen sterilization patients at the beginning of 1914, the impression remains that this doctor had sought to avert future pregnancies not only to preserve the health of her patients but also to forestall the birth of 'dysgenic' children, thereby conforming to the beliefs of most other doctors, women doctors included, who propounded eugenic ideas.[76] Certainly, her assistant, Dr Hengge, who had countersigned many of her recommendations for Porro, stated that her patients typically belonged to 'those classes who were malnourished and therefore especially exposed to morbidity and degeneration'.[77] Among Adams Lehmann's noted indications for sterilizing her patients were findings such as 'extreme nervousness' (*Nervenschwäche*) or 'intelligence deficit' (*Intelligenzstörung*), which were at that time deemed to be hereditary, leading to 'inferior' children. Moreover, of those nineteen women at least two were extraordinarily young for this most final of all contraceptive methods to be contemplated: a 23-year-old wife of a manual worker with only one child, and a single childless actress (who had undergone one previous termination) of twenty-eight; certainly the former case suggests that a hysterectomy was less a last resort than a eugenic measure to prevent permanently the birth of less 'desirable' offspring.[78]

Adams Lehmann's case is testimony to the contradictory nature of academic medicine and its attitude to and practice of abortion. On the one hand, we witness a doctor with a very high level of professional expertise, a feminist and socialist with a rare idealism to strive for women's rights and gender as well as class equality. On the other hand, her medical practice all but contradicted her professed aims: her neglecting to obtain informed consent before operations conveys a disregard for human rights and the very bodily autonomy which feminist abortion campaigners fought for and which was expressed most succinctly in the KPD slogan 'Your Body Belongs to You!'.[79] As far as can be ascertained, Adams Lehmann was one of only two women doctors in Imperial or Weimar Germany who ever had to defend themselves against accusations of having procured illegal abortions, although of course there might have been others who conducted abortions but were never detected.[80] She was, however, not alone in practising sterilization in conjunction with abortion; criminal files are testimony to such practices by other doctors.[81] In some cases, sterilization seems to have been performed on eugenic grounds. The well-known feminist doctors Lotte Fink and Hertha Riese are good examples. They headed the Frankfurt sex advice centre of the radical sex reform organization League for the Protection of Motherhood, and referred a large number of women to the Frankfurt university hospital for termination. Like Adams Lehmann, they also recommended that a third of these patients be sterilized at the same time. In just five years they were responsible for the tubal ligation of as many as 435 women; whether these women gave their informed consent is not known. Their grounds for permanent sterilization were the inefficient use of short-term contraception, for which they blamed their patients' 'indolence', or 'difficult social circumstances'.[82] Although Fink, who wrote about their practice, denied that she and Riese were guided by eugenic principles, the majority of their patients belonged to the very poorest social strata. This and the particular medical assessment would at least suggest that the two doctors were influenced by concern for the individual woman as well as for the genetic quality of the future generation.[83] The fact that Fink was willing to describe their sterilization referrals so readily and enthusiastically in medical journals suggests, moreover, that in the climate of the time sterilization, as long as it was apparently performed in the interest of the patient, was deemed completely acceptable. As far as eugenic sterilization proper was concerned – that is, an operation with the sole or main aim to destroy a woman's fertility permanently to protect the *Volkskörper* – it was illegal but there was increased support during the Depression by doctors and other professionals for its legalization. A survey among doctors of 1930 revealed that a substantial number of surgeons had performed eugenic sterilizations, some of which were almost certainly without consent.[84] By contrast, lay abortionists seldom possessed the necessary knowledge and skills to perform such operations.

Financial considerations

Even though the abortion law reserved especially harsh penalties for abortionists who sought to gain financially by women's plight, and in the revised §218 of 1926 the maximum penalty for commercial abortion was increased from ten to fifteen years' penal servitude,[85] there was a tendency by the courts to overlook this aspect when registered medical practitioners were investigated. Dr Hartmann was originally accused of having performed terminations commercially and a close reading of the witnesses' depositions shows that indeed at least three women patients admitted to having paid Hartmann money. One patient paid 500 Marks in 1920 and in 1921 Maria Leicht, the shop assistant, paid Hartmann as much as 6,000 Marks possibly 7,000 Marks. She also paid a further 5,000 Marks to the Munich surgeon who finally saved her life. Regardless of the impact of inflation, both women's operations were very expensive indeed.[86] As we will see in the next chapter, lay abortionists, in contrast, generally demanded a fraction of this. Although Hartmann's operation on another patient earlier was paid for by the health insurance fund, Hartmann nevertheless charged her 20 Marks per day for her recuperative stay in his 'private clinic', i.e. in his flat. After a stay of eight days, her bill turned out to be hefty.[87] There is no doubt that Hartmann's finances flourished. In 1922, still at the beginning of his career, he and his wife were seen to live comfortably, in a six-roomed flat with a car and an impressive income at their disposal.[88] According to the judicial records of a 1926 abortion case in which Hartmann was also involved, by then he had managed to build a new house for himself, his wife and young child, and was in the process of building a well-equipped private surgery, certainly a sign of a lucrative medical practice.[89]

Hartmann was not the only doctor who was motivated by monetary considerations, something which was usually attributed to quacks. In a rather similar case in 1929 the medical practitioner we have met above, Dr Selo of Krefeld, was also still quite young (only thirty at the time of the illegal abortions for which he was convicted). As with Dr Hartmann, the local Krefeld newspaper described Selo as popular and his trial was also covered by the local press. Selo's reputation was that he had treated his women patients 'always in the most dedicated manner possible'.[90] Nevertheless, he regularly demanded a fee of 100 Reichs Marks to 200 Reichs Marks for each termination, even from women from the very poorest quarters, for whom this constituted several months' wages. For example, he demanded 150 RM from a 26-year-old single domestic servant, even though she presented her insurance certificate. Only after she protested that she only earned 45 RM per month, did he accept 130 RM as 'his rock bottom fee'. Selo was so adamantly opposed to lowering his fees that he preferred to send women away rather than compromise his financial demands. His fees increased depending on the stage of the pregnancy, presumably to compensate for the increased medical risk of terminating a late pregnancy and the possibility of police investigation in case of mishap. Moreover, Selo also committed insurance fraud by charging two health insurance funds for his costs, which his patients had already paid in cash. In the case of the domestic servant mentioned above, he also claimed payment from her sick fund for a fictitious treatment.[91] The habit of charging both patient and insurance fund for an operation was by no means unheard of elsewhere. In another case relating to the last five years of the Weimar Republic, but which was not tried until 1934, the extensive abortion practice of a team of four doctors from Fürstenberg upon Oder, in Brandenburg, was similarly cleverly managed so that each termination was routinely paid twice over.[92]

Hartmann's less than honest marketing ploy, i.e. passing himself off as a gynaecologist, was meant to attract women who found themselves pregnant against their will since abortion had become a very lucrative business in the chaos of the postwar period, when the estimated number of abortions had increased enormously.[93] This kind of indirect marketing was especially advantageous since doctors were officially not allowed to advertise. Hartmann's appearance at the mass rally against §218 in Munich, too, should almost certainly be read as a veiled marketing attempt. This was certainly the view of several newspaper reports, in which it was suggested that Hartmann had used the podium of the demonstration not only to show his commitment to legal reform but also to portray himself as somebody whom many women trusted and who had a successful practice in Rosenheim. In his brief speech he boasted that 'in a single year no fewer than 70 women and girls had approached him to free them from their pregnancies', among them 'even wives of counsellors of justice'. Unfortunately, he said, he had been forced to reject most of these requests.[94]

Indeed, it was not unusual for doctors to try and attract aborting women by whatever means available, especially when young doctors were seeking to build up their own practice in the face of competition. A popular method was to employ midwives, masseuses or nurses as touts for aborting women; another method depended on a whispering campaign.[95] It is possible that a midwife who assisted Hartmann with at least three terminations was also in his employ to refer clients to him. Maybe it was also she who had helped spread the rumour that he was a 'very good gynaecologist' and that this reputation was then passed on as a safe tip to women within the tightly knit neighbourhood network of tenement houses whenever somebody complained about a 'delayed period'.[96] Even those abortion doctors who did not operate commercially, like Adams Lehmann, used intermediaries. There is evidence that in the Red Cross Hospital in which she delivered babies or terminated pregnancies welfare workers supplied her with aborting patients by remonstrating with expectant mothers, 'why they allowed themselves to be burdened with so many children, they should go instead to Dr Lehmann's to put a stop to it'. There were also five midwives who seem to have cooperated with Adams Lehmann and her sympathetic colleagues at the same hospital in a kind of abortion service network, as was the case also with the group of medical practitioners in Fürstenberg upon Oder and many others whose colleagues obliged them with a so-called *Gefälligkeitsattest*, an accomodating certificate.[97] At any rate, the taboo of medical advertising seems to have been easily circumvented.

Medical attitude and medical power

The medical profession's avowed aim, in public, was to gain the right to perform terminations to safeguard public and family health and morality, but, in private, medical attitudes were more ambiguous. Many doctors helped their patients, especially if they were family doctors for the middle classes, some out of sympathy, others so as not to lose their patients' goodwill or to enrich themselves. Many also regarded abortion with disdain and avoided the operation.[98] These latter despised colleagues who transgressed the law in the interest of easy money, decrying them as belonging to 'the despised guild of scrapers' (*Auskratzer*).[99] A widely shared reluctance to perform terminations was probably linked to a deep-seated antipathy to gynaecological intervention. Even obstetrics, a battleground of competition between male obstetricians and female midwives, was traditionally not very popular among (male) doctors, who regarded it as a woman's job. Ornella Moscucci, discussing nineteenth-century English gynaecology, explains that 'the perceived messiness and immodesty of childbirth rendered man-midwifery unpalatable to medical men'.[100] Generally, physical contact with female genitals was a problem for medical men, as indeed it was for their women patients who regarded it as a violation of their modesty. To protect women from such indelicate intervention was after all one of the chief reasons for the campaign for women doctors.[101]

But if childbirth had long been associated in the eyes of male doctors with impropriety, abortion was doubly so: despite evidence to the contrary in the Weimar Republic, it was still commonly associated with illicit sex and the aborting patient with a fallen woman. As I have discussed in more detail elsewhere, medical anthropologists have suggested the continuation of pollution beliefs as an explanation for male unease with women of childbearing age in general and menstruating women in particular.[102] To this day the notion continues that menstrual blood is dirty and sex during the menses is spurned for aesthetic as well as medical reasons. A standard German medical textbook on gynaecology, published in 1924, for example, postulated that during menstruation a woman expels poisonous substances, implying that she could contaminate her surroundings.[103] But abortion must have appeared especially unacceptable, because unlike childbirth, it was not compensated for by bringing about new life. A foetus aborted becomes waste matter and surgeons sought to protect themselves not only from women's bodily fluids and blood but also from contamination from dead material. This explains why doctors attached enormous importance to their surgical techniques of dilation and curettage, which required instruments and prevented their hands from coming into direct contact with 'dirty material'. The late nineteenth-century invention of laminaria tents and tools such as the curette to evacuate the uterus provided a breakthrough which doctors claimed as their prerogative[104] and which established an important distinction between medical and 'quack' abortion. In criminal abortion investigations involving injuries or death, expert witnesses usually interpreted evidence of use of instruments as a sign that 'abortionists without medical knowledge and medical instruments [could] be eliminated', i.e. that it could safely be assumed that a doctor and not a lay practitioner had been involved.[105] But such instruments required great skill and, as we have seen above, it was not uncommon for doctors to use them carelessly or ineptly with the result that wombs were ruptured, intestines punctured, and pelvises infected. Many women suffered agonizing pain, long-term morbidity and, as we have seen, not a few died as a result.

The use of instruments also justified a total anaesthetic, another privilege which doctors had over midwives and especially 'quacks'. Although there was no consensus among experts at the time whether an anaesthetic was required with every curettage, the use of anaesthesia certainly increased medical control by rendering the aborting woman impassive (i.e. into a 'patient') and mute. On occasion this led to an abuse of medical power when an unconscious patient was subjected to abortion and sterilization without consent, as we have seen with Dr Adams Lehmann's practice of sterilizing aborting women, or, even worse, when women were raped by their male doctor. In one case a family doctor from a small town in the Rhineland habitually offered terminations in exchange for sex. Intercourse took place almost immediately and without the precaution of contraception. The aborting women, who were almost without exception very young (that is, between eighteen and twenty-one), were probably too terrified to resist or denounce him. This doctor's rape was acknowledged by the court but not taken into account for the final sentence.[106] Of course, such cases are not representative of the medical profession as a whole; yet, the fact that courts apparently condoned such professional misconduct suggests that it was not uncommon. Most women avoided consulting a doctor, probably well aware of the risks involved when encountering an unknown male doctor on their own, in an emotionally volatile state and asking a favour which laid them open to blackmail, although, as we shall see, they were not necessarily safe in the hands of male lay abortionists either.

Many women, especially of the lower classes, might also have shied away from seeking doctors' help in delicate questions like termination, since they were figures of authority who instilled respect, sometimes even fear, in their patients. The image of the doctor in Keun's novel *Gilgi*, described in the last chapter, acting condescendingly towards a young woman of the lower middle classes at his mercy, was probably not too far-fetched. Some doctors would exploit their power, deciding apparently on a whim which woman seeking a termination was 'deserving', which to be turned away. Interestingly, we know of such unprofessional behaviour from a doctor's own medical diary entries. The diary of a rural practitioner was anonymously and posthumously published by Alfred Grotjahn, the Berlin professor of social hygiene. Grotjahn had originally opposed a liberalized abortion law but had changed his mind when he found how frequently and urgently abortion was sought and granted, even in the countryside. The country practitioner had performed over 400 terminations in just one year, many of them on social, therefore illegal, grounds, but had never been prosecuted.[107] Grotjahn portrayed him as a true friend of the poor. The abortionist's own notes, however, suggest otherwise. He was prone to act capriciously and sometimes even sadistically.

In not a few cases he followed the dictates of his own prejudice rather than the medical evidence before him.[108] As he admitted himself, rather than wait until the situation could be better assessed, he was not above administering a 'precautionary curettage', when he could not diagnose a pregnancy with certainty, only to find after the operation that none had existed. In a single year, at least three women were submitted to a 'libido curettage' to improve their sexual performance; but worse, this doctor also performed 'palliative curettages' to teach his patients, whose pregnancy was uncertain, a lesson 'to take more care in the future'. On these occasions he operated without anaesthetic, probably to heighten the impact. One such case is described in his diary as follows:

> Salesgirl. Not yet 20. Had a boyfriend in the army. I was moved. I do not know if this is true. But I feel sorry for the girl. Examination: uncertain but cannot be excluded. *Abrasio* [termination]. Of course this hurt her very much, but she pulls herself together. I am convinced that she will now take more care. In my experience a palliative curettage has an excellent paedagogical effect with *nulliparas* [women who had never conceived].[109]

Judicial records show that quite a few doctors regularly terminated pregnancies without anaesthesia; one might say that lay abortionists never used them either, but then a medical intervention involved sharp instruments such as the probe or the curette which by their nature were painful to the patient. The testimony of women witnesses tells of the excruciating pain which many suffered as a result.[110]

Such an operation on a fully conscious woman was, of course, special torture when it went wrong. This was the case with one of Hartmann's other patients, Frau Anna Pulver, who suffered appalling injuries. Hartmann's mistakes led to embolism, peritonitis and thrombosis (*Aderverstopfung*) which finally caused her agonizing death.[111] We can only guess why doctors did not routinely adminster anaesthetics but they were probably swayed by financial and practical considerations. Anaesthetics were expensive to adminster since medical regulation required the use of a specialist; a third witness to an illegal operation also increased the risk of detection. Both these points probably persuaded Hartmann to ask his friend, the dentist, or his wife to help, neither of whom was trained for the task.

Women's experience

Aborting women's search for help usually followed the pattern of a self-abortion attempt to start with, then an appeal first to a relative or neighbour, next to a wise woman or wise man and finally, if all else failed or was unavailable, an approach to a (usually male) doctor. Unusually, many of Hartmann's abortion clients seem to have consulted him as their first port of call, although a number seem to have been passed on to him by the two midwives who were in cahoots with him. This may have been because in Rosenheim there were few if any lay abortionists, including midwives, who were prepared to help, or if they existed, they might have preferred to tout for Hartmann rather than risk operating themselves. Or perhaps the reputation of Hartmann, the new young doctor, as a willing accomplice and a 'competent gynaecologist' was sufficient for women not to bother looking further afield. Adams Lehmann was also exceptional in that her abortion patients came to her directly for help. This was because she was well known as a birth control advocate. Furthermore, her surgical skills were renowned and her operations were funded by the health insurance so that there was little point in going elsewhere.

How did women rate Hartmann as an abortionist? Unfortunately the accounts of the police interviews conducted with some of his women patients are very brief and offer little scope for gleaning their attitudes. Apart from one woman or another who expressed her dissatisfaction with Hartmann's treatment either explicitly or implicitly because she had changed to another doctor in town,[112] we can only surmise their reaction by reading between the lines. Opinions among Hartmann's abortion clients probably varied. Some might well have been grateful for his services but others must have found the encounter with him difficult either because the operation was carried out when they were fully conscious or, worse, because he bungled it, as with Maria Leicht and at least two other women patients.[113] Then he surely must have bitterly disappointed their confidence in him, as a 'competent gynaecologist'. Strangely, there is no record of any complaint against Hartmann, not even in extreme cases like that of Maria Leicht. But then this might be explained by fear of being detected in contravention of §218 and of the trial and imprisonment which would follow. In the case of Maria Leicht the expert testimony of Hartmann's surgical skills by the Munich medical committee was a cruel irony. They called Hartmann's attempt to drive her to Munich a 'courageous decision': 'It is solely thanks to this action and the expert operation that the life of the patient which would otherwise have been lost was saved and that she is now completely healthy.' Not a single word was said about the irreparable injury she had sustained. The forensic pathologist who was, as we saw above, much more critical of Hartmann than his mentors in the medical committee, noted sarcastically in the margin of the report the words 'completely healthy': 'sine utero!'.[114]

Whereas in trials of lay abortionists, as we shall see in the next chapter, the aborting women and their concerns were more frequently mentioned, this kind of disregard for the interests of a patient as shown in the investigation of Dr Hartmann is also a feature of medical expert testimonies in other abortion investigations and trials: women were rarely considered as individuals but rather as objects of medical attention; their persons were usually also pathologized and treated without due regard for their personal circumstances. For example, for the 24-year-old single Maria Leicht, an unplanned pregnancy was obviously a real threat. It was likely to endanger her relationship with her boyfriend and she might have risked losing her job. To avert both she decided to persuade her father and her boyfriend to pay Hartmann a small fortune; and she was prepared not only to risk imprisonment herself but also to implicate her boyfriend and father as accomplices, both of whom were liable under §218. It seems that neither she nor her helpers were brought to trial. Having avoided prosecution could, however, hardly have compensated for her terrible injuries and her subsequent permanent infertility. The official reports, however, ignored this personal tragedy completely; what Hartmann himself thought about it is not known.

Patients' individual rights were also often disregarded by doctors who were otherwise known to have been humanitarian: Adams Lehmann was celebrated as a fighter for women's rights and those of the underprivileged. Her decision to sterilize exhausted mothers at the same time as terminating their unplanned pregnancies was, as she suggested herself, motivated by deep sympathy for their biological conundrum: 'Oh, I have to preserve the poor woman for her husband; the man needs a healthy wife; what use are so many children?'[115] The synopsis of her sterilization cases is evidence of Adams Lehmann's conscientious anamnesis, findings and indication; it also suggests that most of her abortion patients were likely to have benefited from a permanent form of contraception. This probable effect alone, however, cannot justify such high-handed decisions and such invasive surgery carried out without previous informed consent. Adams Lehmann's actions were especially unacceptable because some of her sterilization patients were exceptionally young and as yet childless. Moreover, her decision to sterilize was not just informed by medical or social but almost certainly also by eugenic considerations. Even if some, or even all, of these women profited from a hysterectomy, the intervention was probably aimed as much to benefit the *Volkskörper* as the welfare of the individual patient.[116] It is probably no exaggeration to call what Adams Lehmann practised compulsory sterilization by the back door.

Academic medicine in this area at that time was not only rated higher than lay treatment, but also higher than the views of aborting women themselves. The rights of women patients were often, possibly in the great majority of cases, disregarded whenever expert witnesses sought to protect the career of a physician under scrutiny from the law and the medical disciplinary body. It is also clear that from the viewpoint of the aborting woman a termination of pregnancy was not necessarily more effective or safe if performed by a medical practitioner rather than by a layman or -woman. At that time a medical licence was no guarantee of an abortion free from complications, just as the lack of such a licence, as we shall see next, did not necessarily mean a risk to a woman's health or life. The boundary between licensed physicians and unlicensed practitioners – or, in other words, between academic and lay medicine – made much of in the medical literature, was, in this area at least, much more blurred in practise than doctors would have liked. To put it bluntly, as far as termination by a doctor was concerned many medical practitioners were no better than laymen.

This, however, undermined one of the central tenets of their campaign against *Kurierfreiheit*, the right for everyone to practise medicine whether state registered and university trained or not. It was also another reason why doctors were keen to take over this field of reproductive health in which so many lay practitioners were apparently so successful. The profession pursued a dual strategy to exclude the latter: quack abortions (*Pfuscherabtreibungen*) should, they argued, be prosecuted with severity while terminations induced by registered doctors should be made permissable in law. But if this two-pronged fight against quackery and for a medical monopoly of artificial miscarriage was to succeed it was essential to improve medical training in abortion technology and for practitioners to gain experience as fast as possible, even if this proved risky occasionally, at least as indicated by the various expert testimonies condoning the malpractice of doctors like Hartmann. The courts which were willing to accept mitigating circumstances for medical men (and it appeared they were almost always men), but seldom lay practioners, were acting as willing accomplices. Doctors' terminations were often condoned without a strict medical indication even when they had plainly been motivated by financial gain or when they had failed to provide the appropriate care. It was not rare for law courts or investigating magistrates to treat very grave forms of medical malpractice and negligence with extraordinary leniency but, as we shall see next, to habitually prosecute and punish lay abortionists with severity.

Chapter 4

ABORTION IN THE MARKETPLACE: LAY PRACTITIONERS AND DOCTORS COMPETE

The concerted effort made by many members of the medical profession to legalize abortion on medical grounds was closely linked to their campaign against quackery (*Kurpfuscherei*). This was fought against the background of the professionalization of medicine and the quest for medical monopoly in all areas of health care. It signalled the profession's determination to abolish *Kurierfreiheit*, the freedom for anybody to practise healing whether trained or not. Doctors pursued this end overtly through campaigning organizations, medical journals and health exhibitions but also more covertly through the courts by accusing individual lay practitioners of malpractice, generally in cases of sexually transmitted diseases (STD) or abortion.

This chapter will discuss the genesis of *Kurierfreiheit* as part of the process of professionalization of medicine in the nineteenth century and analyse the reasons for the anti-quackery campaign from the turn of the last century to shore up medical influence, especially in the politically sensitive area of reproductive health. I argue that abortion proved a suitable platform for academic medicine to discredit and marginalize lay practitioners in an attempt to medicalize all terminations of pregnancy. Lay abortionists rather than aborting women became the new target of anti-abortionists and abortion reformers alike who usually accused them of leading women astray, of greed and ignorance. This is compared to how lay abortion practice affected women themselves especially with respect to gender, class and culture. Lastly, career paths of 'wise men' and 'wise women' are discussed, as is their safety record, methods used and the price they demanded.

The anti-quackery campaign

The history of this campaign remains relatively underresearched, particularly for the period of the Weimar Republic, and the term 'quackery' remains ill defined.[1] It was used loosely, its meaning varying according to time and place, and it came increasingly to be employed by its detractors and always in a pejorative sense. As Reinhard Spree has pointed out, in the early modern period it still had several meanings, not necessarily always negative: for example, it was used to indicate substandard practice (*Pfuscherei*), or simply that a healer did not belong to the guild, or that a person was practising healing without the relevant professional qualifications. In the late eighteenth and early nineteenth century, quackery had taken on almost wholly negative connotations and was disapproved by the state, which was promoting population growth and public health. Spree argues that despite this, pragmatism dictated that quacks were tolerated, especially in rural districts, because academically trained doctors were scarce and unevenly distributed. It was also difficult to regulate lay medicine, which was often practised out of sight from surveillance, if not clandestinely.[2] Research in other European countries, however, has shown (and later German statistics suggest much the same, as we shall see below) that lay healers were also popular in towns, that they often advertised and practised quite openly and that they were tolerated also whenever they offered specialist services in demand and because of their cultural affinity with their clients.[3] By the end of the nineteenth century doctors, still with the support of the state, had become the chief opponents of quackery; they attempted to stigmatize it primarily as a health hazard. In 1869 the liberal trade regulations of the North German League and, two years later, of the new German Reich, declared medicine a trade open to all, thus legalizing lay healing. Spree argues that the designation 'quackery' henceforth applied technically only to fully trained and registered practitioners, such as nurses or midwives, possibly even doctors, if they dispensed treatment that was illegal or outside their remit, such as abortion.[4] Thus, as we shall see below, midwives who had lost their licence following a conviction for criminal abortion featured as quacks in subsequent judicial records, rather than as deregistered midwives. But in practice, even in courts of law, quackery continued to be understood in a much broader sense, often encompassing all lay healing[5] as well as academic medicine which had embraced alternative methods such as homeopathy or nature therapy. The authoritative *Meyers Konversationslexikon* continued to refer to quackery in this elastic manner. In its 1905 edition it defined quackery as 'the commercial practice of healing without appropriate training'.[6]

Interestingly, German doctors had not always opposed lay healing. It was in fact a medical initiative in the 1860s which led to the law against quackery being revoked in the North German League and subsequently in the Reich. The impetus came from members of the Berlin Medical Society (including Rudolf Virchow) and their campaign was taken up by liberal members of the Prussian Diet, some of whom were also doctors.[7] This led to new trade laws declaring *Kurierfreiheit*; only the title *approbierter Arzt* (qualified registered doctor) was restricted by law to those who had passed the state medical exams. Such official toleration of lay medicine was rare in Europe and could only be found in England and Wales and two small Swiss cantons.

What, then, motivated German doctors to pave the way for *Kurierfreiheit*? Partly pragmatism, partly a large dose of confidence – possibly overconfidence – with a pinch of liberal idealism thrown in. Criminalization of quackery had proved to be ineffective and a new belief in the progress of academic medicine, particularly in the field of bacteriology, persuaded doctors that they need no longer fear competition. Furthermore, they hoped that new science-based medicine attracted quite a different clientele from lay healing. Although research in the Netherlands has shown that lay practitioners also catered for rural and urban elites,[8] which makes it likely that the same was true of Germany, doctors regarded the urban elites as their patients while quacks were thought to care for the lower social strata, predominantly in the countryside. Thus, doctors were confident that, given the choice, the middle classes would always prefer professional rather than lay treatment. Doctors sceptical of *Kurierfreiheit* were won over by promises of important concessions to the profession: full autonomy over training and quality control without state interference; unified professional standards and regulations; abolition of the state *Kurtaxe* (a tax on healing); freedom of movement and choice of medical treatment; and last, but not least, the right for doctors to set their own fees.[9]

This process of professionalization was accompanied by the growing importance of medical societies and the founding, in 1873, of the German Medical Association (*Ärztevereinsbund*). The role of the medical profession in Imperial Germany was also greatly bolstered when in 1883 general health insurance was introduced for between ten and twelve million waged workers. Although lay practitioners were not necessarily excluded, free medical treatment benefited first and foremost qualified doctors with a panel or sick fund practice; this hastened the process of medicalization, the increasing influence of academic medicine within middle- and working-class culture. The extension of the social insurance programme culminated in the Reich Insurance Act of 1913 and increased the number of insured to twenty million (about a third of the entire population).[10] In the Weimar Republic the majority of the working population was brought within reach of free medical treatment. By 1929 compulsory membership, including family members who were also covered, covered two-thirds of the entire population.[11]

This upward trajectory of academic medicine was, however, halted by a so-called 'medical crisis' at the turn of the twentieth century, when there were few tangible successes in new treatments for internal, especially infectious, diseases, then at the forefront of socio-political concerns.[12] Moreover, the confident prediction of the original supporters of *Kurierfreiheit* that academic medicine would gradually replace lay healing, had not come true, as contemporary doctors' associations admitted. The number of quacks had not only not decreased, but had actually risen. In 1903, as a result of medical pressure, the Reichs Chancellor ordered an enquiry into the prevalence of lay healing in German states, which showed a rapid increase year on year.[13] As Cornelia Regin has argued, however, all statistics were highly dubious because of their method of collection and vague definition.[14]

According to Robert Jütte, in 1909 a total of 21,014 laymen and -women practised medicine. Others put the figure at c. 4,500 in 1909 but at over 14,000 by 1931.[15] In Prussia, the number of nonregistered healers was estimated to have risen from just over 4,000 in 1902 to over 6,000 in 1925.[16] In Bavaria their number nearly trebled between 1913 and 1932, from 519 (of which at least 168 were female) to 1,322 in 1932. In 1928 one estimate put the total number of quacks in Germany as a whole at about 50,000.[17] Moreover, quackery was clearly not confined to the countryside, since nearly half of all lay healers now practised in towns; nor did they cater only for the poorer section of the community, as many doctors had wrongly believed; nature therapy and all manner of alternative practices by non-doctors became increasingly popular among the bourgeoisie. This led the Hamburg Medical Association to complain that the 'tendency towards superstition among the population' had welled up after the First World War and was, they claimed, apparent 'even in those classes who otherwise wished to appear educated and enlightened'.[18] The sense of growing competition from quacks drove doctors to accuse them of dangerous practices: a 'death toll of 5,000 lives every year' was alleged publicly and many 'furious' doctors accused individual lay healers of incompetence and malpractice and urged the authorities to prosecute them.[19] The fight against *Kurierfreiheit* led to the founding, in 1904, of the *Deutsche Gesellschaft zur Bekämpfung des Kurpfuschertums e.V.* (DGBK, German Society for the Repression of Quackery), an organization largely made up of doctors. Its aggressive and often vindictive campaigns found much support not just in medical but also in official circles.[20] In 1909 the government tabled a bill to control quackery which was debated twice in the plenary of the Reichstag but was first delayed, then rejected by the Reichstag in 1916 and eventually shelved until February 1939, when the National Socialists introduced the *Heilpraktikergesetz*, the law regulating lay practitioners.[21]

Despite this setback, the anti-quackery campaign made some progress. For example, during the First World War several army commands outlawed lay treatment of STD and the supply of certain drugs, including contraceptives, by non-doctors. After the war, the DGBK used this precedent to petition for a general prohibition of nostrums and the treatment of STD or fertility control by lay practitioners. In 1927 the law to combat STD was an important victory for them since it made the treatment of those infected by STD the prerogative of doctors.[22] Otherwise the DGBK concentrated on repressing quackery by political lobbying, a series of high-profile events and litigation. It succeeded in winning official support for its cause, especially from the Prussian Welfare Ministry and from the former *Oberreichsanwalt*, Dr Ludwig Ebermayer, who at a large public gathering called on the German state to 'protect its population from the pernicious consequences of the *Kurierfreiheit*'.[23] In 1928 the DGBK made the campaign against quackery the subject of a special issue in the official organ of the Prussian Medical Service. Under the banner of 'public enlightenment about the dangers of quackery' the Society organized travelling exhibitions throughout Germany and special 'anti-quackery' training courses for doctors in such high-profile venues as the Berlin Herrenhaus in 1927.[24] They also resorted to libel suits to 'reveal', as they put it, the full extent of 'trickery' behind so-called nature therapy and natural remedies by patent manufacturers and took every opportunity to defend their own 'idealistic and humanitarian' aims against what they described as slanderous attacks by individual lay healers. This paid off on several occasions when judges supported the claims of the Society to be 'genuinely intent on shielding the public from the false belief in products marketed by nature therapists'.[25]

The so-called *Ärzteschwemme*, the glut of doctors at the beginning of the Weimar years, and the alleged rise in the number of lay practitioners made the medical market the site of intense competition. This was blamed partly on the rapidly rising number of newly qualified doctors (from 36,186 in 1921 to 48,507 in 1928), partly on a crisis in the public perception of academic medicine as too 'mechanistic' and not holistic enough. To make matters worse, as a result of the inflation in the early 1920s the number of health insurance doctors was reduced to a ratio of one to 1,000 patients, significantly impeding access to a coveted insurance practice.[26] The Depression, too, at the end of the 1920s hit the profession hard; unprecedented unemployment among their numbers coupled with drastic welfare cuts fuelled a renewed anti-quackery attack. Doctors complained bitterly that *Kurierfreiheit* gave lay practitioners an unfair economic advantage. For example, at an official exhibition in 1927 it was claimed that a medical degree 'took an average of 15,200 hours', whereas lay practitioners were trained, 'if at all, for no more than 6 weeks at the most, or 84 hours'. A university degree in medicine cost '12,800 Marks' but quacks never paid more than '350 Marks'. Doctors also claimed that lay practitioners could earn disproportionately more than they could themselves. In 1927, it was declared that a well-known therapist had advertised for a partner with the promise of a minimum annual income of 12,000 Marks, the implication being that this exceeded the prospects of many members of their own profession.[27]

The issue of abortion provided a perfect platform for the medical profession to flex their muscles and marginalize quacks. It is easy to see why termination of pregnancy became such a focal point. The very high estimates of the annual abortion rate and, worse, its perceived sharp increase ensured its place at the forefront of medico-political debate.[28] Many doctors must have been under considerable pressure to succumb to the pleadings of their female patients, others simply felt compelled to help women in need.[29] Many medics struggling to make ends meet must also have been tempted by what seemed like easy money.[30] There was also the hope that legalization of abortion on therapeutic, and possibly social and ethical, grounds would increase the demand for doctors' services. Moreover, doctors sought to distance themselves from the embarrassing increase in maternal morbidity and mortality by blaming criminal, especially quack abortions.[31] Medical journals made much of each new court case involving lay abortionists. Every quack who inflicted an injury or caused an abortion-related death provided grist for the doctors' mill in their anti-*Kurierfreiheit* campaign.[32] Prominent doctors did their best to discredit quacks who had moved into the area of fertility control.[33] Faced with the problem of maternal mortality, which embarrassed the profession and hindered their programme of obstetric reform and hospitalization of childbirth, socialist doctors were equally ready to demonize 'quack abortionists'. Alfred Dührssen, the left-leaning professor of gynaecology at Berlin University and leading apologist for legalized abortion, claimed that the operations performed by 'midwives, paramedics or lay persons' constituted 'the greatest danger of death for the pregnant woman'.[34]

Not to be outdone, the organized popular health movement also condemned back-street abortions whether performed by doctors or lay persons.[35] To gain respectability they took care to distance themselves from controversial political initiatives, such as the various abortion reform campaigns by the political left. In fact, the largest and most vociferous lay organization, the Central Association for the Parity of Healing Methods (*Zentralverband für Parität der Heilmethoden*), with forty associated societies and about 40,000 individual members by 1919, went as far as refuting that lay healers had ever reserved the right to terminate pregnancies at all: 'In this area we do not want *Kurierfreiheit*', proclaimed an editorial in their official journal. 'Doctors can have their abortion.'[36] They pointed the accusing finger at doctors who, they argued, were the real culprits who indulged in abortion-mongering to enrich themselves. So convinced were they of their own innocence that they called on the government to publish crime statistics distinguishing between qualified physicians and healers indicted for criminal abortions.[37] The Central Association and many other similar organizations took every opportunity to expose the full extent of injuries and death incurred by doctors' bungled abortions so that women might be protected from, as they put it, 'state-registered botchers' (*approbierte Pfuscher*).[38]

Self-induced abortions

This dispute between doctors and lay practitioners helped to obscure the fact that a substantial number of abortions were self-induced. Many women took recourse to this method as the first step towards terminating an unwanted pregnancy. Such self-help was consistently underestimated in official reports but it was very popular amongst the lower classes and in remoter areas of the countryside, especially during the war and the early Weimar years. This is hardly surprising, given that the most frequently used instrument, a syringe

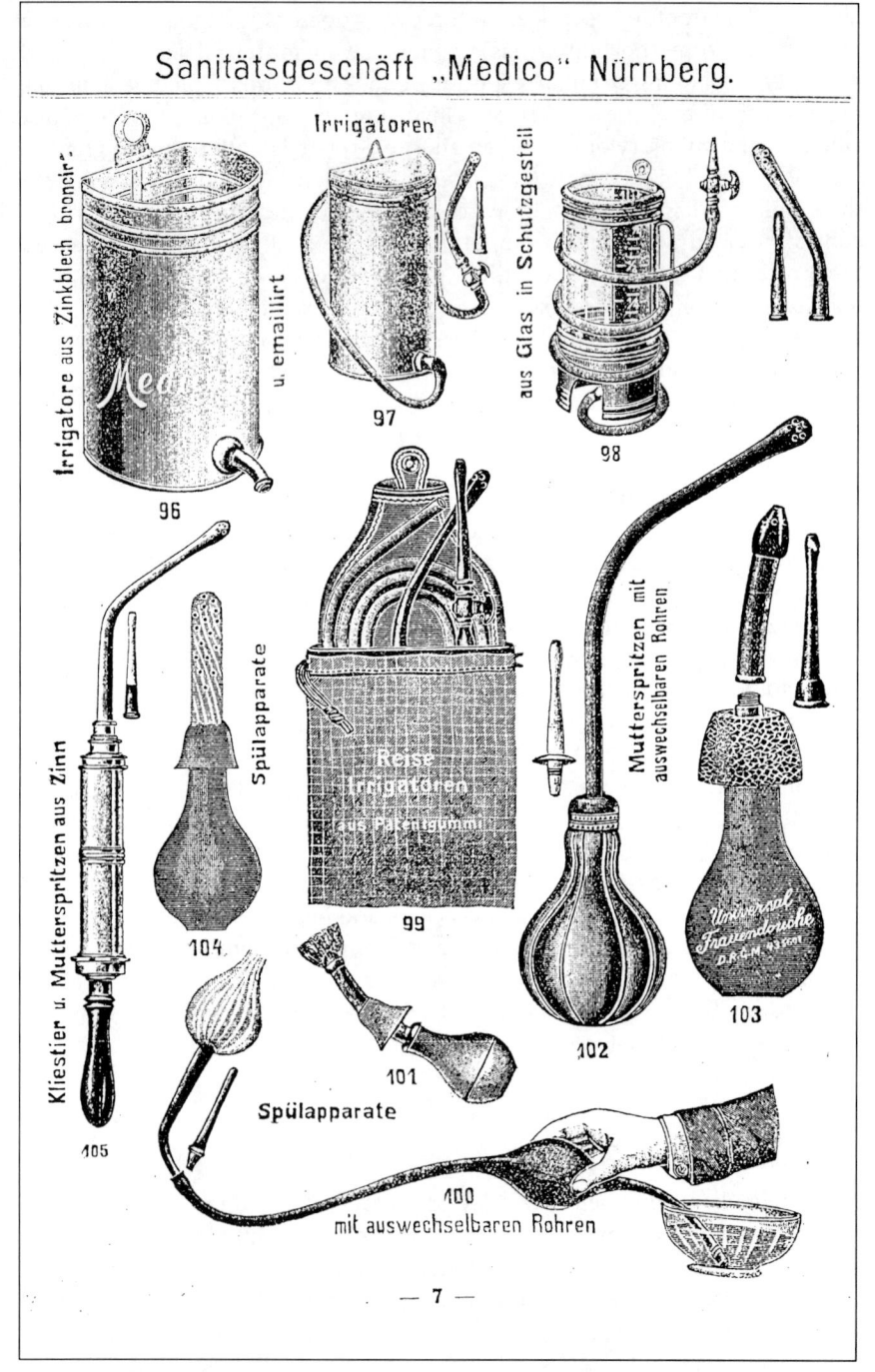

9. *Mutterspritzen* and other douches, from mail-order catalogue *Medico*, Nurnberg

with the telling name of *Mutterspritze*, applied with household soap, was relatively cheap and easily obtainable. Since the early Weimar years, to restore public reproductive health, many sick funds paid for syringes as essential articles of feminine hygiene.[39] They could quite easily be converted into an abortion aid by attaching a long curved catheter, made of glass or, preferably, unbreakable metal or rubber. How to do this safely was usually passed by word of mouth through women's neighbourhood networks or at the workplace, as we shall see in more detail in the next chapter. Some medical practitioners and those clinicians who were able to talk in confidence to their women patients, especially those admitted to hospital after a 'miscarriage', were surprised at how many women had induced their own termination.[40] Self-induced abortions were the hardest to detect since they usually took place without the knowledge of a third party; unless the operation had gone wrong and the woman needed medical help, which made reporting to the police possible, criminal records are therefore not necessarily the best indicators of their prevalence. This notwithstanding, in two industrialized regions of the Rhineland as many as a third of all women prosecuted under §218 during the war had induced their own miscarriage.[41] A number of other small-scale studies suggest that this pattern was repeated elsewhere in other industrialized areas. In Saxony, certainly, a very high proportion of abortions which came to trial in the early Weimar years were self-induced. Typical was the Leipzig case in early 1920 of a young, single dietician who had acquired a syringe for her own use. In the same year, also in Leipzig, a law student, the fiancé of a young female clerk, had procured a *Mutterspritze* and assisted her in using it. In both cases a miscarriage resulted but also a prosecution because the participants were denounced.[42] Other sources suggest an even higher incidence of self-help. Ernst Bumm, the director of the Berlin University Women's Hospital, registered in 1916 that 76 per cent of all abortion-related emergency admissions had confessed to having induced their own miscarriage and a survey conducted in 1922 in Frankfurt a.M. arrived at a figure of 74 per cent.[43] When women failed to achieve the desired result themselves they usually sought help from a third party.[44]

By the mid-1920s the practice of self-abortion had gradually been replaced by, or possibly reverted to, the tendency to consult an abortionist recommended by word of mouth. In the *Landgericht* Mönchen-Gladbach, for example, of all abortions tried, the percentage of miscarriages induced by an abortionist rose from 42 per cent before the war, to 60 per cent during the war, to 82 per cent in 1919–24 and then declined slightly to 74 per cent thereafter.[45] In Duisburg the percentage of aborting women who were tried for having induced their own miscarriage fell from over 30 per cent to 13.7 per cent in the first five years of the Republic, to steadily rise again to just over 20 per cent in the following seven years, but the number of abortions performed for money increased steadily, outstripping all other forms.[46] It is not improbable that doctors numbered among these 'commercial operators' but they appear in criminal records more rarely because prosecutions or convictions often failed for lack of evidence.[47] Despite this uncertainty, judicial material, medical surveys and interviews suggest that the abortion market was dominated not by doctors but by men and women who had no formal training. Ludwig Levy-Lenz, who was in charge of the sex and birth control clinic of Magnus Hirschfeld's Institute of Sexual Science, claimed that in 1928 in Berlin at least half of all abortions were procured by lay practitioners, 30 per cent by women themselves and only about 20 per cent by doctors, a claim which is confirmed by older research based on a complete set of trial records. Even accounting for the fact that doctors' terminations were comparatively hard to detect, their very small proportion of all abortion prosecutions and convictions is telling. The files of the *Landgericht* Mönchen-Gladbach, for example, show that during the Weimar Republic all ten commercial abortionists convicted were non-doctors; exactly the same number and situation was true of the convictions made by the *Landgericht* Gera during the Weimar Republic; in Freiburg i.Br., of seven commercial operators tried and convicted between 1925 and 1930 only one was a doctor; he was convicted for only three abortions whereas the laymen and -women were found guilty for many more: one 'housewife' was convicted for thirty, a nature therapist as many as for forty-one abortions.[48] Since it is more than likely that most of the accomplices convicted of aiding and abetting abortion were non-doctors, the importance of laymen and laywomen inducing miscarriages becomes even more pronounced.[49] Although the trial material I investigated for this study was no longer complete, it mirrored this general pattern of doctors as interlopers in the field of reproduction.[50]

Lay abortionists

Lay abortionists were, however, not only targeted by the medical profession but also by many other, if rather divergent, professional groups, ranging from politicians to churchmen and -women, from lawyers, the Moral Right to socialists, feminists and sex reformers; this was because a significant change had occurred in the perception of abortion itself and the focus had shifted from morality to money. In Imperial Germany it was aborting women themselves who were blamed for an alleged demographic and moral decline. In the Weimar Republic it was those who performed abortions as a business who were held responsible for the prevalence of abortion and the decline in health standards. Before the First World War the typical aborting woman was portrayed as young, single and lower-class, who wanted to rid herself of the fruit of illicit sex; thus she was usually called immoral, feckless and neglectful of her maternal duty. But the social dislocation and economic hardship during and after the war altered this attitude; most people accepted that married women with children, too, opted for termination of unwanted pregnancies as a means of family planning.[51] Despite demands by women (and often by their boyfriends and husbands) to obtain a termination, the 'abortion scourge' was, however, firmly blamed on lay operators.

Quack abortionists were sometimes attacked in the media as if they formed a homogeneous group but the judiciary distinguished between different categories of lay abortionists. The least stigmatized were those relatives, friends or neighbours who helped aborting women out of kindness either by providing an abortifacient or by performing the actual operation. Under the law they were considered accomplices and treated therefore more leniently and their activity was condoned, sometimes even applauded, by the community. The law of 1871 and the revised clause of 1926 provided for the same punishment for an accomplice as for the aborting woman; in practice, accomplices usually were handed down rather more lenient sentences. Husbands or lovers of a woman accused of infraction of §218 often went unpunished if they managed to convince the authorities that they played no role in nor had any knowledge of the abortion. The next category in the hierarchy of disapproval rating were amateurs, men and women who occasionally procured abortions and were paid in kind or in money for their expenses and their efforts (occasionally also for the risk they took) rather than for profit. The authorities prosecuted both these groups but they were concentrating their efforts on rooting out professional abortionists who were involved purely for financial reasons and who would try to persuade women to rid themselves of their undesired pregnancies. After 1926 the judiciary called them *gewerbsmäßig* or 'commercial' abortionists, those lay practitioners (with the occasional renegade doctor among them) who procured terminations as a regular business, sometimes with the help of touts. Doctors liked to call all lay practitioners pejoratively 'quack abortionists' (*kurpfuscherische Fruchtabtreiber*) but in popular parlance they were referred to as *weise Frauen* (wise women) or *Engelmacherinnen* (literally angel makers), reminiscent of the English expression 'graveyard luck', which, as Mary Chamberlain explains, is 'the euphemistic term used to describe those midwives skilled at saving the mother but losing the child'.[52]. This presumed, wrongly, that they were all women. It was the professional or 'commercial' abortionists who came to symbolize corruption and greed in the cinema, on stage and in literature, as we have seen, and were vilified in the public discourse, particularly since aborting women met with more and more public sympathy.

Legal reform reflected and reinforced these new attitudes towards women burdened with unwanted pregnancies. As we have seen, the law of 1871 prescribed a maximum penalty of penal servitude, that is, solitary confinement with hard labour and loss of civil rights of up to five years for both the aborting woman and any accomplice (under §218) and of up to ten years for the abortionist who worked for money (under §219). The amended law of 1926 reduced the maximum penalty dramatically for the aborting woman and any accomplice but increased it for the commercial operator. It also introduced the new definition of 'gainful abortion' to target the professional back-street practitioners, whereas §219 of 1871 simply talked about abortion 'for payment' (*gegen Entgelt*). As a contemporary jurist explained, 'gainful abortion' no longer meant a one-off or occasional operation for payment; the courts now needed to prove 'the intention to make a living from the proceeds of abortion'. Sentencing practice, too, changed, at least as far as aborting women and their accomplices were concerned. Before 1926 penal servitude for the aborting woman was occasionally imposed, while the median penalty was imprisonment of between three months and one year;[53] after the legal reform of 1926, penal servitude was no longer applied and judges showed great leniency to the pregnant woman, especially during the Depression, though this varied according to court, judge and area. For example, in 1920 the *Landgericht* Leipzig sentenced a 20-year-old unmarried female labourer to nine months' imprisonment for having undergone two abortions and for aiding and abetting an abortion of another woman.[54] But another judge of the same court and in the same year sentenced a woman to two years in prison for what seems a lesser crime: a 43-year-old married woman was pregnant twice by her lover, a nature therapist, who also procured her two abortions. She pleaded mitigating circumstances since her boyfriend had apparently insisted on the operations while she had wanted to keep the 'token of their love'. Strangely, the abortionist was given only two months' gaol more than his mistress.[55]

After 1926 aborting women faced far more lenient sentences; for example, the courts of Freiburg in Breisgau reduced sentences for aborting women from six months to circa one month for complete abortion.[56] Elsewhere judges were even more lenient. By the end of the Republic, §218 had fallen into such disrepute that in most cases mitigating circumstances such as economic hardship or the unwelcome prospect of a child outside marriage were routinely taken into account;[57] this resulted in sentences of just a few days for simple abortion, i.e. for the aborting woman, which were often commuted to fines and then suspended. Typically the twenty clients of a well-known Berlin lay professional abortionist tried in 1929 were given short suspended sentences of one or two weeks in prison, or, if convicted for merely attempting abortion, a small fine of 15–30 RM, which could be paid, if necessary, in instalments.[58] Similarly, in East Prussia, in January 1932 the *Amtsgericht* Stromberg sentenced a domestic servant to one month in prison, suspended for four years; in the same year the court of lay assessors in Stettin sentenced a 25-year-old unmarried seamstress to a 30 RM fine or ten days' gaol.[59]

As aborting women were treated with increasing sympathy and amateur abortionists also came off relatively lightly, the ultimate sanction, penal servitude, was reserved for professional abortionists, who made a trade of terminations. According to criminal statistics of 1921 to 1923, the overwhelming majority of all those convicted under §219, i.e. professional abortionists, were sentenced to penal servitude and the proportion was on the increase; in 1921 it amounted to 86 per cent, in 1923 88 per cent and in 1924 as many as 91 per cent of all convicts.[60] Differential treatment of aborting women and their professional helpers was glaring, especially when the penalties for the former were very lenient, even before 1926, as a sensational trial in November 1925 in Berlin Neukölln proved. The main defendant, the caretaker Marie Schild, a professional abortionist, was given a sentence (which took into account an earlier conviction) of two years ten months' penal servitude with three years' loss of civil rights; but her forty-four co-defendants, i.e. her women clients, were convicted only of attempted abortion and were given prison sentences of between five and seven weeks, suspended for three years.[61]

After the reform in 1926 penalties for professional, then called 'commercial', abortionists continued to be severe, yet, contrary to the intention expressed in the new law, there is little evidence to suggest that sentences became even harsher. In October 1926, a few months after the reform, a professional abortionist, a 37-year-old magnetopath (a lay healer who treated patients with the aid of electro-magnetism) from the Palatinate, was sentenced to four years' penal servitude, which was certainly harsh, but it was not his first conviction and in this case his crime was aggravated by manslaughter.[62] Or take the 1927 Munich trial in which the 49-year-old midwife Magdalene Leid received a comparatively mild sentence of two years and seven months in prison, with the loss of all civil rights for three years plus costs. Similarly, in 1930, a Berlin professional abortionist and nature therapist, Fanny Hofstetter, was sentenced to two years' penal servitude for a crime aggravated by possible manslaughter and five previous convictions for offences against §218.[63] Or, in 1932 a Leipzig 74-year-old masseuse received one year and six months' penal servitude for at least five cases of commercial abortion, one of which ended in death. This was also less harsh than many sentences pronounced before 1926, particularly since she had two previous convictions for abortion. And in 1930 the 53-year-old seamstress Albertine Landeck, who stood trial for criminal abortion including one case of manslaughter, was handed down the even more lenient sentence of nine months' imprisonment.[64] Even after Hitler's assumption of power, when abortion of 'desirable stock' was meant to be prosecuted with great severity, surprisingly short prison terms could be handed down.[65]

Gender and the abortionist

The negative and gendered image of lay abortionists in popular culture was pervasive even in those films and novels which were sympathetic to women in need of terminating their unwanted pregnancies. Madame Heye in *Cyankali*, the concierge in *Kreuzzug des Weibes* or the 'real' wise woman in *Madame Lu* were not only portrayed as avaricious and malicious, perpetuating the stereotypical

Cultures of Abortion in Weimar Germany

Dr. Max Hodann, Berlin, der Vorkämpfer der Sexualpädagogik

Dr. Magnus Hirschfeld, Berlin, der Führer der deutschen Sexualforschung

Dr. Helene Stöcker, Berlin, die Gründerin des Bundes für Mutterschutz und Sexualreform

Dr. Heinrich Meng, Stuttgart, Herausgeber einer neuen Art gemeinverständlicher Literatur über Heilkunde und Psychoanalyse

Havelock Ellis, der Senior der internationalen Sexualforschung

Sexualforschung / Gebärzwang und Massenelend

Im preußischen Landtag wurden jüngst Mitteilungen über den gegenwärtigen Stand der Volksgesundheit in Preußen gemacht, die ein erschreckendes Zeugnis für die Verelendung breiter werktätiger Massen ablegen. Die niedrigen Löhne zwingen vielfach zum Kauf minderwertiger Nahrungsmittel. Beweis dafür das Ansteigen der Fleischvergiftungsfälle, im letzten Jahre von 1671 auf 3595. Unzureichende Ernährung ist auch die Ursache für die Ausbreitung vieler Krankheiten und Seuchen namentlich unter den Kindern. So hat z. B. die heimtückische Diphterie 24140 Kinder gegen 30336 im Vorjahre heimgesucht. Ein Drittel aller Tuberkulosefälle in Preußen entfällt auf Kinder im ersten Lebensjahr. Auch die zahlreiche Kropfkrankheit, die zu geistiger Verkümmerung, oft zu Verblödung, führt, nimmt immer mehr zu. Die Säuglingssterblichkeit beziffert sich trotz starken Geburtenrückganges wieder wie im Vorjahre auf 10,1 v. H. Die allgemeine Sterblichkeit ist um 1,2 auf 12,8 pro Tausend gestiegen, Der Geburtenüberschuß verminderte sich von 8,0 im Jahre 1926 auf 6,1 im ersten Halbjahr 1927.

Diese Zahlen reden eine eindringliche Sprache. Sowohl die Zunahme der Sterblichkeit wie das Sinken der Geburten sind auf die allgemeinen schlechten Arbeits- und Wohnungsverhältnisse zurückzuführen. Trotzdem wehrt sich der preußische Wohlfahrtsminister Dr. h. c. Hirtsiefer gegen die geforderten Ausbau der Ehe-

beratungsstellen zu Volks-Sexualberatungsstellen, die der grassierenden lebens- und gesundheitsmordenden kurpfuscherischen Fruchtabtreibung durch eine verständige Propagierung der gesundheitlich einwandfreien Schwangerschaftsverhütung wirksam zu Leibe rücken könnten. Für ihn ist jede künstliche Geburtenbeschränkung ein „Verbrechen am Staate" und sie fördern, hieße „der Unmoral die Hand bieten". Darum ist es um jeden Preis für die Aufrechterhaltung des Gebärzwanges mittels des Paragraph 218 ohne Rücksicht darauf, daß bereits heute unzählige Kinder schon im Mutterleibe hungern, siech werden und, wenn lebend geboren, infolge mangelnder Pflege, Unterernährung und Raumnot einen frühen Tod sterben.

Wie auf allen Gebieten wird sich auch hier der Arbeiterklasse nur selbst helfen können. Die aus ihrer Welt erwachsene, unabhängige Wissenschaft bietet ihr die Waffen der Erkenntnis gegen das verlogene Moralaposteltum der herrschenden Klasse, die für den Gebärzwang eintritt zur dauernden Sicherung einer großen Reservearmee von Proletariern als Lohndrücker und als Kanonenfutter für den kommenden Krieg. Der im Juli stattgefundene Kongreß der Weltliga für Sexualreform gewährte in 40 Vorträgen einen umfassenden Ueberblick über Stand und Forderungen der Sexualreform, Sexualpädagogik, Geburtenregelung und Sexualgesetzgebung.

Es wurden Länderausschüsse für die aktive Arbeit gewählt. Dem deutschen Ausschuß gehören Max Hodann, Helene Stöcker und Heinrich Meng an. Von den Mitgliedern der Ausschüsse anderer Länder seien genannt: Kolontai und Pascha-Osserski-Rußland, Mayreder - Oesterreich, Marguerite-Frankreich, Sanger-Amerika.

Der Kongreß nahm mit Befriedigung davon Kenntnis, daß Sowjetrußland als einziger aller Staaten die Frau von Gesetzen durchgeführt, die dem Stand der Sexualbiologie und Psychologie entsprechen.

Als nun eine praktische Maßnahme sei auf die in Berlin von dem Chefarzt der Berliner Krankenkassen Dr. Benedek, Dr. Hodann und Dr. Schmincke sowie Dr. Stöcker gegründete Sexualberatungsstelle in Neukölln hingewiesen. Eine gründliche Aufklärung über das ganze Problem gibt das in zweiter Auflage erschienene Buch „Gegen den Gebärzwang! Der Kampf um die bewußte Kleinhaltung der Familie" von Emil Höllein. (Verlag E. Höllein, Berlin-Charlottenburg 5, Horstweg 5, Preis kart. 3.— Mark, gebunden 4,50 Mark zuzüglich Porto.)

Typus der gewerbsmäßigen Abtreiberinnen, beide mehrmals bestraft. Ihr schmutziges Handwerk wird erst verschwinden, wenn die Geburtenregelung, wie in der Sowjetunion, den Ärzten freigegeben wird. —

Eine Drahtbürste, die von den „Engelmacherinnen" zur Abtreibung verwendet wird

Ins Wasser
Zeichnung von Zille
„Mutta, ist's ooch nich kalt?"
„Sei ruhig, mein Kind, die Fische leben immer drin!"

Das Wartezimmer der neueingerichteten Sexualberatungsstelle Berlin-Neukölln, Schönstedtstraße 13

Instrumente zur Abtreibung der Leibesfrucht: Katheter zum Ansiechen und Entleeren der befruchteten Gebärmutter, Spülkannen und Spritzen. Mit solchen primitiven und unreinen Instrumenten muß sich die Armut behandeln lassen, während die reichen Damen, vom Gesetz nicht belästigt, in den Sanatorien abtreiben, soviel sie wollen

10. Article about 'sexology, enforced procreation and mass misery', 1928

view peddled in medical circles, by the police and by the print media; they were also all women. This certainly reflected the high incidence of women in criminal prosecutions[66] and also the apparent popularity of female abortionists among women. But although there were many male lay abortionists operating in towns and the countryside, women attracted a disproportionate amount of criticism. This gendered view is not problematized in the contemporary literature but it is probably not too far-fetched to suggest that it derived from expectations and assumptions of femininity. Women were supposed to be maternal, nurturing and life-giving; wise women, however, appeared deviant, killing nascent life (and thereby assisting other women to behave 'unnaturally', too), perpetrating crime and even profiting from it. The typical wise woman was older, postmenopausal and widowed; she undermined traditional gender order, empowered as she was by being freed from reproduction, marital control and monetary strictures. Hence she evoked strong feelings of suspicion and antipathy and was associated with danger and darkness.

An illustrated article in August 1928 from the *Arbeiter Illustrierte Zeitung* (Workers' illustrated newspaper) serves as a good example. Although the author is not named, the provenance and the positive references to sex reform and the Soviet Union suggest it was written by a supporter, possibly member, of the left-wing German sex reform movement. The article discusses the deterioration of public health within the social context of a worsening housing and labour market; it suggests that access to artificial birth control is an important self-help device against 'the maintenance of enforced reproduction'. It praises the recent congress of the World League of Sexual Reform in Copenhagen in July 1928 for having offered 'a comprehensive survey about the state and the aspirations of sex reform, sex pedagogies, birth control and sex legislation'. The Prussian Minister of Welfare, Dr Heinrich Hirtsiefer, a member of the Catholic Centre Party, comes under sustained attack for opposing the replacement of (eugenic) marriage advice centres with proper sex advice centres for everyone despite the fact that this was the only way forward for 'intelligible propagation of safe contraception' (and it is implied that this meant 'advised by a doctor') which alone could eradicate the 'rampant quack abortion so dangerous to life and health'.

While the text of the article singles out the Catholic minister as the culprit responsible for the immiseration of working-class mothers and their children, the visual illustrations point to 'back-street' abortionists who hinder the triumphant progress of enlightened sex reform. Dominating the page are several photographs, among them one of two middle-aged women described in the caption as: 'Typical female commercial abortionists, both have been convicted several times. Their dirty handiwork will only disappear when doctors are permitted to practise birth control as in the Soviet Union.' The photographs of the two *Engelmacherinnen*, as they are also called, are police mug shots, full frontals with faces gazing glumly straight at the reader.

The provenance of such pictures taken when the sitters were suspects in custody intensifies the impression that they are two hardened criminals. Judging from their clothes and physiognomy, both belong to the lower classes; their vacant stare points to a lack of education and moral sensibility. Their association with criminal abortion is suggested by the image of a wire brush, apparently used for abortions, placed directly beneath their photos in the manner of a 'Wanted!' notice for two fugitives. These photos of women convicts are strikingly contrasted with five refined portraits of well-known sex reformers: Max Hodann, Magnus Hirschfeld, Heinrich Meng, Havelock Ellis and, as the sole woman, Helene Stöcker. Their faces are all at a slight angle to the camera or in profile, the classical pose inspired by Roman emperors on coins to dignify the sitter. This and their thoughtful expression and academic titles (with the exception of Ellis) bestow a high degree of respectability.

The largest visual image on the entire newspaper page, almost certainly also taken by a police photographer, depicts abortion implements which in this context appear sinister, like torture instruments. Furthermore, they are imbued with subliminal sexual connotations. Firstly, they are arranged in the shape of a woman's body, with the two irrigator tubes forming breasts and two syringes placed diagonally across them like fetters; the various catheters and syringes below form the pelvis. Secondly, the function of the implements shown below is (according to the caption) 'to pierce and evacuate the fertilized womb', but the visual language seems to suggest violence against the female body since the sharp end of catheters is pointed towards the imaginary vagina and the entrance to the uterus. The caption spells out the class-discriminatory access to abortion, with, 'the poor ... forced to undergo treatment with such primitive and unclean instruments while rich ladies abort entirely untroubled by the law in sanatoria whenever they want.'

Finally, there are three more images; the first is a group photograph of members of the World League for Sex Reform at the recent Copenhagen Congress, apparently with its attendant promise of a brighter future for voluntary parenthood; the second is a drawing by the popular Berlin satirist, Heinrich Zille, which depicts a heavily pregnant proletarian woman heading towards the river to drown herself, her unborn child and her toddler in her arms. This underlines the overall message that only sexual science can save the proletariat from their misery. The last image offers the prospect of a rosy future: a well-appointed waiting room in the newly established sexual advice centre in Berlin-Neukölln.[67]

This page from a communist journal exemplifies the power of the visual image to convey a more persuasive message than the written text peppered with dry statistics of morbidity and mortality among the poor and a rather ponderous rallying cry for sex reform. The visual message is a stark warning against lay abortionists and a strong plea for more power for doctors. In the Weimar Republic even those sex reformers who were not doctors, including some women, maligned lay abortionists: for example, in 1929 a public meeting was organized by the Hamburg branch of Helene Stöcker's *Bund für Mutterschutz und Sexualreform* to protest against the new official draft of the criminal code, especially the section about §218; they deplored the fact that the proposed abortion regulation would not permit doctors to terminate pregnancies on other than strictly health grounds. This, they suggested, would drive 'innumerable women and girls, especially those who fear the shame of an illegal birth, into the hands of unscrupulous quacks'.[68]

It was no coincidence that the lay abortionists displayed in the article from the *Arbeiter Illustrierte Zeitung* were all female. It was widely assumed that wise women rather than wise men were preferred by aborting women and it was not unusual for male entrepreneurs to advertise their abortion services under women's names to improve their chances:

> Frau R.
> gives advice on all intimate matters
> and guarantees absolute discretion.
> Menstrual blockage, discharge, etc.
> treated by unique method,
> safe results guaranteed.
> Practice hours daily 12–3 and 4–7pm.[69]

This was an advertisement like many others placed in local newspapers or specialist journals by midwives or wise women publicizing their illegal services – except that Frau R. was in reality Herr R., a businessman from Thuringia who thought that by posing as a woman he would maximize his chances of selling abortifacients as 'female hygiene' articles and performing abortions. As the police interviews revealed, his tactics bore fruit, attracting at the very least one unmarried woman who expected to find a female practitioner.

Midwives also featured large in these publicity drives. A certain Frau K. appeared daily over a lengthy period in the small-ad section of all four local newspapers in her home town in the Ruhr area. Frau K. described herself as a 'retired midwife' and promised not only a kind welcome for all 'single women and girls', i.e. the group most in need of advice, but also offered 'treatment of women's complaints of all kinds'.[70] Female practitioners seemed to have more credibility with women seeking help because they could be expected as women to sympathize with their clients' fate, particularly since many abortionists were married and had children of their own. Moreover, it was easier to discuss intimate matters with, or be physically examined by, a woman rather than a man, and there was no risk of the abortionist demanding sexual gratification in exchange. There was also often a difference in the way women abortionists approached their task: according to the statements of their patients, it was quite usual for them to massage the patient's abdomen after they had injected the liquid into the uterus. This had the double function of stimulating contractions and calming the patient. Wise women would also normally talk their patients through the operation, soothing their fears and relaxing them; no doubt this facilitated the operation and secured the cooperation of their clients.

Sometimes, women abortionists worked as a team, like the two sisters from the Ruhr area who ran an abortion cooperative in the early 1920s. They were married to manual labourers and had children: one had two grown-up sons, the other six children. They referred clients to each other, 'so that they could make a little money, too'.[71] Or, take the case of the widow of a railway official in her sixties, who also lived in the Ruhr area; she ran an abortion business with her two grown-up daughters and specialized in services for women of the lower classes, such as unmarried domestic servants. The mother was also a fortune-teller who read cards (*Kartenlegerin*) and used her skill to entice her clients to reveal their fear of a possible pregnancy. If a woman admitted this, she was comforted and promised that somebody would help ('there is advice for everything except death'). At this moment her daughter, who lived with her, would appear and offer her services for a lucrative sum; if the client agreed, mother and daughter would operate on the spot. One client admitted in her police statement how she had visited the mother's house to have her fortune told but when she encountered two young women there seeking an abortion she was glad to avail herself of the same opportunity. The fortune-teller's other daughter was also an abortionist/fortune-teller, but in her case she practised palmistry. On one occasion her advice clashed with that of her mother. The daughter counselled one unmarried woman to 'to get rid of the child', contradicting her mother's advice: 'child, leave things be, the lad has money, he could make you happy'.[72]

There was only a small proportion of female abortionists who were also *Kartenlegerinnen* or palmists and this was also the case in the Netherlands;[73] but since *Kartenlegerinnen* were women who attracted exclusively female clients it was not surprising that some combined fortune-telling and procuring miscarriages,[74] or cooperated with an abortionist, rather like midwives did, as we saw in the previous chapter. Telling anxious women their fortune, usually for a small sum of money, helped establish trust between the abortionist and the client and paved the way for the latter to agree paying a far larger sum for a termination of pregnancy. Martha Spitzer, the wife of a caretaker in Berlin Charlottenburg, used to charge only 2 RM in the late 1920s for fortune-telling from cards but as much as 85 RM for an abortion.[75] A domestic servant, 22-year-old Martha Pflanze, for example, had known Frau Spitzer as a *Kartenlegerin* for some years and had had her fortune told by her. In November 1928 she visited her once more but this time she also wanted a physical examination. Frau Spitzer did so and told her that she was pregnant. They both agreed on a sum of 50 RM with Pflanze's wrist watch as security in return for Frau Spitzer terminating her pregnancy.[76] Another client, Maria Schrader, also married to a caretaker in Charlottenburg, however, could not be persuaded. She had gone to Frau Spitzer's and had her cards read by her. Frau Schrader recounted how she was seven months pregnant and Frau Spitzer had told her that, 'I was mad, she would abort it, I should call on her. But I refused and explained that I could not do something like that, my husband would not stand for it, and I wanted to carry the child to term, this was four and a half years ago because the child is now four ... '.[77]

The careers of 'wise women'

For many women of the lower classes, performing abortions seems to have promised a relatively easy way to make a living or to earn extra money, although some women seem to have provided their help out of kindness.[78] Many *Engelmacherinnen* picked up their skills through their own reproductive experiences. Most of them were married with children and they generally possessed a rudimentary knowledge of bringing on a period and usually owned the necessary implements, such as a syringe, kitchen soap and Lysol. Either they had tried to use these on themselves or they had undergone a termination by somebody else and this experience emboldened them to try the same treatment on others. For example, the 38-year-old Leipzig wife of a labourer, Anna Schuster, had an abortion in 1914. She feared that another child would jeopardize her lucrative job as a cleaner in the Leipzig University hospital. So she consulted a woman in Leipzig whom she knew performed abortions and duly paid her 25 Marks 'for expenses' to have her period restored. In 1917, fearing she was in the family way again, Schuster went back for more treatment. Again the intervention was effective but this time she had to pay twice as much plus hand over some household goods. Maybe these expenses encouraged her to try her own luck as an accomplice and later as an abortionist. First she started to lend her syringe to other women, whether for money or out of friendship we do not know; two years later she instructed an acquaintance how to induce a miscarriage and then even performed the operation. She was pleased that 'it had worked so quickly'. She repeated the exercise on other women of her acquaintance and her safety record was good enough to gain her more and more clients by word of mouth before she was apprehended by the police in 1920.[79]

Others acquired their knowledge from books or family members. Frau Spitzer, who in 1930 stood accused of performing over twenty-nine abortions, had learnt her trade from her midwife mother and her midwifery books. Spitzer started to induce miscarriages when her four children were grown up and money was tight, when, according to her police statement, her husband had become a heavy drinker and had cut her housekeeping to a mere 17 RM.[80] Other women took up the trade for similar reasons. The career of a Berlin seamstress, Albertine Landeck, was fairly typical of many other professional abortionists.[81] She was already fifty-three at the time of her trial and the mother of four adult children. After leaving elementary school at the age of fourteen, she had become a domestic servant, later a nanny, but gave up paid work upon her marriage in 1895 aged nineteen. In 1902, now with three children (one of whom later died) she started to work as a seamstress and soon after also as an abortionist. In 1913, aged thirty-seven, she sued for divorce for reasons she did not want to divulge, but her two surviving children stood by her and remained in close touch. In 1925, now forty-nine, she married a manual labourer, Otto Landeck, who brought three children into the marriage, two of whom lived with them in a cramped flat consisting of only two rooms and a kitchen for which the monthly rent was 37 RM. The family budget was stretched since Otto Landeck only earned 37 RM per week and Albertine's contribution from her work as a seamstress and probably also as an abortionist was essential. As is clear from a welfare report by the Red Cross, Landeck's employers and customers held her in high esteem. She was considered dependable and reliable and described as 'honest, hard working, pleasant and good natured'.[82] Landeck's record as an abortionist was equally impressive; her clients trusted her skills and nearly all of her many operations had passed without a hitch. But the abortion-related death of one young woman led to an investigation into her activities and eventually to Landeck's imprisonment. The autopsy revealed that the dead woman was in her sixth month of pregnancy, well beyond the period when the vast majority of abortions were performed and at such a late stage notoriously fraught with complications for anybody to induce an artificial miscarriage; the question this raises is why such an experienced practitioner as Frau Landeck consented to a request which was unreasonable. We can only speculate that she felt overconfident after so many successful operations, was too keen to help, or was possibly fooled by a woman so desperate to avoid the birth of an unwanted child that she concealed the real length of her pregnancy.

For many women, embarking on the career of abortionist was a chance decision which developed out of their lifestyle and an interest in women's health, and quite a few combined it with practising nature therapy. Performing abortions on a professional basis often also evolved from being part of a close-knit network of women in the neighbourhood. Sometimes the pressure put upon them to help acquaintances in trouble turned into blackmail and the threat of being reported to the police unless they agreed. This was cited by some abortionists as their main reason for continuing in the trade.[83] Advanced age seems not to have been a stumbling block; quite the contrary. Older wise women were deemed more compassionate and trustworthy than their younger counterparts. Anna Bregenz, who practised in Leipzig, was sixty-four and recently widowed when in 1922 she decided to combine her career as a nature therapist with an abortion practice. She was still working at the age of seventy-four. In 1930, already aged seventy-two, she expanded her practice by acquiring a high-frequency electric machine for radiotherapy from a doctor who also instructed her in its use. Her frequent lengthy spells in prison (she was sentenced four times for infractions of §219/218) did not deter her from procuring miscarriages for women in need; only her arrest in 1932 and later her conviction and sentence (to eighteen months' penal servitude for abortion aggravated by manslaughter) seems to have ended her career. Educated only to elementary school level she was by all accounts intelligent and eager to learn; she had shown a life-long interest in alternative healing. In the early years of the twentieth century she ran a station inn near Berlin with her husband. When in 1915 he became ill and gave up work they moved to Leipzig. Bregenz, now the only wage earner and having lost her savings in the inflation, sublet a room in their flat and set up her own nature therapy clinic, administering the massages and herbal baths 'so popular in nature therapy'. Judging from her own, her patients' depositions and her account book in 1932, all her patients were women with a variety of ills, such as back pain, rheumatism, nose bleeds and delayed periods who found that Bregenz practised her nature therapies with considerable skill. She regarded 'bringing on a period' in the same way as other treatments to bring relief to her patients and used a similar method, 'body massage'. Bregenz attracted many of her abortion patients by fixing a sign outside her house advertising medicinal massage, a euphemism for abortion well understood in her community. Her patients were routinely offered birth control advice and the chance to buy contraceptives. It was also implied that abortion services were available. Although one of her patients' died after an abortion in 1932 the judge concluded that Bregenz's operation did not cause, but only speeded the demise of the woman who was suffering from an infected appendicitis.[84]

Fanny Hofstetter, another nature therapist/abortionist from Berlin, was considerably younger when in 1925 at the age of forty-three she first got into trouble with the law for violation of §219. But she too had embarked on a new career combining nature therapy with abortion some years earlier following the death of her husband in the First World War, at a time when her three children needed her less. She enrolled in a specialist training institute for nature therapy in Berlin and supplemented this by attending lectures on clinical diagnosis and psychology at the Humboldt University and through private study. Soon she was herself lecturing on nature therapy and women's physical and emotional health. When she witnessed the hardship which many women suffered in the immediate postwar years she became a socialist committed to abortion law reform. She also began to perform terminations of pregnancy; she, too, treated these as an integral part of her healing activity.[85]

This was also the case with another Leipzig nature therapist/abortionist, 35-year-old Hulda Renge, who was also married to a nature therapist. Renge was exceptionally popular and treated her abortion clients with the same respect as her other patients. They all received a comprehensive treatment to bring on a miscarriage: after examining a woman gynaecologically and, if a pregnancy was presumed, she inserted a gauze tampon to stimulate contractions. She also massaged her patient's abdomen and lower back and administered a warm spruce needle bath to relax her and hasten the process of miscarriage. She checked her patients frequently after the operation, between four to eight times and at short intervals, to improve the effectiveness of the treatment and to monitor their progress. She also offered them after-care in their homes where she would perform curettage (rarely done by other lay practitioners) to remove the afterbirth. In the course of their investigation in September 1926 the police found Renge's patient record with details of as many as twenty-five abortion patients in less than two years. These came from a variety of social backgrounds but single and very young women were in the majority. Renge was found guilty of ten cases of abortion, four of which she had performed with her husband, and six cases of attempted abortion; she was sentenced to nine months in prison. All but one of her many operations seem to have been successful and safe, but one patient died; the court left open whether death was caused by Renge's intervention or by a later curettage carried out in hospital.[86]

The safety record of quack abortionists

These brief case studies, which are by no means atypical, present a different picture from the opprobrium with which wise women (and their male equivalents) were regarded in the official discourse. Of course, not a few professional abortionists were ignorant and incompetent, risking their clients' health, fertility and indeed sometimes their lives. A case in point is the 1926 trial concerning one Ludwig Reimer, who practised magnetopathy in the district of Koblenz in the Palatinate. He had previously been convicted for infraction of §219 and had served four years' penal servitude. The severity of this suggests that abortion was aggravated by manslaughter. In 1926 he was reconvicted for the same crime and sentenced again to four years' penal servitude and loss of all civil rights for five years. He had performed a so-called *Eihaustich*, rupturing the amniotic sac with a pointed instrument, on a young woman who had subsequently died of peritonitis. This method of inducing a miscarriage was usually only attempted by doctors because it needed precise gynaecological knowledge, proper aseptic conditions and the appropriate instruments, none of which Reimer possessed; he had chosen to utilize an ordinary goose quill to dilate the cervix and pierce the amniotic sac (*Eiblase*).[87]

Lay abortionists could also prove dangerous when they were reluctant to summon medical help after complications had occurred for fear of prosecution, or out of arrogance or negligence. For example, the 52-year-old

Duisburg nature therapist Heinrich Harker was responsible in January 1926 for the abortion-related death of 18-year-old Anna Berg who died of peritonitis two weeks after her operation. Harker had treated all the members of Anna's family, close neighbours of his. When Anna was feared pregnant by her boyfriend she and her mother turned to the trusted therapist. With the help of forceps he inserted an intrauterine catheter with a cleft top. Anna miscarried the next morning but immediately felt very poorly. Her mother fetched Harker on 25 December; he found her with a very high temperature, a sure sign of septic abortion. Despite this, Harker only called a doctor four days later and then fed her misleading information with the result that she treated Anna initially for influenza. Only when the doctor had correctly diagnosed peritonitis and suspected an artificial miscarriage, was the then gravely ill Anna admitted to hospital on 2 January 1926, where she died two days later.[88]

The Berlin seamstress Albertine Landeck, whom we met above, in a foolhardy attempt to terminate a pregnancy in its sixth month, lacerated the woman's uterus after four or five injections with Lysol and was equally irresponsible in failing to summon medical help when her patient fainted from the severe pain. Instead, Landeck made her get up and travel by bus across Berlin to her mother's in Weissensee 'in case she needed care'. But Erika Hammer's internal injury was developing into peritonitis and when she was finally admitted to hospital for emergency treatment she, too, could no longer be saved. The prosecutor charged Landeck with manslaughter, on the ground that she 'must have been fully conscious of the danger in which she put the other person by such an operation', especially by using Lysol, a very corrosive and harmful chemical which, he said, needed to be appropriately diluted, but in this case obviously was not.[89] A similar case of negligence concerned the Leipzig abortionist, wife of a tram conductor, who was responsible for the death of a young woman when the rubber ball of a syringe she used broke and caused an internal infection.[90]

Judging from their police records, some professional abortionists, both men and women, were also clearly shady characters who had been found guilty of embezzlement, theft or robbery or similar infractions.[91] In one case a 41-year-old trader from Frankfurt am Main had previous convictions for, amongst other things, fraud, theft, bodily harm caused by negligence and unfair competition; he was also an impostor, adopting a false name and title and calling himself gynaecologist and obstetrician and thereby he attracted many women clients and performed at least thirty terminations in nine months.[92] It seems probable that these abortionists were cynical opportunists and regarded inducing miscarriages as an easy way to make money. Moreover, there is no doubt that many professional abortionists were hard-nosed businesswomen and -men.

Veterans of the First World War especially, who had difficulty adjusting to civil life after demobilization, were lured by the prospect of easy money to be made from dispensing fertility control in one form or another. One of those was the plumber, mentioned above, who left active service with a nervous disease but only a small pension. Even the judge accepted that his lack of financial security should be taken into account as mitigating circumstances.[93] Others, like a factory worker from Rheydt in the Rhineland, made use of the medical skills they had acquired during the war; he had learnt how to apply cervical douches to his wife whom he had infected with STD when he was a soldier. There was a decorator from Gera, who had been taught how to induce miscarriages by a French doctor in Toulouse while he was a prisoner of war. On his return home he set up an abortion business with a friend, a glazier. At first only the decorator performed the actual operations, but later his partner thought he had learnt enough by observing and tried his hand, too. As a team they had carried out at least twenty abortions before somebody denounced them to the police.[94]

There were also lay operators who took unfair advantage of women's vulnerability for their own sexual gratification. In 1927 a Rhineland master printer, aged forty-six and married with two children, was on trial for his violation of §218; his women patients reported that he had insisted on sexual intercourse before the operation because 'pregnant women were "too cold" and "needed warming up"'; or, as he told a 17-year-old, sexual intercourse was necessary 'to dilate the cervix'. He also offered to sterilize her. A 1932 trial revealed that a 48-year-old married plumber and father of four children, who also practised medicinal massage and homeopathy, was well known for having sex with his abortion patients, often, in the case of poorer women, in lieu of money. Or take the retired railway shunter, also married with four children and a self-confessed philanderer, who saw the abortion business as a good way 'to establish intimate relations with women'. He seems to have succeeded since he admitted that he 'always felt satisfied' after each abortion.[95]

Although some lay abortionists, like some doctors we have seen, were opportunistic, mercenary, irresponsible and ignorant, they were almost certainly not in the majority. While I have been able to trace many lay abortionists in the surviving archive material, it can be safely assumed that many more, probably the majority of them, escaped public scrutiny thanks to their customers' satisfaction, their safe interventions and the good fortune not to have aroused suspicions in neighbours who harboured ill-feeling towards them; by implication these abortionists remain invisible to me as the historian, too. I can, however, get an idea of just how successful many abortionists were from judicial cases which arose not as a result of injuries or fatalities but because somebody they had quarrelled with notified the police, as was the case with Frau Spitzer.[96] Evidence of the care and skill of the average professional abortionist is also clear from court cases following abortion-related deaths (not necessarily all caused by the abortionist, as was the case with Hulda Renge or Anna Bregenz above) in which scores of other terminations came to light which had been performed entirely without mishap.

The striking popularity of lay abortionists also suggests that their general record was good. In the early 1920s Max Hirsch, the prominent Berlin doctor, gynaecologist and government adviser, declared to the Prussian Medical Council that the majority of lay abortionists performed the operation safely and rarely came to light, precisely because nothing went wrong.[97] The author of a law thesis of 1940, writing in the present tense about professional abortionists of whom the Nazi government disapproved intensely, put it as follows:

> We need to bear in mind that it is especially the commercial abortionists who account for the majority of the *Dunkelziffer* (i.e. the estimated number of unknown cases); thanks to their prudence, experience and precaution they go undetected more frequently than those who perform abortions only occasionally. Often, commercial abortionists attract the attention of the authorities only when a pregnant woman with serious physical injuries receives medical treatment and then, either out of remorse or indignation at the pain inflicted on her or in the delirium of fever, reveals the identity of the perpetrator.[98]

The claims of this author and the gynaecologist Hirsch are validated by the surviving legal records, which often contain the depositions of not only abortionists but also their clients. This excellent source material provides a counterbalance to the stereotypically negative portrayal of 'quack abortionists' in official discussions and works of popular culture.

Those professional operators who feature in trial records were generally from the lower middle classes but there were some who came from all walks of life. For example, of the thirteen professional abortionists convicted by the *Landgericht* Gera in the Weimar years', two were traders and three married to manual workers. The remainder included one merchant (who was also a nature therapist), one plumber, one glazier, one shoemaker (who doubled as a nature therapist), one textile manufacturer (who was also a *Winkeladvokat*, a self-styled lawyer, and worked in an employment office), one wife of a publican, one phrenologist and one care worker. Among the thirty-seven professional abortionists convicted by the *Landgericht* Duisburg (between 1910 and 1935) were twenty-one women: six wives (of miners, manual labourers, coach driver), two unemployed single women, six widows, seven midwives or former midwives; of the sixteen men were five active in the healing trade, one doctor, one chemist, two commercial travellers, two miners, three manual labourers and one hunter (*Kammerjäger*).[99]

They induced miscarriages either in their own homes, or, more usually, in the homes of their clients. Since these came nearly exclusively from the lower classes they were probably less worried about what we today would regard as unprofessional and unhygienic conditions; operations often took place in untidy rooms, on a kitchen table or between two chairs; or, in the countryside, in woods, hay lofts or stables. The trip to and from the abortionist must often have been an anxious one for women, since operations, as we shall see in Chapter 6, were frequently performed after dark by torchlight, which meant a return home late at night through back alleys or along country paths.

A sizeable proportion of professional abortionists were highly skilled and interested in providing help. Among those prosecuted and tried are many midwives or former midwives who not unnaturally displayed a strong interest in women's reproductive health. As we have seen above, depositions referred to abortions by midwives as 'quack abortions' despite the fact that they were performed by qualified and registered practitioners. This was because midwives were barred from inducing artificial miscarriages, even from examining pregnant women internally: if they performed an abortion, they were therefore accused of 'quackery', defined in this case as illegal medical practice. Midwives struck off the register following a conviction for criminal abortion but who continued to deliver babies were also considered quacks whether they performed abortions or not.[100] Since disgraced midwives were deprived of their livelihood, they often had no other option than to become abortionists in order to survive.[101]

Midwives who stood trial for violation of the abortion clause usually received special criticism by the public prosecutor. One such court case of 1926 in Torgau, near Leipzig, created quite a stir and attracted the attention of the Prussian Diet and various influential people. The convicted midwife, Ida Halden, aged forty-four, was by all accounts a well-respected member of the community. She was married to a boot maker and together they had five children aged twelve to twenty-five. She had taken pity on a young domestic servant whose boyfriend had forsaken her when she discovered her pregnancy. Three days after Frau Halden had injected a liquid by means of a syringe, the young woman had miscarried without any after-effects and would have gone undetected had Halden not been denounced by the district medical officer of health (how he heard about this operation is not known), an act which, at least according to the bootmaker, was politically motivated. Halden's husband, and possibly she, too, was an active member of the SPD but the medical officer belonged to the DNVP, the right-wing German National People's Party, and was almost certainly opposed to abortion on principle as well as harbouring resentment towards a well-known left-wing family. In November 1926 Frau Halden was given a suspended sentence of three months in prison. Her campaign to clear her name received support from her local and national party through the intervention of a member of the Prussian Diet.[102] Nevertheless, her plea for pardon was rejected by the *Landgericht* because of their view that, 'It is truly wicked of a midwife to stoop to doing abortions and it seems that this is not the first time. At least she may not have been only motivated by self-interest.' Not only was Frau Halden remanded in custody for three months but the said district medical officer also called for her dismissal as midwife.[103]

Midwives might well have played an even larger part in non-doctor abortions than would appear in the judicial files precisely because it is not always clear whether a defendant who proved to be surprisingly knowledgeable in gynaecology was in fact a trained but de-registered midwife.[104] Take the case of a 46-year-old Polish midwife who lived in Berlin but could not practise there since she had no German licence. She used her skills to help women rid themselves of unwanted pregnancies and was simply known as a wise woman. She had already been convicted as a 'lay person' before 1926 for infractions of §219 when she faced charges again in 1930 for performing an abortion on a 17-year-old domestic servant. She had operated efficiently in her flat and afterwards offered her patient a bed for the night. Next day she accompanied her patient to an acquaintance's house and ordered bed rest – all signs of a conscientious, professional approach. She was given a very lenient sentence of three months in prison apparently because she had not sought abortion clients and had shown great reluctance to oblige those who sought her help.[105] In another case which came before the *Landgericht* Munich in 1926, the former midwife Therese Enderle had previously been convicted under §219 in 1923. She had lost her licence to practise midwifery because of the earlier conviction and was now referred to simply as a professional abortionist. During the judicial inquiry it turned out that Enderle had acted as a trusted and 'very experienced abortionist' for a wide circle of women who were connected by kinship, friendship or neighbourhood. It would seem therefore that inducing miscarriages had become her main source of income once she had lost her midwifery licence. Her willingness to help and her excellent safety record (her interventions caused no ill effects and failed only once to induce the desired miscarriage), based on her knowledge and experience as a midwife, no doubt ensured her wide popularity.[106]

Not only midwives, but also many nature therapists, wise women and wise men, had a good 'safety' record. A remarkable number of non-doctors carried out their abortion practice systematically and responsibly in a way which was usually only associated with doctors: they kept records, followed a tested procedure, used anti- and asepsis (by sterilizing their hands and their instruments and employing antiseptic creams or liquids on their clients). They also often displayed considerable gynaecological skills, as the legal historian Jahns was ready to admit: 'Commercial abortion needs to be taken especially seriously because it will be imitated ... acquaintances often accompany the woman to the abortionist, not only to encourage her, but probably also out of curiosity and to gain experience themselves for the future.'[107]

The 30-year-old homeopath Schenker from Königsberg is a case in point. He also fell into practising abortion through his wartime experiences but he displayed an unusual sense of idealistic mission. He was tried in July 1932 for fifty-one cases of commercial abortion and nineteen cases of attempted commercial abortion, and was described in the *Königsberger Volkszeitung*, as typical ... of the post-war period [as somebody] who could never properly find his feet. In the spring of 1918, as a very young man of 16 he became a soldier. First he was stationed near Verdun, later he joined the medical corps, subsequently he worked in the field hospital in Schaulen, in the Baltic area.[108]

Schenker apparently learnt his trade as a skilled abortionist in this hospital and was persuaded there to become a homeopath. He was inspired by the director, a well-known Munich gynaecologist, not named, who also served the civilian population by delivering babies and terminating numerous pregnancies. Once demobilized, Schenker remained attached to the army; but in January 1928, when he was twenty-six, he started to practise homeopathy in Königsberg. Only a few years later a left-leaning newspaper called him 'the best homeopath in Königsberg'. In 1927 he had already launched his career as abortionist, first helping fiancées of colleagues in the army, later women from all walks of life, even, so he claimed, wives of lawyers. Although he had not studied medicine formally, according to the press reports his work was 'sound and skilful' and never caused any serious complications. Commenting on the trial, the communist *Rote Fahne* praised him for having 'won the confidence of the labouring class in Königsberg, where he is known as a man of conviction [*Überzeugungstäter*]. He has always set his fee according to the social position of those desperately seeking his help'.[109]

One of the most sensational abortion investigations to take place during the Weimar Republic was that of the Berlin pharmacist Heiser in 1924, with the trial following in 1927. Heiser combined idealism with business acumen. He was a member of the SPD and helped predominantly lower-class women. He also founded a lay organization for birth control (Workers' Association for Birth Control) as a useful outlet to sell his brands of contraceptives and he ran a beauty institute 'Mutabor', the venue for his abortion operations. The trial startled contemporary commentators by the extraordinary number of his clients but also impressed them with his surgical standards which put many a clinician to shame. Although Heiser was finally convicted for 300 criminal abortions, he had boasted about 11,000 abortions which had apparently been entirely successful, having achieved the desired terminations of pregnancy without any injury or death.[110] Like any conscientious doctor, Heiser had kept detailed records of all his operations. He had also used an apparently revolutionary new method which avoided potentially risky instrumental interventions and reduced the pain experienced by women who underwent a curettage. Heiser invented a herbal paste (later produced by a firm in Berlin and marketed with the name of Interruptin), which stimulated the uterus into contractions that eventually expelled the foetus naturally. This proved to be the only really significant new development in abortion technology during the interwar period. Initially Heiser kept the composition of his paste secret; but ironically, given the troubled relationship between academic medicine and lay abortionists, it was adopted, before it could be patented by Heiser, by most leading gynaecologists in Germany and abroad and was advertised in

Germany under the name of Provocol; in England and the U.S.A. it was traded under the name of 'Leunbach's Paste'.[111]

Heiser and Schenker were not the only male non-doctors practising abortion who were trained to work in one form or another in the health sector. In Saxony nature therapists were particularly strongly represented among the professional abortionists, no doubt because of Saxony's traditional support for alternative health and strong labour movement, but possibly also because of the high proportion of women employed in industry who traditionally consulted lay rather than academic healers.[112] For example, of the eight court cases with completely preserved records which were administered by the public prosecutor's office of Leipzig during the Weimar years, five featured abortionists who were masseurs and nature therapists.[113] But elsewhere the same trend can be registered: among the twenty-four surviving files of those convicted under §219 or (after 1926) §218 in Prussia and seeking pardon, the proportion is similarly high: six were doctors, one was a midwife; of the remaining seventeen cases there were five abortionists who were either trained to work in the health sector or were connected to it; two homeopaths, two nature therapists and one man who worked for a lay birth control league, the League for Motherhood Protection, where he was almost certainly trained to administer contraceptives and to terminate pregnancies. In the files of the *Landgericht* Gera, five of the thirteen convicted professional abortionists were nature therapists or connected to the healing trade in one form or another. In seven of the cases suspected but not tried, five were nature therapists. In Duisburg five of the fifteen male abortionists were nature therapists, and of the twenty-two female abortionists seven were former midwives. On closer inspection, some other women had links with the healing trade.[114] Training in health care and experience of work in the health sector plus a commitment to healing was likely to have enhanced their skills and safety record.

Even abortionists with no connection to the health sector could be medically adept and conscientious. An example of impressive skill and care exercised by a lay abortionist is that of a 36-year-old miner's wife from Hindenburg, Silesia, Johanna Anders, who stood trial in 1930. Her practice came to the attention of the authorities not because any of her patients required emergency hospital treatment but because of the chance discovery of a buried foetus. The ensuing criminal investigations revealed that Frau Anders practised not for monetary gain but for idealistic reasons. She was a socialist freethinker and campaigned energetically for women's reproductive rights; she put her beliefs into practice and was found to have helped no less than 150 women rid themselves of unwanted pregnancies. Like Heiser (and many of the other professional abortionists), to prevent mishap she conscientiously kept records for all her patients, a fact which benefited them medically but led to her (and probably to their) downfall in the court of law. She did not cause a single complication or injury and the few testimonies from her clients which have been located express their gratitude and praise of her treatment. There is no evidence that she had any formal medical training, although in the light of the remarks about midwifery above, it cannot entirely be ruled out; she took extraordinary care in procuring a miscarriage and using the appropriate medical instruments, such as a syringe with a long catheter and a speculum. She also provided aseptic and antiseptic conditions which enabled her unblemished track record and ensured her popularity. There is, however, a hint that Frau Anders had a real interest in the scientific aspects of obstetrics because a foetus preserved in spirit as a specimen was found on her desk.[115]

Frau Anders' achievements were also matched by the Berlin concierge and fortune-teller Frau Spitzer, who in 1929 was convicted for criminal commercial abortions on twenty-nine counts. Asked by the judge why she kept an account book with her customers' names, addresses and the sums of money demanded for the operation, she said, 'I protest having carried out abortions for money ... I only asked them [her women patients] to note down their addresses so that I could check how they were doing after the operation.'[116] Frau Spitzer did indeed visit her patients to see whether they had recovered from their miscarriages and whether the afterbirth had been expelled. This and the next statement (reduced in the judicial record to just one short sentence) were much more her own concern, and of course that of the women clients, rather than the judiciary's. After all, Frau Spitzer's reputation and her ability to make money from her abortion practice rested on her record of medical success. Frau Spitzer declared: 'I have never heard that a single person has died as a consequence of the operation.'[117] This is a rather understated reference to her considerable achievement that the many abortions she had induced had never caused any injury, let alone death, and that her female patients expressed their satisfaction, frequently adding that they experienced no discomfiture. Frau Spitzer's record was thus admirable despite the fact that she had not studied medicine or midwifery. As noted above, she was entirely self-taught, having learnt about anatomy and abortion from the manuals of her mother, a trained midwife. Hers was a proud achievement as it was a necessary one, since she knew full well that abortion which ended in death would invariably lead to detection and a long prison sentence. Another lay abortionist with an impressive safety record was the wife of a carpenter from a village near Limburg in Hesse (discussed in detail in Chapter 6). But there were probably many other wise women and wise men whose high level of skills and care ensured that they remained unknown to the authorities and thereby anonymous for the historian.

Methods and money

There were numerous medical terminations performed safely in teaching hospitals, even if it was true that many abortions were carried out by medical students, and by those medical practitioners who were inclined to help with or without pay, whose number was probably growing.[118] Nevertheless, it is probably safe to suggest that lay practitioners with extensive abortion experience were a safer option than doctors at a time when many of them had never been taught abortion techniques in medical school and when many general practitioners were not only ill-prepared but also unwilling to risk their careers.[119]

Closely linked to the issue of safety and comfort was the fact that doctors and lay practitioners also used different methods to induce a miscarriage. The standard approach by academic medicine was dilatation and curettage (D and C). First, the cervix was dilated with metal dilators (*Hegarsche Zange*), or gauze tampons (*Laminarstift*) which swelled up; some doctors also used a sharp instrument to rupture the membranes (*Eihaustich*) to bring on contractions. This was usually, though not always, followed by the scraping of foetal and placental tissue out of the womb with a curette, a sharp little knife, an operation which was normally considered too painful and too dangerous to perform without an anaesthetic.[120] The increased use of

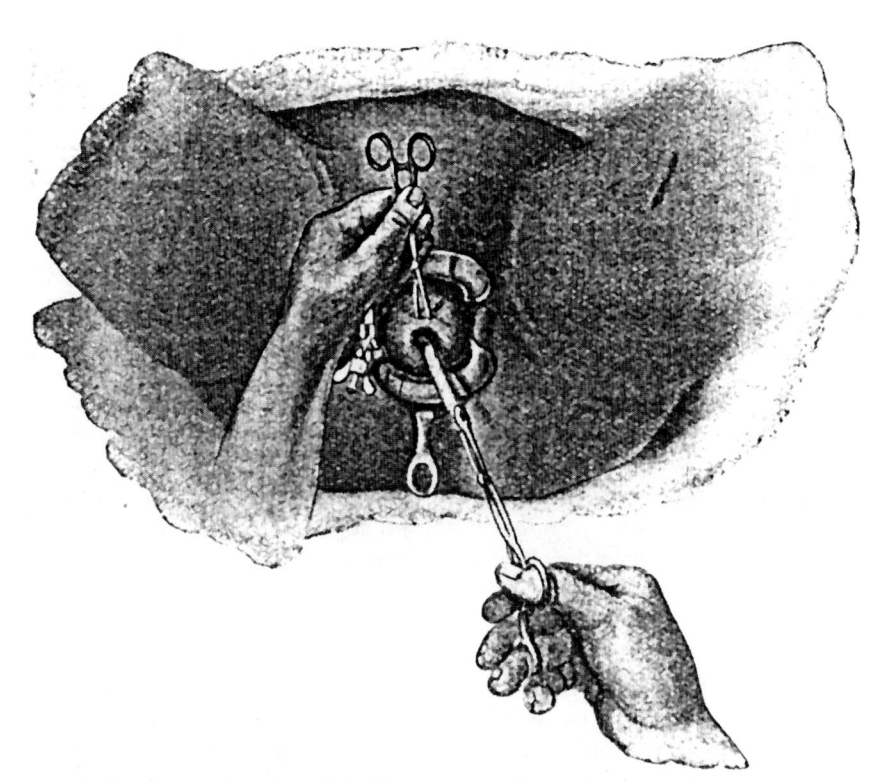

11. Artificial miscarriage, guidelines for doctors by Prof Dr Georg Winter, 1927

instruments in medical termination also caused a rise in abortion-related deaths.[121] Apart from the use of the curette, the use of anaesthesia formed the main distinction between treatment by doctors and that by lay practitioners. As we have seen, many women feared being unconscious and exposed to possible abuse.[122] As we have seen above, some lay abortionists also abused their patients but they were more restricted because they rarely possessed the means to administer anaesthesia or the medical know-how to perform sterilization.

Lay practitioners in fact had to rely on the cooperation of the pregnant woman. That is why so many used massage of the abdomen and talking to relax them and make their work easier. Although it is possible that some midwives used some of the same instruments as doctors, such as speculums, uterine probes, dilators and curettes, I have found no evidence that they did so. Whenever there is an indication of their methods, they used the same as lay abortionists, injecting the uterus with boiled water, a soap solution, Lysol or alum by means of a syringe fitted with a long catheter. Some also dilated the cervix with a gauze tampon.

Lay abortionists were also popular because they charged substantially less than doctors. After the inflation of 1923 doctors charged between 80 and 200 RM, the equivalent of a manual worker's wages for two months, even when their patients were from the poorer sections of society. Quite a few doctors turned women away if they could not pay in advance. In the same period laymen and -women asked between 5 and 50 RM as a rule, on average 25 RM. Others expected the patient to give what she could, accepted payment in instalments and often had to be content with only a fraction of what had been agreed.[123] Some were also willing to receive payment in kind, especially during the inflationary period. For example, a wise woman in Kiel who was tried in 1927 was remunerated in money or groceries; in another case from 1917 a woman abortionist from Leipzig had asked 50 Marks plus '10 pieces of soap and six good towels'.[124] In the early 1920s the carpenter's wife from Limburg settled for small sums of cash or 'a few pounds of flour' or 'a jug of Schnapps', but her husband had to work hard, calling on clients often, sometimes threateningly, to make sure the promises were honoured.[125]

Negotiating payment was often uncomfortable especially when the aborting woman was very poor and had no support from the father of her expected child and when the abortionist demanded a large sum and on-the-spot payment. But the exchange of money itself also guaranteed a greater sense of equality between patient and lay healer. Whereas the judiciary and medical profession decried abortion performed for money and demanded harsher penalties for professional operators, the exchange of money established a contract between the healer selling a service and the pregnant woman paying for the fulfilment of her request. Those of us nowadays who are supporters of a national health service are suspicious about attempts to make individuals responsible for their own health and pay for treatment; we see it as a veiled attack on the principle of free access to health care. But at a time when termination of an unwanted pregnancy (unless medical grounds could be demonstrated) was officially regarded as criminal and health insurance funds therefore refused to pay for it, the exchange of money or payment in kind could also mean empowerment for women in need of help. In fact, it increased the status of both parties. Payment to the abortionist was in recognition of services rendered and of a definite skill. In this spirit some wise women described their services matter-of-factly as 'work' and *Broterwerb*, a means to earn their living for which they naturally expected to be paid. Thus, many spoke of their activities quite openly, even to their own children who discussed their mother's work in the playground.[126] Some also regarded their abortion practice as a kind of 'community service'. They talked of their duty to help, as was the case with two socialists who campaigned to reform the abortion law. The payments they received were often simply to cover expenses.[127]

The act of remunerating the abortionist also bestowed agency on women. By contrast, they appeared as supplicants before a doctor, who always remained the expert and arbiter even when charging a fee, and who could easily turn their request down, as happened to Gilgi in the eponymous novel. But by paying the lay abortionist, pregnant women became clients who had to be taken seriously. They could influence the level and conditions of pay, often paying in instalments, and delaying payment until after the operation and sometimes not paying the full amount, something that doctors did not permit. Women could often also influence the circumstances of the operation: where it was to take place, when and who would be there to assist.[128]

Class differences and shared culture

For all these reasons aborting women from the poorer sections of the population usually chose lay practitioners as their accomplices.[129] They simply felt more comfortable with quacks who were much closer to them socially than members of the medical profession. While doctors were nearly always recruited from the middle classes, lay practitioners came from a similar social background to their clients and shared the same values and attitudes towards life and especially family limitation.[130] This was a great bonus for women at a sensitive time when some feared social stigma and most craved sympathy and support. Conservative doctors often rejected abortion on moral grounds; left-leaning medical practitioners were often more sympathetic but felt hemmed in by the law. Lay abortionists, on the other hand, were either in it for the money and impervious to the finer ethics of the question or shared their clients' view that an unplanned pregnancy was bad luck. Rather than pass judgement, they did what they were paid to do.[131]

The difficult 'medical' encounter with a practitioner when the subject was an intimate and often embarrassing sexual issue was also easier with lay healers because they spoke the same language; medical terminology, by contrast, was couched in scientific-positivist terms which made little sense to patients, especially those with limited formal education. Doctors referred to curettage or artificial miscarriage while many women and lay practitioners, especially if they were female, talked about 'unblocking the monthly flow' or similar concepts and considered this preventive medicine, something which chimed with notions of popular remedies.[132] And of course, it was much more comfortable to have oneself examined genitally and one's stomach prodded and massaged by a woman abortionist, who were in plenty supply among lay practitioners but extremely rare within the medical profession.[133]

This shared experience of abortion as a natural, even everyday occurrence and as an accepted form of birth control meant that wise women and wise men were often proud of and admired for their skill, which they sometimes taught to a friend or neighbour as a special favour. It was not rare for members of a working-class community to ask to watch an abortion in order to learn about it for themselves.[134] Thus, abortion was often performed in secret but nevertheless remained an issue discussed openly within the family, neighbourhood, particularly the working-class neighbourhood, and at the workplace. While this kind of gossip sometimes led to denunciation and prosecution, it also ensured a vital flow of information within the community, as we shall see in the next two chapters.

◌ Chapter 5 ◌

WOMEN'S OWN VOICES: FEMALE PERCEPTIONS OF ABORTION

The abundance of official publications on abortion in Weimar Germany ensures that the views of doctors, jurists and churchmen on the subject are well represented in recent historiography, yet we know very little about what the very people who were at the centre of the debate thought: ordinary women. It is a curious omission since during the Republic many hundreds of thousands of women of childbearing age experienced abortion first-hand or at close quarters. This chapter seeks to make amends by letting the protagonists speak. The process of uncovering women's own voices, however, is fraught with difficulty because of the dearth of records and the nature of the sources available, a corollary of the criminal status of the act. A rare exception is the publication in 1913 by the Berlin medical practitioner and sexologist Max Marcuse, which was based on interviews conducted with his working-class women patients. They reveal a subculture of proletarian fertility control which seems to have had little to do with dominant ideas current at the time, such as practising abortion as a matter of course or sending the husband to other women to prevent more children being born.[1] Only a few historians have attempted to reclaim women's memories of abortion through oral history[2] which is not surprising in view of the sensitivity of the subject, which requires a special trust between interviewer and respondent. Added to this is the difficulty of recalling an event which happened so many years ago and whose memory was probably influenced by the subsequent public debate. But historians also did not avail themselves of the rich source of judicial abortion files relating to the Weimar period which is here for the first time evaluated systematically. The research for this chapter is based in the main on police interviews or court records of women suspected or accused of violation of §218, supplemented wherever possible by medical casebooks, newspaper articles, diaries, letters and publicity material for abortifacients and abortion services.

While denominational, geographical, urban/rural and age differences seem to be evenly represented in these sources, types of class and educational background are not. Overall, those women accused or convicted of simple abortion under §218 who came from the lower social strata massively outweigh those from the more privileged classes. This does not, of course, mean that the middle and upper classes were not terminating their unwanted pregnancies;[3] rather that their behaviour was regulated more informally within their circle of relatives, friends and professional aides and that they were able to seek help more discreetly. It is very likely that educated and well-to-do women had the influence, confidence and money to persuade their family doctor to terminate an undesired pregnancy or refer them to a colleague who was willing and skilled to help. Medical practitioners could legitimate such operations more easily than lay abortionists by certifying the required medical grounds and having a friendly colleague countersign it. Although most doctors rejected criminal abortions publicly, many were prepared to assist their own patients in private. As we have seen, less privileged women tended to seek assistance from lay abortionists who were more easily detected, thereby also exposing their clients to police surveillance and potential prosecution. This explains why working-class rather than bourgeois women's behaviour was usually criminalized.[4] This chapter will thus explore the views of almost exclusively lower-class aborting women.

Uncovering women's attitudes, however, is a challenge. In Marcuse's 1913 survey they are condensed and paraphrased by the doctor; the criminal sources also rarely allow us to hear women's views directly. Usually they are mediated and interpreted by police or lawyers and their clerks; the search for their true expressions and feelings is difficult, involving guesswork and careful reconstruction. The process means looking at the various layers of meaning inherent in the judicial process, the assumptions made by the police, lawyers and medical experts and the more hidden meaning found in the often incoherent and unwitting testimony contained in statements by accused women and their accomplices. The picture which gradually emerges is one of tensions: between modernity and tradition and between women's perceptions of conception and pregnancy, on the one hand, and theories propounded by doctors and lawyers, on the other. However, it took some time for these contradictions to become clear to me. At first I tended to dismiss women's alternative views as mere tactics to avoid imprisonment, protesting their innocence through ignorance. I learnt to accept them for what they were – different views – when I understood that I was no objective observer, since I had internalized the theories of modern medical science objectifying the process of gestation, which was formerly a private event. As Barbara Duden has argued, it is now taken for granted that a foetus is an independent 'person even in the first phases of its existence';[5] and medical imaging techniques illustrate this by compelling photographs of the unborn showing even tiny embryos as recognizable beings. It is difficult to respect that women's own lived bodily experience in the past was quite different. Only by distancing myself from scientific pronouncements did I begin to take seriously many an accused woman's protestations that she had neither been pregnant nor attempted an abortion. Slowly I began to appreciate that women in the 1920s and early 1930s still often relied entirely on the evidence of their own bodies to know what 'state' they were in. Of course, in the Weimar years before chemical pregnancy kits were available, doctors' diagnoses of pregnancy were by no means more scientific in practice than women's own hunches; doctors had to rely on what they felt with their hands and saw with their eyes. But in contrast, women experienced their own bodily changes directly and somatically and consequently often had difficulties expressing them in words.

This chapter focuses on how women perceived menstruation, conception and abortion and the way they conveyed sensory experiences in words, both adopting and contesting orthodox medical discourse by employing expressions of earlier times which were also used by abortion entrepreneurs. I argue below that women accused of abortion spoke in two quite different ways: many participated in 'a new mentality of modernity';[6] that is, they were apparently familiar with the scientific medical language of reproduction and fertility control through their consumption of popular culture and their participation in the welfare state, visiting sick fund doctors, sex advice centres or ante- and postnatal welfare clinics. Many women used a thoroughly modern vocabulary which fitted the official terminology, even though we cannot be certain that they meant the same things by them as doctors or lawyers did. Many women, on the other hand, remained tenaciously attached to older notions of menstruation, articulating ideas which had fallen out of use in medical textbooks although they were conspicuous in advertisements for abortifacients and abortion services which inundated the local press. Moreover, occasionally the very woman who had given a thoroughly well-informed statement befitting the modernity of Weimar Germany, in a later interview lapsed bewilderingly into a traditional mode of expression, evoking ideas and images from the natural world as if modern objective science had not yet existed. How this occurred and what this might signify is at the core of this chapter.

I will begin by exploring the representation of the aborting woman as a criminal by the law enforcement agencies and contrast this subsequently to women's own experience of terminations. Finally, women's sensory perceptions will be analysed with reference to common patois terms revealing a working-class culture in which abortion had a completely different meaning from medico-legal pronouncements.

The construction of the criminal in abortion trials

A criminal abortion case consists of at least two competing discourses, i.e. the legal and judicial discourse, one the one hand, and the statements of the aborting woman whose agenda was usually quite different, on the other. Its interpretation involves taking seriously details recounted by the accused which were irrelevant in law but which mattered in the everyday lives of women. The question of authenticity of defendants' voices is problematic for a number of reasons, most obviously the desire by the accused to escape prosecution or punishment and the fact that women's views are always mediated through the language of the clerk and shaped by the set of questions posed. Nevertheless, given that every opinion is situated and all individuals can only be understood in relation to their circumstances and to those persons with whom they live in close contact, to their education and the culture around them, I aim to reconstruct here as far as possible the opinion of women accused of abortion by carefully peeling away the layers of official language and making visible the framework of questions und suggestions within which their stories were told. On a number of occasions, the opinions of female defendants were recorded verbatim, as for example when women had written to their boyfriends before they were apprehended by the police who confiscated them as incriminating material. Such evidence can reveal women's thoughts and feelings about their bodies, their sexuality and their fertility.[7] We see, later in this chapter, that defendants sometimes seem to address their audience directly when they changed tack in an interview and talked in a language quite different from that used by the police or by the courts.

The trial of a well-known lay abortionist and her many women clients, which opened in Berlin in 1929, offers a good illustration of the very different concerns of women and the police. It started when in June of that year an anonymous note was received by the local police. Written in pencil on a scrap of paper in an uneven hand and composed in shaky grammar, it read as follows:

> In the interest of the general public something should be done quickly to stop the dealings of Frau Martha Spitzer of Berlinerst. 156. She charges 2 Marks for fortune-telling with cards [*Kartenlegen*] which she uses to exploit people's emotional state which is after all why they are driven to go to a fortune-teller in the first place and she promises women that she can help them with sympathy [sic]. For this kind of swindle Spitzer charges 30–80 Marks. To women who recognize this swindle too late and ask for their money back she is insolent enough to deny outright that she ever received any. Spitzer lures mostly wives whose husbands have deserted them and young girls to whom she restores their sweethearts or else she promises to get rid of him [sic] when those concerned want to get rid of their lover. On these occasions women have to hand over material, for example items of underwear [*Wäschestücke*] from their men folk. She says she needs this so that she can work better against them. This sacrifice, as she calls it, must on no

account be touched by the owners of the underwear: this is a trick so that as much as possible [of the items] are handed over to her. Those who cannot pay in one lump sum must pay in instalments and to get her money on time Frau Spitzer threatens women with misfortune if they do not pay on time but those who pay are promised instant relief ...

The letter continues with an urgent plea to the police to search Frau Spitzer's home as soon as possible because it contained plenty of evidence which might be concealed if they delayed. And as an afterthought the writer added:

> ... another thing, if women threaten her with the police she declares that nobody can harm her. She has so many friends among the police whom she has helped to restore their wives to them and she carries with her a little silk pouch with the figure of Lucifer and whatever all the other devils are called that is why nobody can harm her not even in the courts. She says she has often been in court for abortions and similar matters and no judge could touch her thanks to this protection. This is how this woman carries on with her foul work and the time has now come to stop her from harming even more people. Who knows how many years the woman has been carrying on like this and how many people have already been harmed ... What I say will be confirmed by the house search I still want to keep my name secret because Frau Spitzer attacks you in the middle of the street ... [8]

This then was the denunciation of a well-known female healer and abortionist to the police for fraud. The author of the note wanted to remain anonymous, possibly because of the fear of being bewitched by Frau Spitzer ('Frau Spitzer threatens women with misfortune ...'); but it was later revealed that it was a certain Frau Winzer, whom Frau Spitzer herself suspected because she had had an argument with her in the street. Frau Winzer had threatened to make sure that Frau Spitzer ended up in *Zuchthaus* (penal servitude).

This note offers historians a rare glimpse into the proletarian milieu. It also reveals the surprising extent to which alternative medicine, superstition, active witchcraft (as well as abortion) was practised in a working-class community at a time of arguably the first modern welfare state in history, i.e. when the majority of the population was insured for free medical care under Germany's wide-ranging health insurance system. The letter quoted above and the various records of police and judicial interrogations which supplement it reveal the complex meanings of abortion associated with quite different acts and purposes, depending on the vantage point. The letter is doubly rare, because it affords us an uninterrupted personal view, i.e. we hear a woman's voice unmediated since the letter was unprompted by official enquiries, even though it was addressed to the authorities. We thus see very clearly that Frau Winzer's agenda was entirely different from that of the subsequent police action. Frau Winzer had no problem with Frau Spitzer's abortion practice and referred to it only in passing ('she has often been in court for abortions and similar matters ...'). The police, however, appropriated the denunciation for their own purposes: ignoring the complaint of fraud, Frau Winzer's main concern, but a comparatively minor charge, they concentrated instead on the incidental allusion to criminal abortion, a serious charge, especially for commercial operators after the law reform of 1926. The letter had almost certainly been motivated by revenge: Frau Winzer's lover or husband had not been returned to her or, alternatively, if she had come to hate him, because Spitzer had failed to bring about his death. She had probably paid what she regarded as good money, or she had paid a first instalment and Frau Spitzer had tackled her on the street for the outstanding sum, which started off the altercation between them. Revenge by a former client or friend was in fact one of the two chief reasons why illegal abortions and abortionists came to the notice of the authorities when they had hitherto been shielded by the protective silence of their neighbourhood. The other main reason was when the operation resulted in a serious injury and necessitated emergency medical help, or caused the death of the aborting woman, which invariably led to an official investigation.

In order to understand the difference between the female working-class culture in which abortion was a fairly routine event and an official culture in which it was a criminal and moral offence and considered a threat to public health and population strength, it is important to note that Frau Winzer had only complained about Frau Spitzer's fortune-telling and sympathetic magic. She herself had most probably used these services and felt let down by them. Instead of turning to another, more effective fortune-teller she turned to the police to seek revenge for her sense of betrayal. This demonstrates, by the way, that the police were not always considered the hostile arm of state authority but that the working classes made use of them when it suited them. The police, however, had a different remit and used Frau Winzer's complaint for their own ends, namely to suppress the practice of criminal abortion rather than lend support to Frau Winzer's complaint of this fortune-teller's apparently fraudulent claims. They decided to keep an eye on Frau Spitzer and eventually they searched her home for incriminating evidence of abortion activities. In this they were successful: hidden behind Frau Spitzer's stove were a number of notebooks containing the addresses of female abortion patients and the sums of money they had agreed to pay. There were also a number of women's photographs, though sadly these did not survive. The end result was that this successful wise woman, as she was called in the neighbourhood, was charged, tried and convicted for having procured at least twenty criminal abortions on a commercial basis and for attempting to perform an abortion on nine other women, although the actual number of abortions performed by Spitzer was probably much higher.[9]

Frau Spitzer's prosecution sparked off a massive police operation to trace, interrogate and bring to trial twenty-nine of her alleged abortion clients. Unlike the law in some other European countries, where the aborting woman was treated only as a trial witness,[10] in Germany she was also tried as a defendant and usually received a prison sentence, although, especially after 1926, this was often suspended or commuted to a fine. For the historian this has the advantage that German abortion cases yield extraordinarily rich information about many women's intimate histories: we have available to us not just Frau Spitzer's testimony but also those of her twenty-nine co-defendants who will be the main focus here, about whom we have full statements of their interviews with the police, the pretrial investigations and the cross-examinations conducted during the course of the trial.

In order to distil a woman's true voice from such documents, careful attention needs to be paid to the way the criminal case was constructed. Naturally, in the records the defendants' own words are obscured by the bureaucratic language and concerns. In the arena of the police station or the court room defendants always appear to be on the losing end of an unequal power relationship. But female defendants faced an additional disadvantage. Normally the women in the dock were interrogated and judged exclusively by men, who were unlikely to have had any first-hand experience of or sympathy with the dilemma of an unwanted pregnancy and the decision to terminate it. At this time the police, public prosecutors, judges and medical experts were always male and even among jurors women were rare. Typically, in February 1929, in a preliminary examination in Munich of a woman lay abortionist and her clients, one of the aborting women, the 22-year-old embroiderer Martha Nagel, was interrogated in the courtroom by a male examining magistrate and a male clerk. During the trial proper, which took place in Munich at the end of April 1929, Nagel and her three co-defendants faced six men in the court of lay assessors: two judges, two lay assessors, the public prosecutor and the clerk. In addition there were three male solicitors acting as defence counsels and three male witnesses; a further male figure of authority, the expert witness, was not called. Moreover, the session was open to the public for a short time and exposed the defendants to the glare of the public, although the presiding judge presently ordered it be conducted behind closed doors, a normal procedure in such cases.[11]

At the criminal proceedings of the *Landgericht* III (regional superior court) in Berlin in 1930 Frau Spitzer and her patients had to face no less than ten men: three male judges, a public prosecutor, a trainee lawyer (*Referendar*) and five male jurors. The sixth juror was a woman. As we have seen, judgements were based on a law of half a century earlier, even though it was revised in 1926, which reflected the ideology of a patriarchal society according to which the role of women was to be largely confined to the home without any substantial influence on law making or law enforcement. In the 1920s the abortion law was widely believed to be out of date, but the judiciary in the Weimar Republic was well known for its right-wing and conservative attitudes. This, together with the male preponderance in the law enforcement process and the obvious class difference between the judiciary and the average aborting woman, served to inhibit female defendants. Women sought to secure mitigating circumstances for their actions, for example, by pointing to the underlying meaning and logic of bringing on a late period, or terminating an undesired pregnancy, but these were at best irrelevant to the law and at worst aggravated their legal position.[12] The police and the courts, on the other hand, strove to establish legal facts which often mattered very little to women defendants; this almost certainly affected their statements.[13]

Of course, there were other reasons why accused women might have felt too intimidated to speak their minds freely: any woman suspected or accused of abortion faced an uncomfortable police interrogation and a lengthy spell in prison on remand; if she was tried before 1926 she had to fear a prison sentence which could entail not only emotional distress and family dissolution but also professional ruin and social disgrace. While termination of an unwanted pregnancy was not necessarily frowned upon in working-class communities, a criminal conviction and a prison sentence often was. In the dock, or in the police station beforehand, a suspect's dignity and privacy came under attack, her sex life and personal history being considered fair game by a police officer determined to elicit a confession or a public prosecutor intent on undermining her credibility before the jury. The female defendant faced the humiliation of being cross-examined about the intimate circumstances of how she came to be pregnant and minute details of the gynaecological intervention. In the absence of reliable pregnancy tests, women charged under §218 were forced to comment in detail on the nature of aborted matter to prove, beyond doubt, that they had been pregnant in the first place rather than simply having attempted to bring on a late period. Courts often showed considerable leniency if there was some doubt about this point, even though the law of 1871 implicitly, and the amended law of 1926 explicitly, proscribed the 'impossible attempt', that is an attempt when a woman had not conceived or when the method chosen was inappropriate for the purpose.[14] The historian Leslie Reagan describes similar denigration of aborting women in early twentieth-century America, where harassment by police officers and prosecutors constituted their real punishment since in the U.S.A., when aborting women acted as witnesses in trials against abortionists, they were exempt from prison sentences or fines.[15]

It was the added pressure of their entire personal life coming under close scrutiny which was to prove intolerable to many women. In the trial of Frau Spitzer and her patients, Anna Koch is a good example of a defendant for whom the embarrassing criminal investigations probably proved too much. She had only recently arrived in Berlin from Breslau and had taken a manual job. She was twenty-six and single when she found herself pregnant by a married man. When questioned by the police Anna seems to have admitted to her termination straight away. The police, however, were not satisfied and extracted the following confession from her: 'Last year I had sexual intercourse with a gentleman whose name and address I can no longer recall. Since my period was not as heavy as usual I presumed I was pregnant

... I could not marry the man who had made me pregnant ... ' Possibly in response to promptings by the police and in an attempt to come up with mitigating circumstances for her deed (in this case the fear of dysgenic offspring), she added: 'It was only after I became involved with him that I realized that he was a heavy drinker. Otherwise I would have had the child.'[16] Anna was then asked to describe in detail Frau Spitzer's three attempts at procuring the abortion as well as the precise sensations she felt. Rather than endure the trial Anna gassed herself whilst in custody. How her suicide was possible in remand prison is not recorded.

Anna Koch's probable sense of humiliation can only be understood if we appreciate that in criminal investigations of this kind those accused of having undergone a criminal abortion stood before their male inquisitors as young women (Frau Spitzer's clients were either in their twenties or early thirties, as were most aborting women) known to have been sexually active and whose sexuality was associated with deviance either because of abortion or because of an illicit liaison whose details were always required to be told. Courts also often availed themselves of reports by social workers who had visited the defendant's home to establish evidence of her 'respectable' or 'disreputable' social and sexual behaviour.[17] It is in fact quite justifiable to suggest that women were often accused not so much of abortion but of leading what was considered a loose and antisocial life. A woman who terminated a pregnancy but who was otherwise regarded as respectable was usually treated with more leniency than a woman whose domestic arrangements met with opprobrium, although, as we shall see in Chapter 6, single aborting women were often treated more leniently, too.[18]

There was also evidence of gender prejudice on the part of the judiciary who discriminated against women's evidence in court. This was evidently based on traditional beliefs in essentialist gender roles, such as that women were ruled by their emotions and that only men could form rational judgements; or that women's innate character was caring and motherly and consequently aborting women violated both nature and law; or that men were assertive and active, but women were passive and submissive. For example, in a case of 1924,[19] the unexpected acquittal of a gynaecologist accused of criminal abortion with manslaughter was based primarily on the judge's decision to disregard as 'unreliable' the damaging evidence given by five of the doctor's women patients. This was because the judge contended that women usually confuse fact and fantasy. He explained that

> the defendant, Dr Bauer does not seem very credible and ... the court is utterly convinced that he was indeed capable of having committed the criminal offences he is accused of; even though almost all the evidence speaks against him and although his co-defendants [i.e. his patients] and another female witness appeared infinitely more credible than Dr Bauer – nevertheless one cannot totally ignore that persons who have became pregnant illegitimately are especially prone to imagine events and subsequently believe strongly that they are true and then

testify with genuine conviction objective non-truths as if they have actually taken place. This consideration alone persuaded the court to rule that Dr Bauer is not proven guilty beyond all doubt. He is thus acquitted on the grounds of insufficient evidence.[20]

There can be no doubt that women's stories would be influenced by this kind of put-down in court. But their words were also often shaped by the specific questions asked by their male interrogators who followed a set pattern of enquiry and the rephrasing of the answers in legal language by the official clerks. The explanation of defendants was generally disregarded by interrogators, who were primarily concerned with effective policing and prosecution and the apportionment of guilt. Their purpose was to discover who had decided on the abortion in the first place and who knew about it, or helped with it, in order to prosecute all those guilty of inciting, aiding and abetting, all punishable under German law. For example, husbands or boyfriends who had suggested doing away with an unwanted pregnancy were considered guilty of incitement. Or there were investigations into the precise financial transactions between the aborting woman and her abortionist since, as we have seen, abortion on a commercial basis carried more severe penalties.

The experience of abortion

The notion of 'experience' is controversial in postmodern historical writing which questions the 'reality' and 'materiality' of the body and thinks of it rather as part of discourse. Certainly Kathleen Canning and others have argued forcefully about the importance of discursive conditions and illustrated how they shaped women's history.[21] But paying heed to discourse and deconstructuralist thinking does not necessarily mean we have to exclude the concept of 'experience' which is, as one historian put it, 'never completely dissolved in discourse and language', as long as we take care to situate 'experience' properly, i.e. we recognize that it is always 'culturally and discursively mediated'.[22] This is exactly what I have in mind in the following. Women's utterances, both those which expressed Weimar modernity and those which harked back to traditional notions about how they felt about abortion have to be understood against the background of dramatic changes affecting their social position. Long term developments towards women's emancipation during Imperial Germany are well documented.[23] There is no doubt that the First World War and the Revolution crucially altered German women's understanding of their role in society: it raised their expectations of civil rights, paid work, a say in family and sexual matters and erotic pleasure. Their right – not only their need – to control fertility was widely claimed by Weimar's young women and powerfully manifested in the rapidly declining birth rate and the apparent surge of abortions.[24] Notions of equality and women's newfound self-confidence in public life were, however, tempered by a reemerging ideology of maternity and the pursuit of a qualitative population policy, signifying discursive intervention of the body politic on the body female; this sometimes made some women accused of abortion defensive and they apologized for their action.

But, on the other hand, many ordinary women clung to traditional beliefs of the body in the face of quickly changing scientific theories; to appreciate how attractive old notions of fertility remained, we need to avoid presentist ideas, especially how pregnancy is today registered and verified. The historians of a recent volume on the life of the unborn have argued that a 'distance from the modern scientifically mediated thought process' is necessary to comprehend properly women's past perceptions.[25] In her work on the eighteenth century Barbara Duden emphasizes women's 'stubborn certainty' (*störrische Gewissheit*) that 'only they, only each one knew for herself and could only know, in what state she found herself'.[26] Other historians have similarly pleaded that due respect be accorded to women's own 'somatic perceptions' in the past.[27] Michael Stolberg has shown how tenaciously women defended their own views of reproduction against the dominant opinions imposed on them. Even though the lay public was usually remarkably quick to accept new medical doctrines, eighteenth-century women continued to rate menstruation positively, since it heralded the absence of pregnancy, in the face of new medical orthodoxies which ascribed negative characteristics to it.[28]

The trial records used for my project show that this tendency continued well into the twentieth century: many of the aborting women displayed the same kind of *Eigensinn*, the obstinacy to adhere to notions of physical health and fertility which concurred with their own bodily experience rather than (sometimes as well as) with scientific dogma, making this a grey area where hunches rather than (apparent) scientific certainty ruled. Such oppositional perceptions were often hidden behind the 'rationalized verdict' of policemen and prosecutors and it is incumbent on the historian to make the former visible. In her study of nineteenth-century Bavarian rural communities Regina Schulte faced similar methodological problems. She distinguished between different layers of text in criminal trials; firstly the *manifest layer* of the official language of the trial judge, the police and various experts; and secondly, and counterbalancing it, the *latent layer* which included the 'raw material' of the experience of the offenders and witnesses.[29] In the trial records investigated for this book women's sense perceptions were also obscured by the apparently high degree of medicalization of society, that is the permeation and internalization of scientific medical ideas by the general public, including, as we have seen, its representation in popular culture in Weimar Germany.[30] At first sight, women seemed to express their notions of pregnancy and abortion in a manner which was remarkably close to medical orthodoxy. So deceptive was this apparent conformity that on first encountering women's testimonies I could not find an 'authentic voice' among those accused. Only when I had problematized my own immersion in scientific logic did I begin to hear a different message. The difficulty researchers have in admitting their own cultural presuppositions is well documented by the medical anthropologist Emily Martin. When she set out to study the influence of cultural assumptions on the way American women of today experience menstruation, childbirth and the menopause she, too, was at first disappointed by the result of her interviews. Unlike her earlier fieldwork in Taiwan, her American informants did not cause her the same 'puzzlement' as did women in 'exotic' Taiwan. The Americans told stories which seemed 'like so much common sense', based as they were on sound scientific facts. Only when it dawned on Martin that so-called facts were no more than 'cultural organizations of experience' did she began to question scientific views and at the same time grasp the existence of alternative perceptions of women's bodily changes. Martin's interviewees had indeed often challenged received opinions but had done so unconsciously and often only in throw-away remarks.[31]

In this project, too, the testimony of aborting women appeared at first sight to make 'so much common sense'. Only a more careful and sensitive search for what Schulte calls the 'latent layer' revealed the existence, or rather coexistence of deeper, often quite unconscious views, sometimes offered as an afterthought, an alternative vision and resistance to dominant beliefs and assumptions. Many women did not distinguish between contraception and abortion[32] and held on to their own lived physical experience of a delayed period and an early pregnancy as a continuum rather than the clear demarcation which academic medicine postulated and on which the criminalization of abortion was predicated. But women often conveyed their sensory perceptions and interpretations in contradictory and ambiguous ways: many talked about their own or their friends' abortions in 'sensible' terms which the authorities could 'understand'. Other women, or sometimes the same ones on a separate occasion, offered quite different stories, in which another reality emerged that was disconnected from the law and often expressed in euphemisms, similar to those found in advertisements for feminine hygiene and reminiscent of traditional explanations of bodily changes.[33] Below, I shall trace how far the understanding of individual women was shaped by scientific theory (or its interpretation by police or court clerks) and how far it adhered to older notions of gynaecology scarcely touched by medical doctrine.

As we have seen previously, there was a discursive obsession with issues of birth control in general and abortion in particular in the pronatalist/eugenic climate of the Weimar Republic. §218 had not only emerged as a controversial subject of health policy but was also instrumentalized by political parties to woo female voters, and the topic of abortion was also eagerly incorporated into the popular culture of which women were major consumers. But this surely is not sufficient to explain the fact that many aborting women in the dock seem to have used language borrowed from the official medico-legal discourse about pregnancy, abortion and §218. Even if they were caught up in their own logic as to why another child was undesirable, most women referred time and again to medical criteria of a diagnosis of pregnancy and used the appropriate technical terms to describe their abortion. They admitted the deed, even voicing the very word, 'abortion', which incriminated them most, but probably hoped their confession would lessen their sentence.

A case from Bavaria is a good example of defendants' medicalized vocabulary. It should be explained here that their references to 'fruit' instead of foetus does not signify an archaic language but reflects the fact that this term was used in German official language, as it was in the wording of §218. On the afternoon of 3 February 1926 a woman went to the police station in the west of Munich to denounce her niece's fiancé, the 45-year-old locksmith Ernst Spundt. She accused him of performing an abortion on her niece, 28-year-old unmarried cook Franziska Stanner. The woman explained that her niece was injured and might die if nobody intervened. The following morning at 5 a.m. the police raided Erich Spundt's flat, where they found him in bed asleep with Franziska Stanner and arrested them both. Although her fiancé denied everything, Stanner seems to have freely confessed her abortion to the police. She said:

> I have entertained a relationship with Spundt since September 1925 and I have lived with him permanently since November. Shortly after I met him I started sexual relations with him. Before this he promised to marry me. We could not marry because we did not have enough money. I felt pregnant for about one and a half months, but cannot give a precise date. My monthly periods are usually irregular, sometimes every three, sometimes every four weeks. As far as I can recall I had my last period c.25 December. About 6 to 8 weeks ago, again I cannot remember the precise date, my lover suggested that I should have douches. I did not want this at first but bit by bit he got me to agree and one evening I had the douches ... I have kept the syringe in my suitcase because I believed my lover also aborts children [sic!] elsewhere. I thought so because several people told me that my lover had previously aborted the fruits of several women and had been in prison for it. He only gave me one douche and a few days later my period had returned.[34]

A little later that morning Franziska Stanner was produced again in the police station and added the following to her earlier statement:

> I told Spundt about my pregnancy ... Three days after the douche I had contractions and my period showed up. The fruit was about as large as a chicken's egg. It was expelled after I had been bleeding for 2 or 3 days. I did not make a payment to Spundt and he did not ask for one. It is true that I went to see Dr Thalheimer when I realized that my afterbirth had not come away. He removed the afterbirth and told me that I was injured inside ...[35]

In the afternoon of the same day Ernst Spundt's former lodger Frau Rosa Tritt was also questioned by the police since Franziska Stanner's aunt had also denounced her. At first Tritt denied that Spundt had performed an abortion on her but when the latter admitted it she gave the following statement:

> I will now frankly admit that in June [19]24 I felt pregnant and that I allowed Spundt to perform an operation with the intent to abort the fruit. I became aware of my pregnancy because I had missed my period, suffered frequent nausea and the missing period. It existed for c. one and a half months ... [Thereupon she described the abortion] ... the following day the fruit was aborted consisting of blood blots, shreds of skin and mucous membranes ... [36]

The three people involved in abortions talked in what seems to us today perfectly straightforward language, readily adopting medical terms like 'aborted fruit' and 'afterbirth', a testimony of medicalization. Their confessions led to a trial and Spundt's conviction and sentence of one year, six months in prison, with a more lenient sentence for his fiancée and lodger.[37]

Or take another abortion trial from Munich, also from 1926, in which familiarity with medical ideas are evident. The case concerned a lay abortionist, the train driver Anton Schnaller, who had picked up relevant gynaecological skills during his wartime service in Belgium. After his return from the front he practised his know-how on his wife and mistresses alike. Questioned in April 1925 by the police, Therese, Schnaller's first wife, admitted that she knew all about her menstrual cycle and the signs of pregnancy (she had 'after all given birth to four children') and her recall, after five years, of the details of the subsequent termination seems faultless and impressive for somebody unlikely to have had more than elementary schooling, growing up, as she did, in a small village. Shortly after her husband had returned from Belgium in November 1918, 'I had sexual relations with him and a few days later vomiting occurred. My monthly bleeding failed to show. I was therefore convinced I was pregnant and told my husband so.' She resisted her husband's pressure to have an abortion until in her fourth month of pregnancy. When she finally agreed she was dispatched to buy a catheter which 'was red and 30 cm long with a wire attached'.

> On the following day, it was a Thursday between 2 and 4 o'clock, my husband applied a douche with the catheter in the sitting room in our flat with me lying on the sofa. I do not know about a speculum. My husband had a glass tube with a diameter of c.3cm. At the moment I do not know whether he owned this glass tube which he then inserted into my genitals. I am not sure whether he was searching for the womb. He inserted the catheter into my genitals and I suffered very bad pain and felt as if the waters had broken immediately and I began to feel unwell. The bleeding did not return. After two days the miscarriage occurred. I asked the midwife Ermen to assist me. I never felt any quickening with this pregnancy. Apparently the midwife took the fruit to the maternity hospital.

After Therese's use of highly compromising words ('abortion', 'catheter' and 'fruit') which confirmed her guilt under §218 as well as her familiarity with the names of abortion instruments (although the policeman's questions might have prompted her), she confessed to another three terminations also performed by her husband. Evidently asked what had been expelled in the operation she said:

> The miscarried fruits consisted of blood clots roughly the size of a chicken's egg. A human form was not recognizable. One just felt that something had clotted ... I admit that I have incriminated myself by this statement. But I cannot help it. I speak the truth. It is certainly not an act of revenge against my husband.[38]

This was almost certainly disingenuous since Therese Schnaller had certainly also incriminated her husband and by all accounts wanted to discredit him. He was after all shortly to divorce her and marry his long-term mistress. Therese also exposed a whole network of aborting women, abortionists and intermediaries in Munich and the surrounding villages.[39] As a consequence many women were interrogated by the police. They, too, demonstrated in their statements how modern were their ideas of reproduction. One of those implicated was 26-year-old Rosa Marker, who at the time of the abortion was single but in the meantime had married another machinist and was living in Englschalking, a village near Munich. She had had a termination by a midwife in central Munich, a certain Frau Engelhard. This midwife had been recommended by Frau Schnaller when she worked as a seamstress in Rosa's family. Schnaller had not only diagnosed Rosa's pregnancy but also accompanied her to the operation. Engelhard had in fact previously helped Rosa's sister Anna when she was 'three months pregnant'. Rosa described her own abortion to the police, recounting how the midwife had inserted a 'thin little tube into her genitalia'. When the police officer asked her to describe it more precisely she said she could not. She was shown a box with various abortion instruments such as speculums, catheters and the like and she took a catheter and said that was what had been used.

> I left the tube sticking in my genitals for 6-8 hours. Next day I started to bleed again. It was not different from other periods, it did not last longer nor was it heavier than normal. I did not see a fruit or any blocked blood. I can no longer say today what I paid Engelhard [the midwife]. I think I gave her some flour.

Rosa Marker rather naïvely sought to excuse her termination by explaining that her relationship with her then boyfriend had ended and that she 'did not at the time understand the full consequences of her action'. This last admission was almost certainly a rejoinder to a question by the police.[40] This defendant's ignorance of the various abortion instruments used was probably rather untypical for the time.

Many of the other women accused as a result of Therese Schnaller's confessions appeared much more knowing about procedures. So confident were they in recognizing the signs of pregnancy that they did not bother to have a doctor confirm it before arranging for a termination, just consulting him for after-care. A Frau Sachse, aged thirty-five and with three surviving children, told the police:

> I think I became pregnant in August or September 1925; I was afraid that I was pregnant because I had missed my monthly bleeding twice. Since I also suffered from vomiting and dizziness I was convinced of my pregnancy. I did not bother with a medical examination to test for pregnancy ...
> The miscarried blood was blocked a little bit and contained bits of flesh and membrane. I did not see the fruit but suspected one. As a result of the miscarriage I had to stay in bed for about 2 weeks and asked the medical practitioner Dr S. for assistance.[41]

In the police investigation leading to the 1930 Berlin trial of the 'wise woman' Martha Spitzer and her clients, many women suspects also repeated the official terminology of pregnancy and termination when they related their own experience. The 24-year-old wife of a manual worker, Margarete Schmalzer, mother of a three-year-old-child, described her situation to the interrogating police officer as follows:

> At the beginning of 1928 I had missed my period three times. My husband had made me pregnant. I can no longer state the precise dates when my period stopped. Since I did not own my own home and had to work it occurred to me to have my pregnancy terminated. I could not have a second child because of our poor circumstances.[42]

The curiously staccato rhythm of her narrative suggests strongly that she did not so much tell her story as answer specific questions from the police officer. It is noticeable how her answers conformed to official notions of pregnancy diagnosis and criminal abortion at a time when social grounds for a termination were not regarded as legitimate. Margarete Schmalzer's interview with the detective sergeant continued in a similar vein and she offered a wealth of incriminating evidence. She had gone to Frau Spitzer of whom she knew that she 'also did abortions' and asked her, to 'help' her. Frau Spitzer 'consented to carry out the operation'. Asked by a criminal police officer to describe the abortion process itself Schmalzer seems to have had no problem remembering details. She said she was asked to lie 'on two chairs pushed together', whereupon Spitzer placed 'a bucket with lukewarm soapy water under her buttocks'. Spitzer used 'a ball syringe with two rubber tubes attached':

> On one end there was a long thin nickel tube. After locating the womb with a finger she inserted this through the vagina into the womb. She put the other end of the tube in the soapy water and squeezed the rubber ball several times.

In the evening after the third attempt 'bleeding occurred and the fruit miscarried. It was roughly 10 cm long'.[43] Here Margarete Schmalzer expressed herself almost as a doctor would have talked about one of his patients.

Such statements as these seem to indicate that the medico-legal culture had entered the consciousness of even lower-class women with limited education and who were mostly still young. Admittedly, after more than two years Schmalzer could no longer remember exactly when her last period had been (something which was actually untypical in such trials). Nevertheless, Schmalzer remembered in detail how she knew she was pregnant, how the termination was performed and what the aborted matter looked like. Of course, such statements might merely have been the result of leading questions suspects or defendants had been asked by the police or the investigating magistrate, which are unfortunately not recorded. The question is whether their original stories, which we also do not have, conveyed a different meaning and were simply translated into appropriate official language.

These suppositions seem probable, particularly since Frau Schmalzer expressed herself similarly to other defendants in the same case. The 30-year-old wife of an unemployed manual worker, also one of Spitzer's clients, also spoke in a precise and matter-of-fact way: 'I missed my period three times.' As a result of her visit to Frau Spitzer, she said, 'I miscarried a foetus ... it was about 7 cm long, the afterbirth was expelled at the same time.'[44] Just as in the medical approach an embryo was treated like a body whose removal necessitated a curette or a similar instrument, these women seemed to share the notion of a solid, measurable object in their body and also after their termination. Sometimes in the course of their interrogation women even bestowed on the aborted matter a gender and age: in a trial in 1926 in Munich, for example, one woman defendant reported the following: 'I saw the miscarried fruit, it was of the male gender and approximately 4 months old.'[45] Naturally the specific questions and the wording of the recording clerk at the police station of the court affected women's statements. It seems, however, that the wording of the questions women were asked was dependent less on the idiosyncratic idioms used by the individual clerk than on the nature of official language since very similar statements have been recorded by different clerks in different courts and areas as, for example, in the criminal investigations at the *Landgericht* of Berlin, Munich or Wiesbaden.[46]

Notwithstanding the likelihood that the agenda of the interrogator influenced women's accounts, I maintain that the officially transcribed statements can still give us valuable insights into many women's attitudes. What these reveal is their awareness of their monthly cycle, the consistency and size of the aborted matter and the methods of the termination. They also testify to many women's readiness to objectify a very personal experience, an essential ingredient of the scientific discourse and a sign of modern thinking in the welfare state of the

Weimar Republic. The use of medical terms in the statements of the accused may also not necessarily have been due to the clerk's intervention, especially since many women behaved far from passively in interviews but were fiercely determined to challenge underlying assumptions and leading questions. There are quite a few incidents of defendants, even of a young age, putting across strong views even under cross-examination. They protested vigorously against inaccurate statements produced by the scribe and demanded the wording be changed. For example, in the 1926 Munich trial against the train driver Schnaller no less than four female witnesses or defendants retracted previous incriminating statements because they had been made, they alleged, 'under duress'. In one instance the pressure felt was due to the 'gruffness' of the crime officer, in another to an alleged threat of 'arrest' or 'imprisonment and other things … '.[47] Some women also protested their innocence outspokenly and angrily. One defendant in the Spitzer case, for example, was only twenty-five and as a white-collar worker probably not highly educated, yet she was so outraged at having been wrongly implicated in the abortion scandal that she demanded compensation for slander.[48] Many suspects were confident enough to reject the official version of their interviews. Another of Spitzer's clients, 28-year-old white-collar worker Hildegard Deuter, adamantly refused to accept guilt: 'I deny that I had an operation by the defendant Spitzer with the intention of terminating a pregnancy.' She insisted that she had only visited Frau Spitzer because she had 'missed her period' and because this still had not come after several weeks and also because she 'felt physically unwell'. Apparently Frau Spitzer had inquired if she was pregnant, to which she answered in the negative. There was, she told the police, 'no question of this possibility' since she had had 'no sexual congress'. Frau Spitzer had merely prescribed tea and warm baths 'with the result that very soon my period was restored'.[49] Other defendants in the same trial also fought back.[50] Or an accused woman would admit to a miscarriage but steadfastly deny that either she or her partner had done anything to bring this about.[51] In the trial of a Munich photographer, August Wüst, his 27-year-old girlfriend, the bookkeeper Karoline Deisch, denied accusations by the police with great panache. She rejected any suggestion that she was expecting Wüst's child or that she had 'experienced a miscarriage' with his help. 'It is a downright lie to say that Wüst terminated my pregnancy.' Obviously believing that the term 'lover' smacked of impropriety, she was also indignant that the police used it when referring to Wüst and declared she 'won't have it'.[52]

Such examples of public courage show the new type of assertive woman who defends her rights in adversity. This would suggest that at least some of the statements have been handed down to us unadulterated and that at least some of the accused used medico-legal terms of their own volition. If this was so, it could be evidence of the modern 'sober' outlook on life, which was often described by the concept of 'rationalization of sexuality'[53] and associated with the New Woman of the Weimar Republic;[54] it was frequently maligned by contemporary churchmen, economists and populationists as a sign of national degeneration, the decline of moral standards and a subversion of the 'natural' gender order. Conservative forces in particular claimed that in the increasingly secularized society reproduction was no longer a result of divine planning or fate but had become entirely subordinate to the personal will.[55] As Georg Winter, the doyen of German gynaecology, has put it:

> In the rationalized climate of today women have stripped pregnancy of its ethical value and its sanctity and it now has been reduced to a mere function of the female genitals; now there are demands of the right of free disposal over the growing foetus like over any other limb of the body.[56]

Maybe it is not too far-fetched to recognize this 'rationalized' type in a good many of the young female defendants in abortion trials, who seemed to be claiming that to control their biological fate was their right; they were not prepared to submit to unwanted pregnancies and, in a largely medicalized society, they were in command of the precise dates of their monthly periods almost as if they had kept book on it; they also reacted surprisingly quickly and decisively as soon as they noticed a delay. Many women waited for only a few weeks, some only days before they acted. The 20-year-old sales assistant Martha Kraft from Leipzig attempted a self-abortion only a few weeks after her period had been due and the young, single, working-class patients of the nature therapist Hulda Renge approached her generally after only two to three weeks of waiting for theirs. The 34-year-old wife of a Saxon publican consulted a wise woman a mere 'eight days after her stuff was missing'.[57] This promptness in dealing with the problem of an unwanted pregnancy is noticeable in many judicial cases, not least in the 1924 trial against the carpenter, Adolf Kastner and his wife Hermine from Nauheim in Hesse, the central subject of Chapter 6. Even though we usually think of the 1920s New Woman as a phenomenon of the city, this case (and others, too) from Hessian villages shows that during the Weimar Republic women in rural communities, too, strove to be masters of their bodies.

Such attitudes notwithstanding, other depositions by women suspected or accused of criminal abortion betray an alternative consciousness based on a different bodily experience than that expressed in medical terminology. These statements are reminiscent of a much older attitude belonging to the time before the scientific paradigmatic change which declared that life started at the moment of conception. In academic medical textbooks menstruation and pregnancy were portrayed as opposites, as were pregnancy and abortion. In many interrogations, however, women ignored the black-and-white distinctions drawn by the courts and police. Their blurring of the boundaries reflected the gradual and fluid changes of the monthly cycle. In clear contravention of medical orthodoxy an astonishing number of women spoke of the phenomenon of delayed menses and their restoration as if this was quite separate from pregnancy. Many never mentioned 'pregnancy' or 'abortion', only 'blocked menses' (*Blutstockung*) and 'obstruction' of menstruation (*Regelstockung*). Interestingly, sometimes the two languages of science and of sensory perception were used interchangeably or consecutively within the same interview even though they seemed to contradict each other. Karoline Deisch, the girlfriend of the Munich photographer August Wüst, whom we met above, stated that 'as far as I can remember today my monthly bleeding had been missing twice and naturally I feared I was pregnant, especially since I was suffering from vomiting and from nausea.' She claimed she would have liked a child but that she had given in to Wüst's pressure to do something about it since he suffered from STD and she was afraid a child 'would also contract syphilis'. Subsequently, she said, Wüst had operated on her. After this statement in medicalized language, however, Deisch added the following in a very different vein: 'It is true the expelled blood was a little clotted [*gestockt*] but I should add that during my other periods the blood was often curdled. I did not see any fruit nor did I expect one.' She furthermore asserted that although she had 'feared a pregnancy' she had no 'certainty that she was actually in the family way' and that it 'may perhaps have been a case of blocked menses'.[58] Frau Rolf, another of August Wüst's 'patients', declared that she had a miscarriage, 'which occurred as a result of Wüst's intervention'. Afterwards 'a fruit was not detected' whereas 'blocked blood' was.[59]

In a case of 1932 from Upper Bavaria which was, however, only tried in 1934, we can witness the same confusing habit of the aborting woman employing in turn the official and then the alternative discourse about pregnancy and abortion. Hildegard Schäfer, a 20-year-old single chambermaid from the village of Garching, was suspected of self-abortion and of aiding a girlfriend to terminate her pregnancy. In her police interrogation in August 1934 Hildegard admitted the following:

> I have entertained sexual relations with the married wood dealer Johann Ferch in Wald on the Alz for approximately one year because of his constant insistence and because of his promise that I could marry his son if I agreed to a sexual liaison with him. At the same time I was having a love affair with the son, Johann Ferch, 19 years of age. I had sexual relations with both, father and son (Ferch). This was in 1932. On the day before the onset of my menstrual period I had sexual intercourse with Ferch Johann jun. which was not without its consequences. After this intercourse my monthly bleeding ceased. A week later I became convinced that I was pregnant.'[60]

This statement bears all the hallmarks of having been coaxed out of Hildegard with leading questions and then translated into official abortion narrative. She went on to relate how she told first the son and then his father about her state, how both had reacted with dismay and had admitted their guilt. The father suggested she should give birth secretly in Munich and 'find a place for the child there and not tell anybody anything about it'. Her young lover, however, wanted to help her 'abort the fruit'. Here Hildegard admitted to a pregnancy and discussed the possible birth or an abortion in 'common sense' medical terms.

Imperceptibly, however, in the course of her statement she slipped into a different language, mixing traditional with modern concepts, which the police recorded as follows: she recounted again how the younger Johann reacted when she 'had informed him': 'He said, that I absolutely had to put things right. He gave me 10 Reichs Marks with the remark that I should buy a syringe or have one bought.'

She described how she went to see the two sisters Maria and Anna Überling. 'At the time I wasn't my normal self because of my condition and I said so to the Überlings.' They said: 'Never mind, it really isn't so bad, it can easily be sorted out, after all you can get rid of it.' When Hildegard went to fetch milk one Wednesday evening she passed Maria's home and decided to call on her, whereupon Maria administered douches of boiled soapy water: 'After 3 days on a Saturday the douches took effect, that is my monthly bleeding was restored. There was no sign of any miscarriage. It was a menstrual period but a little heavier than usual ... '[61]

Hildegard mentioned neither a foetus nor an abortion; indeed any idea of an abortion was completely dismissed. The argument that this was entirely tactical to avoid prosecution can be disregarded as Hildegard had already implicated herself in her earlier statement above. Hildegard stuck to her narrative of 'blocked menses' in a subsequent interrogation by another police superintendent in which neither pregnancy nor abortion was ever mentioned. She merely said that she had missed her monthly period and that her boyfriend Johann F. had remarked to her when they were bathing 'we should do something immediately to bring on your period'. She had told her close friend Maria Überling, who lived next door and with whom she 'normally had her menstrual period at the same time', that 'this time she'd been caught out' (*hereingesaust*). Maria had reassured her 'not to be scared, if she had a douche immediately, everything would come right again'. 'On the next evening but one, after the douching, [my] bleeding returned and the flow was no heavier than a normal period. I had not been aware of anything you could call a real miscarriage, nothing had come out apart from blood. Since then I've had no pain.'[62]

In contrast to this Bavarian case, the Berlin clients of Frau Spitzer mentioned the words, 'pregnancy' and 'abortion' extraordinarily frequently. But they, too, occasionally used more popular alternative terms. Frieda Mager was a 35-year-old former concierge married to an electrical engineer with whom she had a seven-year old child. She had known Frau Spitzer for nine years. She said that one day she had met her 'unexpectedly in the market' and told her that 'her monthly period was several days overdue and that it had become pretty irregular ever since she had developed heart problems'. Frau Spitzer offered to give her 'douches'. 'The next day', said Frieda Mager, 'my monthly sickness returned. As I had had a cold I assumed that it had been blocked menses, [and presumably in answer to a direct question] I did not feel pregnant.' At a later date she met another acquaintance, Frau Natter, who told her 'that her period was several days late and she worried that she was pregnant'. Frieda encouraged Natter 'to wait and see, maybe it is only an obstruction' and told her about her experience with Frau Spitzer.[63]

Other female suspects in this or other cases did not necessarily use the expression 'blocked menses' or 'obstruction of menstruation' (*Blutstockung*) but they did avoid any reference to 'pregnancy' or 'abortion' and mentioned exclusively 'a late period', 'a cessation of menses', that they 'failed being indisposed' (*ausgebliebenes Unwohl*) or simply 'I told her [the woman abortionist] how things were', and after the douching 'my menses were restored'.[64] Of course, experienced abortionists responded to women's language with similar expressions. Hulda Renge, the Leipzig wise woman, soothed her customers' anxieties about their missing period by promising that she would 'try and make sure that it came back'. Her clients invariably said that 'she did not say whether I was pregnant or not', or 'she never said anything about pregnancy' but 'that [my] period will come any day now'.[65]

Whether this choice of word was being used tactically or not, here is evidence of an alternative language of somatic perceptions on the part of women which may well originally have been used by more women in their statement but which had subsequently become obscured or entirely obliterated in the course of the police or court interrogations, in which carefully leading questions were asked and women's own accounts were turned into an official abortion narrative. Just occasionally it seems some women's traditional notions and images seeped through to reveal different perceptions.

'Blocked menses' (*Blutstockung*) as a popular lay concept

In Weimar Germany, women were not the only ones to refer to 'blocked menses' explicitly or implicitly. Many men used very similar descriptions and when they heard that their wives' or girlfriends' period was late they frequently adopted somatic terms: a 20-year-old mother's help (*Haustochter*) from Upper Bavaria told the police that her male cousin thought that she looked 'unwell' and that 'something was up with her' (*[dass] bei mir die Sache nicht mehr sauber ist*).[66] Women also heard medical men using terms like 'blocked menses'. Thus, in 1929 a 22-year-old embroiderer from Munich reported in court that when her period had failed to show up for a whole month she had gone to a doctor and asked him to check whether she was pregnant. He 'could not give me a definite answer and advised me to take warm hip or foot baths; that way the period would be restored, if it was merely disrupted'. But the period did not return and the young woman induced her own miscarriage by douching, which she freely admitted.[67] It is more than likely that the doctor referred to blocked menses to gain time (the patient had only missed one period) and to avoid legal consequences; he may also have tried to encourage his patient to consider self-help, which advice she obviously followed.

In the Rhineland Dr Bauer, the former director of the Bochum maternity hospital was well known for his commercial abortion practice. One witness told the court that, 'when you go to Dr Bauer you only need to mention the word "blocked menses". Then he gets the picture. But if by any chance you say something about pregnancy then he would not want to help.' Similarly, a medical practitioner from Upper Bavaria told a patient after she had suffered a miscarriage that he had found a 'residue of blocked blood' which needed 'scraping out'.[68] In both cases this seems to have been a procedural precaution to stave off potential prosecutions and protect a lucrative abortion business. Nevertheless, the notion of 'obstructed menses' can also be found within medical circles when such tactical considerations were not necessary. I have also traced at least one forensic pathologist who used this expression when giving his expert opinion.[69]

Moreover, this traditional concept was used by the medical profession in their encounter with female patients because it corresponded to women's perceptions of their bodily changes but also because doctors, even gynaecologists, did not always find it easy to diagnose conception. Despite the rapid development in reproductive science at that time no reliable or fail-safe diagnostic method existed to determine pregnancy in its early stages. Although the medical profession insisted officially on a clear demarcation between pregnancy and a delayed period, without a 'scientific' pregnancy test it followed that a distinction between abortion and 'bringing on blocked menses' was at the time little more than a juridical/medical construct. For many women the boundary was as blurred as the legal/ethical difference between abortifacients and contraceptives. The former were outlawed while the latter were permissible. In daily life and general medical practice, however, the apparently firm distinction was much less clear-cut. By the 1927 law to combat STD it became permissible for the first time to 'advertise and exhibit publicly' prophylactics, which included contraceptives. But these latter often had the double function of preventing conception and stimulating miscarriage. Douching with a *Mutterspritze* into the vagina (or even into the uterus) or having a uterine coil fitted were both considered acceptable contraceptive methods but they could cause a termination of pregnancy if applied after conception had taken place.[70] As we have seen in Chapter 2, some medical practitioners erred on the side of caution and performed a dilatation and curettage even when their diagnosis of a pregnancy was uncertain only to find after the operation that no pregnancy had existed at all.

Even though attempted abortion was also punishable in law, courts generally treated it as a lesser offence than a 'completed abortion'. It was because of the diagnostic uncertainties that the law enforcement agencies normally tried to establish whether an aborting woman had actually been pregnant. In judicial investigations and trials a definite retrospective diagnosis was only possible when an autopsy had been carried out, or when doctors confirmed an error, both of which were comparatively rare. Most judgements were based on the aborting women's own statements after they had been pressed to describe the precise procedure and outcome of interventions by themselves or a third party. If they had miscarried 'clots of blood' (*Blutstücke*), the existence of a foetus and therefore an abortion was presumed; but if the accused spoke of 'normal menses restored' then it was considered only as an attempt after a wrongly assumed pregnancy.[71]

The clients of Frau Spitzer, the Berlin abortionist and fortune-teller in the trial of 1929, were typically cross-examined rigorously in this respect but their depositions were for the most part interpreted generously. A 48-year-old married businesswoman, Martha Detmold, stated that she had no children because her husband had been ill for a long time but that she had had sexual relations with another man. When her period was late she had assumed that she 'had fallen' (*verfallen*). Her lover suggested that Frau Spitzer could help. As soon as Spitzer set eyes on Detmold she also pronounced her 'fallen' and said that she could tell from her complexion. After four to five weeks' treatment with douches administered by Spitzer, Detmold reported: 'my menses were restored, they were exactly like normal, my bleeding was not heavier than usual. Neither did I lose a fruit. For this reason I assumed that I never had been pregnant. I am 49 and believe I am in the menopause.' Detmold added that her period was sometimes ten weeks late. Even though she used the expression 'fallen', a synonym of being pregnant, on two occasions, the examining magistrate heeded her description of her menstruation and gave her the benefit of the doubt.[72]

Another client, Martha Niederer, already had three children aged between eight and eleven years with her foreman husband. In her police interrogation she said that Frau Spitzer, 'told me that we should get on with it, she meant that she would get rid of the pregnancy. Next day my period resumed no heavier than normal, I did not lose a fruit or any clots of blood.'[73] Here, too, both Niederer and Spitzer had obviously assumed a pregnancy but the court declared it only a case of 'attempted abortion'.[74]

Of course it is not unlikely that all these defendants and many others were seeking to take advantage of medico-legal uncertainties by making appropriate statements and thereby avoiding harsh sentences. They were almost certainly aware of legal procedures since abortion trials received wide coverage in the local press. Yet, as we have seen above, references to blocked menses and detailed descriptions of 'normal' monthly periods also fitted the everyday reality of menstruation for women and therefore should not necessarily be dismissed as calculation but accepted as a testimony to their lived experience. Commercial traders of abortifacients recognized this only too well and advertised their wares euphemistically as remedies to 'relieve menstrual blockage'. As will become clear below, there was, besides the obvious commercial motive, another reason for this, exactly as there was for women's somatic expressions.

Advertising abortifacients

The similarity between the way female defendants in abortion trials described their sensory perceptions when their period was late and the manner in which mail-order firms and door-to-door salesmen advertised abortifacients is striking, though perhaps not surprising, given that many entrepreneurs were part of the working-class culture and therefore familiar with popular terms; they also knew that in order to earn their clients' trust they must speak their language. A typical advertisement for an abortion service or abortifacient ran like this:

> **'ATTENTION! FOR SAFE KEEPING!**
> **Women awake!**
> ... If your monthly *period is blocked* or has completely stopped don't worry ... *salvation* and new hope is in the exclusive gift of my tested preparations ... Within only *one hour*. Place your confidence in me and turn to an experienced woman then you, too, can be helped. You will be eternally grateful ...
> Nearly every day unsolicited letters of thanks are received.
> *Guaranteed harmless! No interruption of your work! [Ohne Berufsstörung!]*
> IN A PLAIN WRAPPER. CASH ON DELIVERY.
> Frau A. Liermann, Hamburg P 6
> Schanzenstrasse 68.[75]

Similar advertising copy appeared in the mid-1920s in various German towns in a multitude of leaflets and small ads in journals and newspapers. Frau Liermann, the signatory of the above advertisement, was one of several hundred small entrepreneurs trying to exploit the rapidly rising number of women seeking terminations of pregnancy after the First World War. The trade in abortifacients is reminiscent of that in contraceptives, which had become big business in the prewar years stimulated by Neomalthusian propaganda.[76] It was also not dissimilar from the situation in other countries.[77] The files in the archive of the Munich police headquarters allow us to reconstruct the career of a fairly typical pedlar in abortifacients. Frau Liermann's decision to enter this trade was no doubt motivated by her personal circumstances. She was twenty-eight, a divorcée for two years who presumably needed to earn a living. Resident in Hamburg, the German mail-order capital for 'hygienic articles', she was almost certainly attracted to this business through proximity and by the prospect of easy money; acquaintances who were already part of this world might have encouraged her, or she might herself have obtained abortifacients by mail order. It was not unusual for women to operate in the market for abortifacients; in fact, quite the contrary.

Most of the surviving publicity material was signed by women. We know that Frau Liermann was active in Hanover, Hamburg und Ansbach and possibly in other towns, too; she distributed her leaflets individually to front doors in blocks of flats or in bundles at the foot of communal staircases.[78] Her advertising copy followed the kind of stock text found on other similar leaflets, such as those distributed on behalf of a 'Frau Elisabeth Siemsen, former district midwife', also from Hamburg,[79] and in small ads in local newspapers and journals for remedies against 'blocked menses'. In 1923, for example, a Frau Nagel, also resident in Hamburg, advertised in the hairdressing trade journal *Deutsche Friseur Post*; she invited women 'whose menstruation was obstructed or had ceased altogether ... to order her special product. These advertisements also appeared in the *Süddeutsche Wäschereizeitung* (South German Laundry Journal), in only very slightly altered form.[80] Sometimes such ads were couched in emotive terms addressing 'unfortunate women and desperate girls', mentioning 'tears' and 'sleepless nights' when 'menses were blocked' or a 'period was disturbed'.[81] Most publicity copy, however, stuck to standard, obviously well-tested phrases and commonly overlapped in three important aspects, as was the case in other countries, too.[82] Firstly, the words 'pregnancy' and 'abortion' were conspicuous by their absence; secondly, promises were abundant and usually made by female traders; thirdly, products on offer were usually neither abortifacient nor harmful. There were good reasons for all three aspects.

As to the first, the use of euphemisms was necessitated by police surveillance because the trade in abortifacients was illegal.[83] The copy of Frau Liermann's leaflets have been preserved because she had come to the attention of the police. She got off with a warning because the use of euphemistic language in her leaflets allowed her to talk her way out of the accusation that she peddled abortifacients; she assured the police that her products were merely 'remedies for pathological period irregularities' and consisted of 'footbath salts, menstruation powder, female tea [*Frauentee*] and menstruation drops'.[84] Offering remedies for 'obstructions of menses', 'blockages of menstruation', 'monthly disturbances' or simply 'women's afflictions' rather than mentioning 'unwanted pregnancies' was legally necessary but also chimed in with women's own perception and terminology, as we have seen.[85]

As to the second point, advertisers were keen to convey the reliability of their products: 'no need to be afraid' since they were 'harmless', 'proven many times over' and praised in 'many grateful letters'. It was predominantly the lower classes, especially female wage workers, who were targeted, as the frequent references to speedy treatment (in 'only a few hours' or 'next day') and 'no interruption of work' testify; they were promised 'discreet' delivery to protect them from gossip.

Customers were courted by another ploy: the great majority of traders presented themselves as women, especially midwives or, more frequently, 'former midwives' in an attempt to exploit the well-known preference by women for female abortionists.[86] On close inspection, however, many a female dealer turned out to be male. 'Frau Elisabeth Siemsen, former district midwife, Hamburg', was a case in point. Police investigations exposed a male trader named Metz who obtained his products 'for period irregularities' from another man, a wholesaler located on the *Reeperbahn*, Hamburg's notorious red-light district. A certain Frau Siemsen had indeed once owned the firm and had also trained in midwifery without ever practising it, preferring to sell 'menstruation remedies' instead. Her name was simply used to boost business. When Metz bought the business he retained the original name for the same reason.[87]

As to the third point above: for legal and practical reasons it was too risky to sell by mail order products that were sufficiently toxic to cause a miscarriage. Toxic products were classified as *Geheimmittel* (restricted medicine), their ingredients were kept under lock and key and therefore usually out of reach of untrained traders. That is also why mail-order business people always denied that their products were abortifacients. The druggist Thiele told the police that his products, the women's tea 'Loretto' and the menstruation powder 'Silva' were harmless and incapable of terminating pregnancies. Another owner of a mail-order firm, Nikolaus Rauh, defended himself similarly: his drops consisted, he said, of '70 per cent spirit of wine, lemon balm, cinnamon, lemon peel, cloves, nutmeg and coriander' and apparently conformed to the 'spirit of Carmelite of the German Pharmacopeia' (*Arzneibuch*); moreover, he claimed, they were available 'in nearly all pharmacies, druggists, and sanitary shops'. He was almost certainly telling the truth, as the Reich Health Office testified that most confiscated drugs 'to cure irregular menses' were perfectly innocuous:

> The products are generally known to be harmless and totally unsuitable for terminating pathological period irregularities, let alone a pregnancy, because of their composition and the manner of their application. But they are bought by the public as abortifacients and are also offered to them as such. Thus the public feels cheated and deceived.[88]

The files do not tell us whether the police instigated proceedings for offences against False Claims which, at least in theory, might well have resulted in the paradoxical situation where traders were prosecuted because their products were *not* abortifacients. In practice I have traced only a single case and this was in respect of contraceptives.[89] But then abortifacient potions, powders and teas were not the main concern of district medical officers of health or police inspectors; their efforts were concentrated on preventing the sale of appliances such as intrauterine catheters and *Mutterspritzen* which could be had at chemists' and also through mail order.[90]

In his police interrogation the Hamburg trader Rauh defended his practice by declaring:

> I only advertise and sell menstruation drops for complaints relating to irregular menses. These irregularities are not uncommon in adolescence or during the menopause. Colds, leucorrhea, greensickness, anxiety, even a simple change of air can cause irregular menstruation. My drops provide great relief from abdominal pain before and during menstruation and for the conditions mentioned above.[91]

Did his products really relieve problems of 'irregular menses' or was his explanation merely an excuse to avoid prosecution? I would suggest it was both. Of course traders were well versed in legal loopholes and tried to protect themselves from prosecution. But we should also interpret the flood of publicity material which, according to the police, inundated rural and urban Germany during the Weimar years, as a sign that the success of this business was predicated on its appeal to women. This was due in no small measure to the fact that traders spoke the same language as their clients and knew how to express empathy with anxious women whose menses were overdue. Abortion trials reveal the importance of these products as the first remedies to which women turned in their attempt to reverse 'blocked menstruation'. Advertisements brought into the public arena the vocabulary of sensory perceptions used by women in everyday life; they could therefore be regarded as the public face of a female subculture, reflecting and reinforcing an alternative view of women's reproductive problems.

Women's sensory perceptions

For many women in the early twentieth century, especially if they did not desire a child, the notion of 'blocked menses' seems to have corresponded more accurately to how they perceived their bodily changes than terms like 'pregnancy' or 'gestation' used in the official discourse. Doctors and others steeped in scientific thinking nearly always regarded a missed period as a sign of pregnancy but women often saw it quite differently. Although many women rushed to find help to unblock their menses, the notion that a late period could or would probably turn into an unwanted pregnancy in the near future and eventually into the burden of a child appeared either as too distant or too unpleasant to countenance. The scientific rationale demanded a projection of the future onto the present: but many women would not grasp the physical reality of an embryo in their belly at a time when there were no visible and tangible signs of it. According to medical teaching a foetus in the womb was viable from conception but this had little resonance with many women especially if they were worried that they were pregnant:

they did not permit themselves to imagine a 'fruit' (*Frucht*) in their womb nor a future human being when their menstrual bleeding was late; they recognized only what they could actually see and feel: the lack of blood stains. This raised the alarm that something needed to be done whatever its cause.

Of course, there were other physiological indications that something was not quite right: 'morning sickness, back pain, loss of appetite',[92] 'frequent abdominal pain' or 'constant pain', a 'bloated stomach' or a 'swollen breast'.[93] But the most important sign by far for many reluctant mothers was when 'their menses were ... not as heavy as normal,'[94] were missing or had ceased, a warning to seek help. For third persons, too, one of the most recognizable signs of a woman in trouble came when no 'menstruation laundry' was in evidence.[95] In a 1924 trial the case was discussed of a domestic servant, Elfriede Joachim, who had died as a result of a doctor's botched termination. Questioned by the examining magistrate whether Joachim had actually been pregnant, her former employer answered this in the negative; there were no visibile signs of pregnancy and she had been 'completely healthy'; she had carried out 'heavy labour as normal'. The other servants of the household, however, disagreed; they claimed Joachim was 'fallen' since they had not noticed 'any traces of blood in her laundry'.[96] Or in a 1926 trial a certain Frau Spanger from a village in Upper Bavaria was suspected of having arranged a medical termination for a farmer's daughter, Elisabeth Stauer. In her defence Spanger described how she had tried to ascertain 'how it was with Liesel'.

> I then went down to her and remonstrated with her and told her she should tell me about it, perhaps she could be helped since later on it would be too late to help. I only said this to find out for certain if something was the matter or not. But father and daughter laughed and Liesel showed me her slip which was stained with menstrual blood ... [97]

Occasionally during a police or court interrogation women admitted to an abortion and apologized for their 'misdeed', saying they had not known at the time it was wrong. But if we read between the lines of their statements – often composed in response to a leading question and reworded in officialese – many women's judgements of their actions differed radically from the official discourse in that they usually did not regard the 'bringing on a period' as a 'crime against life' (*Verbrechen wider das Leben*) as the Church or the law pronounced it, or a 'criminal abortion' as doctors referred to it. The medical sexologist Max Marcuse had already observed during the First World War that 'Frauen aus dem Volke' (women of the people) 'could not see anything remotely immoral' in abortion.[98] On the contrary, the act of reversing a 'menstrual blockage' seemed natural and necessary. Unless a child was desired menstruation was traditionally interpreted in the popular imagination as a sign of a healthy female body; its absence heralded ill health as well as an unplanned and unwanted pregnancy. In the words of the medical historian

Michael Stolberg, 'for hundreds of years menstruation was described as an essential, beneficial evacuation, and the decrease or total suppression of the menstrual flow was considered one of the principal causes of female disease'. Significantly women held on to this belief despite the best efforts of medical science from the Enlightenment onwards, which tended increasingly to stress the negative effects of menstruation until this came to be considered eventually as a 'major source of irritation'. The notion that menstruation was a 'purifying, cathartic process', freeing and cleansing their bodies 'from impurities and peccant matters',[99] continued to have currency even in the twentieth century and underpinned the statements of many of the women above accused of abortion. This was of course not confined to Germany.

Leslie Reagan, in her study of abortion in nineteenth- and twentieth-century America, has also located such concepts. She asserts that the notions of 'blocked menses and quickening must be taken seriously by late twentieth-century observers ... blocked menses cannot be dismissed as an excuse made by women who knew they were pregnant'.[100] The anthropologist Emily Martin has provided us with a powerful analysis of late twentieth-century American women's socialization and conformity to medical culture. When she dug deeper into the meaning they had attached to certain concepts she found very different visions of how they experienced their own bodies. Often, as an aside, they revealed a 'sensory and emotional experience' which was at odds with medical accounts and those of the larger society; while medicine associated menstruation with 'disorder' and 'failed production' and society linked it with shame and disgust, women themselves often felt positively about it since it signified they were not pregnant. Their ability to perceive menstruation in opposition to the 'hegemonic scientific views of women's bodies' meant they could talk quite neutrally about 'the phenomenology of menstruation', that is, describe the physical sensation of menstruation and the appearance and smell of the menstrual flow.[101]

For women who did not desire a child and who stood accused in the files studied for this book, the act of restoring their monthly bleeding was indeed perceived as a release. It liberated them from 'the blockage', 'a predicament' (*eine Verlegenheit*), or simply from 'a matter' which they wanted 'removed' rather like an ulcer.[102] One woman from Bochum put it like this: 'I was at Bauer's [a well-known abortionist] and I am rid of it.'[103] Another defendant in the same trial said that she had been to the doctor and 'I'm tipping out' (*ich kippe*). She explained that 'to tip out' was an expression used in this area to describe the imminent start of a miscarriage'[104] but the use was not confined to the Rhineland; the Berlin working-class women interviewed in 1914 by Marcuse also used the same expression. To tip out evokes notions of cleansing the body of waste material.[105]

Only if we appreciate the positive associations of restoring menstruation can we understand that for women employing this term in police stations and court it was not just tactical expediency but also an accurate description of their sensory perception. Thus, the medical understanding of menstruation as pathological was contested. While in the medicalized official discourse 'being indisposed' (*sich unwohl fühlen*) was a euphemism for women's monthly period,[106] reluctant mothers felt unwell not when they menstruated but when their period was 'overdue' or their 'stuff had failed to come' (*ihr Zeug ist ausgeblieben*).[107] It was then that they quite literally 'missed' an essential ingredient of their well-being, their monthly blood. An obstruction or blockage of the menses (*Blutstörung* or *Blutstockung*) was thus perceived as a worrisome imbalance in the body, an irregularity in the physical rhythm which needed to be put right. Working-class, though not usually middle-class, women who feared a pregnancy thought of these symptoms as an illness. Consequently they described themselves as 'fallen' (*verfallen*), thus using a metaphor of ruin (*Verfall*) and downfall (*Fall*).[108] Interestingly, these sentiments were expressed irrespective of denomination; in fact, religious affiliation seems not to have been a significant influence in how proletarian women thought about abortion or indeed acted on it. These notions also constituted a powerful contestation of the ideology of motherhood in religious and conservative circles according to which pregnancy signified 'good hope' (*gute Hoffnung*) and children were always to be celebrated as a blessing (*Kindersegen*).

Those few middle-class women whose investigations for offences against §218 have been located, expressed themselves differently though also negatively. A 20-year-old office clerk from Saxony likened the event of her missing period (or pregnancy) to something terrible and literally unspeakable (*Unsäglichem*) which had befallen her. The idea was so gruesome that it provoked in her a death wish. In her letter to her lover, a 31-year-old law student at Leipzig University, Philipp Breuer, she described her feelings:

> Philipp! My dear, kind Philipp, what would you say or do if as a consequence of our relationship – I don't dare to write it ... well, if something terrible happened?! It will not flow out of my pen und yet it wrests itself from my lips like a scream. Philipp, my love, already 4 weeks have passed, no – when I have always felt it coming at least 8 days earlier ... . How unendingly terrible is it to awake from a sweet dream. I can already see the grey spectre in front of my eyes and tears blur it ... I am so afraid, Philipp, what will become of us? ... Do you know, Philipp, what I would like now? Become seriously ill and die the next day.[109]

But if the absence of monthly blood was perceived as an illness or a misfortune it follows that the operation to 'bring on the menses' was a cure. After a successful intervention many women experienced 'a huge relief' (*eine große Linderung*) and helpers, too, could appreciate this moment. One 'wise woman' who witnessed the happy outcome of her operation with her own eyes, soothed her client with the words: 'now everything is fine, now it's alright again ... '[110] For aborting women the sign of bleeding was greeted with joy and relief signifying the end of physical and psychic problems. When women called their bleeding normal they might also have meant that they felt their body had resumed its normal function and that they were feeling well again.

Blood, therefore, was for many women not embarrassing but welcome and the monthly cycle was a frequent topic of conversation within female circles. A late period or its arrival was freely talked about in all social situations, whether at the weekly goose market, the workplace, a tea party or in the stairwell, in the back yard of a tenement block or in a shop.[111] It formed a natural topic of a woman's everyday life and showed that there was little fear of denunciations within family and neighbourhood circles. If a denunciation did occur it was usually a consequence of a quarrel followed by an act of revenge, as we have seen with the denunciation of Frau Spitzer above, or a sudden disturbance in the structure of communal life.[112]

The positive meaning attached to the act of 'unblocking' the menstrual blood was reinforced by an adherence to the traditional belief that the bodily juices needed to be in flux. It was thought that menstrual blood needed to be encouraged to flow, be it by a potion, or, most frequently, by injecting a liquid into the womb.[113] Douching with soapy water or Lysol was considered restorative, associated as it was with personal hygiene in a number of interconnected ways; and hygiene had an extraordinarily high status within Weimar health policy, hailed as a social ideal in the numerous and ambitious government campaigns, especially in the popular health exhibitions of the 1920s. For one thing, syringes were prescribed by doctors for 'female hygiene' and also popularized by Neomalthusians as contraceptive devices, available at all pharmacists' and chemists' shops.[114] In the form of *Mutterspritzen*, with the additional extension of a long catheter so that they could reach the womb (*Gebärmutter*), they were employed to stimulate the menstrual flow. The positive role of 'bringing on a period' was furthermore strengthened by its association with disinfectants. The use of soapy water, or on occasion Lysol, had a practical and a symbolic function. Both acted as germicides and stimulated the uterus to contract and expel 'waste'; their symbolic importance was their 'cleansing' and, paradoxically, life-preserving image. Within the household carbolic soap kept bodies and laundry clean; Lysol was a household disinfectant protecting healthy bodies from germs, women in childbirth from puerperal fever and newborn babies from infection. It was prescribed in midwifery for safe deliveries.[115]

The refusal of many female defendants in abortion investigations to recognize nascent life in their own body is also evident in the manner in which they attempted to bring on their period and in the unsentimental way they talked about and disposed of what they had expelled. Once a woman missed her period she usually tried to stimulate menstruation by taking one of the many widely marketed remedies for 'blocked blood', followed, if necessary by the application of a douche by herself or a friend/relative and, if this still did not succeed, by a professional abortionist.[116] Many women reported extraordinarily speedy results after douching: 'I started bleeding again the very next day', or even 'my period returned the same night'.[117] While doctors, lawyers or churchmen pathologized, criminalized or moralized about the act, many women talked quite matter-of-factly of what they saw and felt during and after the operation, even though, of course, their statements may well also have been influenced by leading questions in the police station or court. If the period was abnormal, containing thick substances, the contents were described as 'little clots of blood' or as 'longish pieces of flesh'[118] and likened to animal or plant shapes: 'like a chicken's egg'[119] or a 'blood clot the size of a little apple'.[120] Rarely did they perceive what had been expelled as an embryo, let alone a child, but they thought of it rather as a normal monthly period or as 'waste' to be disposed of unceremoniously: it was put into the chamber pot, thrown into the lavatory, or buried in the ground outside.[121]

A client of Frau Spitzer reported how she had been told by her 'to return with it [the expelled matter] so that she could see whether everything had come out [*abgegangen*]. But I did not find her at home, so I threw the fruit into the loo'.[122] Schmalzer, another of Spitzer's clients, thought nothing of carrying an aborted foetus through the streets of Berlin and back home again, eventually disposing of it as if it were a normal bodily waste. A 19-year-old domestic servant, another of Frau Spitzer's patients, thought it quite natural to ask a friend to run this errand for her. She and her friend had originally gone together to Frau Spitzer to have their pregnancies terminated. In fact, each helped with the other's operation. But in the case of the friend the miscarriage had not occurred yet and since she was going back to Frau Spitzer for a second attempt, she did not appear to mind taking her friend's parcel (the aborted foetus) along.[123] The 20-year-old daughter of a forester, Berta Graml, from a village in upper Bavaria, expelled 'a clump of blocked blood' which she buried 'in the woods near Frauendorf'. She said 'it was just discharge [*Abgang*] like others frequently have'.[124] The farm girl Frieda Zirnbiegl from Wald an der Alz, Upper Bavaria, shared a room with Erika, the 12-year-old daughter of her employer. When Frieda was douching herself with a syringe, Erika was in her bed in the same room. Frieda recounted that she 'could not do it by herself' and asked the 12-year-old to pass over her chamber pot into which she then put the miscarried matter. Towards 10 o'clock on the same evening her boyfriend came to her room to 'pay his nightly visit'. Frieda wanted to show him the 'discharge' but 'he did not want to know about it'.[125]

So determined were many women to regard 'restoring their period' as a positive event that they often denied any discomfort, although it is well known that any artificial miscarriage can be painful. In the next chapter we shall encounter the trial of a Hesse carpenter and his wife in which only two of the more than fifty aborting women tried had suffered any injury and all defendants emphasized the absence of pain. The few who alluded to discomfort likened it to normal aches 'as during a period'.[126] It is also surprising how few women expressed any fear of the potential danger of these gynaecological interventions, a rather startling fact given that this aspect, at least as far as abortions performed by laymen and -women was concerned, was given so much attention in the official discourse and played a major role in the campaigns for abortion law reform.[127]

Many women were eager enough to have the name and address of an abortionist at the ready in case they ever needed it. Frau Margarete Schmalzer, one of Frau Spitzer's patients, revealed how an abortion was often planned for long before the need arose. She explained how she came across Spitzer's name as an abortionist. 'I became aware of Frau Spitzer through Frau Schmidt (who lived just round the corner). I spoke to Frau Schmidt and in the course of a conversation she mentioned that Frau Spitzer also did abortions. At that time I was not yet pregnant.'[128] So here we learn about not just the existence of a female network of self-help but also about long-term family planning. I found other examples of such a preventive strategy.[129] A network of communication within working-class communities was useful for passing on information about reliable 'help' and arranging appointments. We see this clearly in the 'monster trial' from rural Hesse in the next chapter but it was also common in big cities like Berlin, Munich or in the Rhineland and Saxony.[130] It is not clear whether information was paid for or given freely but certain trials suggest that the former was by no means rare.[131] The path to an abortionist often involved many people, both men and women, as did the operation itself: as we shall see in more detail in the next chapter, it was often carried out in the presence of husbands, boyfriends, relatives or friends, who often assisted the abortionist with practical help. In this respect the experience of an abortion was not so different from that of a home delivery.

In this chapter I have tried to explore the various ways in which women talked about periods missed and their restoration and how their terms differed from the official abortion discourse. We have seen that while some women apparently adopted a modern, medicalized language, others contested medical, legal or religious idioms and expressed their own remarkably independent views which were more in keeping with older notions of female fertility. But such distinctions are not always obvious in judicial files because many responses must have been coloured by the promptings of police and lawyers who were also seeking to make women's statements conform to official linguistic norms.

From at least the nineteenth century medical men and lawyers had been attempting to regulate reproductive decisions and thereby assume control over the female body. They defined the time of conception, and as a consequence the legality or illegality of a pregnancy terminated, in such a way that it was only verifiable by scientific means (although not yet achieved in the Weimar period) and not by a woman's perceived changes to her own body. Or doctors compiled a catalogue of grounds, on the whole to do with medical conditions, for the justification of a termination which was accepted by jurists but rarely corresponded to female needs. Typical female arguments for abortion, as recorded in interrogations and cross-examinations, were: economic hardship, fear of loss of employment,[132] homelessness, parental objection to a planned marriage, or a lover's refusal to marry, shame,[133] a completed family or simply the wish not to have a child.[134] Such motivations appeared compelling and logical to the aborting woman but carried little weight in courts.

Many women seemed familiar with scientific concepts but the abundance of a medicalized language used by female defendants is probably also due to the influence of the authorities in judging the behaviour of aborting women and a result of the interrogator's questions or the clerk's interpretation. But there were usually signs of women's alternative perceptions once the questions which law enforcement officials asked of the accused were reconstructed and the efforts of the clerks edited out; by reading between the lines, women's own voices can be detected. Many continued to inhabit a world in which their bodily changes were perceived quite differently from the way the police, doctors or law courts saw them, even though they often appeared quite comfortable using a medical discourse. We might wonder how this was possible. I believe the explanation is that women's expressions were as ambiguous as their experience. On the one hand, they had become familiar with medico-legal concepts and expressions as was only to be expected of citizens of the early twentieth century, especially in the Weimar welfare state; on the other hand, we should not assume that all women were completely medicalized. The contradictions between different statements and the steadfast retention of such unscientific notions as 'blocked blood', and its reversal by douching, suggests that many women did not mean the same when using medical language, particularly since it concerned mostly working-class women. They might have used it but not necessarily internalized it.

Thus, a pregnancy and its termination did not necessarily have the same meaning for doctors (and jurists) as for those most immediately affected by it; for women an unwanted pregnancy was often thought of as a misfortune akin to a family tragedy that had befallen them, just like an illness for which a cure was needed. To return to the letter quoted near the beginning of this chapter which denunciated Frau Spitzer as a fraud, abortion was only one of many strategies to maintain the general well-being of a woman and her family. Frau Spitzer's clients, ordinary Berlin working-class women, seemed engaged in the pursuit of domestic peace (*häusliches Glück*), irrespective of how this was defined.[135] When it was disturbed, whether by the desertion of a boyfriend or husband, the illness of a mother, the thwarted hope for a child or the fear of an unwelcome pregnancy, an appropriate remedy was sought. The fact that this could range from fortune-telling to magic charms, secret potions to sympathetic magic or abortion, seemed to make good sense to these women even if it aroused the suspicion and censure of the law enforcement agencies intent on controlling what they regarded as women's irresponsible and unlawful approach to sexuality and reproduction and convinced that quack abortions needed to be eradicated by all means at their disposal.

Working-class women simply wanted to be prepared for all eventualities within their domestic sphere. When they were intent on preventing an unwanted pregnancy, it mattered little whether their period was simply delayed or whether they were definitely pregnant. This may also explain the paradox of why so many interrogated women adopted the language of the very authorities who were out to prosecute and punish them: the criminal police, the medical experts and the prosecutors and judges. Just as the female talk about pregnancy and termination often appears contradictory, the experience of being overdue with their monthly period must have appeared baffling and complex to many women themselves. As Alf Lüdtke has put it in a different context, every experience consists of a jumble of different ingredients which are wholly consciously steered to the advantage of the person herself, but which are also nourished by unconscious fears and fantasies, by symbols and cultural patterns of perception.[136] My attempt to excavate a woman's voice in the judicial statements resulted in such a 'jumble' of perceptions, images and figures of speech. The different ways of talking and the different experiences of a late menstruation and its restoration should not necessarily, however, always be interpreted as contradictions but rather as a coexistence, a patchwork quilt of various expressions and perceptions: whether a delay of the monthly blood was read as a sign of a blocked period or an early pregnancy depended on the emotional state, the socioeconomic circumstances and the particular situation a woman found herself in and it could change according to mood and calculation. For this the euphemisms of the commercial terminology were as useful as the scientific concepts of doctors or the legal language of the police or the courts.

◈ Chapter 6 ◈

ABORTION AS AN EVERYDAY EXPERIENCE IN VILLAGE LIFE: A CASE STUDY FROM HESSE

On 19 August 1924, the 26-year-old decorator Willy Stammer gave the following statement to the examining magistrate of the court of lay assessors at the Landgericht Limburg, Hesse:

> In 1921 I had a relationship with Hedwig Zeiger which also involved sex. One day that summer ... Zeiger told me that her period was late; I had no money and no accommodation of my own. So I arranged for Zeiger to have the matter removed by Frau Kastner. I took Zeiger to Nauheim to the Kastners where we met the couple. Frau Kastner proceeded to inject into Zeiger's vagina a liquid which she had taken from a little flask. Zeiger meanwhile lay on the table. To begin with Kastner inserted a tube into her vagina and inserted the syringe through this tube. After the douching Zeiger had some pain, she had to sit on a chair for a while. But then we walked back together to Dauborn. Frau Kastner demanded from me 20 or 25 Marks; I paid this sum in several instalments. During the operation I stood in the room. Whether Herr Kastner was present I cannot remember. Next day Zeiger told me that her period had returned and that the bleeding was normal just like with a period.[1]

Hedwig, Willy Stammer's then girlfriend, was twenty-one at the time and a domestic servant. Her own statement concurred largely with Willy's but she added that he and Herr Kastner had stood next to the table on which the operation had taken place.[2]

In what the press called a 'monster case', Willy and Hedwig were just two of ninety-three defendants tried in court in December 1924 for criminal abortion. Apart from the abortionist, Frau Hermine Kastner and her accomplice, her husband Adolf, fifty-four women and thirty-seven husbands or lovers faced charges: the women for having undergone an abortion, the men for aiding and abetting them. Impressive as this array of accused is, the real number of women who underwent an abortion performed by the Kastners was likely to have been larger still, since it was more than likely that not all abortions came to the notice of the authorities. The trial took place in Limburg in the Prussian province of Hesse-Nassau, 45 km north of Frankfurt; the aborting women, however, resided in seventeen villages to the south and southeast of Limburg, the so-called *Limburger Becken* (Limburg basin).

Willy Stammer lived in Dauborn, one of the larger and better-off communities which was also the home of the majority of the aborting women (altogether twenty-one). It was a sign of the intricate network of kin and work relationships within these villages that Stammer had been actively involved not just in organizing the abortion for his girlfriend described above but also of his subsequent girlfriend and, as a mediator, for two other women of his acquaintance and not his girlfriends. In April 1923 he had engaged the services of Frau Kastner for 23-year-old Wilhelmine, his new love. When she became pregnant for a second time they married, but she later miscarried by 'falling twice'. Later in 1923 Willy turned to Frau Kastner again, this time to help the two other women: in the summer his sister and in December to assist the wife of a Dauborn farmer for whom Willy 'slaughtered'. Frau Kastner's intervention with Hedwig, Wilhelmine, his sister and the farmer's wife had been entirely successful. Kastner always followed the same procedure, administering a douche of boiled water or alum and keeping to a fairly strict hygienic regime. Her other patients were even more satisfied than Hedwig had been, feeling no pain at all after the operation and also finding that their periods had already returned the next day or soon after. Indeed Frau Kastner's record was impressive since none of the forty-seven abortions she was charged with had caused a single death and only two women had suffered minor side-effects. Their exemplary track record notwithstanding, the Kastners' sentence proved to be severe. Hermine Kastner, as the chief defendant, received three years' penal servitude with five years' loss of civil rights for 'performing abortions for monetary gain' in forty-seven cases; her husband, as her accomplice, received three years' gaol with three years' loss of civil rights. Since the Kastners were only thirty-seven years old with four children ranging in age from nine to seventeen, their gaol sentence was obviously a tragedy for the whole family, the more so since both Hermine and Adolf had been in remand prison for many weeks before the trial which also cost Adolf his job.

In contrast to its strict treatment of the abortionists the court admitted mitigating circumstances for all the aborting women by granting them the benefit of the doubt as to whether they had actually been pregnant at the time of their operation. As the judge explained, this was because all Frau Kastner's clients without exception had sought her help at a very early stage in their menstrual cycle when 'even a physician can hardly diagnose with any degree of certainty whether a conception has taken place'. Consequently these female defendants were tried for 'attempted abortion', a definition which was not explicitly contained in the abortion law but was recognized by courts in practice and by precedent and subsequently recognized explicitly as an offence when the law was amended in 1926. Other mitigating circumstances were also taken into account: single women were treated more leniently if circumstances ruled out a marriage and because of the social stigma of a child born out of wedlock. Married women were granted mitigating circumstances if they already had a large number of children. The judge also recognized the negative influence of 'general economic hardship, the difficult employment and economic situation', since 'by far the greatest majority of cases had occurred during the time of severe inflation', the 'demoralization after the war and the postwar period' and 'the ready availability and cheap opportunity' of an abortion service which had 'severely curtailed the inhibition for this crime'.[3]

Such sympathy with the lot of these women and men notwithstanding, the great majority of the defendants were found guilty and in accordance with the unreformed law the sentences were substantial. In particular, husbands and lovers who had arranged abortions for their wives or girlfriends were punished severely. For example, Willy Stammer received one year, six months' imprisonment for aiding and abetting abortion on four counts; his sister's husband and the Dauborn farmer eight months' and nine months' imprisonment respectively. The aborting women, though punished more leniently, still received prison terms ranging from four (for single women) to six months' gaol (for married women). Had they been tried after the law was amended in May 1926 they might well have come out with very negligible prison terms or even just a small fine.

The sentences caused an outcry among the community and everyone who had been convicted lodged an appeal. Most did so through a lawyer, but others had relatives write on their behalf and some wrote their own letters. The majority of the appeals secured commuted sentences. In the letters there were clear signs of anger and dismay felt at the way the court had decided the fate of the defendants. Furthermore, the widespread practice of abortion amongst the seventeen villages, blatantly contravening §§218, 219, was evidence of disrespect of the abortion law; but maybe the clearest sign of this nonchalant attitude on the part of the villagers was that the Kastners' abortion practice had been protected by a veil of silence for nearly four years, something which did not go unnoticed by the judge: 'Despite the fact that [Frau Kastner's activities] were an open secret in the named [seventeen] villages and beyond, the appropriate law enforcement agencies did not know about them because there was no denouncement at first.'[4]

A close analysis of the Limburg case reveals that a number of previous assumptions of attitudes to and the practice of abortion need revising, for example the belief expressed by commentators at the time and upheld by most historians, that attitudes and prevalence differed between town and countryside; according to women's marital status, age and class; according to religious denomination; between academic and lay medicine; and last but by no means least, according to gender. The Limburg trial shows that in the

1920s large-scale abortion was by no means confined to German cities but was rife in the countryside, too. It also proves that every type of woman sought help from lay abortionists, not only the poor and the unmarried. The Kastners' clientele was remarkably heterogeneous, comprising women both married and single, old and young, rich and poor.

It also shows a blurring of denominational differences: both Protestants and Catholics seemed to have had few scruples in employing abortion as an important, if not the most important, method of fertility control. It is relatively easy to recognize the denominational influence because of the historic demarcation between Catholic and Protestant villages. Niederbrechen, Oberbrechen and Werschau had remained Roman Catholic after the Reformation while other villages like Dauborn, Nauheim, Kirheim, Heringen and Neesbach had become Protestant. This clear-cut division had been maintained, albeit with a sprinkling of the other denomination and a very small number of Jewish inhabitants. This meant that Protestant and Catholic religious cultures existed separately although in close proximity to each other, enabling the historian to look for possible differences. In fact, this case study does not reveal any clear difference in attitude: there was no indication that Protestants were less inhibited than Catholics in practising abortion nor did the latter display any sense of moral outrage at aborting women or remorse about their own abortions; this was despite the fact that abortion continued to be considered murder in Roman Catholic doctrine.

The contemporary official opinion that only academic medicine could guarantee safe terminations is strikingly contradicted by Frau Kastner's remarkable medical successes. As the depositions in this trial show, lay abortionists – even if, like Frau Kastner, they lacked any conventional medical training – could be a safe option and, as Chapters 3 and 4 have demonstrated, possibly even outperform inexperienced doctors.

Lastly, this case from Hesse shows very clearly that the practice of illegal abortions was not part of a separate female culture of reproduction occurring without reference to men, as Angus McLaren has suggested for earlier centuries.[5] On the contrary, the Limburg trial reveals how much men were involved in the process, either by close emotional and practical cooperation with women or by imposing their will on the situation. It was relatively rare that women decided to go it alone without calling on the support of their male partner; men however, sometimes arranged an abortion unilaterally and against the wishes of the woman. This was when they tried to defend their honour and avert being trapped into an undesirable marriage. But generally decisions were taken together and aborting women could count on the help of their boyfriends/husbands in negotiating the day, time and cost of the operation, which often made a considerable claim on their time and energy. Men would usually accompany their women to the appointed place and remain in attendance giving moral and practical support. Since it was Frau Kastner's habit to operate at night – presumably to avoid detection and to have the support of her own husband available – men would shine the torch to help her insert the syringe with precision, especially when Herr Kastner was unavailable. Consequently men had no difficulty describing the manner of the abortion in great detail and the reaction of their wives or sweethearts; they knew whether they had been frightened, felt pain and whether their 'period blood' had returned and how this manifested itself.

The same gender cooperation was also manifest in the Kastners' partnership. Hermine Kastner could usually count on her husband to accompany her on the way to her clients on a Sunday evening because he did not want her to walk there and back alone; but Adolf's role extended to preparing for the operation by boiling instruments and providing water for her to wash her hands. During the operation he would hold the torch for her and sometimes he held the patient's head to calm her. He also acted as her accountant, negotiating the fee and collecting money in advance or outstanding sums when poorer clients paid in instalments.

Rural communities in decline

The economic situation of the seventeen villages involved in the abortion trial provides a good indication of the breakdown of boundaries, in the way rural/urban life and agricultural/industrial work was increasingly interlinked. In the 1920s the undulating countryside of the Golden Valley and the villages in the wooded southwest of Limburg, famous for its natural beauty, its fruit production and its ancient history, may have appeared like a perfect rural idyll. This was, however, misleading. They could only survive by increasingly deploying labour to the industrial centres which came within reach when the railway network expanded at the end of the nineteenth century. While traditional agricultural life appeared to continue undisturbed in these ancient communities, its survival hung in the balance because of the decline of the rural economy.

The villages in question are part of the *Unterlahnkreis* spreading between Limburg in the northwest and the Taunus hills in the northeast to the margins of the industrial centres of Frankfurt in the southeast and Wiesbaden to the southwest. In the nineteenth century these villages belonged administratively to the electoral Duchy of Hesse founded in 1815. In 1866 after the Austro-Prussian War the duchy was annexed by Prussia because it had sided with the losing Austrians. From then on it became part of the newly founded Prussian province of Hesse-Nassau. Many of the villages dated as far back as, in the case of Oberbrechen, the eighth century and consisted of attractive half-timbered houses with slate roofs.[6] Farmhouses were renowned for their large inner courtyards reached through imposing three-metre-high carved double gates. Round the courtyard were

Cultures of Abortion in Weimar Germany

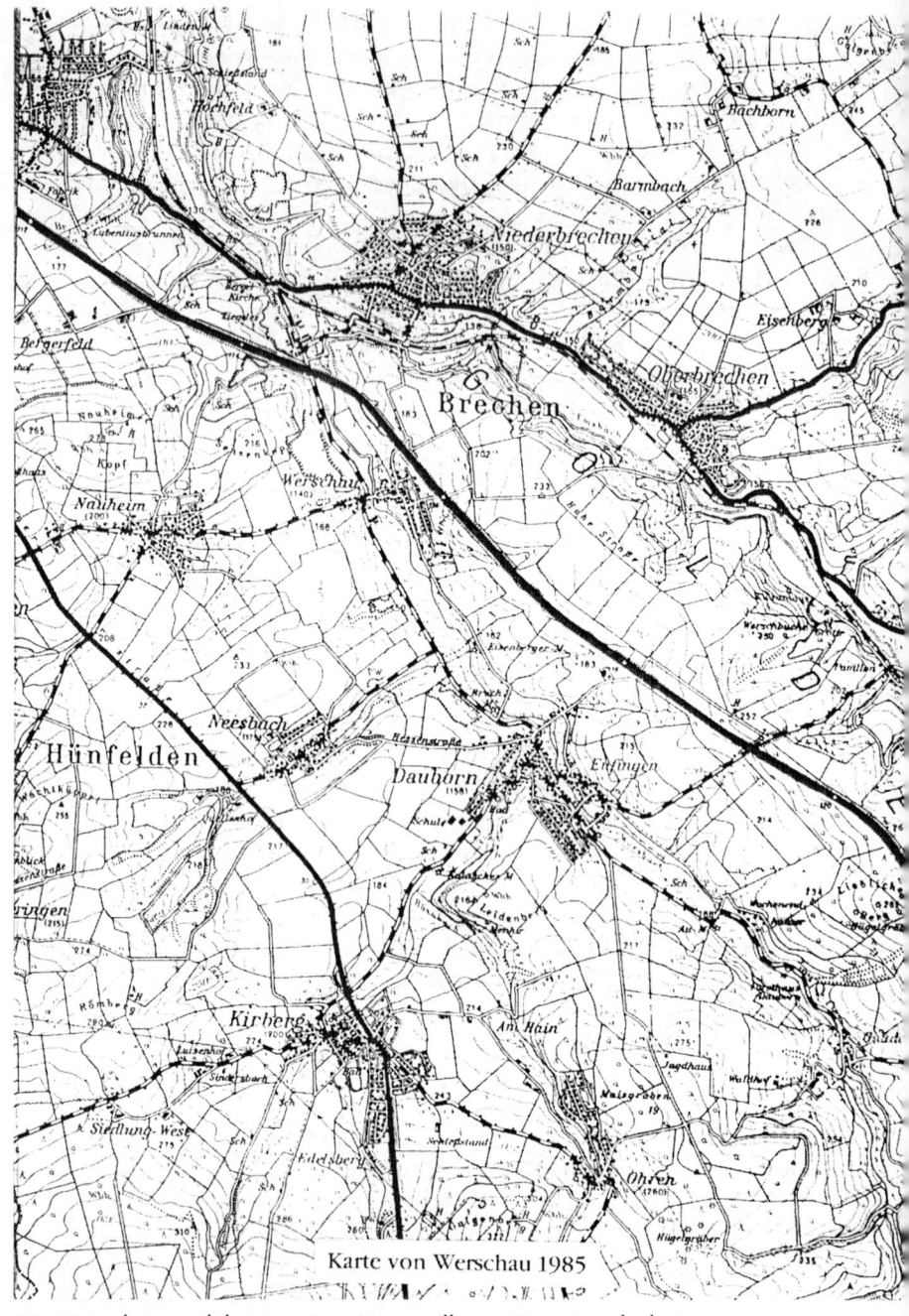

Karte von Werschau 1985

12. Map of some of the seventeen Hesse villages. From top clockwise: Niederbrechen, Oberbrechen, Dauborn, Kirberg, Neesbach, Nauheim, Werschau. Limburg is to the north west along the railway.

13. Timbered buildings in Nauheim as it is today

14. Oberbrechen seen from a field above the village

galleried passages used for drying fruit, vegetables or clothes. Villagers were proud of their history, as testified by the numerous *Heimatverbände* (heritage associations), *Heimatfeste* (local festivals), *Verschönerungsvereine* (societies for the improvement of local amenities), and a number of vocational and art associations like *Schweinezuchtvereine* (associations of pig farmers), *Turnvereine* (gym clubs), *Gesangvereine* (choral societies). The socioeconomic structure was determined by the topographical features – gently undulating land, fertile clay soil good for growing wheat, rye, oats, root crops, fruit, even a quantity of wine sold in the great towns of the Rhine, Main and the Ruhr area. There was also a fair amount of woodland, which afforded the villagers the necessary firewood and building materials.[7] Villages situated near rivers, such as Niederbrechen and Oberbrechen on the Emsbach or Dauborn and Werschau on the Wörsbach, possessed a number of important mills. A significant income in the 1920s was still derived from agriculture and farming formed the basis of the villagers' self-perception. This was despite the fact that since the turn of the twentieth century the majority could no longer make a living from it and had to rely increasingly on industry in the larger conurbations to the south or the northwest, hence the increasing interrelationship between agriculture and industry.

But why did agriculture decline? The most important reason was *Realteilung*, the law of heredity introduced by Napoleon decreeing that estates be divided equally between all heirs, leading to the division of land into ever-smaller plots. As a result most farmers had far too little arable or grazing land to be profitable. Large-scale farming became so rare that a Dauborn farmer who owned 22 *Morgen* (c.17 hectares) of land, certainly not a huge amount, 'belonged' in the eyes of his peers 'to the wealthy farmers' in the area.[8] After the rationalization of land distribution in 1925 the average farm size comprised only 25 acres (c.10 hectares) arable land and 10 acres (c.4 hectares) grazing land but it could not stop the decline of farming. For example, in 1900 Niederbrechen still had ninety farms which were all family-run and -owned but by 1925 the number had shrunk to eighty-one of which only sixty-nine had more than 6.25 hectares, the rest considerably less.[9] Elsewhere the story was similar.[10]

There were numerous schemes to halt the trend, such as the increasing practice of family limitation, to prevent the division of the land, or the attempt to join together various pieces of land. For the latter farmers sought to buy land from their siblings or acquire it through an unashamedly commercial marriage policy: the preference was to marry a relative who could bring back bits of inherited land.[11] In Protestant Ohren, for example, a village 5 km south of Nauheim, a noticeable reduction in the recorded number of schoolchildren would suggest the adoption of birth control: in 1910, 389 villagers had eighty-six children of school age, but in 1925 with a more or less stable population (382) the number of schoolchildren had more than halved (to only thirty-six).[12] Catholic villages like Werschau displayed the same trend: here a

Abortion in Village Life: Case Study from Hesse

15. Werschau seen with a donkey in the foreground

declining birth rate was indicated by the fact that a rise in the number of households (from eighty-five in 1910 to ninety-five by 1925) had nevertheless resulted in a decrease of the total population from 414 to 411.[13]

The economic downward trend could be countered by some villages like Dauborn, (and to some extent Kirberg), which possessed an important source of extra income from distilling spirits out of fruit and rye with added aniseed water. Nearly all landholders had the licence to distil. Before the First World War there were around 100 distillers in operation and they produced and sold nearly 1 million litres of drinkable spirit, with thirty-five per cent alcohol. The residue from spirit making, called *Maische* or *Schlempe*, was an additional bonus as it was fed to the cattle, which produced richer milk, and it also fattened oxen and pigs. Several distillers apparently became millionaires, but their fortunes dwindled during the war when the copper containers used for distilling were requisitioned. The inflation of the German currency which started during the war also hit distillers very hard and they lost most of their money.[14]

With a dwindling number of middle-sized farmers, most of the land was owned and worked by smallholders. In general they owned less than 2 hectares (just under 5 acres) and they had to rely on odd jobs to see them through.[15] Typically, Werschau had 420 inhabitants consisting of thirty farmers, twenty-two men employed in the building trade such as bricklayers, joiners, cabinet makers, decorators etc., three publicans, two each of grocers, tailors, shoemakers, bakers, one smith, one wheelwright, five pensioners, one labourer.[16] In Dauborn there was the same pattern. A great many carpenters, shoemakers, tailors, coopers and cartwrights worked generally in one-man outfits which did not provide enough income for an independent existence and necessitated a little agriculture on the side. The proportionally large number of shoemakers in Dauborn can be explained by the fact that there were 250–300 farmhands and maids who annually received hand-made shoes as part of their wages and who also had these repaired in the village.[17]

The listing of rural trades in the local address book or the depositions, however, gives a misleading impression. Many, if not most, of these craftsmen had become industrial workers, often employed as unskilled labourers working outside the area, and were no longer able to pursue their trade within the village community. Since the turn of the last century the large number of construction workers among the villagers depended on employment in the Low Countries or the industrialized Rhine and Ruhr.[18] In 1900, for example, Oberbrechen listed 117 assorted decorators, joiners, plasterers and bricklayers etc. who often spent ten to eleven months away from home 'at great cost to family life'.[19] But increasingly the Unterlahn communities became closely connected to the industrial centres in the south, especially to the chemical giant Höchst, in the town of Höchst, near Frankfurt am Main. This was made possible when the railway linking Limburg with Frankfurt was built in the 1870s.[20] Originally this was single-track only; a second track was built in

16. Oxcart in Dauborn, 1936

1921 which was later to be complemented by another one connecting Limburg and Wiesbaden.[21] The station in Niederbrechen built in the 1870s served all the surrounding villages like Nauheim, Werschau, Dauborn and Neesbach, provided railways users had a bicycle or could make use of the postal van or a friendly farmer's ox cart. There were obviously enough commuters to warrant the building of a large waiting room and a large shed for bicycles.[22]

Adolf Kastner, the husband of the abortionist Hermine, too, had obtained a position as a joiner not just outside his home village Nauheim but in Höchst, although he had a very small holding in Nauheim. He was designated as a 'joiner' but his weekly wage slip of 138.61 RM in July 1924 suggests that he received the wages of an unskilled worker.[23] The chemical concern Höchst was one of the biggest employers in the region and its workforce was drawn to a large extent from outlying areas, within a travelling distance of well over an hour, especially from the northwest, where Nauheim and the other villages covered by the abortion trial were situated.[24] Adolf Kastner's journey to work involved a 5 km ride to the station and a roughly 90-minute rail journey to Höchst. This was inconvenient, time-consuming and too expensive for him to return home every day; therefore, like many of his colleagues who lived in the villages discussed in this case study, he stayed in lodgings near work during the week. Adolf's absence left Hermine to look after her four children and the smallholding on her own. It also explains why Hermine preferred to perform abortions on a Sunday evening when her husband was at hand. But he also helped the business from his workplace by recruiting potential customers through his colleagues.

Female communication networks

Women, too, took to the railways occasionally. Hermine Kastner, for example, visited her husband fairly regularly in Höchst and she was unlikely to have been the only wife to do so. She also travelled the 6 km distance to Limburg, the capital of the region. It was there that she bought abortifacients, syringes and a speculum. However, on the whole women tended to stay rooted in village life, caring for their families, the household, the plot of land and their animals.[25] The absence of so many men might well have engendered tension in family life but it also increased female power: it was up to women to make decisions about the running of the home, take charge of their everyday life, maintain social contacts and run a business, as Frau Kastner did. A preponderance of women increased their reliance on each other through a network of self-help, especially in areas of reproduction. An informal exchange of information concerning sexuality and family limitation, even if this is usually pejoratively called 'gossip', had important bearings on the quality of women's lives. Women kept up to date with village 'gossip' through a network of communication built round kinship and neighbourly contact. Since most people remained in the village where they were born or, even if women moved upon marriage, they moved within a relatively small radius to a neighbouring village, such ties remained strong throughout life. Adolf Kastner was untypical in that he moved to his wife's birthplace in Nauheim; but Nauheim was only just over 3 km removed from his birthplace of Dauborn. Hermine Kastner thus remained close to her family and friends from childhood. Her younger sister Emilie, too, continued to reside in Nauheim after her marriage and although her brother Karl had moved to Hofen, his wife's village, at a distance of 10 km further away than many of the other seventeen villages in the trial, he was still within relatively easy reach. Others, like Adolf Kastner's colleague in Höchst, Edmund Blaser, continued to live in Dauborn, where he was born; he married a woman who was also from Dauborn so that his relationship with kin and neighbours continued uninterrupted even after he found work at Höchst.

The female communication network was also enhanced by women's daily habits and routine chores. The layout of the topography, villages and farms facilitated such contacts between women. For example, Dauborn and Kirberg possessed many wells still in good working order today; some of these were so-called *Laufbrunnen* with continuously running water fed through wooden pipes by a spring located outside the village wall; others were *Schöpfbrunnen* with standing water where women dipped their bucket in to take water home. Many houses in the early 1920s had no running water and wells obviously constituted an important daily meeting place for women. In Nauheim no wells survive and it is possible that there were either very few or even none. Hermine Kastner, who needed to go elsewhere for water, in fact relied on her immediate neighbours. Other simple tasks, such as sweeping outside the house or fetching bread from the village baker afforded other opportunities to meet neighbours and indulge in 'gossip'. Frequent interaction between women of different generations and marital status meant that worries about late periods could be voiced in passing and vital information, like how best to bring them on, could be exchanged. The depositions in the trial are evidence of the ease with which the name and address of Hermine Kastner as a reliable abortionist was obtained and passed on.

Word-of-mouth recommendation of Frau Kastner worked smoothly within a village community, but how did this spread to the other sixteen villages from which Frau Kastner drew her clients? The depositions reveal frequent visits by Frau Kastner to other villages and visits by inhabitants from neighbouring villages to Nauheim where she lived. Such movement between communities was stimulated by simple errands to collect or deliver fruit or other goods or by visits to friends and family. Since very few people owned a car and there was no bus service in the area, the most popular way to move about was on foot or, in the case of the younger generation, by bicycle. The fastest means to get from place to place was along the many paths between fields linking neighbouring villages, which were kept open by the local authorities.[26] The mode of walking or cycling facilitated easy communication between passers-by or provided an easy opportunity for assignations whose intimate nature demanded that they appeared to have come about by chance. The depositions show that many a potential customer did indeed 'happen' upon Frau Kastner as she walked between her home and some other village. For example, Auguste Stahl, the wife of a tailor from Werschau, said she had met Hermine Kastner 'occasionally on the path from Neesbach to Werschau'. In January 1924, when times were still hard after the hyper-inflation and her husband was out of work, Stahl feared she was pregnant with a second child. She set out in search of Frau Kastner and duly met her on the path from Nauheim to Werschau, where she was able to settle all the necessary details for a termination. Soon afterwards she used the same strategy to arrange an abortion for one of her friends.[27] The Kirberg butcher, Richard Band, too, set out to find Frau Kastner on one of these field paths when he and his fiancée needed her help. He knew Frau Kastner from sight and met her one day 'by chance on the path from Dauborn to Werschau'.[28]

Particularly when the corn stood high, these paths were secluded and they offered a relatively safe space to negotiate abortion business. They were also the preferred route to travel to the appointed place of the operation. Richard Band and his fiancée were just one of many who cycled along the path the 4 km from Kirberg to Frau Kastner's home in Nauheim where the douche was administered. Immediately afterwards they cycled back home the same way when 'bleeding occurred'.[29] And Willy Stammer walked with his girlfriend Hedwig the 3.5 km along the path to the Kastners in Nauheim and back again from Dauborn where they both worked and lived. Presumably he repeated this trip when he accompanied his future wife to Nauheim for the same purpose. The Dauborn baker Albert Grau and his wife Elise followed this example, also walking back home immediately after the intervention.[30] If, as happened occasionally, Frau Kastner operated in her client's home she would also always walk and she did so, for obvious reasons, 'always ... in the evening'.[31]

Given the popularity of this personal method of communication and travel it is not surprising to learn (see Table 6.1) that the geographical distribution of Frau Kastner's clients is in direct proportion to (a) the size of their village and (b) its distance from the Kastners' home in Nauheim. For example, by far the largest cluster of defendants in the Limburg trial lived in Dauborn, which was not only relatively large but also within easy walking distance from Nauheim. Neesbach and Werschau, in third and fifth place resepctively in the hierarchy of number of defendants, were closer but also much smaller than Dauborn. Naturally, the villages furthest from Nauheim, like Flacht, Kaltenholzhausen and Wolfenhausen mustered only one defendant each. Distance obviously mattered for getting to the Kastners but also for word of mouth to travel about their practice and skill. Beuerbach is an exception. It was more than twice the distance from Nauheim than Dauborn and had relatively few inhabitants, yet it is represented by three defendants: two aborting women and the husband of one of them as an accomplice. This was possibly a consequence of a chance meeting, an existing link between the Kastners or a satisfied customer in this village and somebody who had heard about this case. (See Plate 12 for a map of the area.)

Table 6.1 The seventeen villages in order of number of defendants in the trial (The distance between Nauheim and the villages is based on the field paths, except when villages were too far to be reached on foot)

1.	**Dauborn,** *39 defendants* (22 aborting women, 17 husbands/boyfriends plus 1 aborting woman born here but living in Düsseldorf); c.3.5 km SE; birthplace of Adolf Kastner; 1,412 inh. (1,380 Prot., 21 Jews, 11 Cath.), Protestant vicar.
2.	**Nauheim** (the Kastners' place of residence), *15 defendants* (9 aborting women, 6 husbands); 574 inh. (572 Prot., 2 Cath.).
3.	**Neesbach,** *9 defendants* (4 aborting women, 2 husbands, 3 boyfriends/seducers); 2 km S; 451 inh. (all Prot.).
4.	**Kirberg,** *5 defendants* (3 aborting women, 1 husband, 1 boyfriend); c.4 km S; 1,011 inh. (998 Prot., 8 Cath., 5 Jews); seat of area constabulary; Prot. vicar.
5.	**Werschau,** *4 defendants* (2 aborting women, 1 husband, 1 boyfriend, plus 1 boyfriend born there but now in Düsseldorf), 2 km E; 414 inh. (407 Cath., 7 Prot.); Cath. priest.

Abortion in Village Life: Case Study from Hesse

6.	**Beuerbach**, 3 *defendants* (2 aborting women, 1 husband) c.9 km S; 453 inh. (all Prot.).
7.	**Niederbrechen**, 3 *defendants* (1 aborting woman, 2 boyfriends) c.4.5 km NE; 2,138 inh. (2,120 Cath., 18 Prot.); railway station; Cath. priest.
8.	**Oberbrechen**, 2 *defendants* (1 aborting woman, 1 boyfriend); c.6 km E; 1,303 inh. (1,239 Cath., 43 Prot., 21 Jews); constabulary, Cath. priest.
9.	**Weyer**, 2 *defendants* (2 aborting women); c.7 km E; 806 inh. (781 Prot., 19 Jews, 8 Cath.).
10.	**Hahnstätten**, 2 *defendants* (2 aborting women); c.5 km SW; 1,251 inh. (1,200 Prot., 51 Cath.).
11.	**Heringen**, 2 *defendants* (1 aborting woman and her husband); c.3.5 km S; 680 inh. (all Protestant); Prot. vicar.
	The remaining villages had each a single woman defendant:
12.	**Flacht**, c.7km W; 697 inh. (660 Prot., 30 Jews, 7 Cath.).
13.	**Hofen**, nr. Dehrn, c.10km N; 275 inh. (270 Prot., 5 Cath.)
14.	**Kaltenholzhausen**, c.4km SW; 434 Prot.
15.	**Nied**, nr. Höchst, 8,553 inh. (4,150 Cath., 3,900 Prot., 3 Jews, 50 other Christians., 450 without religion).
16.	**Oberneisen**, c.4 km W; 615 inh. (610 Prot., 5 Cath.).
17.	**Wolfenhausen**, c.10 km E; 822 inh. (811 Prot., 5 Cath., 6 Jews).

Source: GSABD, Rep 84a, 17109, B1. 4–30, Bischöfliche Kanzlei, Limburg (ed.), *Schematismus der Diözese Limburg 1927* (Limburg, 1927).

Apart from geographical proximity, family and work relationship were likely to have played an important role in spreading Frau Kastner's net of customers. For example, Dauborn, where most defendants lived, was also the birthplace of Adolf Kastner and where Hermine had worked as a domestic servant before they married. Obviously, their relatives, friends and acquaintances there turned to them for help when they needed it. Indeed Hermine Kastner's career was launched when a member of her own family was in difficulty. Her very first case concerned her brother's future wife, Philippine, who lived some distance away, c.10 km north of Nauheim, in Hofen. Later on Hermine also assisted her sister Emilie and two of her cousins, Hermine Bauer and Emilie Lauter, all of whom lived in Nauheim, Hermine's birthplace and also her home after her marriage. Subsequent abortion business occurred as a result of family relations of satisfied customers. As we have seen at the beginning of this chapter, Willy Stammer recommended Hermine Kastner's services first to his sister and later also to his brother Otto, as well as to his workmate, the farmer from Dauborn whose wife needed help.

Neighbourhood contacts, too, played their part in Frau Kastner's enterprise. Frau Enkel, for example, who wanted to rid herself of her third pregnancy, knew Frau Kastner because 'she lived two houses on from us' and she 'visited our house every day' mainly 'to fetch water'. Frau Enkel was obviously satisfied because she in turn sent Hermine Kastner her cousin, Frieda Schild from Flacht. Frieda had come specially to Nauheim for this reason and the operation duly took place at the Enkels' house.[32] Luise Zeiger, too, benefited from being a neighbour of the abortionist. She lived opposite Frau Kastner and saw her daily. Luise was married to a day labourer-cum-nightwatchman with two children aged nine and eighteen. She was thirty-nine but her husband was already sixty. When she feared she was pregnant again she naturally turned to Hermine and soon found herself relieved on this account.[33] In many cases neighbourly advice proved to be vital; for example, Philippine Reuter, a housekeeper in her early twenties, was expecting a child by her employer, a young farmer, who refused to marry her. Philippine confided in her neighbour and was told, 'don't be so stupid, go to Nauheim to Frau Kastner!'[34]

It is possible to trace neighbourhood links among Frau Kastner's clients in Dauborn through the address book of 1928. Even allowing for the fact that a number of people might have moved between 1924 and 1928 (which was unlikely) and others were not registered because they were only renting temporary accommodation, the accumulation of defendants in certain roads is striking. Arbsenstraße is a good example: No. 5 belonged to the bricklayer August Buch and his wife; five houses on was the abode of the electrical engineer Edmund Blaser, a colleague of Herr Kastner; opposite him that of Alwin Krumm, a manual worker; the farmer and distiller Wilhelm Prasser and his wife lived in no. 23 and four houses up the road was the farm of Gustav Pust – all these were clients of Frau Kastner because their wives or mistresses underwent a termination. Laistrasse, a road characterized by much smaller houses, was where many other clients lived: the families of the baker Grau, the manual worker Paul Kachel and the butcher Johann Schepf. Round the corner lived the family of the carpenter Wilhelm Hanf in the Schulstrasse and next door to them the bricklayer Wilhelm Pust, and so on.[35]

Workplace contacts of Adolf Kastner, especially when they also shared train journeys to Höchst, also proved profitable for Hermine's abortion business. For example, Emilie Glau of Neesbach became a customer because her husband worked with Kastner. Sometimes Hermine made contact with Adolf's colleagues when she travelled to meet him in Höchst. In 1919 the mechanic Edmund Blaser had met her on such an occasion and she had recommended family limitation to him in the strongest possible terms in connection with his wife and sister.[36] Adolf's school friends were another good source for business. For example, Gustav Pust, a Dauborn farmer, had attended Adolf's class at primary school. Pust was married with three children but in 1922 got a farm maid from Beuerbach into trouble. When she apparently had 'threatened to harm herself' because her period was late, he arranged for Frau Kastner to give her a douche.[37]

Reproductive *Eigensinn*

How do we explain the persistently high incidence of abortion in this part of Hesse-Nassau during the four years from 1920 to 1924? The answer rests with structural long-term causes, more short-term causes, and personal reasons. Long-term economic developments associated with the particular stage of transition from industrialization to postindustrialization had damaged prospects in agriculture all over Germany but had a particularly marked effect on the communities in and around the Golden Valley, marginalized as they were in the now largely urbanized industrial economy of the area.

Among the short-term causes was the dislocation suffered in the aftermath of the First World War; the correlation between this period and the date when Frau Kastner started her abortion career is surely evidence of this. The war had not only cost many villagers their health or life but it had brought a significant decline in standards of living; the after-effects of the blockade on health in general and nutrition in particular were noticeable in rural communities.[38] In 1920 Oberbrechen, for example, founded a committee for food distribution.[39] One chronicle describes the desperate food situation during the war:

> The population sought to improve the food situation by keeping pigs, goats and hares, to grow more rape, by extracting oil from beech nuts, and by making use of every suitable spot possible for growing things. The situation in the winter of 1916/17 was particularly threatening. In these months it was so cold that the Elbbach was covered with a thick sheet of ice for five weeks and in many cellars the stored potatoes froze. People had to make do with swedes as their staple food.[40]

Food rationing introduced during the war remained in place after it. Food remained scarce, as was coal, electricity, gas and housing.

Frau Kastner's activity also coincided precisely with the period of the German inflation and, in 1923, hyper-inflation, leaving a legacy of economic insecurity and hardship for everyone in Germany.[41] Villagers took to barter so that eggs, grain or alcohol replaced money. This is also how Frau Kastner was remunerated for her services. With the total cost of living index rising fast during 1920 to 1922 and reaching fantastical heights during 1923, even rural populations could not escape. In October 1923 in Runikel, east of Limburg, a pound of butter cost six million Marks, whereas in 1916/17 after only two years of the wartime inflation it had still only cost 20 Marks.[42] In Oberbrechen in October of 1920 the price of potatoes was fixed at 20 Marks a ton whereas 'in normal times' this was no more than 2–4 Marks. In February 1921 and again in January 1922 the price of firewood was fixed, too, but during this time it had risen almost 200 per cent. In March 1923 the parish councillors of

Oberbrechen felt themselves compelled to organize a collection for the poor of the community. In Werschau in August 1924, in the immediate aftermath of hyper-inflation and stabilization of the currency the 'great majority of the working population was unemployed'.[43] The depositions in the Limburg trial give a vivid picture of individual and family livelihoods destroyed by the inflation: it had prevented countless marriages, delayed the starting of families and left many a couple in despair when a further child was on the way and they did not know how to feed another mouth.[44] Moreover, in July 1923 Limburg and its surroundings were occupied by French troops, thus draining community resources still further; in August 1923 French soldiers had also occupied Oberbrechen and Dauborn (the latter occupied mainly by Moroccans). This was greeted with passive resistance by the inhabitants, with the result that many workers were expelled from the area and their families were forced to move to the unoccupied area of the Oberlahnkreis.[45]

There was another cultural reason why so many local men and women deliberately flouted §218. The economic interrelationship between town and countryside discussed above resulted in the imposition of the norms of civil society onto village life; for example, medical, political, moral and juridical discourse developed on a national level entered village talk through newspapers, journals, books, radio and films; it was also mediated by members of the professional classes who lived in the villages, such as the doctor, the teacher, the priest and the lawyer. In addition, employees in Höchst and other industrial concerns were increasingly influenced by new ideas as they were subject to union and factory rules, subscribed to factory insurance and were protected by factory inspectors.[46] Herr Kastner, for example, received industrial health insurance through his job at Höchst.

But the Limburg trial shows how the local residents had regained what in German historiography is called their *Eigensinn*, an obstinacy or determination to do it their own way and if necessary go against the ways of the state when this appeared hostile. Wolfgang Kaschuba and Carola Lipp introduced the concept of 'life in two worlds' (1982). They argued that men forced to live an *arbeiterbäuerliche Doppelexistenz*, a kind of double life as both industrial and also agricultural workers, were confronted with the contradictionary lifestyles of 'traditional' village life and 'modern' industrial work. Kaschuba and Lipp affirmed that this did not mean that the traditional was simply replaced by the modern, rather that both worlds reinforced each other: industrial employment helped maintain agricultural smallholdings which could secure a household in times of crisis, and the communal ties within villages acted as a counterbalance to the sense of alienation in industry. Villagers, it is claimed, developed an *Eigensinn* which was not, Kaschuba and Lipp stressed, a passive adherence to tradition but an active attempt to adapt to changing attractions and demands of modern industrial life. But it was also a stubbornness to retain what German anthropologists have called 'their symbolic autonomy' over the material order imposed on them from outside.[47]

The display of a certain resistance to the dominant ideology implied that abortion, especially if it was performed on demand by a lay practitioner, was an expression of *Eigensinn*. The penal law and the Church may have called abortion 'murder of nascent life' but to the communities of the Limburger basin, negotiating between 'traditional' interests and outside demands, the act of bringing on a late period or terminating an unwanted pregnancy was simply a practical way to retain a measure of control over their precarious lives, balancing a healthy sex life with the need to adapt family size to the available resources. Finally, an almost complete absence of references to contraception in the trial proceedings and the individual depositions suggests that the preference of abortion over conception control was another form of rebellion. While in the climate of crisis during the early years of the Republic artificial contraception had slowly become acceptable in official circles, abortion as a means of family limitation had officially remained tainted by danger, illegality and promiscuity.[48] Yet, for country women of either Catholic or Protestant creed, abortion was not only a fall-back strategy when all else had failed but offered exactly the kind of flexibility they required in their uncertain lives: it offered a solution to a problem when it manifested itself without the need to buy expensive contraceptives on a regular basis or having to rely on men's cooperation at times when this might not have been guaranteed.

Rebellious women and men

Female defendants in the Limburg trial were, it seemed, rebellious when it came to flouting criminal law and state authority; they were also very much in charge of their bodies. It is striking how very early Frau Kastner's clients sought her help.[49] They were obviously acutely aware of their menstrual cycle and recognized the first signs of pregnancy. In most cases their menses were only one or two weeks late but sometimes help was sought after only three days! Such haste shows not only alertness to physical change but also a remarkable resolve to stay on top of their fertility and their life. Many women and men also displayed considerable chutzpah in defending their actions against anybody who questioned them, as we will see below. In his letter of appeal against the harsh punishment dealt out by the assize court, the lawyer acting on behalf of a large number of the defendants sought to excuse his clients' actions by transferring all blame to the abortionist who, he said, made the operation readily available:

> Here in the countryside was an opportunity, of which the rural population normally is ignorant. If Frau Kastner had not been known as an abortionist, then none of these men and women would have appeared in front of a judge. None of them would have dreamt of turning to a colleague of Frau Kastner or of attending an unscrupulous doctor in a city.[50]

This argument was no doubt the correct line for a lawyer to take, seeking to secure a reduction in sentence for his clients; but the notion of innocent rural folks led astray by a corrupt operator does not ring true. While Frau Kastner did go round proselytizing for birth control,[51] local women and men who availed themselves of the Kastners' services exemplified the kind of *Eigensinn* mentioned above, and their decision to ignore religious dogma and criminal law could and should be read as a rebellion against the bourgeois state.

Eigensinn was also displayed in the determination of the majority of defendants to revise their sentence. Of the eighty-seven convicted in Limburg in December 1924, sixty-eight (or 78 per cent) appealed against their sentences – an impressive proportion, especially considering that one woman had died in the meantime (not related to her abortion) and another had become ill and her appeal was heard separately.[52] While the main defendant, Hermine Kastner as the commercial abortionist, failed to have her sentence reduced and in fact had it increased (from five years, six months' gaol to three years' penal servitude with solitary confinement and hard labour), the aborting women and their accomplices were much more successful. Of the sixty-eight appeals fifty-four (or 79 per cent) succeeded in having their sentence commuted and some were even acquitted.[53] There were hardly any signs of humility or remorse. Lawyers' letters or those written by individual defendants to the appeal court displayed considerable indignation and a determination to avoid any kind of penalty – either because they claimed that they never had an abortion or that the operation had been entirely justified.[54] One woman from Oberbrechen complained bitterly that she was arrested and imprisoned on remand for a whole week although 'entirely innocent'. She claimed her doctor could easily have clarified the misunderstanding and she demanded compensation.[55] Other women admitted to an abortion but either considered it a very minor offence or found nothing wrong with it. In a handwritten letter of appeal the wife of the Nauheim nightwatchman demanded a remission of punishment: 'My sentence [of two months' gaol] seems far too high in the light of the trivial nature of my offence.' The court had failed to take her many mitigating circumstances into account; she had terminated her pregnancy not for any selfish motives but because of hardship. She already had two children when in 1920 she suddenly feared she might be pregnant again. Her husband was twenty-one years her senior and had suffered from ill health throughout her marriage which had diminished his ability to hold down a proper job. Now he was suffering from stomach cancer and heart disease (indeed he died four years after the trial). She recounted how in 1920 in her worried state she had confided in her neighbour, Frau Kastner, whom she saw every day. The latter had consoled her and offered to syringe her; she had had no qualms about accepting this, certain that this was permissible. Even now she was convinced that she had in fact not been really pregnant since her monthly bleeding had returned after the syringing and proceeded as normal without any pain.[56]

Another woman, Ida Treib, pleaded for leniency on the grounds of having 'already too many children'. She recounted how she had given birth to nine children, of whom only five had survived. She was married to a labourer who was a war invalid and no longer able to undertake heavy work; this and the fact that they did not own 'a single plot of land' had left them poor and living in very cramped conditions. In 1921, 'during the expensive times', she found that her period was three days late. She had thought she could no longer conceive (she was already forty), she 'was near despair' with worry and sought solace from Frau Kastner who duly administered a douche.[57] Frau Treib's appeal was unsuccessful and she subsequently employed a lawyer to write again on her behalf.[58]

Many women also wrote appeals on behalf of their husbands or sons who had been convicted for aiding or abetting abortion. For example, the wife of a bricklayer, herself found guilty of abortion, wrote at least three times to the court to have her husband at least temporarily released; he was sorely needed because their daughter was seriously ill. When this was unsuccessful, she wrote again, pleading that he was indispensable because they had to 'thresh several more times'. She also mortgaged several plots of land as bail for her husband but apparently to no avail.[59] The mother of Willy Stammer, with whom this chapter began, appealed for her son's release on a number of grounds: poverty, her old age (she was sixty), having reared seven children and lost one son to the war effort. Her request was successful and Willy Stammer was duly released on 2 March 1925.[60]

In contrast to most women, men generally engaged lawyers to appeal for them, probably indicating men's easier access to money. Lawyers who defended male clients usually sought to place the blame on women. If male defendants were unmarried the blame would usually fall on their girlfriends; if married men were involved, Frau Kastner or a woman friend were held responsible. For example, the lawyer representing a young farmer from Kirberg insisted that his client had nothing to do with his girlfriend's abortion. He 'had simply told her he could not marry her', and she would have known this since 'she was only a maid'. This lawyer even took the Limburg judge to task:

> The fact that a young farmer from a well-to-do household does not marry the domestic servant is so normal that it is taken for granted by all maids. Only somebody who does not know the rural customs could have composed such a statement of reasons for the verdict. A seduction through deception is not applicable here. The judge enters territories here which simply do not accord with reality.[61]

Indeed, in September 1925 the appeal court reversed the original verdict and acquitted the farmer as well as five other men.[62] Another lawyer employed the tactic of character assassination of the aborting woman. He appealed on behalf of a Dauborn farmer convicted of aiding the abortion of his mistress.

The lawyer suggested she was untrustworthy and immoral. This was no doubt a strategy to deflect opprobrium from his client, who had entered into sexual relations with the maid of another farmer despite being a married man with three children. The lawyer claimed his client 'did not seduce Minna Baum. She had already lost her virginity and has had sex on several occasions. Amongst the young men she had the reputation as somebody "who is available". His client was forced to obtain Frau Kastner's services when Minna became pregnant because the maid threatened to drown herself.[63]

When the same lawyer appealed on behalf of a wealthy farmer and miller, Arthur Knaus, he transferred the blame from the aborting woman, because she was the farmer's wife, to the abortionist. The lawyer alleged that the abortion had been performed entirely on Frau Kastner's initiative and his client had never asked for it; he had simply mentioned his wife's condition to Frau Kastner in passing.[64]

The subversion of the state-imposed ban on abortion was not confined to a certain class or type of woman. Frau Kastner's clients comprised a cross-section of the whole community. Not only did they hail from seventeen different villages but also from a variety of social backgrounds, marital status, age groups and, as we have seen, religious beliefs. What bound them together were the difficult economic conditions and social upheaval after the war; but of course different women (and different men) had their own particular set of circumstances which led them to risk detection and imprisonment. The existence of a large family among the poor was always a prime reason to call in Frau Kastner once a new pregnancy was suspected and this, of course, related to older women. Ida Treib, mentioned above, was amongst the oldest of Hermine Kastner's customers, very poor and with five children to feed and clothe; for her it was essential to practise family limitation. Or take the Dauborn baker's wife with four children between the ages of one and seven. In 1921, at a time of rapid price rises and a declining business, a fifth child could not be countenanced.[65] Another Dauborn villager, Luise Schlachter, had as many as ten children to look after, ranging in age between eighteen months and eighteen years old. At the beginning of the First World War she had married a farmer and cartwright with three children. She was twenty-three and he forty-one. By 1923, still only aged thirty-one, she had borne him another seven children. In the spring of 1923, almost at the height of the inflation, she feared she was with child again and turned to Frau Kastner. The latter had apparently admonished her to intervene on five or six previous occasions. 'I should get rid of the thing [die Sache wegmachen], I should not be so stupid, rich farmers would never have so many children.'[66]

But younger women with fewer children also practised family limitation by means of abortion. Emilie Glau, for example, was only twenty-eight with two children when she had a termination. During the war, at the age of twenty-three she had married a blue-collar worker. He was employed by Höchst and was away from home during the week. Within five years she had borne him three children though her eldest had not survived. In 1919 when Emilie was expecting her second child Frau Kastner had also tried to intervene. 'She said we were stupid to go on making [sic!] children because we were poor, but I said I was glad because my first child had died.' In May 1924, however, when Emilie's period was late, she approached Frau Kastner again but was turned down unexpectedly. Frau Kastner had simply said, 'I will not do this any more.' In retrospect her refusal was hardly surprising since prosecution proceedings had started against her by then and by the end of the same month she was imprisoned on remand. Consequently Emilie had tried to induce her own miscarriage with a syringe she owned but she was unsuccessful and at the time of her police interview in August 1924 she was several months into her fourth pregnancy.[67]

While the poor showed all the signs of beginning to plan their families, wealthier families, usually farmers, had practised this for some time, no doubt because of the law of inheritance, the pressure of economic circumstances and possibly also because of women's aspirations for themselves and their children. Well-to-do women were quite likely to have used contraceptives but they also availed themselves of the services of Frau Kastner whenever an unwanted pregnancy occurred, often feigning health reasons. A good example is Pauline Hahn, wife of a Dauborn farmer who was considered to be well off on account of his 11 Morgen (roughly 9 acres) of land. Aged thirty-five, a full-time housewife with domestic help and with only one two-year old child, she might have been expected to welcome more children. Yet, Pauline had a new pregnancy terminated. When questioned by the examining magistrate she referred to a difficult birth and feared complications with a second birth. Her family doctor, Dr Hilfrich, confirmed her medical history. What he did not explain was why he had apparently condoned a lay abortionist to induce the miscarriage. Pauline had indeed consulted Frau Kastner rather than her family doctor. It is not clear whether Dr Hilfrich was not qualified to perform the operation himself, unwilling to risk prosecution or whether he simply sanctioned his influential patient's action in retrospect to protect her.[68] Whatever the reason, by not upholding the official medical guidelines, this general practitioner also served to undermine the law and its representatives.

The story and the excuse of Emilie, the wife of another well-to-do Dauborn farmer and miller, Arthur Knaus, was almost identical. Emilie was even younger, only twenty-nine and with one child, but she had lost another who had died. Emilie also sought to excuse the termination of her third pregnancy by referring to complications during labour. But she could not count on the support of a family doctor to justify her termination and her midwife, Dorothea Stautz, in fact denied she had had difficult births.[69] The wife of a third well-to-do Dauborn farmer, Wilhelm Prasser, also underwent a termination. She did not excuse this on the grounds of health. She stated that she already had two small children and simply did not want another although she was only twenty-five. When she feared she was pregnant again in December 1923 she remembered 'that there was talk that he [Willy Stammer, employed by her husband as a butcher] had to do with such things'. So she 'asked him one day to send Frau Kastner to me'. The operation was duly carried out at the Prassers' farm on the evening of 24 December with both Kastners in attendance. Since Christmas is celebrated on that evening in Germany the operation was obviously deemed urgent or else this time was purposely chosen to conceal an illegal action.[70]

Relations between the sexes

The majority of aborting women in the Limburg trial were married and had completed their families. Generally they made the decision to undergo an abortion but their husbands usually supported them in this and often also assisted in the operation itself. Sometimes women chose a time for their abortion when they knew their husbands would be absent so as to protect them from prosecution;[71] or in their depositions they denied their husbands' or boyfriends' active involvement for fear of implicating them as accomplices in the crime. Nevertheless, men's support in the preparation and the process of abortion often revealed itself in the depositions, given away carelessly or, possibly, deliberately in the mistaken belief that frank admissions would lead to lower penalties. Emilie Knaus, whom we met above, for example, did not have to worry on her own how best to rid herself of an unwanted pregnancy. Her husband not only applauded her strategy but also found the abortionist. In his statement he admitted that it was he who had consulted Willy Stammer and negotiated with the Kastners.

There was also cooperation between couples who were engaged to be married. Rosa Karl, a domestic servant from Oberbrechen, stated that the decision to 'abort the foetus' was taken by her and her fiancé Karl, a turner, and that it was he who arranged and paid for the operation; he also walked her to the appointed place in Werschau, waited for her and walked her back home again afterwards. Karl delivered three-quarters of a ton of wheat in payment for Frau Kastner's service.[72] Where some male defendants remained coy about admitting their involvement, it was revealed by Frau Kastner's own police statement. She reported, amongst others, that Willy Stammer had done all the necessary preparation for the operation on his present wife and had held the lamp during the actual abortion. The same was true of Otto Stammer, Willy's brother, a bricklayer, who also organized, paid for and assisted in the abortion of his girlfriend Minna, a domestic servant from Beuerbach.[73] Similarly, the Dauborn baker Albert Grau was said by Frau Kastner to have paved the way for his wife's operation and, since this took place in the small hours of the morning, 'between 12 and 1', he had also 'held the lamp'.[74]

Frau Kastner's deposition also showed that some husbands had attempted to syringe their wives themselves, then turned to her when they had failed.[75] Not infrequently male defendants admitted their own involvement. For example, Gottfried Schepf, a Dauborn decorator, talked quite freely about how his wife had charged him with the task of calling Frau Kastner when she feared she was pregnant again in the spring of 1923. 'At first I was reluctant to do so, later I called her by asking Herr Kastner. They both came and the two women went to the bedroom, I wanted to stay in the sitting room but Frau Kastner called me to hold the lamp.'[76] The Kirberg butcher Richard Band told the police how he had searched for Frau Kastner to help his then girlfriend, now wife, Helene. He was concerned that an abortion would be dangerous, but 'she dispelled these fears, she would only inject a salt solution which was nothing to fear ... I stood at the head of my wife during the operation ... '.[77]

Husbands or boyfriends, certainly if their relationships were affectionate, shared women's burden of reproductive responsibility, witnessing their fears and supporting them in the anxious wait for the operation. Men were also often present in the abortion room, assisting Frau Kastner and thus contributing to the success of the operation. Thus they lived through the trauma of discovering an unplanned pregnancy and shared feelings of relief when it was terminated without incurring injuries. These common experiences are witness to a surprisingly close relationship between the sexes and may well have contributed to cementing them further.

The story was, however, quite different when single women fell pregnant and could not count on the continuing support of their lovers. Then the dominant theme was strife, vengeance and retribution and the tone was always bitter and full of despair. Most expectant unwed women felt cheated and abandoned and they often submitted to an abortion under duress from their boyfriends. In the Limburg trial eighteen – or about a third of all female defendants – belonged to this group made up mostly of farm maids (six), but also domestic servants (four), young women still living at home (three), widows (two), and a seamstress, a postal assistant and a housekeeper. A few of these did later marry the men who they thought had impregnated them, though they were the exception. A pregnancy of a single woman was usually terminated for quite different reasons from those of her married counterparts. When it did not hasten the date of a marriage or indeed provide the main reason for one, it invariably spelled the end of a relationship. Men seized upon the opportunity of getting out of an unwelcome obligation when they had no wish to marry, or indeed could not do so because they were already married or engaged to somebody else. In these cases the power of decision making over the foetus rested with men who often enforced their will on their mistresses, especially when they felt their reputation was at stake.[78]

In the case of the commercial traveller Paul Hauf, the pregnancy of his mistress Emma Belser would have exposed him as a cheat and a liar for having deceived both Emma and his official fiancée. Another defendant, the young Kirberg farmer Theodor Büttner, insisted 'the matter should be removed' after he had impregnated his mother's housekeeper. He felt his honour was endangered since he could never marry beneath him: 'I could not do this to my mother'.[79] This pursuit of preserving male honour seems to have overridden any other principle such as loyalty, trust or charity, and former girlfriends were easily sacrificed as a result. Thus, Emma Belser was most reluctant to undergo an abortion but finally consented to go to Frau Kastner. Her lover had arranged it and paid for it but he subsequently disappeared from her life completely.[80]

The 23-year-old Philippine Reiter was even blackmailed by her lover to make her agree to a termination. She told the police that he had said that 'he will not marry me, he will shoot a bullet into his head, the thing must go'. Philippine simply waited until her period was missing for the second time. Maybe she was living in hope that he would change his mind, maybe she had nowhere to turn to. But when her former lover repeated his threat she sought advice from a friend, who encouraged her to try and negotiate with the farmer; if he refused to marry her then he should at least pay alimony for the child. But Theodor Büttner simply went on the offensive: 'Rubbish, in this case I shall find some boys whom I will give something [money] so that they will state they also had sex with you.' This was a reference to the infamous law of *Einrede des Mehrverkehrs*, which released men from the obligation of alimony if they could prove that their pregnant mistress had also had sexual relations with other men at the same time. Phillipine did not dare tell her own family of her predicament, especially since her brother's honour also seemed in jeopardy; she told the police: 'I feared my brother would shoot me.' Instead she confided in a neighbour, the wife of a bricklayer, who had seven children of her own. The latter told Philippine: 'Don't be so stupid, go to Nauheim to Frau Kastner', which Philippine did and very successful her visit proved to be: 'The blood came back two weeks after the operation. It was quite normal … '.[81]

Lina Geist, a 23-year-old domestic servant employed in the iron mill in Dauborn found herself in a similarly hopeless situation. She may well have indulged in casual sex since she only knew the first name, Alwin, of the young man, a 22-year-old manual worker. She reported that when she told him she might be with child he had become very angry, chiding her for not telling him earlier because 'then it would have been easier to get rid of it'. Lina said that she had been keen to marry but he 'insisted on doing away with it'. In his own deposition Alwin stated: 'I told Geist I would rather shoot myself than marry her'. According to Lina, Alwin was so determined to have the child aborted that he pursued Lina relentlessly to obtain her consent. Every evening he appeared below the window of her bedchamber and whistled up to her, demanding she come down and listen to his arguments.

This was a rather cruel reversal of the well-known custom of *Fensterln*, when young farm hands appear under the window of farm maids at night to court them and gain admission to their bed; in this case Alwin's motive was rather the opposite, intending to break his bond and preserve his honour by destroying the evidence of his involvement with Lina. She remained steadfast, refusing to go down to him until one evening one of her former woman colleagues turned up pleading with her to meet Alwin. In her deposition Lina said that 'he would shoot me in the grass if I did not go'. The meaning of this is not entirely clear but there seems little doubt that it meant a threat of violence. In her statement Lina said that she finally gave in and accompanied Alwin to Frau Kastner, albeit very reluctantly, and found all the necessary arrangements had been made. According to Lina, Alwin literally manhandled her into the operation. Hermine Kastner's statement confirmed this: 'At first she [Lina] baulked at it, but then she came round.' Lina's matter-of-fact description may well have played down a very frightening encounter. She stated: 'I did not know them. It was late at night. I was still not happy and wanted to talk to Frau Kastner first but Alwin said now there is no running away. Alwin held my head from behind ... '. After the intervention Alwin paid Frau Kastner 1,000 Marks and in the following April married another woman, also called Lina.[82]

Willy Stammer's girlfriend, the 21-year-old Hedwig Zeiger, was also reluctant to have her pregnancy terminated and it was again the man who insisted on the operation. But unlike Lina's short-lived affair, Hedwig's relationship with Willy had lasted for over two years. It seems therefore only reasonable for her to have entertained the hope of marriage when in the summer of 1923 her period was late by two weeks and she thought she was expecting a child. According to her police interview, Willy, however, maintained that marriage was impossible since 'the times were too bad' and he organized for Hermine Kastner to administer a douche to the reluctant Hedwig. Frau Kastner confirmed that the operation was Stammer's idea alone and in her 'presence Stammer talked her [Hedwig] into it'. Hedwig's pregnancy and her abortion ended their relationship and only six months later, 'bad times' notwithstanding, Willy married his new girlfriend Wilhelmine, then pregnant for the second time, after an earlier termination by Frau Kastner.[83]

Women who had affairs with married men faced a similar fate but unlike the women with unmarried boyfriends, they were unlikely to have expected anything different. The case of the farm maid, Wilhelmine Karg, is instructive. Her lover was her employer, a Neesbach farmer, who was married but still without children. His mother's maiden name and his age suggest that he could well have been a first cousin of Hermine Kastner and that therefore he probably knew who to turn to for help. Frau Kastner duly removed the evidence of the farmer's infidelity and his honour was restored, at least until he faced trial. It looks as if his marriage survived since nine years after the trial a daughter was born to the farmer and his wife.[84] A slightly different pattern of decision making occurred when a farm maid, Ida Schatz, was impregnated by her employer, the farmer Meyer in Kirberg. In this case the necessary arrangements for a termination were made by the young woman's mother; she apparently happened upon Frau Kastner 'in the field'. The 22-year-old had, she said, been seduced one night when the farmer's children were ill and his wife was therefore sleeping downstairs. The maid's room, however, was right next to the farmer's bedroom. He had then bribed Ida with money to keep quiet about it. The maid obviously did not and told her mother, who in turn discussed the incident and the outcome with both the farmer and his wife. Strangely, none of these in their police interviews referred to the act of seduction or possibly rape and neither the farmer's infidelity nor the subsequent abortion seemed to have unduly disturbed the farmer's wife or Ida's mother. But Ida's own story is more ambiguous:

> It was in the second night that I stayed there, that the husband Meyer came into my bed. He woke me from my sleep. I told him off, this was not done, he should be ashamed to come to a maid who had only been with him for two days. Meyer told me to be quiet, he would give me some money. Thereupon I no longer resisted. I was then fully awake ...

She then described the sexual act.

> When it was all over I tapped with a stick on the floor in order to call up Frau Meyer. Frau Meyer did come. I told her what her husband had done. Frau Meyer thought, I should leave it for now until the next morning. The next morning we quarrelled about this. The husband Meyer insisted my claims were untrue. Thereupon I left the service with Meyer the next day. About four weeks later I missed my period. I told my mother whom I had already told what Meyer had done to me. The mother said I should leave it ...

Ida's mother had indeed dismissed her daughter's accusations. When asked by the examining magistrate she said, 'the statement by my daughter that she stayed only a few days with Meyer is wrong. My daughter does not know what she says. She is not normal'. She admitted that Frau Kastner declined to help at first because she felt, Ida 'would denounce her'. Nevertheless, Frau Kastner seemed to have changed her mind and apparently turned up one evening with her husband and carried out the termination. Ida herself described the effects of the douching in dramatic terms; the morning after the intervention she suffered severe pains and strong bleeding. 'The blood was black and there were little clumps in it as large as a thumb nail'. Ida's mother's description of this was equally graphic: Ida apparently 'lost a whole piece (*Fetzen*) of blood, as big as half a hand'.[85]

Examples such as these conform to the view of single pregnant women as victims of callous men who had first seduced and then abandoned them. The Limburg trial complicates this stereotypical picture by showing that some of the female defendants either had resisted marriage when they were pregnant and had instead opted for an abortion or else were indeed well supported by their boyfriends in their hour of need. The girlfriend of Otto Stammer, a Dauborn bricklayer and Willy's brother, is an example of a young woman who seems to have been too independent to adopt the safe option of marriage. Minna was only twenty-two and worked as a domestic servant. She had been Otto's girlfriend for two years and after a year their relationship had become intimate. In March 1924 her menses were one week late and she feared pregnancy. According to Otto's statement to the investigating magistrate, he 'wanted her to have the child and ... wanted to marry her'. Of course, this could well have been a tactical exercise to extradite him from the charge of aiding and abetting an abortion. But Minna herself exonerated him, affirming that the decision not to marry and to seek an abortion was hers alone on the grounds of her youth and the worsening economic situation.[86]

Rosa Kraus's case demonstrates the extent to which unmarried couples could cooperate and support each other. Rosa was only twenty-one and still lived at home with her parents in Oberbrechen but she had a steady and intimate relationship with Karl, an Oberbrechen turner. In January 1924 her period was two weeks late. Although Rosa and Karl were engaged they 'both decided to abort the fruit' rather than have a shot-gun marriage. Frau Kastner duly carried out the operation in Werschau, in the house of an acquaintance, probably because they did not want to alert or involve Rosa's parents. Subsequently Karl delivered three-quarters of a ton of wheat to an inn in Werschau for the Kastners as payment.[87] At the time of the trial in December of that year Rosa was still not married. In a number of other cases women had in fact married the man after having terminated a pregnancy as a result of their affair. Helene Band was one of them. In April 1923 she had married her fiancé Richard, the Kirberg butcher. This was seven months after she had a douche administered by Frau Kastner because her period was late 'by about 8 days'. She wanted 'to have the matter taken away' and Richard had agreed. According to her deposition, her parents had been opposed to Richard as a husband. Richard had not only found Frau Kastner, negotiated the fee but also supported her throughout the operation. 'My [future] husband stood next to me during this. Both Kastners were in the room. Then we cycled on to Kirberg, already on the way bleeding occurred, maybe already in the house of the Kastners ... '[88]

Of the fifty-four female defendants in the Limburg trial only one married woman had terminated a pregnancy as a result of an extramarital affair – Anna Katharina, the 35-year-old wife of the Werschau head postmaster (*Oberpostinspektor*). After ten years of marriage, in March 1924 and only three months after the birth of her third child, she had started an affair with a local carpenter, seven years her junior. She told him that she no longer had sex with her husband as 'she has no need for so many children'. But when she thought she might be pregnant again by her lover (she had relied on a false concept of the 'safe' period in her menstrual cycle) she had apparently attempted to placate him by telling him she 'did not worry about [her] husband since [she] also had intercourse with him'. It was she who made all the necessary arrangements for the termination. The young carpenter was eager to help and readily consented to walk her to the Kastners, especially 'because it was evening and [she] was afraid to go there by herself. I did not mind'. The operation proceeded the following day in Werschau on the first floor of the carpentry workshop. It had gone well and Anna's menses had 'returned the same night like a normal period'.[89]

The career of a successful abortionist

Among the German lay abortionists Hermine Kastner must be rated as the very best. She stood accused of having terminated the pregnancies of forty-seven women[90] but there was no evidence of a single case in which the woman had subsequently died or suffered any long-term detriment. It was a rare achievement among doctors who were active in the abortion business and even among gynaecologists (see Chapter 3). The effectiveness of Frau Kastner's operations also suggests that not every case of her interventions had come to light and that she was very likely to have performed more operations, rendering her achievement even more impressive. It was not by chance that during her trial the medical officer of health in Limburg, Ernst Tennbaum, went out of his way to praise her extraordinary medical know-how and hygienic care:

> I noticed the very great skill of the defendant [Frau Kastner] in these cases, since it is extremely difficult to insert the syringe into the uterus and to find the cervix with the speculum, especially since there is no assistance. One needs very good light for this. In order to syringe the cervix one needs an extraordinary skill.[91]

There is evidence that Hermine Kastner and her husband, who assisted her in many operations, considered themselves as health professionals. They were aware of the risks of late abortions. Hermine knew enough gynaecology to avoid operating beyond the very early weeks of pregnancy and always tried to establish the length of gestation. 'I asked people at the beginning when their period had stopped. If it had stopped for more than 10 weeks I did not do anything.'[92]

She and Adolf also kept medical notes about each case, possibly like doctors to help deal with mishaps and also to keep accounts of outstanding payments. In this they acted like other lay operators, as we have seen in Chapter 4. And yet, Hermine Kastner became the community abortionist by chance. Her interest in birth control and abortion was probably triggered by her own experience of having a large family. She was only twenty when her first child was born and by the age of twenty-eight found herself mother of four. Furthermore, the timing of the birth of her children must have made this a problematic experience. Her last child was born in 1915, a year after the outbreak of the First World War when her husband, then also twenty-eight, had almost certainly been drafted into the army and was away from home, leaving her to cope alone. We do not know whether she welcomed her four pregnancies or felt them a burden. Caring for a large family during the war on her own, however, was bound to have been a difficult task and, judging from Hermine's energetic proselytizing for birth control after the war, it seems safe to assume the latter. According to her own testimony she had used 'prophylactics' herself, almost certainly to prevent the birth of more children.[93] Certainly by 1919 there are indications that she felt emboldened to advise others on this topic. Apparently when one of her husband's colleagues at Höchst and his wife were expecting a second child Hermine berated them or others who burdened themselves with a *Bunkert*, a child born out of wedlock, when they could easily have prevented this.[94]

The step from recommending birth control to 'helping to bring on a late period' through douching was rated as momentous by the law enforcement agencies but probably seemed fairly logical to Hermine Kastner herself. She was self-taught and seems to have learnt her trade as a lay abortionist haphazardly and by trial and error, except that she was too gifted and maybe too fortunate not to have committed any major blunders. She said herself: 'I did not have any special knowledge ... I did not possess books or other literature.'[95] At first she simply administered abortifacients. In fact she had consulted the pharmacist in Limburg who sold her an abortifacient tea. When this failed to produce the desired result and she went back, the assistant there suggested a syringe and probably recommended soapy water. 'I came to the deed through my sister-in-law, Frau Staub ... this was talked about and neighbours came and other people too and asked me to help them ... First I only did it out of pity, later on because people threatened to report me ... '

She told the investigating police officer in August 1924 how she went about helping Philippine, the then 24-year-old farm maid and girlfriend of her brother Karl, a mason. She travelled to Limburg to get some abortifacient pills at the chemist Rexel. They failed, however, to bring on Philippine's period; so Hermine went back to buy more of the pills. But 'the Rexel's apprentice' recommended she 'try warm douching'. By her own confession, it was sheer luck that she learnt of this method of inducing a miscarriage. 'I had no idea that you could abort by douching. I had never tried this on myself, I used prophylactics.'[96] Little did a young apprentice know that he had just launched the career of one the most successful – or notorious – lay abortionists in the area. Hermine, however, still had a lot to learn. At first she bought too small a syringe, an 'ear syringe whose middle piece was made of glass' and tried to apply this without a speculum. She said: 'I could see the cervix through the catheter. I know that I was acting unlawfully. I did not act out of hardship. I put the payment towards the household expenses.'[97]

She carried out the procedure on Philippine in the Kastner home. Philippine had 'crouched down but it did not really work. She asked for the syringe and tried to do it herself. In my presence she syringed her vagina several times, I can't remember with what, probably warm water.'[98] But to no avail. As a result the two women had quarrelled and Hermine's brother had hurriedly married Philippine to legitimate the expected child.

In spite of this failure Hermine's readiness to help with unwanted pregnancies spread quickly. Her second client materialized almost immediately and provided her with her first success story. She was Frieda, the niece of one of Hermine's neighbours in Nauheim from whom she often fetched water. Frieda's period had been '8 or 10 days late and her mother had thrown her out'. Frieda's aunt in Nauheim knew Frau Kastner 'had made injections for [Philippine]' and had no doubt invited her niece to stay so that Frau Kastner could attempt an abortion on Frieda. Hermine did as she was asked. She found Frieda alone in the house 'sitting in the kitchen crying', fetched her little syringe and injected her with alum solution. She left the syringe with Frieda so that she could repeat the douching. Only a few days later Frieda told Hermine that 'she felt fine and went home'. In Hermine's own words, 'these two cases must have been talked about because more and more people came and asked for help'. Frieda apparently had broken the syringe and her aunt bought a new one for Hermine Kastner, which constituted her only 'payment'.[99]

Remunerating Hermine's services with a new or sometimes better instrument was the norm early on in her career. For example, her third abortion client in the autumn of 1920 was the wife of a colleague of Herr Kastner. Her husband was so grateful for Hermine's effective help that he gave her his own speculum. Hermine neither charged for her work nor was offered money, which made sense since her early customers were either relatives (her sister-in-law, sister and cousin), wives of her husband's colleagues or neighbours and friends to whom she gave her services entirely free, probably because she relied on their help, such as obtaining water.

Only when her business contacts reached beyond this small circle of personal acquaintances did the nature of her activity change from an act of friendship or neighbourly help to one of a professional service. In her deposition, Hermine said: 'I have never demanded payment but only wanted to help people [einen Gefallen tun]; they have, however, often given me money or fresh produce [Früchte] themselves.'[100] Naturally, it was of the utmost importance for her to dispel the impression of having been paid properly since the law reserved the severest penalty for any person who performed abortions as a trade. But Hermine used every opportunity to stress that she never asked for money and many of her customers confirmed this.[101] She also implied that she had no need of extra money because her husband had been employed at Höchst for ten years. In 1918 they had been able to purchase a small house (two up, two down). They also had the use of a bit of land consisting of two 'gelehnte' (leased) plots of 50 rods for vegetables and potatoes, a goat and a pig.[102]

Eventually, however, Hermine's clients began to offer gifts, such as a pot of home-made pear jam (Birnenkraut), a local delicacy, or 'two eggs and a tiny bit of money'. This was followed by satisfied customers starting to pay in cash. Hermine stated that the married publican from Dauborn 'gave my husband a sum of money, how much I do not know, it was worth five or six loaves of bread'.[103] Some clients continued to offer nothing in return for Hermine's douching, others paid money, in increasingly large sums as the inflation mounted. At the peak of the hyper-inflation, in November 1923, a Neesbach farmer, for example, paid as much as 9 million Marks for his girlfriend but of course at that time it did not amount to very much at all. It made more sense to pay in kind and indeed most customers seem to have adopted this strategy during high inflation.[104] For example, the wife of a shoemaker paid half a pound of butter; another customer paid with 'several pounds of sausages bit by bit'; and immediately after the reform of the currency, the wife of a farmer gave a jug of *Schnapps* and one gold Mark. Others preferred to help 'the Kastners at work', such as a Nauheim farmer who 'planted a field of potatoes for us'; another farmer made Herr Kastner a handle for his axe and later also delivered 50-60 pounds of oats, which, however, at least according to Adolf Kastner, was 'so bad that the chickens would hardly eat it'.[105]

This pattern was typical of the rest of her patients; some offering nothing, others paying in kind or with money. Hermine Kastner claimed that 'with the payment for abortions [she had] never bought anything' but used it for housekeeping.[106] Her reputation spread from satisfied customers slowly but surely from relative and neighbour to people not personally known to her, from her own village of Nauheim and Adolf's birthplace of Dauborn to all the villages in the neighbourhood. Equipped with a proper syringe and speculum since the autumn of 1920, she developed a routine which proved almost infallible: her patient was asked to lie on a table and Hermine, using her instruments which she had earlier cleaned with plain water, injected salt water or alum into her patient's womb; this caused contractions and led to the expulsion of the fruit, or if the woman was not pregnant, brought on her period. Either Adolf Kastner or the woman's husband or boyfriend held the lamp to help Hermine operate with precision. Her grateful customers ensured that her 'activity was well-known in the entire area'.[107]

Denunciation

If so many villagers had been helped by the Kastners and were therefore implicated why then did their practice come to the notice of the authorities? The Kastners, like most other abortionists who worked efficiently and safely, were detected not through incriminating evidence (as for example when a patient had needed emergency medical treatment) but through a denunciation. While local gossip had been vital for a steady supply of customers it was, of course, also the means of the Kastners' downfall. Too many people knew about their activities including at least one local doctor who had been in the habit of supplying his patients with abortifacients such as douches and syringes and very likely directed them to the Kastners when these implements had failed.

But the shroud of silence protecting the Kastners within their community was rendered useless once a person decided to inform the police. The official investigation was duly put into motion after an anonymous letter was received on 5 May 1924. It read as follows (the translation follows the ungrammatical style of the original German):

> Tell you by this letter that family Gastner [sic] in Nauheim constantly offend against the law because of abortion. Request urgent investigation by the secret police [sic] who will go to them for the same reason, he must of course take care before he acts. Detailed information will be given after the arrest, even doctors fear for their lives if they report it.[108]

The surviving records do not reveal either the author of this note or where it was delivered. But it is probable that it was handed to the gendarme of the parish of Oberbrechen, Singelmann, who then passed it on to the public prosecutor. We can surmise this because three weeks later Frau Kastner's solicitor alleged that Singelmann had boasted as early as 10 May that 'he would make sure that Frau Kastner was arrested'. This gendarme was also said to have alerted a local doctor to examine the wife of the postal clerk Ferdinand Schuster in Werschau because he suspected her of 'having aborted a foetus with the help of the wife of Adolf Kastner in Nauheim', since the former was 'bleeding profusely'. In his report the doctor concluded that an abortion had indeed recently taken place. Interestingly, he suggested that such abortions were 'mostly performed by *Eihausstich*', by loosening the egg with a sharp object, a method Hermine Kastner never used.[109]

It is not clear who had it in for the Kastners. Usually such denunciations were sparked off by a quarrel or the dissatisfaction of a customer with the abortion services rendered or a request refused. The letter writer accused the Kastners not only of criminal abortion but also hinted at their potential violence, which might suggest that the writer had been in a serious quarrel with the couple or, maybe more plausibly, that the writer did not want to divulge his or her own identity for fear of any kind of reprisal. The fact that the name of Kastner was misspelt suggests either that the author did not know the couple very well or had little education. The awkward, ungrammatical style and lack of punctuation would suggest the latter. It certainly points to someone not used to writing letters, possibly a farmhand or a maid. But then many inhabitants of the villages in question would have fitted that description and quite a number of the Kastners' clients could have been seeking revenge.

Take the love affair of Philipp Seifert, the 25-year-old Werschau carpenter, with his neighbour, ten years his senior, the wife of the head postmaster,

Ferdinand Schuster mentioned above. This relationship had started either in February (according to him) or in March 1924 (according to her) and had led to a pregnancy. One of the witnesses at the subsequent trial was a widow, Margarete Schuster, who ran a tavern in Werschau and was very likely the mother of the post office clerk. The outraged mother of a cuckolded husband might well have sought redress by denouncing Frau Kastner and thereby securing punishment for the unfaithful wife and her lover.[110] There is a further probable link between Margarete Schuster and the wife of a Werschau tailor, Auguste Maria Stahl, whose mother was née Schuster. Not only did Auguste Maria have an abortion by Frau Kastner, she also lent her house to the Oberbrechen housemaid Rosa Kraus for her termination. Rosa's fiancé paid the Kastners in wheat which he left at the pub of the widow Schuster. Rosa was one of only two of Frau Kastner's clients who suffered from minor after-effects of the operation. She fell ill with peritonitis two weeks after the douching and although she stated that she suffered no ill effects from this, she was treated by Dr Hilfrich who had apparently 'referred' her to Frau Kastner for the termination in the first place and who appeared as a witness at the trial.[111] Personal feuds probably eventually involved many more people than the original number since the kin relationships were so intricate within the villages. Take another trial witness, a Werschau dressmaker, Fräulein Ender; she was very likely a cousin of Auguste Maria Stahl because the latter's maiden name was also Ender; and a further trial witness from Werschau was Fräulein Franzika Seifert, who was probably the sister or cousin of Philipp Seifert, the lover of the wife of the post office clerk.

There were fourteen trial witnesses altogether: two gendarmes, a midwife, three doctors and eight nonprofessional witnesses. Significantly, seven of the latter lived in Werschau, which might well suggest that this village was the origin of malicious rumour and eventually denunciation. The other patient of Frau Kastner who suffered from mild peritonitis after the termination was the wife of one of the wealthier farmers in Dauborn. She had consulted her family doctor in Dauborn, Dr Riedel, before he moved to Hanover. Dr Riedel and the midwife Stautz of Dauborn looked after her[112] and both also acted as witnesses in the trial; either or both might well have supported a campaign against the Kastners once the police had become involved.

But there is a further clue, namely that the person who denounced Hermine Kastner was a woman who had requested her help and had been rebuffed. Hermine had done her best to take care not to get involved with clients who were unreliable in this respect.[113] There was at least one person to whom Hermine had apparently refused to administer a douche: this was the mentally handicapped farmhand Ida Schatz. Ida's own mother had maintained that Frau Kastner had at first declined her request for an abortion for her daughter (although she had later relented) because Ida 'was a gossip [*schwatzhaft*] and would blab about it and she would go to prison'.[114] As we have seen above, Ida had claimed she was raped by her employer at the end of 1922 but this story was dismissed both by Ida's mother, her employer's wife and finally also by the district medical officer appearing as an expert witness at the trial.[115] It might well have been Ida who had written the letter of denunciation above. After all, she had also denounced (falsely as it turned out) another Dauborn farmhand, Minna Stautz, for having had an abortion. Moreover, Ida appeared as the first defendant on the official judicial list of aborting women.[116]

Whoever wrote the letter to the gendarmerie at Oberbrechen in May 1924, it started an immediate police investigation and spelled the end of the Kastners' abortion career, Adolf's job at Höchst, their family life and their freedom. A few days after the letter was received Frau Kastner was taken into remand even though her solicitor pleaded that she was 'urgently needed at home with her four children' and she posed 'no risk of absconding'.[117] Strangely, it took another two months for her husband to be questioned by the police. He refuted all accusations of having induced abortions himself or having aided or abetted his wife. He also claimed ignorance of his wife's activities.[118] Further investigations followed, however: on 2 August 1924 the charge against him was drawn up and on 19 December 1924 he was convicted of aiding and abetting in fifteen cases of attempted abortion. As we have seen above, his sentence was harsh. Hermine Kastner's penalty as the main defendant was even more severe. The judge attributed to both a *ehrlose Gesinnung* (base character) but took into account extenuating circumstances and refrained from sentencing them to penal servitude. He acknowledged several factors for this: once their abortion activity had become known they were trapped in this activity through the pressure of blackmail on them; they rarely asked for or received recompense (and if they did it was of little material value); they, Frau Kastner in particular had made an extensive confession which made the investigation possible in the first place; especially Frau Kastner 'realized the baseness of her activities' and 'showed genuine repentence'.[119] Notwithstanding this, in the summer of 1925 the public prosecutor appealed against this sentence; he dismissed the mitigating circumstances and increased Frau Kastner's sentence: from simple imprisonment (albeit for five years) to three years' penal servitude, i.e. solitary confinement with hard labour.[120] Adolf Kastner was released early from prison on 3 November 1926 by a petition for pardon and found work in Limburg, but only for 94 Pfennig hourly pay. Despite Hermine Kastner's request to be considered for early release, supported by the mayor and the counsellor of orphans, she was forced to serve her sentence in full.[121] On my research trip to the area I came across her grave in the churchyard of Nauheim and was gratified to read that she lived to the ripe old age of eighty-one, by which we may deduce that she had returned home after her release. Her husband's name, however, was missing from her grave, indicating, perhaps, that her marriage had not endured her long absence.

Conclusions

Although the Limburg case is unusual for the number of abortions induced and their provision by a couple rather than one individual, it was also typical in that it showed abortion as a routine event; the dominant role of lay abortionists; generally high standards of lay medical skill; the active role of neighbourhood networks; the interplay of trust and commercial considerations; and reasonably high gynaecological knowledge amongst even the most poorly educated women. All this suggests that the portrayal of abortion, the practitioner and the aborting woman was generally wide of the mark in both dominant medico-poltical discourse and in popular culture.

Although artificial birth control was not, or only rarely, employed, it is very probable that coitus interruptus was being practised by these villagers, but this was unreliable and necessitated careful planning and a high degree of cooperation from the male partner. Artificial contraception was expensive and required the help of a doctor, a time-consuming affair even if a local doctor could be found with the necessary knowledge and inclination to advise. Birth control clinics, which sprang up all over Germany after the inflation, were still relatively unknown at the time of the Kastners' practice and anyhow in the main limited to towns and cities. This left abortion as the preferred strategy, which was already apparent in Marcuse's first survey among Berlin proletarian circles.[122] Women only needed to seek help if their period was late and provided they watched their dates carefully, which they seem to have done. So-called period remedies rarely helped; douching oneself was popular during the First World War, less so in subsequent years; terminations was relatively simple and safe, certainly in the hands of an experienced, conscientious and skilled operator such as Frau Kastner obviously was. Her intervention was also cheap, as we have seen; at first a labour of love and later, at c.25 Marks, very good value. As the inflation worsened after 1921 the Kastners' remuneration changed from money to payment in kind.

There is no evidence that the women of these seventeen villages took part in the vociferous campaigns waged by thousands of ordinary women all over Germany to change the abortion law or join those parties of the left who promised to do so. Nevertheless, the startling flouting of the law and of religious dogma by these fifty-four female defendants (and many more who protected them in the local community) should, I would argue, be regarded as an act of rebellion against outside interference, and an act of civil disobedience.

As we saw in the previous chapter, although the words 'abortion' and 'pregnant' appear in depositions they were most probably inserted by police or court clerks. Judging from quite different terms used in examples of direct speech which were included, local men and women referred to 'having the matter removed' and 'missing periods'. I want to suggest that it was also evidence that women refused to accept official notions of biomedicine and personal guilt when they were seeking a practical solution to a potential problem, namely, bringing on their menses when these were blocked or delayed. The existence of a 'wise woman' who was easily persuaded to help rendered the whole process comparatively easy.

Hermine Kastner, far from being the villain, as her kind was usually portrayed in government and medical literature but also, as we have seen in Chapter 2, in popular culture and historiography, was looked upon at worst as a woman who knew what she was doing, at best as a helpmeet in times of trouble. At the height of their practice the Kastners were in fact providing a service to their immediate and wider communities, in times of economic crisis a service no less valuable than the midwife's in better times. The presence of so many men as defendants in the trial reflects their intimate involvement in decisions about family planning and their implementation at every stage, and refutes the idea that this aspect of sexuality belonged to a separate women's sphere.

Chapter 7

ABORTION IN EARLY TWENTIETH-CENTURY GERMANY: CONTINUITY AND CHANGE

*T*his book has explored women's reproductive body not only as discursively constituted but also as material and subjective. It counters a trend by gender historians in the last decade or so when body history was written exclusively about a symbolic body, as it is publicly represented, or the social body, that is, the body politic as it is symbolically made up of numerous individual bodies. 'The body as experience' explored, for example, by Barbara Duden over many years is usually avoided.[1] According to Kathleen Canning, there are a number of reasons for this. Scholars fear to fall into the trap of essentialism, i.e. understanding bodily experiences solely in biological terms and thereby linking them to nature rather than to culture. The crucial influence of Michel Foucault's analysis of gender and sexuality boosted the discursive approach and so does the greater availability of sources which 'chart the discursive construction of male and female bodies at the levels of state, social reform, science, medicine, or law'. Sources which 'offer insights into the body as a site of experience, memory or subjectivity' are far rarer and more difficult to locate.[2] But recently a number of feminist scholars, amongst them Canning herself, have attempted to inject corporeality into the abstract notion of the symbolic body, thereby replacing the passive body, an object of public surveillance, by one which is also understood as a site of agency, subjective interpretation and resistance.[3]

Cultures of Abortion in Weimar Germany also aims to link the experiential with the symbolic and discursive dimension of body history, showing how abortion was portrayed, practised and punished in Weimar Germany, but also, more importantly, how it was experienced and talked about by aborting women themselves. Abortion is thus explored both in the way it manifested itself publicly – as, for example, in sentencing policy or in medical discussions – and the way it was experienced privately by the historical actors, aborting women and their helpers. The story told is composed of many different narratives and informed by different viewpoints which are important for a cultural approach to this subject, the attempt to interpret the tapestry of different meanings by women and men involved in reproductive decisions.

When this project was conceived, Foucault's groundbreaking *History of Sexuality* was one of the major inspirations for a discursive approach and a constructionist explanation of the body and now that my project has come to an end, many of his ideas still hold good. Foucault famously postulated that 'sexuality must not be thought of as a kind of natural given which power tries to hold in check, or as an obscure domain which knowledge tries gradually to uncover. It is the name that can be given to a historical construct.'[4] This definition revolutionized the study of sexuality which before had often been perceived as an essential and therefore unchanging biological process. Following Foucault and later constructionists, abortion should equally be conceived as a social construct, both in the way it was represented and talked about but also in the way it was defined. The meaning of abortion not only changed over time but differed also according to gender, class, location, religious denomination etc. although as we have seen, perceptions differed often less than previously thought. I do not, of course, suggest, that abortion is not anchored in a material order (abortion was a process involving objects, payment, people) or that it is not grounded in biology (for example, women's menstruation was restored); it was performed on particular occasions in certain ways with specific instruments or potions; and abortion is after all bounded by physiological phenomena such as conception and childbirth. But these physiological and material aspects are themselves open to cultural interpretation in the way they are defined and regulated, desired or feared, valued or denigrated, which renders the meaning of abortion unstable and contingent on specific contexts. It is here that this study takes issue with positivist notions of medical progress and historians of medicine who discuss scientific discoveries of reproduction as if they were part of a linear development, an upward trajectory towards the scientific truth, and as if procreation belonged to a constant biology, a 'universalized body'.

I have argued that abortion was and remains today a highly contentious issue fought over by competing groups for the right to define, organize, mediate and regulate it.[5] As Jeffrey Weeks puts it in relation to sexuality, the way it is constructed 'is a product of negotiation, struggle and human agency'.[6] In this book I have investigated the complexity of the cultures of abortion by interrogating what it meant for and how it was practised by different social actors. Instead of relying solely on authoritative accounts by law makers and policy makers which have not always responded to historical or social change, I have also drawn on the assumptions and linguistic practices of those usually marginalized in the historical analysis: aborting women, lay abortionists, pedlars of patent medicines as well as those who presented abortion in different media of popular culture. These ideological struggles are important for their own sake but they also act as a probe into the way Weimar medical cultures were organized, challenged and reconstituted. In the 1920s and early 1930s German doctors, lawyers, politicians and the Churches strove to impose their own bourgeois norms upon the meaning of conception, pregnancy and miscarriage and devised rules for reproductive behaviour. Their prescriptions were challenged more or less openly by lay practitioners, working-class women, and their accomplices. Proletarian women especially displayed alternative forms of knowledge and adhered to trusted older notions of fertility and procreation while at the same time applying modern techniques.

My exploration of the cultural clashes over abortion has also revealed much about Weimar society and culture in general: it illuminated and redefined the polar relationships between men and women, middle and working classes, town and countryside, academic and lay medicine and the dominant abortion discourse, popular practices and its representation in mass culture. Last but by no means least, this study invites the reader to reexamine critically the way Weimar society is portrayed in historiography, especially its modernity, and to revisit the perennial question of continuity and change in modern German history: how significant was the shift in attitude to and practice of fertility control from Imperial to Weimar Germany, on the one hand, and from Weimar to Nazi Germany, on the other?

Gender roles and gender relations

From the findings of her oral history project about contraceptive practice in England and Wales during the first half of the twentieth century, Kate Fisher challenges the view that birth control was first and foremost a 'woman's question' or that women were responsible for the dramatic increase in the use of it. Rather than wives exerting influence on their husbands to use condoms, or 'insisting upon abstinence, turning to abortion, or adopting female methods such as caps', it was 'primarily husbands, not wives, who took responsibility for birth control strategies'. Women, Fisher claims, 'were reluctant to take an active role in the management and enforcement of birth control strategy', because they deemed this as a 'transgression of their passive and naive sexual personas'.[7] Fisher's image of women's submissiveness echoes the portrayal of working-class women's passivity in the abortion narratives of Weimar popular culture. Victimhood and vulnerability characterizes them on screen, stage and in fiction: from the proletarian mother of four in *Kreuzzug des Weibes* and Hete, the tormented and tragic heroine in *Cyankali*, or the destitute Herta in *Gilgi, eine von uns*, to the miserable protagonist of *Maria und der Paragraph*, women who found themselves pregnant against their will either took their own life or were mortally injured by botched abortions. Without much agency these women were crushed by their apparent biological fate. Contemporary reviews of the film *Cyankali* applauded such portrayal since it was thought it reflected the 'bitter truth'. One critic praised the way, 'an entire family living in poverty and destitution is hurled against the cliff of the clause [§218] and then smashed to pieces'.[8]

In contrast, middle-class protagonists like the young teacher or the 'modern woman' in *Kreuzzug* represent the New Woman as they manage to secure a 'safe' medical termination and thus retain some control over their own body. But they achieve this at a cost and their transgression is punished. The young teacher's body is doubly expropriated, first through rape and then by having conceived a dysgenic foetus, the sole reason why she qualifies for an abortion. Likewise, the character of the 'modern woman' is condemned for the pursuit of pleasure. As von Keitz points out, she comes across as mannish in her determination to keep her figure, making her husband look effeminate as he expresses joy at his impending fatherhood in a childlike war dance.[9] Other New Woman characters like Gilgi, the heroine of Keun's eponymous novel, or Helene in Baum's novel *stud.chem Helene Willfüer* survive their reproductive dilemma with feistiness and keep their ambitions intact but are burdened with single motherhood. As Krisztina Robert suggests in respect of post-First World War Britain, popular culture 'served as an arena of symbolic agitation where women's new gender roles, identities and relations were debated, constructed and contested through symbolic portrayals'.[10] This is true of Weimar Germany where aborting women portrayed in popular culture generally suffered because their desire for bodily autonomy was at odds with a still largely patriarchal society.

All the films, plays and novels I examined were remarkable in that without exception they supported abortion law reform; they all contained important ideas which questioned or subverted the dominant ideology of abortion but they were reined in by a general fear of censorship. It is instructive to be reminded of the seven-year battle with the censorship authorities waged by the director Georg Jacoby during and after the First World War to secure a licence for his abortion film *Moral und Sittlichkeit* (Sexual mores and morality), now no longer available. In 1924 it was passed and screened as *Muß die Frau Mutter werden?* (Does a woman have to become a mother?), but almost immediately banned again. It was reworked and finally released as *Frauen, hütet Eure Mutterschaft!* (Women, guard your motherhood!). As this title suggests, the censors had not only succeeded in destroying the anti-§218 message of the original script but also in 'bending it into its opposite meaning'.[11] No wonder that, as von Keitz suggests, producers and distributors tended to bow to rather than fight 'this manipulative practice by censorship authorities to ensure that films with controversial subject matter managed to get into cinemas at all'.[12] Since censors always checked the script particularly carefully, directors decided to portray transgressive behaviour on the silver screen visually rather than verbally, through a particular camera angle or through associations established by montage, while the text of the sub- or intertitles stayed within the boundaries of conventionality. In literature challenges to hegemonic discourses appear tucked away in inner monologues or asides. Abortion narratives in popular culture were thus neither at the forefront of a new ethic nor were they purely backward looking; instead they can best be described as mediating between a dominant ideology critical of lay abortionists and aborting women, on the one hand, and a popular acceptance of them, on the other.

The film *Kuhle Wampe oder Wem gehört die Welt?* is the exception to this rule. It did not feature abortion explicitly, but simply implied it as if it were completely normal. As a result it was neither pathologized nor was young Anni, the proletarian heroine, punished. In true communist style she learns to mistrust conventional rules about women's proper role and comes out fighting for a better world. She first agrees to a shot-gun engagement when she discovers she is pregnant, but then liberates herself from the shackles of petty bourgeois respectability, calls it off, and, having successfully rid herself of her pregnancy, gets on with her life in the communist youth movement and finally renews her relationship with her former boyfriend.

Anni's implied matter-of-fact approach to abortion chimes best with many of the women who had to defend themselves against the accusations of police and the courts. Rather than appearing passive, as in Fisher's interviews, or victimized, as in most popular cultural productions, they come across as active agents capable of exercising control over their fertility and their lives. Of course, my sample is self-selected in that the women examined stood accused of offences against §218 and were therefore involved in practising birth control. But German women's agency in this respect is also confirmed by surveys carried out just before or during the First World War by the Berlin dermatologist and sexologist Max Marcuse, and the Würzburg professor of gynaecology Oskar Polano.

Marcuse interviewed 100 of his proletarian female patients at his Berlin general practice. Framing his questions in such as way as to convey the assumption that contraception had been practised and pregnancies had been terminated as a matter of course, he managed to elicit extraordinarily frank answers. He found that ninety-eight women respondents thought his 'assumptions entirely natural if they related to themselves and harmless and understandable if they related to others'. Only three of Marcuse's 100 patients left contraception to their husbands and were ignorant of their precise method. All others showed that they had helped shape marital reproductive strategies either by their precise knowledge of their husbands' precautionary methods or by habitually using female contraception themselves, such as douching after intercourse or having a cap fitted. Forty women readily admitted to having had one or several abortions, apparently without 'embarrassment and inhibition', some even against their husband's wishes. Their determination to limit family size and the manner in which they inferred that birth control was their natural right is testimony to women's agency.[13]

In contrast, Marcuse's attempt to conduct the same survey on married male patients encountered great reticence even when he enquired about the relatively safe subject of contraception. Questions about abortion were warded off with replies such as, 'I don't worry about that', or 'that is my wife's business'. Only the special conditions afforded by the war, when Marcuse was in charge of a reserve army field hospital, gave him the chance of meeting more willing respondents: he selected 293 married soldiers who were well enough to be interviewed. This survey confirms that almost half of the soldiers' wives had taken on or at least shared the responsibility for family planning and, since the soldiers were not specifically asked about this, there may have been more. Typically, couples' birth control strategies ranged from husbands in charge with back-up measures by wives to wives having sole responsibility. For example, a 31-year-old postman told Marcuse that his wife applied a douche after every coitus and now had a coil inserted, too; or a 40-year-old construction worker with three children whose wife had had three miscarriages practised coitus interruptus but his wife douched immediately afterwards in case of doubt; a 27-year-old musician admitted that he did not always practise coitus interruptus but that his 26-year-old wife 'is on her guard against it'. Or a 25-year-old cashier, married for one year, no children but two miscarriages (one because the 'wife had got rid of it') admitted that only his wife used contraception. A milling cutter whose first marriage was contracted when he was aged twenty-two used no contraception at all but his wife had 'tipped' every year. This marriage ended in divorce because of adultery.[14]

Polano conducted his survey in 1914 on 500 women patients at his clinic in Würzburg; the great majority of his interviewees were married, lower-class and Catholic and it is therefore a useful counterpart to Marcuse's Berlin sample of mostly Protestant women. Polano's report omits the respondents' answers, which precludes gleaning information about husbands' and wives' gendered attitudes. But similarly to Marcuse's Berlin women, 339 of Polano's interviewees who admitted to contraception could name the precise method or appliance used by their husbands. One hundred and sixteen women said they and their husbands did not practise birth control for a variety of reasons, such as 'the desire to have children or indifference' (94), the belief that it was sinful (26), or because they were widowed or divorced (12) and husbands' refusal to cooperate with wives' express wishes (12). Only fifteen married and two single women appeared ignorant of birth control.[15]

The majority of women in my research for this book were very much part of the decision-making process about reproductive strategies, and many were in charge. What is more, their *Eigensinn* (obstinacy), in this respect showed that they resisted the dictates of medical authority both in the way they perceived abortion and in the manner of its execution. Many steadfastedly clung to the notion of blocked menses, or, as it was expressed in Marcuse's survey, 'bad blood', in the face of different medical and legal definitions and in the intimidating setting of police stations or courts of law. Marcuse, out of empathy with his proletarian women patients and possibly also because he knew the limits of medical knowledge, thought this was 'not entirely without good reason'.[16] Many women refused to regard abortion as either the killing of an unborn child or a life-threatening calamity but as an everyday occurrence, even liberation from the burden of an unwanted pregnancy which was potentially disastrous in uncertain times. Women's mass violation of §218 during the Weimar Republic was in itself a sign of resistance against figures of authority, from policeman to teacher and priest. The 'scourge of abortion' much decried by the contemporary moral right but also by many liberals and men of the left, was little less than a mass rebellion against the draconian clause §218, even if judges were applying it more leniently than they were entitled to, especially in the later Weimar years. Moreover, the will to retain control over their body drove thousands of women onto the streets to demonstrate in favour of the decriminalization of abortion and it led them to petition politicians and parliament to this end.[17] Exhortations to the contrary in newspapers, travelling exhibitions, pamphlets and, as we have seen, in popular culture notwithstanding, women turned to pedlars of abortifacients, quacks and even fortune-tellers for help with unplanned pregnancies.

Yet, Kate Fisher's insistence that before the Second World War in England and Wales both husband and wife saw birth control 'as part of the male world, and a man's duty' is a useful reminder that men's role in this respect should not be overlooked. I have found plenty of evidence of men imposing their will on women, sometimes forcing them to terminate a pregnancy if this was inconvenient for the man and yet desired by the woman. There is, however, more evidence of close cooperation between husband and wife and between a young woman and her fiancé or lover, and this was true among both the working and the middle classes. According to Fisher, in England and Wales many married couples did not seem to have discussed birth control issues until well after the Second World War because it was unquestionably understood to be a man's responsibility and also because women regarded 'the act of planning ... as cold, calculating, and an unnatural approach to family building'.[18] Furthermore, all matters sexual were a cause of acute embarrassment for British working-class couples. According to the academic and writer Richard Hoggart (b.1918) they were very shy about certain aspects, such as talking about sex normally, or being seen naked, or even undressing before sex.[19] The sexual culture in late Imperial and Weimar Germany was markedly different: abortion featured large in many of the most popular plays, films and fiction and although censorship forced authors and scriptwriters to toe the line in some respects, the subject itself got plenty of airing. Marcuse's 1917 survey of 300 soldiers' marriages clearly shows that most men and women discussed reproduction and family limitation; even more respondents might have indicated that this was the case had they been asked about it. Well over half the answers suggest that family size and birth control was planned together either by explicitly saying so or by implying it by a precise knowledge of the wife's contraceptive method and the absence of criticism of it. Take the example of the 24-year-old postman from a small town in the Lausitz, married for three years with one child; this had arrived unplanned but now he and his wife wanted to avoid another. They had 'immediately agreed that later there was still time for the matter of having children'. In those cases where a child or more children were desired, husbands' responses show that this wish was supported by the wife.[20]

The German birth rate declined rapidly, from 31.7 per cent in the years 1906-10 to 18.4 per cent in the years 1926-30, a result of a decline in both marital and extramarital fertility. This meant a very visible decline in the average number of children per family: from 4.7 (for marriages contracted before 1905) and 3.6 (for those contracted in 1910-15) to only 2 (for marriages contracted between 1925 and 1929), much lower than the equivalent figures in England and Wales.[21] The rapidity of this demographic change was hardly possible without marital cooperation, although mentally and physically disabled veterans must have contributed to it perhaps more than was officially conceded.[22] The decline in the number of children born outside wedlock shows that single women also knew about contraception or, more likely, had access to abortion. As we have seen, however, responsibility for fertility control was also shared between the unmarried. Family planning, including abortion, may well have brought couples closer. The Hesse case study presented in Chapter 6 shows clearly the extent to which many husbands or boyfriends were involved in the planning and execution of a termination; they were often present during the operation, holding a torch to provide light for the abortionist and thus could not but witness the visceral aspects of an obstetric operation men were usually shielded from at that time; they also registered their wives' or lovers' physical and psychological reactions to it. The surviving correspondence between women who feared an unwanted pregnancy and their lovers reveals how well informed many men were about the gynaecological aspects of women's bodies but also how emotionally committed they were to help bring about a solution to their dilemma. This was to be found among all classes and in towns as well as countryside.[23] Such mutuality signified an important shift in the relationship between men and women: they talked openly about matters which their parents' generation probably found too embarrassing or distasteful to mention freely and they supported each other when the need arose. It also meant a transformation of the politics of marriage or gender relations: thanks to their growing awareness of their economic, political and social power women had become more assertive in controlling their fertility while at the same time it highlighted, as Linda Gordon suggested, 'men's diminishing social power in the family'.[24] On the other hand, women might well have resented the assumption that birth control was to be their responsibility rather than their partners', and that men should be allowed to be sexually active without such responsibilities, a point made both by Fisher and by Hera Cook in her discussion of English sex and marriage manuals after the Second World War.[25] In unmarried relationships in particular, honour played an important role. A woman's honour was damaged if her boyfriend deserted her once she was pregnant, but honour was equally important for men's strategies, which depended greatly on cultural norms of class differences between the couple and the promises given at the outset of the relationship. Much more needs to be known about men's motives and the role of masculinity in reproduction and fertility control and this would be a fertile ground for future research.

The blurring of boundaries

This study has shown that in some important respects the boundaries were blurred between the genders but also between other dichotomies. This was certainly the case with academic versus lay medicine, at least with respect to abortion. Here doctors enjoyed a privileged status above lay practitioners when it came to health policy, legislation and sentencing; members of the medical profession also enjoyed a high status in bourgeois society in contrast to their lay colleagues. Contemporary medical discourse and, under its influence, political debates presented medical termination and quack abortion as polar opposites: the former safe and clean, the latter a dirty and dangerous business. The image of the greedy, malicious and shady wise woman in the films and literature examined here furnished a dramatic counterfoil to the stereotypical innocent woman victim. In practice the story was much less black and white. Abortion was by no means medicalized in the Weimar Republic; women learnt about methods of self-help (as was popular especially during the war) from a family member, neighbour, work colleague, pedlar of abortifacients or the local pharmacist (the way Frau Kastner in Hesse was launched in her career as one of the most successful abortionists at the time); if self-help or assistance from an informal network of kin or local relationships failed, women turned to a variety of professional abortionists, such as midwives or wise women. Doctors were only one source of help among many and, as this book suggests, the least important for lower-class women. This made sense since the apparently clear-cut boundaries between medical and lay know-how and skills were far less distinct than academic medicine liked to claim. Many a medical practitioner proved a less safe option than an experienced and conscientious lay operator. The elite discourse suggested that criminal abortion was the preserve of lay practitioners while doctors stayed above the law. But the hostility voiced by the medical profession against illegal abortion in public has obscured the extent of medical involvement in private practice. Commercial abortion, singled out by politicians and others as the core of the 'abortion problem' and therefore the main target for policing, prosecution and punishment, turned out, much to the embarrassment of the medical establishment, to extend not only to quacks but also to doctors. The former worked for money but so did many doctors, and both categories of abortionists contained their fair share of avaricious, disreputable and ruthless as well as idealistic and conscientious practitioners.

The relationship between academic and lay medicine in this field was also complicated by gender and medical politics. The number of female doctors known to have practised terminations is negligible in spite of women doctors' participation in the campaigns for abortion law reform. The reasons for this have been explored elsewhere but it was most probably linked to their prioritization of professional interests over feminist ideals.[26] As we have seen, one of the most prominent women gynaecologists, Adams Lehmann, had invoked in her writings a woman's right to bodily autonomy and yet had herself offended against its most basic principle by carrying out sterilizations without prior informed consent. In contrast, women were well represented among lay abortionists and were often preferred by aborting women to male practitioners. A number of manufacturers and pedlars of abortifacients thought it worthwhile to give themselves women's names in their advertisements as a boost to their credibility with female customers. The general public seemed to have imagined the abortion market to consist exclusively of women, as the common terms for lay abortionists were clearly gendered: *Weise Frau* was the name used by aborting women while the general public or the press preferred the pejorative *Engelmacherin*, denoting a woman who produced angels and, by implication, killed the unborn child. It was most probably Protestant in origin since in Catholic beliefs only baptized children went up to heaven while those who remained unbaptized, such as the unborn, went into purgatory. It smacks of anachronism at a time when a human foetus was scientifically defined and had long since ceased to be a creature of God. No such colourful descriptions existed for male lay abortionists although on rare occasions *Weiser Mann* was used and although they existed in large numbers and were popular particularly among men who found they had inadvertently impregnated their wives or girlfriends. Representations of lay abortionists in the examples of popular culture examined were also misleading since the villain was invariably a female abortionist, from Madame Heye in *Cyankali*, the concierge in *Kreuzzug* to the exotic widow Mulacka in *Madame Lu*. In newspapers and journals, too, wise women were the main target of public disapproval of 'quack abortion' and it is easy to see why. A woman assisting another woman to destroy the seed of maternity undermined what for many still constituted woman's 'natural role' and chimed in with the critics of the emancipated New Woman who they feared would bring about sexual anarchy.

The public vilification of quacks by doctors was not only motivated by concern to protect women's health but also, though less publicized, by professional interests, namely doctors' quest for a monopoly in the important area of reproduction and fertility control, where lay practitioners, especially midwives, proved to be serious competition and a hindrance to the professionalization of childbirth and abortion. 'Scientific' methods of inducing miscarriages by using instruments and anaesthesia rendered the operation respectable. This helped overcome many doctors' physical scruples and established a clear distinction between medical and quack practice. Doctors' pursuit of market domination was bolstered by legal change, especially the decree permitting therapeutic terminations which implied a medical monopoly. Some feature films like *Kreuzzug* celebrated the figure of the medic as the man of honour whose humanitarian help was restricted by the existing law. Yet, the majority of working-class women continued to look for help from lay abortionists, not only because they proved cheaper but also because they were culturally more accessible and sympathetic, sharing for the most part, their clients' attitudes regarding the definition and morality of abortion.

A number of contemporary commentators suggested that contraceptive habits were crucially influenced by denomination and region. As early as 1912 a prominent economist blamed Protestant and the presumed atheistic Social Democratic influence for the declining birth rate, while a year later a medical study contended that it was Jewish mixed marriages which had produced the lowest marital fertility.[27] This study, however, has not revealed any significant differences in the abortion behaviour of different religious groups. Given that during the Weimar Republic the Catholic Church much more than the Protestant, retained its condemnation of artificial miscarriage as murder, it is surprising to find that women of all denominations resorted to illegal abortion; generally they also defined and defended their actions without clear references to their religious beliefs. The Hesse case study in Chapter 6 is particularly relevant here since the Kastners' clients came from some predominantly Protestant villages and others which were almost exclusively Roman Catholic without any corresponding dichotomy in attitudes. The abortion case material from Catholic Upper Bavaria similarly shows little evidence of religious scruples. Marcuse's study of 300 soldiers suggests that the difference in birth control culture among Protestants and Catholics was narrowing. He found that of the ninety-seven couples who had never used contraception, sixty-one were Protestant, seventeen were Catholic, three 'purely Jewish', ten Catholic-Protestant, one Christian-Jewish and five where both or one partner was a non-believer. When he looked at their answers more precisely he could not detect any religious sentiments among the Protestant couples though there were with six of the Catholic couples.[28] According to Polano's survey, of the

161 women (32 per cent of a total of 500) who did not practise birth control, 130 (or 81 per cent) were Catholic and only twenty-two (14 per cent) Protestant, with seven of mixed denomination (4 per cent) and a single Jewish woman. Yet, of the 339 women (68 per cent) who practised birth control, 224 (66 per cent) were Catholic, sixty-one (18 per cent) Protestant, seven belonged to mixed marriages and one was Jewish. The denominational breakdown showed that of 350 Catholic women, 224 practised birth control (64 per cent) compared to 61 of 83 Protestants (73 per cent), suggesting a cultural gap, though a surprisingly small one.[29]

Weimar culture was predominantly urban and discussions of modernity usually focus on cities[30] and, like Weimar politics did, too, largely neglect the countryside. Surprisingly, however, novels like *Madam Bäuerin* by Lena Christ (1920) suggest that modernity and the New Woman also existed outside city life. Christ's heroine moves from a town to the countryside, where she espouses progressive ideas and a modern lifestyle and is critical of traditional values and customs.[31] Polano and Marcuse examined the relationship between town and countryside and its influence on the contraceptive culture and both suggest that the rural-urban dichotomy is too crude to be helpful. In Polano's sample more women lived in the countryside; of these 59 per cent, that is, a small majority, used birth control compared to 70 per cent, i.e nearly two-thirds, of the urban women. Nevertheless, Polano found that class was a more important variable than geography since manual workers who lived in villages were responsible for the high percentage of rural birth control practice while the independent farmers were much less inclined to plan their families.[32] Marcuse's survey of 300 soldiers contained only a small rural sample but he, too, argued that 'domicile alone cannot justify characterizing a marriage as rural' and he mentions a number of external influences which 'today render the psyche of the rural population into an urban one', such as the profession of the husband, of the wife, of both fathers, the places of birth, the region of the present place of residence etc. Quoting a contemporary study of Baden, he noted that an important influence was the urbanization of the male generation and the fact that most young men lost their 'sexual naiveté during their military service'.[33] My own research shows a similar picture: the various Hesse villagers making use of the abortion service of Frau Kastner displayed the same attitude to abortion as did women in cities like Berlin or Munich. The Hesse villages, however, were very closely connected to the industrial centres in the Rhineland and around Frankfurt through the annual or weekly migrant work of most of the men. Women, too, travelled to see their husbands at their workplace or to the nearest market town for shopping. Even aborting women from the Bavarian countryside who themselves worked on the land and whose boyfriends or husbands were agricultural labourers were visibly influenced by urban, middle-class culture through relatives in town or the presence of the teacher, policeman, doctor and judge.

Of all the oppositional polarities, the differences between lower and middle classes proved of greatest importance. It was national economists like Julius Wolf or Paul Mombert who had developed the theory that wealth and the declining birth rate were causally linked. Mombert stated that fertility declined in parallel to rising wealth and social status',[34] an observation which seemed to be borne out in the statistics of the marital birth rate differentiated by class: among higher civil servants the average number of children was 3.5 for marriages contracted before 1905 but only 1.6 for those contracted between 1925 and 1929 compared to the number of children born to labourers of 4.5 and 2.1 in the same periods.[35] Class differences were also noticeable in the way abortion was practised and prosecuted. Contemporaries usually perceived abortion as a class-specific problem. One of the very first petitions to decriminalize it, sent by a group of women to the Prussian Minister of Justice, referred to 'wealthy childless women' who could afford a termination and to poor women who were criminalized.[36] Both the KPD and the SPD fought for legal reform on the grounds of class discrimination;[37] in the cultural sphere productions like *Kreuzzug*, *Cyankali*, *Madame Lu* or *Maria und der Paragraph* echoed and reinforced this notion, although others like *Gilgi* or *stud.chem. Helene Willfüer* showed that white-collar workers like Gilgi or academic women like Helene also found it impossible, or difficult, to rid themselves of an unwanted pregnancy. In 1914 Max Hirsch, another doctor and sexologist practising in Berlin, claimed that abortion among the lower classes was the main method of fertility control and that contraception was limited to the upper classes.[38] The criminal court cases examined for this book suggest that prosecutions for violation of §218 were heavily stacked against the poor. Bourgeois women certainly practised abortion, too, but they were underrepresented in crime statistics and this was for two reasons: well-to-do and educated women found it easier then lower-class women to obtain discreet help from a doctor and they had easier access to effective contraception, such as the Mensinga diaphragm, the cervical cap or the coil which usually needed fitting and regular check-ups by a doctor. This accords with Polano's findings: 81 per cent of all wives of civil servants in his randomly selected sample had used contraceptives compared to only 72 per cent of workers' wives.[39] The physical circumstances and the rhythm of daily life made it far easier for the middle classes to practise birth control more assiduously compared to the lower classes who lacked the necessary privacy, being hampered by cramped living conditions, and who often had no access to running water and heating etc. The many birth control clinics which sprang up in Weimar Germany after the end of the inflationary period catered not just for the middle classes but also for the working classes, yet those in charge found that the latter continued to prefer non-appliance methods such as coitus interruptus which cost nothing and which needed no complicated preparations.[40] A number of doctors developed their own expensive patented brands of female contraceptives, such as the Gräfenberg ring made of gold, or cervical caps in platinum which suggests that they were clearly aimed at the rich.[41] Finally, lower-class women, more than their middle-class counterpoints, refused to be colonized by bourgeois ethical norms defining what constituted appropriate sexual behaviour: the biographical references to women defendants show that premarital sexual relations or the custom of 'tipping' unwanted pregnancies were frowned upon by middle-class commentators but among the poor were widely practised and accepted, often considered entirely rational, even the norm. Marcuse was astonished to find that abortion was often practised not 'as a later replacement for contraception but very often very early on as the method of choice'.[42]

Continuity and change

There is no doubt that the influence of the First World War on body history was enormous. For example, Max Hirsch, the Berlin doctor and sexologist, thought the war and the revolution had produced 'profoundly changed attitudes, life circumstances, and led to moral and economic decline'.[43] Elisabeth Domansky argued that the war had eroded the German family; the 'gendered mobilization of German society for total war' which also frequently included children and young people drafted in for public works, separated men, women and children from their families. Men's murderous experiences at the front rendered many families fatherless or undermined male authority in the home which was also challenged by 'women's and children's experience with self-sufficiency during the war'.[44] The refiguration of gender roles during the war also transformed men's and women's role in public life during the Republic, especially in the labour market and in politics. As Kathleen Canning has put it, the result of these multiple social changes was

> the emergence of a new female body – that of the female citizen. The body of the new *Staatsbürgerin* figures prominently during the early years of the republic, from the writing of the Weimar constitution to the campaigns of the reconstituted political parties in 1919 and 1920, to the new arenas of popular culture, consumption and mass entertainment, and to the visions of an expanded and effective welfare state.[45]

In the face of a rapidly declining birth rate and the slaughter of over two million young men in the trenches, the war had also put a new premium on women's procreative capabilities. In the interventionist Weimar welfare state young women's bodies became both a site of intervention and of power, to be disciplined by stringent regulation and to be rewarded materially and symbolically. This and their new civil rights emboldened women from all walks of life to voice their demands publicly.[46] In 1919 Adele Schreiber-Krieger, radical feminist and SPD member of the Reichstag's population select committee, called the phenomenon of the rapidly declining national fertility 'the greatest, non-violent revolution' by women, and one which 'put the key to the control of life firmly into the hands of mothers. Thus a woman in bondage becomes master and determines the fate of the family, the *Volk* and humanity'.[47] It is no coincidence that among the very first petitions sent to the Constituent Assembly was by a group of Berlin women, without party affiliation, to 'curb coercive procreation in Germany' and to decriminalize abortion, for single women and for mothers of three children'.[48] Weimar's modernity, which encouraged a 'rationalization of sexuality' – that is, a belief that the reproductive process should be controlled to suit the economic conditions and personal preferences – led to the lowest birth rate in the Western world. It also heralded a new hedonism in women's sexuality and a shift in the power of gender relations. As ever more women from the lower classes opted for abortion as their birth control method of choice, official disapproval waned, too.

Members of the medical and legal professions and the law enforcement authorities reluctantly came to tolerate, sometimes even support, abortion law reform in view of the apparent rise in abortions. The draconian penalties prescribed by the Wilhelmine criminal code were substantially modified in 1926 in favour of the aborting woman; the new law scapegoated professional abortionists instead; this was followed in 1927 by the permission of therapeutic abortion by decree. In Imperial Germany and the early Weimar years the police made many raids on suspected doctors' or quack practices but in post-inflation Weimar prosecutions generally occurred only after an abortion-related death or injury was detected or after a denunciation. This meant that the gap between theory and practice or elite attitudes to §218 and popular ideology narrowed. Even the great pillars of sexual morality, the Protestant Church, to a larger extent, and the Roman Catholic Church, to a lesser extent, and their affiliated denominational societies felt compelled to adapt to the growing popularity of family limitation in Weimar Germany in order to retain their influence in the new republic and popular support in an increasingly secular age.[49]

Individual doctors were increasingly willing to brave the storm of indignation from their invariably conservative national and local medical societies by publicly defending their own practice of terminating pregnancies on economic and social grounds, which was still illegal. Testimony of this are the highly publicized abortion trials involving doctors during the second half of the Republic, most famously the case in 1931 of the two communists Else Kienle and Friedrich Wolf, the doctor/playwright we met in Chapter 2.[50] The rural practitioner who became well known by the posthumous publication of his case material by Alfred Grotjahn was not the only one to practise terminations undetected. Another doctor from a small industrial town somewhere in Germany was able to perform abortions undisturbed by the law. In 1932 he confided to Dr Käte Frankenthal, doctor and member of the Prussian Diet for the Socialist Workers Party, that since 1922 he had performed more than 1,500 terminations. Although his patients were predominantly poor he had also helped wives and daughters of industrialists, entrepreneurs, police officers, teachers and even National Socialists.[51] In 1927 two doctors from Rheydt in the Rhineland, an area with a high number of female industrial workers, thought that agreeing to women's abortion requests was no more than a reasonable response to social hardship or, more radically, a woman's right. Although the account of this trial is found in a legal thesis of 1940, which is therefore infused with National Socialist ideology,[52] especially in its condemnation of the alleged communist propaganda resulting from the case, it is still valuable for the statistics and direct and indirect statements that it contains. In this trial the witness statements of several midwives and a medical colleague all agreed in one respect, namely that

> the opinion of men and women had changed fundamentally since the war. As soon as they sensed a second pregnancy women planned how to rid themselves of it out of a general distaste for the burden of children. Among working-class women and commercial abortionists alike, communist propaganda against §218 had a major effect. Women declared they would treat their body as they saw fit and nobody else had the right to determine whether the child should be carried to term.

The working-class women accused of abortion in this trial thought that to give birth to an unwanted child was sheer stupidity. 'You are mad to want another child, why don't you go to [one of the two doctors on trial] and ask him to remove it for you!'.[53]

Towards the late 1920s punitive policy softened considerably, showing to what degree 'the practice of award of punishment is influenced by cultural trends and changing world view'.[54] The German criminologist Exner conducted a study of the average penalties meted out for simple and commercial abortion within Germany as a whole during the single year of 1927. This showed that most sentences for both 'simple' and 'commercial' abortion were extraordinarily lenient. He regarded this as the result of 'a moral response to the ethics of every-day-life' since the popular moral judgement of this [particular] crime is based on the principle: understanding means condoning.'[55]

Abortion in Nazi Germany

This coming together of popular practice and official policy seemed to come to a sudden halt with Hitler's assumption of power. Abortion became an important tool in the National Socialists' increasingly repressive population policy: Gabriele Czarnowski refers to it as a highly sophisticated selective programme of state-regulated reproduction according to eugenic/racist principles. It covered the entire spectrum from prosecuting and prohibiting abortion of those regarded as eugenically desirable children to permitting and enforcing it when 'undesirable' offspring were involved. Nazi population planners set out to destroy the subculture of clandestine abortion which they considered had spiralled out of control during the 'libertine' years of the Weimar Republic. The new regime introduced the necessary measures against voluntary abortion without delay. As early as May 1933 advertisements for abortion services and abortifacients were banned, an attempt to stop once and for all their widespread use of the Weimar years. At its nadir, during the Second World War the law of 1943 'To Protect Marriage, Family and Motherhood' introduced capital punishment in certain cases for hardened abortionists. This meant the killing of those who had in their turn 'killed genetically valuable' foetal life. Czarnowski certainly found a number of cases where abortionists, among them former midwives, were executed.[56] The new 1943 law also had a detrimental effect on simple abortions, that is by 'Aryan' German women who did not involve commercial operators. The normal penalty for simple abortion for a woman went up to a whole year's imprisonment and that for aiding frequently exceeded this.[57] My own research corroborates this; for example, at the beginning of June, exactly three months after the new law had come into operation, a 19-year-old domestic servant was sentenced to one year in gaol for having terminated her pregnancy, the result of a brief dalliance with a soldier on holiday in her village. Her mother, an unmarried washerwoman of forty-seven, had assisted her daughter by supplying a syringe and was sentenced even more harshly, to 15 months' imprisonment. A Dutchman who lived in the same village and had also aided in the abortion received the same penalty. The judge explained that the sentences were so harsh because the new law dictated this kind of judgement.[58]

Although the Nazi regime legalized abortion on medical grounds for the first time (as opposed to permitting it by decree of the Supreme Court, as was the case in 1927), Czarnowski argues persuasively that this apparently liberal measure was in reality repressive owing to the stringent and punitive procedure of assessment and registration. The year 1935 saw the introduction of mandatory registration and identification of every termination, miscarriage and premature birth, which made detection of criminal abortion easier. By 1936 or 1937 policing had been sharpened and Himmler had established his Headquarters to Combat Homosexuality and Abortion within the Department of Criminal investigation. Its effectiveness is easily apparent from the increase in the number of criminal investigations into potential abortion infringements and the rising proportion of all investigations. Between Weimar and Nazi Germany the proportion of abortion cases of all criminal investigations in the *Landgericht* Mönchen-Gladbach went up from 9 per cent during the Weimar years to 11 per cent in the first six years of the Nazi regime, with an enormous increase in 1937.[59] The records of the *Landgericht* Duisburg show a similar increase.[60] And there were other legal measures to curb abortion if practised by individual women as voluntary birth control, hidden in new laws which had, on the surface, little to do with abortion (such as that against Dangerous Habitual Offenders of 1933), and the police had their own means of 'protective custody' which usually involved concentration camps.[61]

While the assessment centres put as many obstacles as possible in the way of German women of 'sound' stock seeking to terminate unwanted pregnancies, they facilitated mass abortions on Polish and Russian forced women labourers. This was the other side of the coin of Nazi abortion policy. Their programme of negative eugenics, which had the professed aim to 'cleanse the racial body' of 'inferior individuals', led to compulsory abortion for 'hereditarily diseased' women and those of 'alien races'. In July 1933, the 'Law for the Prevention of Hereditarily Diseased Progeny' paved the way for compulsory eugenic sterilization,[62] which was swiftly supplemented by the legalization of abortion on eugenic grounds. This occurred in two stages: firstly, clandestinely in a confidential memorandum sent in 1933 by the head of the Reich Medical board to all doctors in Germany and without informing the judiciary but with the apparent backing of Hitler; secondly, by incorporating this principle into the amended Sterilization Law of 1935.[63] While the new abortion law of March 1943 introduced more severe penalties for those who performed abortions on women deemed of 'desirable' stock, it abrogated penalties if this was not the case. Polish and Czech aborting women and their accomplices, for example, were not prosecuted in German courts, nor were German abortionists who performed the operation on foreign women or those, like Jewish women, whose progeny was deemed 'undesirable'.[64]

My research has also unearthed the fact that the 1943 law caused frequent retrials when a public prosecutor pressed for a more severe sentence on aborting women and her accomplices. Thus, in October 1943, the *Landgericht* Trier increased the gaol term from four to six months for a 17-year-old female manual worker despite her employer's concern at the loss of a valuable worker and recognition of 'emotional problems caused by a pregnancy when so young and despite possessing a clean police record, her full confession and her evident remorse'. The judge ruled that 'in view of the long war and the considerable loss of valuable human life the vital strength [*Lebenskraft*] of the German *Volk* deserves increased protection and that, in contrast to opinions held before, the particular reprehensible and unacceptable nature of crimes against foetal life have come to be fully appreciated by the community'. The sentence of the young woman's accomplice, a father of three small children, was even raised from eight months' gaol to twelve months' penal servitude, on the grounds that he 'should have known that every attempt to perform an abortion on a genetically valuable woman expecting a desirable valuable child is to be regarded a crime against the vital strength of the German people'.[65]

Statistics of individual courts' records show that the determination to hand out much tougher sanctions on abortion was put into practice. In the *Landgericht* Duisburg, for example, during the last five years of the Weimar Republic only one single person was sentenced to penal servitude (under two years) but in the first years after January 1933 no less than sixteen people were thus sentenced, nine of whom to penal servitude of more than two years. At the same time the length of prison sentences also went up markedly.[66] In the *Landgericht* and *Amtsgericht* Freiburg i.Br., during the second part of the Weimar years (and the early parts of the Nazi period), two-thirds of all abortion cases were tried as misdemeanours by courts of lay assessors with a maximum penalty of three months' gaol (but in practice weeks or days or even fines were meted out), but between 1935 and 1945 as many as 12.3 per cent were tried by jury courts with much harsher penalties being meted out.[67] The same trend was noticeable in Mönchen-Gladbach.[68] In a typical case from the *Landgericht* Braunschweig from October 1942 a 27-year-old married woman had a brief affair with a lorry driver while her husband was in the army and when she suspected she was pregnant she arranged for a termination. She was sentenced to twelve months' imprisonment for this while her lover, who supplied an inappropriate instrument, went scot-free. In another case, also from 1942, an unfaithful wife received a penalty of five months' gaol simply for an attempted abortion which might well have been a natural miscarriage.[69]

Women's accomplices, their unpaid helpers, were also more severely punished, as the records of the *Landgericht* Freiburg well illustrate: prior to 1933 the vast majority received sentences of less than three months; after 1933 this gradually reversed and by 1936 the majority of accomplices were sentenced to between three and twelve months. In Mönchen-Gladbach the average length of sentence more than doubled.[70] An abortion case tried by the *Landgericht* Trier in 1938 shows how the courts inflicted increasingly harsh sentences on all involved: a 20-year-old woman, engaged to a bricklayer whom she subsequently married, had a pregnancy terminated in 1936 by a railway employee and one year later sought his help again but this time his attempts were unsuccessful and she bore a child. She received a month's prison sentence for one full and one attempted abortion, 'despite her youth and the hardship she suffered'. In the same trial a young woman living at home had been expecting an illegitimate child by a miller who said he could not marry her because he had no money. Through a friend, a local farmer, he arranged a termination by a widow. The young woman was sentenced to four months in goal. As with the other aborting woman mentioned above, the judge allowed that she had acted under duress but insisted that 'despite the mitigating circumstances the punishment should be appreciable because of the detrimental effect her actions had on the *Volk*'. The miller received a prison sentence of three months and three weeks, which was almost as harsh as that of his girlfriend, by way of punishment for his 'disgraceful behaviour' towards her, by impregnating her 'to fulfil his sexual drive', yet refusing to marry her. As for the two professional abortionists, the railwayman was sentenced to a total of three years in gaol, for one completed and one attempted abortion and for aiding with an attempted abortion on a second woman. Even though he had not acted for financial gain he had done so 'not out of compassion but to satisfy his carnal lust' (he had also forced his client to have sex with him) and had carried out his trade 'during office hours and in official railway accommodation'. His mitigating circumstances were the fact that he had no police record, his advanced age (despite being only forty) and the fact that 'he has shown himself a man in life', surely a reference to his wartime service. The harshest punishment by far was reserved for the widow: she was sentenced to a total of three years' penal servitude and a loss of all civil rights for five years for the full abortion on the young woman and two cases of attempted abortion on a domestic servant. The judge wanted her punished severely because she had 'carried out her criminal trade to the detriment of the national community even though her economic position did not force her seek an additional income. This was aggravated by the fact that she already had a four months' goal sentence for procuring.'[71]

Not surprisingly, the penalties for commercial abortionists went up markedly. A case from the *Schwurgericht* Trier from October 1937 shows this well: an agricultural vineyard worker also ran an abortion business with his wife. He was found guilty of three cases of commercial abortion and received the severe sentence of six years' penal servitude and loss of civil rights; his wife was sentenced to two years' penal servitude and loss of civil rights.[72] In another case, from Braunschweig, the commercial abortionist was a divorced woman of seventy-three who had a police record for offences against §218. The court considered her 'a dangerous habitual criminal', 'completely incorrigible' and a 'serious danger to the German *Volk*'. A severe sentence was demanded and duly meted out: five years' penal servitude and loss of civil rights for the same period of time.[73]

Many of the trials of the Nazi years I have investigated also show that men who had impregnated women and then aided an abortion – or, even worse, instigated the operation in the first place – were punished severely. For example, in March 1933, a 22-year-old woman from a village near Aachen was sentenced to six months' gaol for having undergone an abortion but her boyfriend was given eight months' goal for aiding and abetting and for his 'base motives since he did not want to marry her'; even when 'she withdrew her sexual favours from him' he preferred to denounce her to the police for having an abortion rather than do the honourable thing by her.[74] In the later years of the Third Reich men were punished severely for 'avoiding [their] duty as procreator[s] of children', as proved by the case of the lover of a divorcée who received fifteen months' imprisonment for helping his girlfriend with six abortions, though she was only sentenced to ten months in gaol[75] or, similarly, when the penalty for an agricultural worker from a village near Trier for aiding with his girlfriend's attempted and unsuccessful abortion (owing to inappropriate means) was one year in gaol, while she received only nine months. The judgement was, however, revised downwards on appeal but he still received two months more in gaol than she did.[76]

No doubt as a consequence of the increased level of monitoring, doctors and other health professionals noticed a more marked tendency towards self-abortion in the Nazi era than was the case during the Weimar Republic when it was much easier to enlist the help of a professional abortionist. Some doctors commented on the surprising skill which women displayed in finding their cervix and the care they took to operate in sterile conditions.[77] Certainly, the files from the period of the Second World War in particular, show the high prevalence of self-abortions.[78] Against the background of war when so many men were away at the front and a significant number of married women seemed to have started affairs with other men, or single women with married men, a number of abortion trials document the determination of women to avoid raising children born out of wedlock. But the authorities, worried about population loss and racial purity, saw it differently. Illegitimacy (as long as the progeny was thought 'eugenically desirable'), the courts now argued, was not a valid ground for abortion because, as one judge of the Cologne *Landgericht* put it, 'in today's times everything possible will be done to alleviate the situation of the unmarried mother, to bestow on her the full dignity and honour of motherhood in the eyes of the public'. Never mind that the 21-year-old woman was not only unmarried but also had lost both parents and had never had any brush with the police before. The judge freely admitted 'emotional hardship' was outweighed by crude populationist concerns. Or, as the *Amtsgericht* Rostock declared in June 1941, in the case of a 40-year-old divorcée who had an affair with a married man, her abortion must be judged a serious crime since this was 'an age in which prejudice against illegitimacy is no longer important'.[79] And, in the name of preserving the existing children of 'Aryan German parents', aborting women were given extra-long sentences if they were deemed to have neglected their children while on wartime quests for sexual adventure,[80] a paradoxical judgement since these children would be much more neglected when deprived of their mothers in gaol.

Yet, despite such signs of a determined crackdown on abortion as voluntary birth control it is perhaps surprising to find some evidence of continuity between Weimar and Nazi abortion judicial practice, for a number of reasons. Firstly, as Czarnowski has asserted, only a small proportion of putative criminal abortions was ever investigated under National Socialist rule because there were never enough funds available to investigate all the registered cases of terminations and miscarriages. Secondly, Nazi sentencing policy became much harsher in theory but was in practice tempered by a number of amnesties benefiting both aborting women and their accomplices, in cases when the expected prison term did not exceed a certain duration, the exact length of which varied over time.[81] What is more, during the early years of the Third Reich judicial practice resembled that of the Weimar era quite closely. Contrary to official threats, some judges seem to have condoned infractions of §218 and handed down surprisingly mild sentences for aborting women and abortionists alike on the grounds of often spurious-sounding mitigating circumstances. These latter seem either to have masked attitudes which were still more in tune with Weimar liberalism, while at the same time paying lip service to Nazi ideas, or they were driven by expediency rather than populationist concerns. Explanations proffered included one of chronology, i.e. that the deed had taken place during the decadent Weimar years when minds were perverted and sensibilities warped, or during the very early years of Nazi rule when the new ideology had not yet had time to enlighten the populace. Typically, one judge commenting on an abortion case of 1932, tried during the Nazi rule, thought

> the accused was quite right to point out that her deed, or rather her submitting to it, had taken place at a time when the community in which she lived did not regard it as unethical (1932) and since then the state has failed to change people's mind by the appropriate public enlightenment. Even if this incontrovertible fact cannot entirely exonerate the accused it must, however, serve as mitigating circumstances.[82]

In a case from October 1933, where the infraction of §218 had occurred at the very beginning of the Nazi regime, a homeopath was convicted of commercial abortion and manslaughter. His penalty consisted merely of imprisonment for two years, six months, presumably for the same reasons as above.[83] In another case from 1937, a husband-and-wife team of professional abortionists were convicted on at least four counts of abortion performed together and the husband for a further two cases performed by himself. Astonishingly, they were both spared penal servitude and received instead three and four years' gaol respectively. The judge held that they should be punished severely for not having operated with due care but that, on the other hand, they had

> carried out their criminal acts in the years 1927 to 1928, that is at a time, when the strict National Socialist view of the totally reprehensible nature of abortion had not yet penetrated to the general public; when, on the contrary, energetic propaganda on the part of certain factions for the complete decriminalization of abortion had become widespread, that means circumstances in which the defendants' deed could have appeared in a less reprehensible light. Thus, the deeds committed ... could not be judged as severely as would be today. That is why the defendants were granted mitigating circumstances and penal servitude was not imposed.[84]

Expediency was clearly the main reason for mild sentences in a well-known case tried in January 1935 in Frankfurt upon Oder: four doctors from Fürstenberg upon Oder, a medical officer of health and three family doctors, were accused of having cooperated in an abortion business; issuing false medical certificates for each other's operations; and entering misleading data in their medical diaries. Moreover they had been found guilty of deceiving health insurance funds by double charging them and their patients. Each was suspected of performing illegal terminations on many women, the medical officer of health in most, but not all, cases before 1933; his three colleagues after Hitler came to power. The sentences of these four doctors no longer referred to the most damaging aspects of the charge: abortion for financial gain and insurance fraud; consequently they were spared harsh sentences and, what is more, they served only a fraction of their time in prison either because they were pardoned or their prison term was commuted to a fine. The official reason was either that the charge was invalidated by the statute of limitation (five years) or, in the cases of the three medical practitioners, that it was committed in the first few months of the Nazi regime 'at a time when the political situation was still very fluid and the strict National Socialist attitude towards termination of pregnancy had not yet made its way into medical circles in a sufficiently desirable manner'. The more plausible explanation is the fact that the authorities had realized with some embarrassment that the criminal investigation of these four doctors would deprive the local population of all medical help. Thus, the arrest of the fourth doctor was delayed until a locum was secured. The decision in subsequent years not to strike their names off the medical register was surely taken for the same reason.[85]

Continuity with Imperial Germany

While I want to stress the significant liberal tendencies which developed in the sentencing practice of the postinflation Weimar years and connect them to a greater openness to modernity in general and reproductive self-determination in particular, there are important continuities also between Imperial and Weimar Germany in reproductive practices. The effect of the First World War should not be exaggerated. The continuity in working-class patterns of fertility control from late Imperial to Weimar Germany is striking, with a persistence of age-old trusted methods such as coitus interruptus and abortion alongside newer methods, although infanticide was much rarer than in the nineteenth century. There was no sharp break with women's previous strategy in that they had also taken control of their reproductive choices before the war.

Two of Weimar's potent symbols of modernity, the New Woman and the concept of rationalized sexuality, too, often turn out to be more ambiguous when tested against both popular culture and the statements of hundreds of aborting women here examined. While fictional heroines like Gilgi and Helene Willfüer celebrate the emancipated woman, the typical image of the proletarian protagonist in literary or cinematic abortion narratives hardly resembled that of the economically independent and sexually assertive woman; nor did the lower-class victims of §218 in popular culture display the rebelliousness against husband or the state which comes across in Marcuse's and Polano's surveys or when women defended their abortion in front of the police or the judge. Popular fiction or film preferred to present women from the lower orders in their more traditional roles as suffering mothers and as victims of the vicissitudes of fertility control.

As Elizabeth Harvey has put it, 'if the "new woman" was one powerful symbol of cultural change, Berlin came to embody it in terms of geographical location. The capital of the republic became the site on which competing and conflicting visions of its modernity were – at least partially – realized'.[86] Asserting bodily autonomy was as much a characteristic of emancipated women as their role in consumerism and the new mass culture. Aborting women who sought to control their body and their sexual relationships pursued their aim in a strikingly unsentimental fashion, for example when they disposed of their foetus as if it was so much waste, or when they terminated a pregnancy against the will of their male partner. Here women were not unlike what Helmuth Lethen called the 'cold persona' of male intellectuals who hid their emotions behind a mask of detached cynicism.[87] Yet, most of these women eschewed 'scientific' contraceptives in favour of what doctors repudiated as 'primitive' and unreliable methods of postcoital douching or, more importantly, abortion, albeit practised with modern methods like the syringe. While women defendants generally seemed to be familiar with medical concepts of pregnancy and termination they also adhered to older interpretations: a delayed period could mean several things, from a physical disturbance, a sign of being unwell to a misfortune that had befallen them or their entire family. In this they echoed the eighteenth-century female patients of the physician Storch, examined by Barbara Duden; they, too, understood a lack of menstrual flow in a variety of ways: as an illness, an unborn child, or a *Mondkalb*, that is a 'mole' or a 'shadow sibling' of a real conception.[88] If late blood is perceived as a misfortune, a visit to a fortune-teller does not seem illogical. The Berlin concierge who was a popular abortionist as well as a *Kartenlegerin* and offered sympathetic magic was only one of many wise women who catered for their clients' physical and emotional needs, as in other parts of Germany. It shows that 1920s and early 1930s Berlin, the byword for modernity, continued to offer space to practices we associate with premodern times, and that women who 'rationalized' their sexuality were still attracted to enchantment and magic. If such views appear strange to some of us today, it is proof that the historian needs an imaginative sympathy with and respect for the sensibilities of the subjects under scrutiny; rationality comes in different guises, and wonder and awe are compatible with a scientific worldview.[89]

ABBREVIATIONS

AG	Amtsgericht
ASDKB	Archiv der Stiftung Deutsche Kinemathek Berlin
BABL	Bundesarchiv Berlin-Lichterfelde
BAFAB	Bundesarchiv-Filmarchiv Berlin
BLHAP	Brandenburgisches Landeshauptarchiv Potsdam
Cath.	Catholic
EPA	Erich-Piscator-Archiv
FWA	Friedrich-Wolf-Archiv
GSABD	Geheimes Staatsarchiv Preussischer Kulturbesitz Berlin-Dahlem
HASK	Historisches Archiv der Stadt Köln
HHSAW	Hessisches Haupstaatsarchiv Wiesbaden
inh.	inhabitants
KPD	Kommunistische Partei Deutschlands
LAB	Landesarchiv Berlin
LG	Landgericht
LHAK	Landeshauptarchiv Koblenz
NRWHSAD	Nordrhein-Westfälisches Hauptstaatsarchiv Düsseldorf
Prot.	Protestant
SAdK	Stiftung Archiv der Akademie der Künste Berlin
SAM	Staatsarchiv München
SHSAD	Sächsisches Hauptstaatsarchiv Dresden
SPD	Sozialdemokratische Partei Deutschlands
St.anw.	Staatsanwaltschaft

Preface Notes

1. In the USA, legalization occurred in 1973 with *Roe v. Wade*; in Great Britain in 1967 by David Steele's private member's bill; in the German Democratic Republic in 1972 and in the Federal Republic of Germany in 1976.
2. Suzanne Goldenberg, 'State's Abortion Ban Fires First Shot in a Long War over Women's Rights', *Guardian*, 8 March 2006.
3. E.g., The Alton Bill of 1987 and 1995, a new bill in 2005; cf. attempts to relax abortion legislation by Frank Dobson in early 1998 (*Guardian*, 19 January 1998); The Pro Choice Forum, a group of UK academics, try to counter calls to outlaw late abortions, see Anna Fazackerley, 'Call to Axe Abortion Law', *Times Higher*, 21 January 2005; Polly Curtis, Health Correspondent, 'Abortions at Home Are Safe – Pilot Study', *Guardian*, 16 February 2006, front page; Zoe Williams, 'Time to Speak Up. Abortion Is Not Evil', *Guardian*, 27 January 2006, an eight-page special in G2.
4. Giles Tremlet, 'Catholic Church Fights to Keep its Grip as Portugal Votes on Legalizing Abortion', *Guardian*, 9 February 2007, 27; Giles Tremlett, 'Catholic Portugal Votes to Allow Abortion in Early Pregnancy', *Guardian*, 12 February 2007, 17.
5. 'Reizthema Abtreibung. Paragraph 218 spaltet die Koalition', *Der Spiegel*, 45.20, 13 May 1991, cover story; Ian Traynor, 'Catholics Defy Pope on Abortion', *Guardian*, 26 January 1998; Ian Traynor, 'German Bishops Hedge on Abortion', *Guardian*, 28 January 1998.
6. Despite pressure, he has so far not moved away from the official line which opposes all abortion since 'human life' is 'a primordial value which must be protected and promoted' from the beginning, see The Holy See, *Sacred Congregation for the Doctrine of the Faith. Declaration on Procured Abortion*, Doctrine of Faith, endorsed by Pope Paul VI, 28 June 1974.

Chapter 1 Notes

1. BABL, 2013, B1. 45, *Vorwärts*, 18 April 1918; ibid., 2017, *Münchener Post*, 9 July 1918. Cf. Cornelie Usborne, 'Body Biological to Body Politic: Women's Demands for Reproductive Self-determination in the First World War and Early Weimar Germany', in Geoff Eley and Jan Palmowski (eds), *Citizenship and National Identity in Twentieth-Century Germany* (Palo Alto, Ca., forthcoming).
2. See Cornelie Usborne, *The Politics of the Body. Women's Reproductive Rights and Duties* (London and Ann Arbor, 1992), appendix 1: According to the penal code of 1871 the abortion law was as follows:

    §218: A pregnant woman who has an abortion or who has her foetus [in German *Frucht*, fruit] destroyed in the womb is to be sentenced to penal servitude for up to five years. If there are mitigating circumstances the penalty is reduced to a minimum of six months' imprisonment. The same penalty applies to any person helping to procure an abortion or to destroy a fruit in the womb with the consent of the pregnant woman.

    §219: Any person helping to procure an abortion for money is to be sentenced to penal servitude of up to ten years.

    §220: Any person who procures an abortion without the knowledge or consent of the woman is to be sentenced to penal servitude for not less than two years. If the operation results in the death of the woman, penal servitude for not less than ten years, or for life, is prescribed. Attempts are punishable.
3. BABL, R 1501, 9347, B1. 45.
4. GSABD, Rep 84a, 8231, B1. 84.
5. Gisela von Streitberg, cited by Ute Gerhard-Teuscher, 'Frauenbewegung und §218', in Gisela Staupe and Lisa Vieth (eds), *Unter allen Umständen. Zur Geschichte der Abtreibung*

(Dresden and Berlin, 1993), 104–13; Helene Stöcker, *Die Liebe und die Frauen* (Minden, 1906).
6. See Julie Eichholz, *Frauenforderungen zur Strafrechts-Reform. Kritik und Vorschläge. Nach den Beschlüssen der Rechtskommission des BDF* (Mannheim, n.d.), 30, cited in Gerhard-Teuscher, 'Frauenbewegung und §218', 109.
7. See Usborne, *Politics of the Body*.
8. Hans-Jürgen Arendt, 'Eine demokratische Massenbewegung unter der Führung der KPD im Frühjahr 1931. Die Volksaktion gegen den Paragraphen 218 und gegen die päpstliche Enzyklika Casti Connubi', *Zeitschrift für Geschichtswissenschaft*, 19 (1917), 213–123; BABL, R 86, 2379, vol. 5; GSABD, Rep 219, 57; cf. Atina Grossmann, *Reforming Sex. The German Movement for Birth Control and Abortion Reform 1920–1950* (New York and Oxford, 1995), 86.
9. See Usborne, *Politics of the Body*; Grossmann, *Reforming Sex*.
10. Caroll Smith-Rosenberg, 'The Abortion Movement and the AMA, 1850–1880', in idem, *Disorderly Conduct, Visions of Gender in Victorian America* (New York, 1985), 217–244, 218; cf. Willem de Blécourt, 'Cultures of Abortion in The Hague in the Early Twentieth Century', in Franz X. Eder, Lesley Hall and Gert Hekma (eds), *Sexual Cultures in Europe. Themes in Sexuality* (Manchester and New York, 1999), 195–212.
11. See Eduard Seidler, 'Das 19. Jahrhundert. Zur Vorgeschichte des Paragraphen 218', in Robert Jütte (ed.), *Geschichte der Abtreibung von der Antike bis zur Gegenwart* (Munich, 1993), 133; Barbara Duden, *Disembodying Women. Perspectives of Pregnancy and the Unborn* (Harvard, 1993), 60.
12. Seidler, 'Das 19. Jahrhundert', 134.
13. The law of 18 May 1926 (see Usborne, *Politics of the Body*, appendix 1):
    §218 [the new single clause]:
    A woman who kills her fruit (foetus) by abortion or permits this by somebody else will be punished with imprisonment.
    The same penalty applies to any person helping to procure an abortion or to kill a fruit. Attempted abortion is punishable.
    Anybody who procures an abortion without consent or for money will be punished with penal servitude. The penalty also applies to any person who has supplied abortifacients for money. Under mitigating circumstances the penalty is reduced to imprisonment of not less than three months.
14. 'Entscheidungen des Reichsgerichts', Strafsachen, vol. 61, 243ff.: The decree of 11 March 1927.
15. Gabriele Czarnowski, 'Women's Crimes, State Crimes: Abortion in Nazi Germany', in Margaret L. Arnot and Cornelie Usborne (eds), *Gender and Crime in Modern Europe* (London, 1999), 238–56, 241–44; idem, 'Frauen als Mütter der "Rasse". Abtreibungsverfolgung und Zwangseingriff im Nationalsozialismus', in Gisela Staupe and Lisa Vieth (eds), *Unter allen Umständen* (Dresden and Berlin, 1993), 58–73, 59.
16. Donna Harsch, 'Society, the State, and Abortion in East Germany, 1950–1972', *The American Historical Review*, 102 (1997), 53–84.
17. Cornelie Usborne, *Frauenkörper – Volkskörper. Geburtenkontrolle und Bevölkerungspolitik in der Weimarer Republik* (Münster, 1994), 273–74.
18. Gabriele Czarnowski, 'Abortion as Political Conflict in the Unified Germany', *Parliamentary Affairs: A Journal of Comparative Politics*, 47 (1994), 252–67.
19. See Seidler, 'Das 19. Jahrhundert', 120–39; Angus McLaren, *A History of Contraception from Antiquity to the Present Day* (Oxford, 1990), 82–84.
20. See Seidler, 'Das 19.Jahrhundert', 120–139, 123ff.; Nick Hopwood, 'Producing Development: The Anatomy of Human Embryos and the Norms of Wilhelm His', *Bulletin of the History of Medicine*, 74 (2000), 29–79, 74; Scott F. Gilbert (ed.), *A Conceptual History of Modern Embryology* (Baltimore, 1991); Barbara Duden, '"Ein falsch Gewächs, ein unzeitig Wesen, gestocktes Blut". Zur Geschichte von Wahrnehmung und Sichtweise der Leibesfrucht', in Staupe and Vieth (eds), *Unter anderen Umständen*, 27–35; Duden, *Der*

Frauenleib als öffentlicher Ort. Vom Mißbrauch des Begriffs Leben (Hamburg and Zurich, 1991), 71.
21. Seidler, 'Das 19. Jahrhundert', 124.
22. Usborne, *Politics of the Body*, esp. ch. 2; idem, 'The Christian Churches and the Regulation of Sexuality in Weimar Germany', in Jim Obelkevich, Lyndal Roper and Raphael Samuel (eds), *Disciplines of Faith: Studies in Religion, Politics and Patriarchy* (London, 1987), 99–112.
23. Joseph Mayer, 'Katholische Sexualethik und Strafrechtsreform', *Mitteilungen des Reichsfrauenbeirats der Deutschen Zentrumspartei*, 4 (1929), 1–11, 11.
24. Wilhelm Lütgert, 'Die Stellung der Evangelischen Kirche', in Arbeitsgemeinschaft für Volksgesundung e.V. (ed.), 'Paragraph 218. Sinn und Problematik der Abtreibungsparagraphen', *Schriften zur Volksgesundung*, 17 (1931), 23–28.
25. Friedrich Lönne, *Das Problem der Fruchtabtreibung vom medizinischen, juristischen und nationalökonomischen Standpunkt* (Berlin, 1924), 16.
26. Alf Labhardt, 'Die Gefahren der künstlichen Eingriffe in das keimende Leben', *Das kommende Geschlecht, Zeitschrift für Familienpflege und geschlechtliche Volkserziehung auf biologischer und ethischer Grundlage*, 1 (1921), 72–80, 74.
27. Alfred Dührssen, 'Die Reform des §218 (unter Berücksichtigung der Strafrechtsentwürfe von 1919 und 1925)', *Sexus IV* (Leipzig, 1926), 48–121, 52.
28. Wilhelm Liepmann, *Die Abtreibung* (Berlin and Vienna, 1927), 1–2; Georg Winter, 'Strittige Punkte in der Behandlung des fieberhaften Abortes', *Medizinische Welt*, 1 (1927), 1040–43.
29. Georg Winter, 'Abtreibung oder künstlicher Abort?', *Medizinische Welt*, 1 (1927), 52–54.
30. E.g. Alfred Grotjahn and Gustav Radbruch, *Die Abtreibung der Leibesfrucht. Zwei Gutachten* (Berlin, 1921); Max Hirsch, *Fruchtabtreibung und Präventivverkehr im Zusammenhang mit dem Geburtenrückgang* (Würzburg, 1914).
31. Angus McLaren, *Birth Control in Nineteenth-Century England* (New York, 1978), 231.
32. Smith-Rosenberg, 'The Abortion Movement', 217.
33. McLaren, *Birth Control*, 14.
34. Norman Himes, *A Medical History of Contraception* (London, 1936, repr. 1963); J.A. Banks, *Prosperity and Parenthood: A Study of Family Planning among the Victorian Middle Class* (London, 1954).
35. E.g. John T. Noonan Jr (ed.), *The Morality of Abortion: Legal and Historical Perspectives* (Cambridge, Mass., 1970).
36. John E. Knodel, *The Decline of Fertility in Germany, 1871–1939* (Princeton, NJ, 1974).
37. Himes, *A Medical History of Contraception*, 238; R. and K. Titmuss, *Parents Revolt: A Study of the Declining Birth Rate in Acquisitive Societies* (London, 1942), 66, 73.
38. Luc Jochimsen, *Paragraph 218. Dokumentation eines hundertjährigen Elends* (Hamburg, 1971); Petra Schneider, *Weg mit dem Paragraphen 218! Die Massenbewegung gegen das Abtreibungsverbot in der Weimarer Republik* (Berlin, 1975).
39. E.g. the authors of the volume of essays edited by Susanne von Paczensky and Renate Sadrozinski (eds), *Die Neuen Moralisten. §218 – vom leichtfertigen Umgang mit einem Jahrhundertthema* (Reinbek, 1984); idem, *§218. Zu Lasten der Frauen* (Reinbek, 1988), especially the contribution by Barbara Duden; Christiane Dienel, 'Das 20. Jahrhundert (I). Frauenbewegung, Klassenjustiz und das Recht auf Selbstbestimmung der Frau', in Jütte, *Geschichte der Abtreibung*, 140–169; the contributions in Staupe and Vieth (eds), *Unter allen Umständen*, esp. Kristine von Soden, '"§218 – streichen, nicht ändern!" Abtreibung und Geburtenregelung in der Weimarer Republik', 36–51.
40. Esp. Duden, 'Ein falsch Gewächs', 27–35.
41. Linda Gordon, *Woman's Body, Woman's Right: A Social History of Birth Control in America* (Harmondsworth, 1977); Sheila Rowbotham, *A New World For Women. Stella Browne: Socialist Feminist* (London, 1977).
42. Gordon, *Woman's Body, Woman's Right*, xiii.
43. E.g. James Reed, *From Private Vice to Public Virtue. The Birth Control Movement and American Society since 1830* (New York, 1978).

44. McLaren, *Birth Control*; Smith-Rosenberg, 'The Abortion Movement'; Rosalind Pollock Petchesky, *Abortion and Woman's Choice* (London, 1986); Barbara Brookes, *Abortion in England 1900–1967* (London, 1988); idem, 'The Illegal Operation. Abortion 1919–39', in London Feminist History Group (ed.), *The Sexual Dynamics of History* (London, 1983), 165–76.
45. Petchesky, *Abortion and Woman's Choice*, xxiii.
46. Ibid., vii.
47. E.g. McLaren, *Birth Control*, see especially 12–13; Brookes, *Abortion in England*; Patricia Knight, 'Women and Abortion in Victorian and Edwardian England', *History Workshop Journal*, 4 (1977), 57–69.
48. E.g. for Germany: Usborne, *Politics of the Body*; Anna Bergmann, *Die verhütete Sexualität. Die Anfänge der modernen Geburtenkontrolle* (Hamburg, 1992) and her revised edition *Die verhütete Sexualität. Die medizinische Bemächtigung des Lebens* (Berlin, 1998); Grossmann, *Reforming Sex*. For Austria: Karin Lehner, *Verpönte Eingriffe. Sozialdemokratische Reformbestrebungen zu den Abtreibungsbestimmungen in der Zwischenkriegszeit* (Vienna, 1989). For Switzerland: Annemarie Ryter, 'Abtreibung in der Unterschicht zu Beginn des Jahrhunderts. Eine empirische Untersuchung von Strafgerichtsakten des Staatsarchivs Basel-Stadt', unpubl. MA dissertation (*Lizentiatsarbeit*), (University of Basle, 1983). Sometimes abortion has not been given sufficient consideration, see Karen Hagemann, *Frauenalltag und Männerpolitik. Alltagsleben und gesellschaftliches Handeln von Arbeiterfrauen in der Weimarer Republik* (Bonn, 1990), a book of nearly 900 pages which dedicates only fourteen pages to women's experience of abortion, most of them gleaned from medical or official sources and only two cases of oral history.
49. Edward Shorter, *A History of Women's Bodies* (London, 1982), xi.
50. Petchesky, *Abortion and Woman's Choice*, 31.
51. James Woycke, *Birth Control in Germany 1871–1933* (London, 1988).
52. Ibid., 89.
53. Smith-Rosenberg, 'The Abortion Movement', 217.
54. See my review of Woycke's book in *German History*, 8 (1990), 101–03.
55. Paul Weindling's review in *The Times Higher Education Supplement*, 21 October 1988, 19.
56. Paul Weindling, *Health, Race and German Politics between National Unification and Nazism, 1870–1945* (Cambridge, 1989).
57. Bergmann, *Die verhütete Sexualität*, 183; Grossmann, *Reforming Sex* and her numerous earlier articles, e.g., '"Satisfaction is Domestic Happiness": Mass Working-Class Sex Reform Organizations in the Weimar Republic', in Michael N. Dobkowski and Isidor Wallimann (eds), *Towards the Holocaust: The Social and Economic Collapse of the Weimar Republic* (Westport, Conn., 1983), 265–93; Grossmann, 'The New Woman and the Rationalization of Sexuality in Weimar Germany', in Ann Snitow, Christine Stansell and Sharon Thompson (eds), *Powers of Desire: The Politics of Sexuality* (London, 1984), 190–211; Grossmann, 'Berliner Ärztinnen und Volksgesundheit in der Weimarer Republik: Zwischen Sexualreform und Eugenik', in Christine Eifert and Susanne Rouette (eds), *Unter allen Umständen: Frauengeschichte in Berlin* (Berlin, 1986), 183–217; Elisabeth Domansky, 'Militarization and Reproduction in World War I Germany', in Geoff Eley (ed.), *Society, Culture, and State in Germany, 1870–1930* (Ann Arbor, 1996), 427–463; Ute Planert, *Antifeminismus im Kaiserreich. Diskurs, soziale Formation und politische Mentalität* (Göttingen, 1998); idem, 'Der dreifache Körper des Volkes: Sexualität, Biopolitik und die Wissenschaften vom Leben', *Geschichte und Gesellschaft*, 26 (2000), 539–76.
58. Bergmann, *Die verhütete Sexualität*, 1st edn, 183.
59. Günter Jerouscheck, 'Zur Geschichte des Abtreibungsverbots', in Staupe and Vieth (eds), *Unter allen Umständen*, 11–26, 23; idem, *Lebensschutz und Lebensbeginn. Kulturgeschichte des Abtreibungsverbot* (Stuttgart, 1989); idem, 'Die juristische Konstruktion des Abtreibungsverbot', in Ute Gerhard (ed.), *Frauen in der Geschichte des Rechts. Von der frühen Neuzeit bis zur Gegenwart* (Munich, 1997), 248–261.

60. James Mohr, *Abortion in America* (New York and Oxford, 1978), 21, 164.
61. Michele Barrett, *Women's Oppression Today* (London, 1980); Mary O'Brien, *The Politics of Reproduction* (London, 1981); Petchesky, *Abortion and Woman's Choice*.
62. Usborne, *Politics of the Body*; cf. e.g. Grossmann, *Reforming Sex*; Bergmann, *Die verhütete Sexualität*; Christine von Soden, 'Verwünschungen und Prophezeihungen. Die Befürwortung des §218 in der Weimarer Republik', in Susanne von Paczensky (ed.), *Wir sind keine Mörderinnen!* (Reinbek, 1984), 127–37; Woycke, *Birth Control in Germany*; cf. for other Western countries, Brookes, *Abortion in England*; J. Farrell Brodie, *Contraception and Abortion in 19th-century America* (Ithaca and London, 1994); Smith-Rosenberg, 'The Abortion Movement'. Exceptions are e.g. Gisela Bock, *Zwangssterilisation im Nationalsozialismus. Studien zur Rassenpolitik und Frauenpolitik* (Opladen, 1986); Czarnowski, 'Women's Crimes, State Crimes'; the contributions by Larissa Leibrock-Plehn, Karin Stukenbrock and, to some extent, by Christiane Dienel in Jütte, *Geschichte der Abtreibung*, 68–90, 91–119 and 140–68; Knight, 'Women and Abortion'.
63. E.g. Max Marcuse, 'Zur Frage der Verbreitung und Methodik der willkürlichen Geburtenbeschränkung in Berliner Proletarierkreisen', *Sexualprobleme*, 9 (1913), 752–80; idem, *Der eheliche Präventivverkehr. Seine Verbreitung, Verursachung und Methodik. Dargestellt und beleuchtet an 300 Ehen. Ein Beitrag zur Symptomatik und Ätiologie der Geburtenbeschränkung* (Stuttgart, 1917); cf. Robert P. Neumann, 'Industrialization and Sexual Behaviour: Some Aspects of Working-Class Birth Control in Wilhelmine Germany', in Robert Bezucha (ed.), *Modern European Social History* (Lexington, Mass., 1972), 270–98.
64. See Angus McLaren, 'Women's Work and Regulation of Family Size: the Question of Abortion in the Nineteenth Century', *History Workshop Journal*, 4 (1977), 70–81; idem, 'The Early Birth Control Movement: an Example of Medical Self-Help', in John Woodward and David Richards (eds), *Health Care and Popular Medicine in Nineteenth-Century England* (London, 1977), 89–194.
65. Angus McLaren, *Reproductive Rituals: the Perception of Fertility in England from the Sixteenth Century to the Nineteenth Century* (London and New York, 1984) 11.
66. Petchesky, *Abortion and Woman's Choice*, xxii, 51.
67. Usborne, *Politics of the Body*; Knight, 'Women and Abortion' nevertheless comes up with many subtle findings.
68. Hera Cook, *The Long Sexual Revolution. English Women, Sex, and Contraception, 1800–1975* (Oxford, 2004).
69. Knight, 'Women and Abortion'; Mary Chamberlain, *Old Wives Tales. Their History, Remedies and Spells* (London, 1981); Kate Fisher, *Birth Control, Sex, and Marriage in Britain, 1918–1960* (Oxford, 2006) which is based on oral history.
70. Brookes, *Abortion in England*, 29, 36–37; cf. idem, 'Women and Reproduction, 1860–1939', in Jane Lewis (ed.), *Labour and Love. Women's Experience of Home and Family, 1850–1940* (London, 1986), 149–71; idem, 'The Illegal Operation'.
71. Brodie, *Contraception and Abortion*; cf. Mohr, *Abortion in America*; Allan Keller, *Scandalous Lady: The Life and Times of Madame Restell, New York's Most Notorius Abortionist* (New York, 1981).
72. Ursula von Keitz, *Im Schatten des Gesetzes. Schwangerschaftskonflikt und Reproduktion im deutschsprachigen Film, 1918–1933* (Marburg, 2005).
73. Leslie Reagan, *When Abortion Was a Crime. Women, Medicine, and Law in the United States, 1867–1973* (Berkeley, 1997); see also idem, '"About to Meet her Maker". Women, Doctors, Dying Declarations and the State's Investigation of Abortion, Chicago, 1867–1940', *The Journal of American History*, 77 (1991), 1240–64.
74. For a fuller discussion cf. Usborne, *Politics of the Body*, chap. 4.
75. Kristine von Soden, *Die Sexualberatungsstellen der Weimarer Republik, 1919–1933* (Berlin, 1988); idem, 'Auf der Suche nach den fortschrittlichen Ärzten', in von Pazensky and Sadrozinski (eds), *Die neuen Moralisten*, 127–37; von Soden, 'Auf dem Weg zur "neuen Sexualmoral"', in Johanna Geyer-Kordesch and Annette Kuhn (eds), *Frauenkörper, Medizin, Sexualität* (Düsseldorf, 1986), 237–62.
76. Grossmann, *Reforming Sex*, 97, 101, 106.

77. Cf. David Crew, 'Alltagsgeschichte: A New Social History from Below?', *Central European History*, 22 (1992), 394–407; Alf Lüdtke, 'Alltagsgeschichte: Aneignung und Akteure. Oder – es hat noch kaum begonnen!', *Werkstatt Geschichte*, 17 (1997), 83–91; idem, (ed.), *The History of Everyday Life. Reconstructing Historical Experiences and Ways of Life* (Princeton, NJ, 1995).
78. Giovanni Levi, 'On Microhistory', in Peter Burke (ed.), *New Perspectives on Historical Writing* (Cambridge, 1991), 93–113, 95.
79. Peter Burke, *The Historical Anthropology of Early Modern Italy. Essays on Perception and Communication* (Cambridge, 1987), 15; idem, 'Cultural History: Past, Present and Future', *Theoretische geschiednis*, 13 (1986), 187–96, 190; Willem de Blécourt, 'Time and the Anthropologist; or the Psychometry of Historiography', *Focaal, tijdschrift voor antropologie*, 26/27 (1996), 17–24, 18–19.
80. E.g. Duden, '"Ein falsch Gewächs"'; idem, '"Keine Nachsicht gegen das schöne Geschlecht." Wie sich Ärzte die Kontrolle über Gebärmütter aneigneten', in Paczensky and Sadrozinski (eds), § *218*, 114–33; Larissa Leibrock-Plehn, *Hexenkräuter oder Arznei. Die Abteibungsmittel im 16. und 17. Jahrhundert* (Stuttgart, 1992); idem, 'Frühe Neuzeit. Hebammen, Kräutermedizin und weltliche Justiz', in Jütte (ed.), *Geschichte der Abtreibung*, 68–90; Eva Labouvie, *Andere Umstände. Eine Kulturgeschichte der Geburt* (Cologne, 1998) and idem, *Beistand in Kindesnöten. Hebammen und weibliche Kultur auf dem Land, 1550–1910* (Frankfurt a.M., 1999); Ann Oakley, 'Wisewoman and Medicine Man: Changes in the Management of Childbirth', in Juliet Mitchell and Ann Oakley (eds), *The Rights and Wrongs of Women* (London, 1976), 17–58.
81. E.g. The essays in Jürgen Schlumbohm, Barbara Duden, Jacques Gélis and Patrice Veit (eds), *Rituale der Geburt. Eine Kulturgeschichte* (Munich, 1998) and in Barbara Duden, Jürgen Schlumbohm and Patrice Veit (eds), *Geschichte des Ungeborenen. Zur Erfahrungs- und Wissenschaftsgeschichte der Schwangerschaft, 17. – 20. Jahrhundert* (Göttingen, 2002).
82. See Margaret L. Arnot and Cornelie Usborne (eds), *Gender and Crime in Modern Europe* (London 1999), introduction.
83. Regina Schulte, *The Village in Court. Arson, Infanticide, and Poaching in the Court Records of Upper Bavaria, 1848–1910* (Cambridge, 1994), 15–16; cf. idem, 'Infanticide in Bavaria in the Nineteenth Century', in Hans Medick and David Sabean (eds), *Interest and Emotion. Essays on the Study of Family and Kinship* (Cambridge, 1984), 77–102.
84. Emily Martin, *The Woman in the Body. A Cultural Analysis of Reproduction* (Boston, Mass, 1987), 5–23; cf. McLaren, *Reproductive Rituals*.
85. Duden, '"Ein falsch Gewächs"', 27–31; cf. idem, *The Woman Beneath the Skin* (Cambridge and London, 1991); idem, *Disembodying Women*; idem, *Der Griff nach dem ungeborenen Leben. Zur Subjektgenese des Embryos* (Pfaffenweiler, 1993).
86. Kathleen Canning, *Gender History in Practice. Historical Perspectives on Bodies, Class, and Citizenship* (Ithaca and London, 2006), 169–70, 173, 179.
87. Fisher, *Birth Control, Sex and Marriage*.
88. Mohr, *Abortion in America*; Diana Gittings, *Fair Sex: Family Size and Structure, 1900–1939* (London, 1982).
89. Cf. McLaren, *Reproductive Rituals*, 7, 89 mentions a separate culture of women from men, 'a world of female reproductive rituals' that has remained largely hidden. The same is true of Weimar Germany, see Cornelie Usborne, 'Wise Women, Wise men and Abortion in the Weimar Republic: Gender, Class and Medicine' in Lynn Abrams and Elizabeth Harvey (eds), *Gender Relations in German History. Power, Agency and Experience from the Sixteenth to the Twentieth Century* (London, 1996), 143–76; cf. de Blécourt, 'Cultures of Abortion in The Hague'; idem, *Het Amazonenleger. Irreguliere genezeressen in Nederland, 1850–1930* (Amsterdam, 1999), chap. 8.
90. HASK, NL Marx, no. 193, 26 February 1926, 'proposals to protect nascent life', by bishop Dr Joseph Stoffels; ibid., 18 September 1928, minutes of the Magdeburg meeting initiated by the Deutscher Caritas Verband about abortion.

91. Cf. Charles Tilly, *Big Structures, Large Processes, Huge Comparisons* (New York, 1984).
92. Alf Lüdtke, '"Alltagsgeschichte": Verführung oder Chance? Zur Erforschung der Praxis historischer Subjekte', unpublished paper, cited by Geoff Eley, 'Foreword', in Lüdtke, *The History of Everyday Life*, X; cf. idem, 'Alltagsgeschichte: Aneignung und Akteure. Oder – es hat noch kaum begonnen!', *WerkstattGeschichte*, 17 (1997), 83–91.
93. See Detlev J.K. Peukert, *The Weimar Republic. The Crisis of Classical Modernity* (London, 1991); Thomas W. Kniesche and Stephen Brockmann (eds), *Dancing on the Volcano. Essays on the Culture of the Weimar Republic* (Columbia, 1994).
94. See contemporary sources such as Deutscher Textilarbeiterverband (ed.), *Mein Arbeitstag, mein Wochenende. 150 Berichte von Textilarbeiterinnen* (Berlin, 1930); Irmgard Keun, *Gilgi – eine von uns* (Berlin, 1931). See also, Usborne, 'The New Woman and Generation Conflict: Perceptions of Young Women's Sexual Mores in the Weimar Republic', in Mark Roseman (ed.), *Generations in Conflict. Youth Revolt and Generation Formation in Germany, 1770–1968* (Cambridge, 1995), 137–63; Dagmar Reese, Eve Rosenhaft, Carola Sachse and Tilla Siegel (eds), *Rationale Beziehungen? Geschlechterverhältnisse im Rationalisierungsprozeß* (Frankfurt a.M., 1993).
95. Today we are familiar with such habits as part of the New Age movement, which seems to appeal particularly, though not exclusively, to the educated middle classes. In that sense it is obviously different from the strategies pursued by Berlin proletarian women during the 1920s and early 1930s. Cf. Mary Lindemann, *Health and Healing in Eighteenth-Century Germany* (Baltimore and London, 1996).

Chapter 2 Notes

1. Friedrich Wolf, *Cyankali. §218: ein Schauspiel*, (orig. Berlin and Weimar, 1929); the edition used here is based on Emmi Wolf and Klaus Hammer (eds), *Cyankali von Friedrich Wolf. Eine Dokumentation* (Berlin and Weimar, 1978; repr. Stuttgart, 1983).
2. Atina Grossman, however, devotes a short section to some anti-§218 plays, novels and paintings, see *Reforming Sex*, 98ff.
3. Scott Spector, 'Was the Third Reich Movie-Made?', *American Historical Review* 106 (2001), 461–84, 461, 463.
4. Cf. Peukert, *The Weimar Republic*; Elizabeth Harvey, 'Culture and Society in Weimar Germany: the Impact of Modernism and Mass Culture', in Mary Fulbrook (ed.), *German History since 1800* (London, 1997), 279–97.
5. Anton Kaes, 'New Historicism: Writing Literary History in the Postmodern Era', *Monatshefte* 2 (1992), 156, cited in Richard Bodek, *Proletarian Performance in Weimar Berlin: Agitprop, Chorus, and Brecht* (Columbia, 1997), 2–3.
6. Ernst Toller, *Masse Mensch* (Berlin, 1920); Richard Dove, *He Was a German. A Biography of Ernst Toller* (London, 1990).
7. Bertolt Brecht, 'Schwierigkeiten des epischen Theaters', *Frankfurter Zeitung*, 27 November 1927, cited in Anton Kaes, Martin Jay and Edward Dimendberg (eds), *The Weimar Republic Sourcebook* (Berkely, Los Angeles and Oxford, 1994), document 220.
8. Olaf Dohrmann, '"Kämpfer für eine Reform des §218", "Limonade" oder Gretchentragödie? *Cyankali* im sozialhistorischen und intermedialen Kontext', in Malte Hagener (ed.), *Geschlecht in Fesseln. Sexualität zwischen Aufklärung und Ausbeutung im Weimarer Kino 1918–1933* (Munich, 2000), 102–18, 103.
9. Anton Kaes, 'Film in der Weimarer Republik', in Wolfgang Jacobsen, Anton Kaes and Hans Helmut Prinzler (eds), *Geschichte des Deutschen Films* (Stuttgart, 1993), 39, 46; Eberhard Kolb, *The Weimar Republic* (London, 1988), 92; cf. Harvey, 'Culture and Society', 281.
10. E.g. Siegfried Kracauer, *From Caligari to Hitler. A Psychological History of the German Film* (Princeton, 1947, repr. 1974); Lotte Eisner, *The Haunted Screen: Expressionism and the German*

Film and the Influence of Max Reinhardt (Berkeley and Los Angeles, 1969); it is also invoked by Katharina von Ankum, 'Motherhood and the "New Woman"'. Vicki Baum's *stud.chem. Helene Willfüer* and Irmgard Keun's *Gilgi – eine von uns*', *Women in German Yearbook*, 11 (1995), 171–88.

11. Cf. Thomas Elsaesser, *Weimar Cinema and After. Germany's Historical Imaginary* (London and New York, 2000), 3; Lynda Nead, *Myths of Sexuality. Representations of Women in Victorian Britain* (Oxford, 1988), 7.
12. Von Keitz, *Im Schatten des Gesetzes*, 120ff.
13. Ibid., 83ff., 132ff.
14. It was released in 1928 in the U.S.A. as *Unwelcome Children*, see von Keitz, 'Sittenfilm zwischen Markt und Rechtspolitik. Martin Bergers *Kreuzzug des Weibes* (1926) und seine amerikanische Fassung *Unwelcome Children*', in Hagener (ed.), *Geschlecht in Fesseln*, 139–53, 146ff.
15. *Schmiede* (The forge) was produced in 1924 and *Freies Volk* (Free people) in 1925. According to David Welch both showed 'fundamentally reformist tendencies', see Welch, 'The Proletarian Cinema in the Weimar Republic', *Historical Journal of Film, Radio and Television*, 1 (1981), 3–18, 6; cf. the entry 'Martin Berger – Regisseur,' in Hans-Michael Bock (ed.), *Cinegraph. Lexikon zum deutschsprachigen Film* (Munich, 1984).
16. Cf. Usborne, *Politics of the Body*, 183–84.
17. *Film-Kurier*, vol. 8, no. 231, 2 October 1926.
18. Cf. von Keitz, 'Sittenfilm', 143.
19. ASDKB, folder *Kreuzzug des Weibes*.
20. Von Keitz, 'Sittenfilm', 139.
21. *Der Film*, vol. 11, no. 27 (1926), 14; *Reichsfilmblatt* 41 (1926), 24; *Film-Kurier*, vol. 8, no. 231 (1926) and 5 July (1927) n.p.
22. Relatively few films favoured the existing abortion law: *Arme kleine Eva* (Edmund Heuberger, 1931); *Kinderseelen klagen Euch an* (Kurt Bernhardt, 1927) financed by the Catholic church; see von Keitz, *Im Schatten des Gesetzes*, 191ff.
23. Kracauer, *From Caligari to Hitler*, 46, 144.
24. See Usborne, *Politics of the Body*, 183ff.
25. See ibid., 139–41.
26. BAFAB, censorship report 13759, *Kreuzzug*, 2nd act, 24 September 1926.
27. Von Keitz, 'Sittenfilm', 145–46.
28. Keun, *Gilgi*, 191; cf. Usborne, *Politics of the Body*, 116, 120–21, 129.
29. A notable exception is Mike Leigh's 2005 film *Vera Drake*, which represents a wise woman as naïve but essentially idealistic. Her 'employer', a woman from her acquaintance who collects payment from Drake's abortion clients, is the villain here.
30. *Film-Kurier*, vol. 8, no. 231, 2 October 1926, n.p.
31. See Usborne, *Politics of the Body*, chap. 4.
32. Von Keitz, 'Sittenfilm', 147.
33. See. the detailed examination in von Keitz, *Im Schatten des Gesetzes*, 169.
34. When Max and Paul surprise her with stolen food she protests, 'I have been honest for fifty years!.'
35. Keun, *Gilgi*, 189.
36. Barbara Kosta, 'Unruly Daughters and Modernity: Irmgard Keun's *Gilgi – eine von uns*', *The German Quaterly*, 86 (1995), 271–86, 282; cf. Kerstin Barndt, *Sentiment und Sachlichkeit. Der Roman der Neuen Frau in der Weimarer Republik* (Cologne, Weimar and Vienna, 2003), 3. My interpretation here differs from von Ankum's in 'Motherhood and the "New Woman"', 173, who sees this as an advocacy for the 'New Mother' and an 'essentialist femininity' supporting 'patriarchal and capitalist structures'.
37. *Berliner Tageblatt*, 2 October 1926, cited in von Keitz, 'Sittenfilm', 142, n.7.
38. Patrice Petro, *Joyless Street. Women and Melodramatic Representations in Weimar Germany* (Princeton, 1989) xx, xxii: she bases this also on Emilie Altenloh's 1914 study, *Zur*

Notes

Soziologie des Kino: Die Kino-Unternehmung und die sozialen Schichten ihrer Besucher, Diss. Heidelberg (Jena, 1914, reprinted in facsimile Hamburg, 1977).
39. Petro, Joyless Street, 90–91; Lynda King, Best-Sellers By Design. Vicki Baum and the House of Ullstein (Detroit, 1988), 89; cf. Harvey, 'Culture and Society', 282; Barndt, Sentiment und Sachlichkeit, 65.
40. Cf. Barndt, Sentiment und Sachlichkeit, 96ff.
41. Hiltrud Häntzschel, Irmgard Keun (Reinbek, 2001), 33; Barndt, Sentiment und Sachlichkeit, 152; von Keitz, Im Schatten des Gesetzes, 262ff.
42. Barndt, Sentiment und Sachlichkeit, 123.
43. Häntzschel, Irmgard Keun, 31ff.
44. Kosta, 'Unruly Daughters', 272.
45. Keun, Gilgi, 97.
46. See Usborne, 'The New Woman and Generation Conflict'; Stephen Brockmann, 'Weimar Sexual Cynicism', in Kniesche and Brockmann (eds), Dancing on the Volcano, 165–80; Usborne, Politics of the Body, 85ff.; Grossmann, Reforming Sex, chap. 3.
47. Max Brod, 'Die Frau und die neue Sachlichkeit', in Friedrich M. Huebner (ed.), Die Frau von Morgen, wie wir sie wünschen (Leipzig, 1929), 38–48, quoted in Kaes et al. (eds), The Weimar Republic Sourcebook, document 77.
48. Keun, Gilgi, 7.
49. Siegfried Kracauer, 'Die kleinen Ladenmädchen gehen ins Kino', originally published in Frankfurter Zeitung, 11 – 19 March 1927; repr. in idem, Das Ornament der Masse (Frankfurt a.M., 1977), 279–94.
50. Keun, Gilgi, 8, 9.
51. Ibid., 65.
52. Kosta, 'Unruly Daughters', 282; cf. Richard W. McCormick, Gender and Sexuality in Weimar Germany. Film, Literature and 'New Objectivity' (New York, 2001).
53. Ingeborg Franke (Ingeborg von Wangenheim), 'Gilgi – Film, Roman und Wirklichkeit', Der Weg der Frau, 3 (1933) special number 'Angestellte', 3, 6.
54. Kracauer, 'Die kleinen Ladenmädchen'.
55. E.g. Heide Schlüpmann, 'Kinosucht', Frauen und Film, 33, October (1982), 45–52; Petro, Joyless Street, 18ff.
56. Cf. King, Best-Sellers by Design, 40ff.; see the excellent discussion of Heidegger, Benjamin, Kracauer and Simmel in Petro, Joyless Street, 50ff.; cf. Dorothy Rowe, Representing Berlin. Sexuality and the City in Imperial and Weimar Germany (Aldershot, 2003), esp. 90ff.
57. Wolf, Cyankali. §218, 37.
58. Ibid., 38.
59. The title of Wolf, 'Vorspruch für ein Zeittheater', Arbeiterbühne und Film, 17, no. 11 (November 1930) 6–7, cited in Wolf, Cyankali, appendix, 85–86.
60. SAdK, Friedrich-Wolf-Archiv, 153/8. Cf. Dohrmann, 'Kämpfer für eine Reform des Paragraph 218', 104ff.
61. SAdK, Berlin, FWA, 153/8, programme of the Stuttgart theatre.
62. Süddeutsche Arbeiter-Zeitung, cited in Kulturamt der Landeshauptstadt Stuttgart, Stuttgart in Dritten Reich, Friedrich Wolf. Die Jahre in Stuttgart, 1927–1933. Ein Beispiel (Stuttgart, 1983), 140.
63. SAdK, FWA 153/3, Erich Kästner, '§218 Cyankali', Neue Leipziger Zeitung, 14 September 1929; ibid., Süddeutsche Arbeiter-Zeitung, Stuttgart, 12 March 1930.
64. SAdK, FWA 153/3, Hamburgischer Correspondent, 24 March 1930; Ludwig Marcuse, 'Friedrich Wolf: Cyankali Paragraph 218', in Frankfurter Generalanzeiger, 31 October 1929, cited in Kulturamt Stuttgart, Stuttgart in Dritten Reich, 140; Kölner Volkszeitung, 15 November 1929.
65. SAdK, FWA 153/3, Frankfurter Zeitung, 10 November 1929, Dr. Kögel, 'Cyankali – eine juristische Aufklärung. Der Staatsanwalt weist den Dichter zurecht', n.p.
66. See Chapter 1.

Notes

67. SAdK, FWA 153/3, *Frankfurter Zeitung*, 10 November 1929, Dr. Kögel, 'Cyankali – eine juristische Aufklärung. Der Staatsanwalt bringt den Dichter vor Gericht', n.p.; see similar criticism on 7 August 1930 by the Bavarian Ministry of the Interior, cited in Kulturamt Stuttgart, *Stuttgart in Dritten Reich*, 206.
68. SAdK, FWA no. 153/3, *Frankfurter Zeitung*, 13 November 1929, Frau Rechstanwältin Elfriede Cohnen and *Frankfurter Zeitung*, 17 November 1929, reply by Friedrich Wolf.
69. Dohrmann, 'Kämpfer für eine Reform des §218', 105.
70. 'Dass der Film keineswegs Limonade wird', cited in Kulturamt Stuttgart, *Stuttgart im Dritten Reich*, 201–2.
71. Cf. Karl Christian Führer, 'Auf dem Weg zur Massenkultur? Kino und Rundfunk in der Weimarer Republik', *Historische Zeitschrift*, 262 (1996), 739–82, 743.
72. Dohrmann, 'Kämpfer für eine Reform des §218', 102, 106.
73. See ibid., 112.
74. Carl Credé-Hörder, *Volk in Not! Das Unheil des Abtreibungsparagraphen* (Dresden, 1927). SAdK, EPC, no. 69, Credé, *Frauen in Not – §218* (Berlin, 1929).
75. W.L. Guttsman, *Workers' Culture in Weimar Germany. Between Tradition and Commitment* (New York, Oxford and Munich, 1990), 278.
76. SAdK, EPC, no. 69, Gastspiel der Piscatorbühne, Berlin, *§218. Gequälte Menschen*, 4, 5; ibid., Piscator, 'Fundamental statement', 7; cf. Bodek, *Proletarian Performance*, 4.
77. SAdK, EPC, no. 69, *§218. Gequälte Menschen*, 11, 13.
78. SAdK, EPC, no. 69, *Tempo*, Berlin, March 1930.
79. SAdK, EPC, no. 69, 'Gastspiel der Piscatorbühne im Schiller-Theater', *Fremdenblatt*, Hamburg, 14 January 1930.
80. SAdK, EPC, no. 69, cited in *Freie Presse*, Elberfeld, 19 February 1930.
81. SAdK, EPC, no. 69, Alfred Kerr, Credé: 'Paragraph 218', Piscator Bühne. Wallner Theater, *Berliner Tageblatt* , vol. 59, no. 161, Berlin, 4 April 1930.
82. SAdK, EPC, no. 69, 'Frauen in Not', *Berliner Zeitung am Mittag*, Berlin, 4 April 1930; Herbert Ihring, *Berliner Börsen-Courier*, June 1930; Julius Bab, 'Piscator ist wieder da … Wallner-Theater zeigt "§218" (Frauen in Not) von Carl Credé', *Berliner Volkszeitung*, Berlin, April 1930.
83. SAdK, EPC, no. 69, Willy Haas, *Der Montag Morgen*, Berlin, 7 April 1930.
84. SAdK, EPC, no. 69, e.g. *Kölner Tageblatt*, Cologne, 3 February 1930; *Volksstimme*, no. 320, Mannheim, 25 November 1929; cf. Emil Belzner, *Neue Badische Landeszeitung*, 25 November 29 but also the critic of *Wormser Zeitung*, 6 December 1929, who dismissed Piscator's direction as a gimmick which got in the way of Credé's main message; *Lübecker Volksbote*, no. 4, 6 January 1930.
85. E.g. in several municipal theatres in Elberfeld, SAdK, EPC, no. 69, cited in *Freie Presse*, Elberfeld, 19 February 1930.
86. SAdK, EPC, no. 69, *Berliner Zeitung am Mittag*, 4 April 1930; *Rheinische Zeitung*, 39, no. 34, Cologne, 3 February 1930; 'Spektakel im Festhaus. §218', *Wormser Zeitung*, 6 December 1929.
87. Franz Krey, *Maria und der Paragraph. Ein Roman um §218*, Der Rote 1– Mark Roman, vol. 5 (Vienna, Berlin and Zurich, 1931); Wolf, preface, 2.
88. Krey, *Maria und der Paragraph*, 127–28.
89. Cf. Grossman, *Reforming Sex*, 85.
90. SAdK, Erich-Weinert-Archiv, B1. 297.
91. SAdK, Erich-Weinert-Archiv, Erich Weinert, '§218', typescript, later published in *Der Mahnruf* (Berlin, 1929) and *Die Welt am Abend*, 25 March 1931; poem specially translated by Timothy Adès, translator-poet, London, 2006.
92. See Usborne, *Politics of the Body*, 16ff., 157ff.; Privatarchiv Dr Kurt Nemitz Bremen, NL Julius Moses, Julius Moses, *Textilpraxis*, (1927), 76, 82.
93. Harry Zohn, '"A Heart of Gold and a Jaw of Iron": An Introduction to Kurt Tucholsky', in Harry Zohn (ed.), *Germany? Germany! The Kurt Tucholsky Reader* (London, 1990), 13–20.

94. Kurt Tucholsky, 'Die Leibesfrucht spricht' (orig. 1931, repr. Reinbek, 1983), this version trl. Karl F. Ross, in Zohn (ed.), *Germany? Germany!*, 35.
95. Wolf, *Cyankali*, 11, 38 (all page numbers refer to the 1983 reprint).
96. Ibid., 50, 60, 65, 3.
97. Krey, *Maria und der Paragraph*, 48–50, 72–75.
98. Bock (ed.), *Cinegraph*, entry Beß.
99. BAFAB, censorship report 18637, *Frauenarzt Dr. Schäfer*, 11 April 1928.
100. BAFAB, censorship report 22326, *Der Sittenrichter*, 3 May 1929; ASDKB, *Der Sittenrichter*.
101. See Welch, 'The Proletarian Cinema', 5.
102. See Usborne, *Politics of the Body*, 76ff.
103. Kulturamt der Landeshauptstadt Stuttgart, *Stuttgart im Dritten Reich*, 204: in 1930 it was examined on 2 and 11 April, 19 May and 12 September.
104. Kulturamt Stuttgart, *Stuttgart im Dritten Reich*, 204–13. Cf. Dohrmann, 'Kämpfer für eine Reform des §218', 108–9.
105. BAFAB, censorship report, 13848, Arthur Ziem, Internationale Film Exchange, Berlin (world distribution). *Kreuzzug des Weibes*, 24 September 1926. When Conrad Veidt as the public prosecutor refers to the law (paragraph 218/219, crime against nascent life), Maly Delschaft as the teacher replies: 'ach was, das Gesetz trifft die Armen, die Reichen wissen sich ihm zu entziehen!'. This was censored and had to be replaced with: 'ach was, dem Gesetz wissen sich andere ja doch zu entziehen!'. For censorship of rape scene, see von Keitz, 'Sittenfilm', 144.
106. BAFAB, censorship report 18637, *Frauenarzt Dr. Schäfer*, Hegewald-Film Berlin, 11 April 1928.
107. E.g. Beth Irwin Lewis, '*Lustmord*: Inside the Windows of the Metropolis', in von Ankum, *Women in the Metropolis*, 202–32; Maria Tatar, *Lustmord: Sexual Murder in Weimar Germany* (Princeton, 1995); cf. also Stephen Brockmann, 'Weimar Sexual Cynicism', in Kniesche and Brockmann (eds), *Dancing on the Volcano*, 165–80.
108. See Usborne, *Politics of the Body*, 78ff.
109. Cf. Marcuse, 'Zur Frage der Verbreitung und Methodik'.
110. Petro, *Joyless Street*, xxii; cf. von Keitz, 'Sittenfilm', 148, who argues that the central topic of the film *Kreuzzug* is not abortion but 'the exploration of the sphere which can accommodate the male subject's conflicting claims of his heart and his conscience ... '
111. See Usborne, 'The New Woman and Generation Conflict'.
112. See Welch, 'The Proletarian Cinema', 7–9, 13.
113. The various motions of the USPD and the KPD in the Reichstag demanded the decriminalization of and access to abortion as an individual right; see Usborne, *Politics of the Body*, 217–19.
114. Cited in Jill Forbes, 'Retrospective: Kuhle Wampe oder wem gehört die Welt?', *Monthly Film Bulletin*, July 1978, 146.
115. See 'Kuhle Wampe', *Screen*, special issue, vol. 15, no. 2 (1974), 41–73.
116. See Ulli Jung and Stephanie Roll, 'Women Enjoying Being Women. Some Observations on the Occasion of a Retrospective of Franz Hofer's Extant films in Saarbrücken', *Kintop. Jahrbuch zur Erforschung des frühen Films*, 8 (1999), 159–68.
117. BAFAB, censorship report 13759, *Kreuzzug*, 24 September 1926, subtitle, act 1: The storm throws the window in the prosecutor's office open: While the young teacher admires the tempestuous nature, the public prosecutor warns: 3. 'Ja, – Doch der Mensch darf nicht wie sie hemmungslos seinen Trieben folgen. 4. ... jeder Zoll ein Staatsanwalt.' (Yes, but we human beings should not follow our drives as unrestrained as nature.' She: ' ... always a public prosecutor.')
118. Anton Kaes, 'The Debate about Cinema: Charting a Controversy (1909–1929)', *New German Critique*, 40 (1987), 7–33.
119. Heide Schlüpmann, 'Aufklärung als Subkultur. Madame Lu, Die Frau für diskrete Beratung', in Hagener (ed.), *Geschlecht in Fesseln*, 131–53, 131–32.

120. Keun, *Gilgi*, 159: 'Einen kräftigen Schuss Strassenjungenhaftigkeit braucht man als Selbstschutz. Keine Angst vor Worten, keine Angst vor Begriffen – deutsch geredet. Eine böse und ungerechte Wut hat sie auf den harmlosen kleinen Doktor. Mach' dich man nicht so wichtig, du elende in Karbol getauchte Micky Maus, du ... was heisst prachtvoll gebautesn Becken! Ich will kein Kind!'
121. Keun, *Gilgi*, 161: 'Helfen Sie mir, Herr Doktor! Ich habe solches Vertrauen zu Ihnen'; 'hört jeder Arzt gern'; 'ich weiss nicht, was – ich meine – also ich –'; 'Quatsch, das ist mir zu dumm, ich kann das nicht.'
122. Peter Brooks, *The Melodramatic Imagination: Balzac, Henry James, Melodrama and the Mode of Excess* (New Haven, 1976), cited in Petro, *Joyless Street*, 26ff.
123. Petro, *Joyless Street*, 26–27; Barndt, *Sentiment und Sachlichkeit*, 24, 138ff.
124. E.g. Baum's novel *stud.chem. Helene Willfüer* (1928); Braune's novel *Das Mädchen an der Orga Privat* (1925).
125. Cited in Petro, *Joyless Street*, 19–20.

Chapter 3 Notes

1. See Weindling, *Health, Race and German Politics*, esp. 155ff.
2. Bergmann, *Die verhütete Sexualität*, 169ff.; Usborne, *Politics of the Body*, 10ff.
3. E.g. Jean Bornträger, 'Der Geburtenrückgang in Deutschland, seine Bewertung und Bekämpfung', *Veröffentlichungen aus dem Gebiete der Preußischen Medizinalverwaltung*, 1.13 (1912), 36ff.
4. Cf. Robert A. Nye, *Crime, Madness and Politics in Modern France. The Medical Concept of National Decline* (Princeton, 1984).
5. See Usborne, *Politics of the Body*, 10ff.
6. Ludwig Ebermayer, *Arzt und Patient in der Rechtsprechung* (Berlin, 1924), 248.
7. BABL, R 86, 2379, vol. 1, Niederschrift, Reichsgesundheitsrat, 21 December 1917, 15.
8. E.g. Von Soden, *Die Sexualberatungsstellen*, 139–44.
9. See Chapter 1, note 13.
10. Gustav Radbruch, 'Der künstliche Abort im geltenden und künftigen Strafrecht', *Monatsschrift des Bundes Deutscher Ärztinnen*, 5: a termination was not illegal 'if performed by the pregnant woman herself ... or by a third person who was appropriately equipped to judge the situation'.
11. BABL, R 3001, 6232, Bl. 188, decision by the Supreme Court, 20 April, 1928, that no lay person could rely on §54, the emergency clause, since 'non-doctors are generally not in the position to lean on it' and 'if in doubt only a doctor can judge the danger of a pregnancy'.
12. See Chapter 1, note 64; see also Bettina Herrmann, 'Else Kienle (1900–1970) – Ein Ärztin im Mittelpunkt der Abtreibungsdebatte von 1931', in Eva Brinkschulte (ed.), *Weibliche Ärzte: Die Durchsetzung des Berufsbildes in Deutschland* (Berlin, 1993), 114–22; Monika von Oertzen, '"Nicht nur fort sollst du dich pflanzen, sondern hinauf": Die Ärztin und Sexualreformerin Anne-Marie Durand-Wever (1889–1970)', in Brinkschulte (ed.), *Weibliche Ärzte*, 140–52.
13. Cf. for example, GSABD, 84a, the many files of investigations or trials of aborting doctors, e.g. nos 17108; 17112; 17114; especially 17153; 17136; 17148; 17139 etc. Also, BHSAP, Pr.Br.Rep 2A, Reg. Potsd., I Med, No. 10, Bl. 166ff. investigations against Dr. L. F.; Bl. 293, Dr. H. G; LAB, Rep 58, many files of doctors accused of crimes against §218 or §§219/220, e.g. nos 416, 850, 2137, 2494, 2719; BAK, R86, 2379, vol. 1, Reichs Minister of the Interior to the President of the Reichs Health Office, 8 November 1917, case of Prof. Henkel of Jena University.
14. SAM, St.anw. Traunstein, 15634, public prosecutor, Maria L., 10 July 1922, 79–81.
15. Ibid., Bl. 169–169Rs, report by the forensic pathologist at the court, 30 August 1922.

16. Ibid., public prosecutor, B1. 50–51Rs, 17 July 1922.
17. Ibid., B1. 170–171, forensic pathologist, 30 August 1922; ibid., B1. 50–51Rs, public prosectuor, 17 June 1922.
18. Ibid., report by the medical committee, 185.
19. Ibid., letter of the public prosecutor, Traunstein, 31 August 1922; *Rosenheimer Volkszeitung*, no. 131, (September) 1922; and decision of criminal court at the *Landgericht* Traunstein, 29 November 1922.
20. See Usborne, *Politics of the Body*, 181ff.
21. Leo Klauber, 'Die Abtreibung', in Ludwig Levy-Lenz (ed.), *Sexualkatastrophen. Bilder aus dem modernen Geschlechts- und Eheleben* (Leipzig, 1926), 119; see the discussion in the journal *Der Sozialistische Arzt* throughout the 1920s. Left-wing members of the Reichstag who favoured a liberalization of §218 shared this opinion, e.g. Emil Höllein (KPD), see his book, *Gegen den Gebärzwang. Der Kampf um die bewußte Kleinhaltung der Familie* (Berlin, 1928), 174, 179.
22. Dührssen, 'Die Reform des §218', 57, 80, 74.
23. Leo Klauber, *Der Sozialistische Arzt*, August (1928), 3.
24. See Cornelie Usborne, 'Women Doctors and Gender Identity in Weimar Germany (1918–1933)', in Anne Hardy and Lawrence Conrad (eds), *Women and Modern Medicine* (Amsterdam, 2000), 109–26.
25. See Usborne, *Politics of the Body*, chap. 4.
26. SAM, Sta.anw. Traunstein 15634, forensic pathologist, *Landgericht* Traunstein, 30 August 1922, 1.
27. Ibid., deposition Dr Karl Hartmann, *Landgericht* Traunstein, 24 June 1922, 3.
28. Ibid., *Rosenheimer Volkszeitung*, no. 131, September 1922.
29. Ibid., report forensic pathologist, *Landgericht* Traunstein, 30 August 1922, 2.
30. The so-called 'Ärzteschwemme' was often evoked when doctors defended their abortion practice, e.g. case of Dr J. (LAB Rep 58, 2137–2139); cf. Eva-Maria Klasen, 'Die Diskussion über eine Krise der Medizin in Deutschland zwischen 1925 und 1935', unpubl. med. Dissertation, Mainz, 1984.
31. SAM, Sta.anw. Traunstein 15634, resolution by the brush manufacturer Pruckner, Rosenheim, n.d.
32. Ibid. 'Zum Fall DR. H.', no name (probably a trade union paper).
33. Ibid., *Rosenheimer Volkszeitung*, no. 131, September, 1922.
34. Ibid., *München-Augsburger-Abendzeitung*, 12 April 1922; *Bayerische Staatszeitung und Bayerischer Staatsanzeiger*, no. 87 (1922).
35. Ibid., B1. 169–71, report by the forensic pathologist at the Landgericht Traunstein, 30 August 1922.
36. Ibid., B1. 167.
37. Ibid., deposition Hartmann, 24 June 1922, 1.
38. Ibid., 55Rs.
39. E.g. LAB, Rep 58, no. 850, Dr K.M., vol. I and II; ibid., no. 2494, Dr F.S. 1931; ibid., no. 416, Dr E.M.; NRWHSAD, Reg. Dü, 53761, medical practitioner A.H.; ibid., 53762, Dr H. S.
40. SAM, St.anw. Traunstein 15634, B1. 185, Medizinalkomitee der Universität München, 15 November 1922 to the Bayerische Landgericht Traunstein.
41. E.g. Julius Moses, 'Der Kampf um die Aufhebung des Abtreibungsparagraphen', *Biologische Heilkunst*, 10 (1929), 934. Many conservative doctors, on the other hand, often conceded that medical terminations could also be risky: e.g. Sigismund Vollmann, 'Die Bekämpfung der Abtreibungsseuche', *Ärztliches Vereinsblatt für Deutschland* 52, (1925), 45–49; cf. Usborne, 'Abtreibung: Mord, Therapie oder weibliches Selbstbestimmungsrecht? Der Paragraph 218 im medizinischen Diskurs der Weimarer Republik', in Johanna Geyer-Kordesch and Annette Kuhn (eds), *Frauenkörper, Medizin, Sexualität* (Düsseldorf, 1986), 192–236, 203–5.

42. Cf. Georg Winter, 'Strittige Punkte in der Behandlung des fieberhaften Aborts', *Medizinische Welt*, 20 August 1927, 1040; Paul Hüssy, *Begutachtung und gerichtliche Beurteilung von ärztlichen Kunstfehlern auf dem geburtshilfliche-gynäkologischem Gebiete* (Stuttgart, 1935), 8. This has been supported by the many judicial files of doctors who came to the attention of the police because their aborting patients had been seriously injured or had died, e.g. NRWHSAD, Reg. Dü, 53761, Complaints and Investigations of Medical Personnel in the District of Duisburg; idem, Sta.anw. Dü, 7J 298/30, 53762; BLHAP, Rep 3B, IMed 269, Frankf. a.O.
43. Ernst Bumm, 'Not und Fruchtabtreibung', *Münchener Medizinische Wochenschrift*, vol. 70, 1 February (1923), 468–72, 471.
44. Hüssy, *Begutachtung*, 8.
45. BABL, R 86, 21379, vol. 3, his representation 13 November 1925.
46. Sigmund Vollmann, *Die Fruchtabtreibung als Volkskrankheit. Gefahren, Ursachen, Bekämpfung* (Leipzig, 1925), 23.
47. Erich Ebstein (ed.), *Modernes Mittelalter. Eine Anklage auf Grund authentischen Materials von Dr. med. I. St., weiland Arzt in –burg* (Leipzig, 1921).
48. LAB, Rep 58, 850, Dr K.M, 1926; cf. Usborne, 'Abortion for Sale!', 190–91; cf. below, Chapter 4.
49. E.g. the case of a medical practitioner of 1929: he was sentenced to one month's gaol for criminal abortion leading to death, while the midwife's sentence was nine months' gaol for the same offence, see NRWHSAD, Reg. Dü, 53761, 16.
50. Ibid., Bl. 17.
51. GSABD, Rep 84a, no. 17107, Bl. 17, 97.
52. NRWHSAD, Reg. Dü 53761, Bl. 16, trial against Dr W.B.
53. SAM, St.anw. Traunstein 15634, Bl. 157.
54. Ibid., Bl. 128, 83.
55. Ibid., 10 July 1922, no. 7, Kathi B.
56. GSABD, Rep 84a, no. 17107, Bl.103.
57. SAM, St.anw. Mü I, 1834, expert testimony Professor Döderlein; letter Dr Adams Lehmann to the chair of the District Medical Association of Munich, 12 July 1914.
58. In this I agree with Marita Krauss, *Die Frau der Zukunft. Dr. Hope Bridges Adams Lehmann, 1855–1916, Ärztin und Reformerin* (Munich, 2002), 153ff.
59. SAM, Sta.anw. Mü I, 1834, testimony Dr Adams Lehmann, 16 July 1914; cf. Krauss, *Die Frau der Zukunft*, 22–31; see Usborne, *Politics of the Body*, 7.
60. SAM, St.anw. Mü I, 1834, police interviews 6 March 1914, 1–2, and 10 March 1914, 2.
61. Krauss, *Die Frau der Zukunft*, 125ff.
62. SAM, Sta.anw. Mü, I, 1834, interview 6 March 1914, testimony, B.R., referring to an article by a Dr A. Müller, 'Bericht über die am 5. März abgehandelte Versammlung der Vereinigten Münchener Frauenvereine', *Bayerische/Süddeutsche Hebammenzeitung*, 1 April 1914.
63. SAM, Sta.anw. Mü I, 1834, Bl. 4.
64. Ibid., Bl. 12ff, deposition Dr Anton Hengge, 25 July 1914.
65. Ibid., court order, 1 September 1915.
66. Krauss, *Die Frau der Zukunft*, 150.
67. SAM, St.anw. Mü I, 1834, Bl. 12, deposition Dr Anton Hengge, 25 July 1914.
68. Ibid., deposition Adams Lehmann, 16 July 1914, 1.
69. Krauss, *Die Frau der Zukunft*, 143ff.
70. SAM, St.anw. Mü I, 1834, expert report by Professor Döderlein.
71. Ibid., Bl. 65, deposition 25 July 1914.
72. Ibid., letter to the Medical Association of the district of Munich, 12 June 1914.
73. See the various contributions in Arthur Weil (ed.), *Sexualreform und Sexualwissenschaft. Vorträge gehalten auf der 1. Int. Tagung für Sexualreform auf sexualwissenschaftlicher Grundlage in Berlin* (Stuttgart, 1922), 218–37; Ludwig Fraenkel, *Die Empfängnisverhütung, biologische Grundlage, Technik und Indikationen* (Stuttgart, 1932), 175.

74. SAM, St.anw. Mü I, 1834, police interviews, 30 January 1915.
75. SAM, St.anw.Mü, I 1834, letter to the Medical Association of the district of Munich, 12 June 1914.
76. Cf. Usborne, 'Women Doctors and Gender Identity', 117ff.; idem, *Politics of the Body*, 196ff.
77. SAM, St.anw. Mü I, 1834, B1. 12, testimony Dr Anton Hengge, 25 July 1914.
78. Ibid., appendix to letter to Munich Medical Association, 12 June 1914.
79. Usborne, *Politics of the Body*, 180, 196.
80. The other one was Else Kienle, arrested in Stuttgart on 19 February 1931, and charged with providing the necessary certificates for termination and with having performed abortions in her private practice on more than 100 women; see Grossman, *Reforming Sex*, 83f. Cf. Usborne, 'Women Doctors and Gender Identity'.
81. E.g., BABL, R86, 2379, vol. 1, Reichs Minister of the Interior to the President of the Reichs Health Office, 8 November 1917, re case of Professor Henkel of Jena University; GSABD, Rep 84a, 17153, Dr med. St. of Husum, 1930, who was found to have removed 'the complete uterus in five cases, including at least one healthy one'.
82. Lotte Fink, 'Schwangerschaftsunterbrechung und Erfahrung aus Ehe- und Sexualberatung', *Die Ärztin*, 7 (1931) 70–74.
83. Fink, 'Die Tubensterilisation als Mittel der Geburtenregelung. Bericht über 375 Fälle der Ehe- und Seuxalberatungsstelle Frankfurt a.M. (Mutterschutz)', *Medizinische Welt*, (1931), 750–51.
84. See Usborne, *Politics of the Body*, 151ff.
85. See Chapter 1, n. 14.
86. SAM, St.anw. Traunstein, 15634, B1. 88Rs, B1. 89. Anna N.
87. Ibid., B1. 80Rs–81Rs, police interviews.
88. Ibid., judicial enquiry, 22 June 1922.
89. SAM, St.anw. Traunstein, 15658, case against Elisabeth. St., 1926.
90. NRWHSAD, Reg. Dü 53762, trial against medical practitioner Dr Selo, 1930, 'Über die Tragik des Riesenprozesses', *Volkszeitung*, 22 October 1931.
91. Ibid., cases 1, 6 and 7.
92. BLHAP, Rep 3B I Med 281 Frankfurt a.O., Dr K. u. Gen, 1934, B1. 9.
93. See Usborne, *Politics of the Body*, 182.
94. SAM, St.anw. Traunstein 15634, newspaper cuttings, *Münchener Zeitung*, no. 101, 3 and *Bayerische Staatszeitung und Bayerischer Staatsanzeiger*, no. 87, 11 April 1922.
95. Cf. NRWHSAD, St.anw. Dü, 7J 298/30, case against Dr med Georg Kr; cf. Usborne, 'Wise Women', 146–47.
96. SAM, Sta.anw. Traunstein 15634, police interviews, Maria B. B1. 93–101Rs.
97. SAM, St.anw. Mü I, 1834, 6 March 1914, interview midwife Babette R.; BLHAP, Rep 3B, IMed 269, Frankfurt a.O., Dr K. and others, 1934; GHSABD, Rep 84a, 17148, *Berliner Zeitung am Mittag*, 3 November 1931.
98. Vollmann, 'Die Bekämpfung der Abtreibungsseuche', 45.
99. Lönne, *Das Problem der Fruchtabtreibung*, 31.
100. Ornella Moscucci, *The Science of Woman: Gynaecology and Gender in England, 1800–1929* (Cambridge, 1990), 56.
101. See Johanna Bleker, 'Die ersten Ärztinnen und ihre Gesundheitsbücher für Frauen', in Eva Brinkschulte (ed.), *Weibliche Ärzte. Die Durchsetzung des Berufbildes in Deutschland* (Berlin, 1993), 65–83, 67; Oakley, 'Wisewoman and medicine man', 33–34.
102. Cf. Usborne, 'Wise women and wise men', 166–67.
103. Ludwig Fraenkel, 'Physiologie der weiblichen Genitalorgane', in J. Halban and L. Seitz (eds), *Biologie und Pathologie des Weibes* [8 vols] (Berlin and Vienna, 1924–29), vol. 1 (1924), 517–634, 549–50.
104. Cf. Shorter, *A History of Women's Bodies*, 179–207.
105. NRWHSAD, Reg. Dü, 53761, complaints and investigations about medical personnel in the district of Duisburg, penal case of med. practitioner Dr Wilhelm B. 1929.

106. NRWHSAD, St.anw. Kleve, Rep 7, 896; this doctor was prosecuted for illegal abortion on many counts, as well as child abuse and incest, but, strangely, not for rape.
107. Grotjahn and Radbruch, *Die Abtreibung der Leibesfrucht*; Grotjahn, (ed.), *Eine Kartothek zu §218: Ärztliche Berichte aus einer Kleinstadtpraxis über 426 künstliche Aborte in einem Jahr* (Berlin, 1932).
108. Grotjahn, *Eine Kartothek zu* §218, 15, case 3 and 136-37, case 433.
109. Ibid., 17, case 19.
110. E.g. NRWHSAD, Reg. Dü, 53762, trial of Dr Selo of Krefeld, 1930, 3rd case; 'Aus der Politik: Dr Käthe Frankenthal, Anfrage im preußischen Landtag', Korrespondenz des Informationsbüros für Geburtenregelung, no. 2 (1932), 4-9, 7: report about an anonymous doctor in a small industrial town who in 1931 performed terminations on 1,500 women, 'all operations without general or local anaesthetic'.
111. SAM, Sta.anw. Traunstein, 15634, Medizinalkomitee der Univ. Mü, 15 November, 1922, 181Rs, 182.
112. SAM, St.anw. Traunstein 15634, B1. 16ff., police interviews 10 July 1922.
113. Ibid., report by forensic pathologist, 30 August, 1922 and report by medical committee, 15 November, 1922, on Maria L., Anna P., and Marie R.
114. Ibid., B1. 46.
115. SAM, St.anw. Mü I, 1834, deposition Babette R., 6 March, 1914.
116. Ibid., case 16, Frau C. Sch., cook, 37: '3 childbirths, 1 termination, intelligence deficit, Porro'; or case 18, Frau R. P., cook: '29, no childbirth, 1 termination, Porro'. For a discussion of eugenic sterilization, see Usborne, *Politics of the Body*, 151ff.

Chapter 4 Notes

1. The most detailed study is Reinhard Spree, 'Kurpfuscherei-Bekämpfung und ihre soziale Funktionen während des 19. und 20. Jahrhunderts', in Alfons Labisch and Reinhard Spree (eds), *Medizinische Deutungsmacht im sozialen Wandel* (Bonn, 1989), 103-22. See also, Spree, *Soziale Ungleichheit vor Krankheit und Tod. Zur Sozialgeschichte des Gesundheitsbereichs im Deutschen Kaiserreich* (Göttingen, 1981), 140ff.; Martin Dinges (ed.), *Medizinkritische Bewegungen im Deutschen Reich (ca. 1870-ca.1933)* (Stuttgart, 1996); Cornelia Regin, *Selbsthilfe und Gesundheitspolitk. Die Naturheilbewegung im Kaiserreich (1889-1914)* (Stuttgart, 1995), chap. 3; Franz Walter, Viola Denecke and Cornelia Regin, *Sozialistische Gesundheits- und Lebensreformverbände* (Bonn, 1991); Robert Jütte, *Geschichte der Alternativen Medizin. Von der Volksmedizin zu den unkonventionallen Therapien von heute* (Munich, 1996), esp. 32-42; Eberhard Wolff, '"Volksmedizin" - Abschied auf Raten. Vom definitorischen zum heuristischen Begriffsverständnis', *Zeitschrift für Volkskunde*, 94 (1998), 233-57; Lutz Sauerteig, *Krankheit, Sexualität, Gesellschaft. Geschlechtskrankheiten und Gesundheitspolitik in Deutschland im 19. und 20. Jahrhundert* (Stuttgart, 1999), 421ff.; Claudia Huerkamp, 'Medizinische Lebensreform im späten 19. Jahrhundert. Die Naturheilkundebewegung in Deutschland als Protest gegen die naturwissenschaftliche Universitätsmedizin', *Vierteljahresschrift für Sozial- und Wirtschaftsgeschichte*, 73 (1986), 158-82.
2. Spree, 'Kurpfuscherei-Bekämpfung', 108-9.
3. Willem de Blécourt, 'Prosecution and Popularity: the Case of the Dutch Sequah, 1891-1993', in John Woodward and Robert Jütte (eds), *Coping with Sickness. Medicine, Law and Human Rights - Historical Perspectives* (Sheffield, 2000), 75-90; idem, 'Cultures of Abortion in The Hague'; Willem de Blécourt and Cornelie Usborne (eds), *Alternative Medicine in Europe since 1800*, special issue *Medical History*, 43, (3) (1999); Roy Porter, *Quacks, Fakers and Charlatans in English Medicine* (Stroud, 2000).
4. Spree, 'Kurpfuscherei-Bekämpfung', 103.

5. As a 1905 manual put it, it related to all those who practised 'commercially without an academic medical degree and without proper qualifications approved by a state examination body'; see Gaston Vorberg, *Kurpfuscher! Eine zeitgemäße Betrachtung* (Leipzig and Vienna, 1905), 1, cited in Regin, *Selbsthilfe*, 278.
6. See Jütte, *Geschichte der Alternativen Medizin*, 39.
7. Ibid., 36-37.
8. See de Blécourt, 'Prosecution and Popularity'; idem, 'Illegale genezers en nep patienten. Over de aantrekkingskracht van unorthodoxe vormen van geneeskunde rond 1900', *Tijdschrift voor sociale geschiedenis*, 25 (1999), 425-42.
9. See 'Wie und warum die Kurierfreiheit eingeführt wurde', *Medizinalpolitische Rundschau. Zentralblatt für Parität der Heilmethoden*, 20, 31/2 (1927), 138-39.
10. See Spree, *Soziale Ungleichheit*, 140-50; Claudia Huerkamp, *Der Aufstieg der Ärzte im 19. Jahrhundert. Vom gelehrten Stand zum professionellen Experten: Das Beispiel Preußens* (Göttingen, 1985), 364ff.; 'Volk und Arzt', *Medizinalpolitische Rundschau*, 19, 13 (1926), 24.
11. Alfons Labisch, 'From Traditional Individualism to Collective Professionalism: State, Patient, Compulsory Health Insurance, and the Panel Doctor Question in Germany, 1883-1931', in Manfred Berg and Geoffrey Cocks (eds), *Medicine and Modernity. Public Health and Medical Care in Nineteenth- and Twentieth-Century Germany* (Cambridge, 1997), 35-54, 50. Cf. Weindling, *Health, Race and German Politics*, 344ff.
12. See Spree, 'Kurpfuscherei-Bekämpfung', 113.
13. Weindling, *Health, Race and German Politics*, 22.
14. Regin, *Selbsthilfe*, 280-90.
15. Jütte, *Geschichte der Alternativen Medizin*, 41; Alfred Haug, *Die Reichsarbeitsgemeinschaft für eine Neue Deutsche Heilkunde (1935/36)* (Husum, 1985), 31.
16. 'Über die Mißstände auf dem Gebiet der Kurpfuscherei und Maßnahmen zu ihrer Beseitigung', *Veröffentlichungen aus dem Gebiete der Medizinalverwaltung*, 15, 3 (1926), 11.
17. 'Ausübung der Heilkunde durch nichtapprobierte Personen', in Staatsministerium des Innern (ed.), *Berichte über das Bayerische Gesundheitwesen*, vols 41-52 for the years 1914-32, (Munich, 1922-34).
18. Cited in Jütte, *Geschichte der Alternativen Medizin*, 40.
19. Ibid., 41; NRWHSAD, Landgericht Essen, Rep 6, 688, Bl 31: the editor of *Der Volksarzt* only estimated about 6,000 in 1927; GSABD, Rep 84a, no. 1241, Bl 230: May 1928, special issue: this higher estimate by the *Arbeitsgemeinschaft für Lebens- und Heilreform*, in Frankfurt a.M., which was almost certainly opposed to lay medicine, was therefore probably alarmist and too high; Spree, 'Kurpfuscherei-Bekämpfung', 111.
20. BABL, R1501, Med.Polizei, no. 9138, Maßregeln zur Bekämpfung des Kurpfuschertums 1917-1925, Bl, 161; *Medizinpolitische Rundschau*, 19 (1926), 125; cf. Weindling, *Health, Race and German Politics*, 22.
21. 'Entwurf eines Gesetzes gegen Mißstände im Heilgewerbe', 27 April 1910, see BABL, RMdI, 9137, petitions; BABL, R 86, II, 1502, Rep 319, Kurpfuschertum 1916-1931, DGBK Petition to the Bundesrat for a decree against 'Mißstände im Heilgewerbe', 3 May 1916: it was apparently outvoted in the Reichstag on the grounds that many healing talents should not be suppressed just because they had not attended university; that the sound health enlightenment campaign by nature therapy should not be suppressed; that if quackery was to be outlawed there would not be enough doctors, and that this would mean reintroducing *Behandlungszwang* (compulsory treatment) by doctors; and on grounds of democratic principles that everyone had the right to determine his or her own kind of treatment. Manfred Stürzbecher, 'Aus der Vorgeschichte des Heilpraktikergesetzes vom 17.2.1939', *Medizinische Monatsschrift* 7 (1967) 313-20.
22. GSABD, Rep 84a, 1241, vol. 1, Bl. 6-24Rs, 140, 172ff.; There was also a motion tabled in the Prussian Diet in 1925 which was debated in January 1927. For 1927 anti-STD law, see Sauerteig, *Krankheit, Sexualität, Gesellschaft*, 430ff.

23. GSABD, Rep 84a, 1241, vol. 1, Bl. 144, 1925 proposal by the DGBK to induce law courts to appoint medical experts on quackery and the approval by the Ministry on 1 October 1925; ibid., Bl 166, Berliner Medical Society organized a lecture by Ludwig Ebermayer on 9 December 1926 in the big hall of Berlin University.
24. Ibid., Bl. 236, 'Der Kampf gegen die Kurpfuscherei', ten lectures, in *Veröffentlichung auf dem Gebiet der Medizinalverwaltung*, XXVII, 8 (1928); ibid., Bl. 148 medical courses, e.g. February 1926 and February 1927; NRWHSAD, Rep 6, Landgericht Essen, no. 688, Bl. 11.
25. NRWHSAD, Landgericht Essen, Rep 6, no. 688, Bl. 1-11, court case in 1927 *DGBK v. D. Gerpheide*, Essen, nature therapist, editor of the journal *Der Naturarzt* and chair of the *Verband der Heilkundigen Deutschlands* in Essen.
26. Detlef Bothe, *Neue Deutsche Heilkunde, 1933-1945* (Husum: 1991), 28; Haug, *Reichsarbeitsgemeinschaft*, 30.
27. 'Das Kurpfuschertum, ein dunkles Kapitel des 20. Jahrhunderts', *Groß-Berliner Anzeiger*, 113, 9 March 1927: these allegations appeared in an exhibition on quackery in the Prussian Ministry of Public Welfare in 1927; cf. Gunnar Stollberg, 'Die Naturheilvereine im Deutschen Kaiserreich', *Archiv für Sozialgeschichte*, 28 (1988), 287-305.
28. See Usborne, *Politics of the Body*, 182.
29. See letter by Lehfeld to author, autumn 1983, in which he described his own efforts to help women in his Berlin practice.
30. See Weindling, *Health, Race and German Politics*; LAB, Rep 58, 2138, for an example of a doctor performing abortions because he failed to obtain a panel practice.
31. BABL, Reichstag 1919-36, Bl. 130Rs: 'Denkschrift über die gesundheitllichen Verhältnisse des deutschen Volkes in den Jahren 1923 und 1924, Reichstags Printed Matter, 1725, 20 December 1925, 2, 4.
32. E.g. *Der Sozialistische Arzt*, the journal of the Association of Socialist Doctors.
33. Lönne, *Das Problem der Fruchtabtreibung*, 26; Albert Niedermayer, 'Schwangerschaft, Abortus, Geburt', *Handbuch der speziellen Pastoralmedizin*, III (Vienna, 1950).
34. Alfred Dührssen, 'Die Reform des Paragraph 218', *Sexus* IV (Leipzig, 1926), 57, 80, 74; cf. Chapter 3, n. 21.
35. E.g the Central Association for the Parity of Healing Methods and their organ, *Medizinpolitische Rundschau*, 18 (1925), 31-32; 19 (1926), 51, 52.
36. 'Neues von der Abtreibung', *Medizinalpolitische Rundschau*, 19, 7 (1926), 65-66.
37. 'Der neue Strafrechtsentwurf zum Problem der Fruchtabtreibung', *Medizinalpolitische Rundschau*, 18, (1925), 31-32.
38. E.g. *Medizinalpolitische Rundschau*, 19 (1926) 51-52; ibid., 20, 9 (1927), 12; ibid., 21, 34; *Naturärztliche Zeitschrift*, the journal of the *Deutsche Verein der Naturheilkundigen* (German Association of Nature Healers) 24 (1915), 47, 96.
39. See Usborne, *Politics of the Body*, 76f, 106f.
40. Lönne, *Das Problem der Fruchtabtreibung*, 11-12; Max Hirsch, *Die Fruchtabtreibung* (Stuttgart, 1921), 53.
41. Konstantin Inderheggen, *Das Delikt der Abtreibung im Landgerichtsbezirk Mönchen-Gladbach in der Zeit von 1908-1938* (Jena, 1940), 27; Helmuth Jahns, *Das Delikt der Abtreibung im Landgerichtsbezirk Duisburg in der Zeit von 1910-1935* (Düsseldorf, 1938), 5.
42. SHSAD, St.anw. Leipzig, 593, 919.
43. Ernst Bumm, 'Zur Frage des künstlichen Aborts', *Monatszeitschrift für Geburtshilfe und Gynäkologie*, 43 (1916), 385-95; Walter Offermann, 'Beitrag zur Behandlung des fieberhaften Abortes', *Zeitschrift für Geburtshilfe und Gynäkologie*, 79 (1917), 567-78.
44. Offermann, 'Beitrag zur Behandlung des fieberhaften Abortes', 567.
45. Inderheggen, *Abtreibung in M.-Gladbach*, 27; cf. Jahns, *Abtreibung in Duisburg*, 5: between 1908 and 1914 about 4 per cent of all detected abortions had been performed by women alone, just over 50 per cent with the help of accomplices, and just over 40 per cent by commercial abortionists. During the war as many as a third of all abortions were self-induced, only about 8 per cent with accomplices. After the war the first category decreased

Notes

to 20.2 per cent, while the number of 'commercial abortions' increased steadily to become the dominant mode.
46. Jahns, *Abtreibung in Duisburg*, 5.
47. See Werner Krieger, 'Erscheinungsformen und Strafzumessung bei der Abtreibung dargestellt an Hand von Gerichtsakten des Landgerichts und Amtsgerichts Freiburg im Breisgau aus den Jahren 1925-1951', unpubl. legal diss. (Albert-Ludwig-University, Freiburg i.Br., 1952), 45.
48. Ludwig Levy-Lenz, *Wenn Frauen nicht gebären dürfen* (Berlin, 1928), 43; Inderheggen, *Abtreibung in M.-Gladbach*, 106-12; BABL, R 86, 2371, Bl. 153-65, 157; Wolfgang Köhler, *Das Delikt der Abtreibung im Bezirk des Landgerichts Gera in den Jahren 1896-1930* (Jena, 1935); Krieger, 'Erscheinungsformen', 44.
49. For example, in Gera the number of abortions procured by a third party, though not necessarily for money, rose steadily from one in 1919 to forty in 1925 and then decreased somewhat, but remained relatively high, see Köhler, *Abtreibung in Gera*, 13.
50. For example, GSABD, Rep 84a, of twelve cases of abortion by commercial operators, only three referred to doctors; among the material from the public prosecutor's office in Leipzig the proportion was even higher, see SHSAD, St.anw. Leipzig, of eight detailed cases not one involved a medical practitioner: two were self-induced and six performed by non-doctors.
51. In the area of the *Landgericht* Mönchen-Gladbach before the war only 15 per cent of aborting women were married; during the First World War this increased to over 30 per cent; in the first six years of the Republic it decreased to 12 per cent but in the final eight years it went up to nearly a third; Inderheggen, *Abtreibung in Mönchen-Gladbach*, 81.
52. Cf. Chamberlain, *Old Wives' Tales*, 115, 122; Brookes, *Abortion in England*, 35; McLaren, *History of Contraception*, 228, 231.
53. BABL, R 3001, 6232, extract from the crime statistics of the German Reich, 1921 to 1923: in 1921, of 4,248 convicted persons under §218, sixty-nine were sentenced to penal servitude, 4,179 to imprisonment, 1,974 between 3 to 12 months, 1,921 under 3 months; in 1922, of 3,565 persons convicted, 83 were sentenced to penal servitude, 3,465 received a prison sentence, 1,444 for between 3 to 12 months, 1,769 under 3 months; in 1924, 5,296 were convicted, 90 were sentenced to penal servitude, 5,789 to prison, 2,555 for between 3 and 12 months, 2,380 under 3 months.
54. SHSAD, St.anw. Leipzig, 944.
55. Ibid., no. 862.
56. See Krieger, 'Erscheinungsformen', 48: the courts in Freiburg i.Br. regularly handed down a sentence of six months' gaol for complete abortion and one month two weeks to three months for attempted abortion.
57. E.g., Krieger, 'Erscheinungsformen', 49.
58. LAB, Rep 58, 2439.
59. GSABD, Rep 84a, 17159, 17160.
60. BABL, R 3001, 6232, extract from the crime statistics of the German Reich, 1921 to 1923.
61. BABL, R 3001, 6235, '§218 und Ärzteschaft', *Berliner Tageblatt*, 4 November 1925.
62. LHAK, 583.1, 707.
63. LAB, Rep 58, 2431, Bl. 134.
64. LAB, Rep 58, 2442.
65. SHSAD, St.anw. Leipzig, 663, 1926. A criminal inquiry was first started in the autumn of 1926 regarding a nature therapist from Leipzig, Frau Hulda Reiche, and it took until 1933, well into National Socialist rule, for the court of jurors to finally rule; Frau Reiche was convicted for criminal abortion on twenty-five counts and in one case of manslaughter and was sentenced to only nine months' prison with three years' loss of civil rights.
66. For example, in the area of Mönchen-Gladbach a little over half of all abortionists were women during the war and in the first nine years of the Republic; in the last six years the proportion was reversed, cf. Inderheggen, *Abtreibung in M.-Gladbach*, 103-31.
67. *Arbeiter Illustrierte Zeitung*, 30 (1928).

- 246 -

68. BABL, R 3001, 6232, Bl. 202, 211.
69. Advertisement by a certain A.R., cited in Köhler, Abtreibung in Gera, 44-55.
70. Cited in Jahns, Abtreibung in Duisburg, 65.
71. Köhler, Abtreibung in Gera, 45.
72. Inderheggen, Abtreibung in M-Gladbach, 107.
73. See de Blécourt and Usborne, 'Women's Medicine, Women's Culture'; de Blécourt, Het Amazonenleger (Amsterdam, 1999), 149-52.
74. For other such cases, cf. GSABD, Rep 84a, 17122, 17125.
75. LAB, Rep 58, 2439, vol. 1, Bl. 2; Handakten Bl. 13.
76. Ibid., vol. 2.
77. Ibid.
78. See McLaren, History of Contraception, 228.
79. SHSAD, St.anw. Leipzig, 944.
80. LAB, Rep 58, 2439, Bl. 31.
81. LAB, Rep 58, no. 2442, 1929-30.
82. Ibid., Red Cross report, 22 January 1930.
83. E.g. GSABD, Rep 84a, 17125.
84. SHSAD, St.anw. Leipzig, 663, Bl. 1, 45.
85. LAB, Rep 58, 2431.
86. SHSAD, St.anw. Leipzig, 663.
87. LAK, 584.1, 707, 1926.
88. GSABD, Rep 84a, 17113, 1926.
89. LHAB, Rep 58, 2442, Bl. 25-6, indictment, 17 December 1929.
90. SHSAD, St.anw. Leipzig, 656, 1922.
91. E.g. SHSAD, St.anw. Leipzig, 656; GSABD, Rep 84a, 17110, 17116, 17117, 17119, 17124, 17125, 17126.
92. GSABD, Rep 84a, 17133, 1930.
93. Inderheggen, Abtreibung in M-Gladbach, 110-11; 111-12.
94. Ibid., 108-9; Köhler, Abtreibung in Gera, 45.
95. Inderheggen, Abtreibung in M-Gladbach, 110-11, 111-12, 113.
96. There are many cases of a chance discovery where a widespread abortion practice was revealed without any problems at all, see e.g. the case of the homeopath Sch. who had helped at least eighty-four women without any mishap: GSABD, Rep 84a, 17158.
97. BABL, R 86, 2371, Bl. 153-65, 157. The legal historian Inderheggen strongly disapproved of all 'quack abortionists' but conceded that they were much more prevalent than doctors because women thought them more skilled: idem, Abtreibung in M.-Gladbach, 27.
98. Jahns, Abtreibung in Duisburg, 64.
99. Köhler, Abtreibung in Gera, 44; Jahns, Abtreibung in Duisburg, 64.
100. For reform of midwifery and its professionalization process see Stürzbecher, 'Die Bekämpfung des Geburtenrückganges und der Säuglingssterblichkeit', esp. 55-77.
101. For example, in Duisburg a third of all commercial abortionists were midwives and they also had the largest abortion practice: Jahn, Abtreibungen in Duisburg, 65; in Freiburg two out of the seven commercial operators were midwives: Krieger, Abtreibungen in Freiburg, 42-43.
102. GSABD, Rep 84a, 17118, 1928, Bl. 7, 10.
103. Ibid., Bl. 3, 3Rs.
104. In Gera amongst 146 commercial operators no midwives are listed, but some simply called 'married women' might well have been deregistered midwives: Köhler, Abtreibungen in Gera, 12.
105. LAB, Rep 58, 2719.
106. SAM, AG Mü, 16595, eyewitness statement 14 November 1925, Franz F. and depositions by other defendants and witnesses.
107. Jahns, Abtreibung in Duisburg, 64-65.

108. GSABD, Rep 84a, 17158, *Königsberger Volkszeitung*, 13 July 1932.
109. Ibid., *Rote Fahne*, 2 February 1932; *Königsberger Volkszeitung*, 13 July 1932.
110. BABL, R86, 2379, *Vorwärts*, 20 May 1924, 8 October 1924; ibid., 2373, vol. 2; Cf. Grossmann, *Reforming Sex*, 128: she points to a claim that Heiser attempted to rape a young woman from the provinces who had sought his help and that he had also botched her abortion.
111. *Sexual-Hygiene* 1, 4, (January 1929), 32; Sigismund Vollmann, *Deutsches Ärzteblatt* 59 (1932) 68; Elisabeth Prager-Heinrich, *Die Ärztin*, 7 (1931), 18; Hans Leideritz, *Die 'operationslose', indizierte Schwangerschafts-Unterbrechung* (Hamburg, 1932), 30–41; cf. Reagan, *When Abortion Was a Crime*, 156.
112. Cf. Regin, *Selbsthilfe*, esp. 63; Walter, Denecke and Regin (eds), *Sozialistische Gesundheits- und Lebensreformverbände*.
113. SHSAD, St.anw. Leipzig, 862, 919, 641, 663, 778.
114. Köhler, *Abtreibung in Gera*, 44, 48; Jahns, *Abtreibung in Duisburg*, 63–68.
115. BABL, R3001, 6233, vol. 2, Bl. 87–97, 'Matter for discussion in the Reichstag', 26 April 1930, proceedings against Frau Johanna A. in Hindenburg. Despite extensive searches the full judicial records of the trial could not be located and have to be assumed to be lost.
116. LAB, Rep 58, no. 2439, vol. 1, Bl. 31ff.
117. Ibid., Bl. 6, 31.
118. BABL, R 86, 2380, statistics of artificial miscarriages in maternity hospitals, 1929. Clara Bender, *Klinische Wochenschrift* 19 (1925), 933. Credé, *Volk in Not! Das Unheil der Abtreibungsparagraphen*,15.
119. LHAK, 403, 13425, Bl. 704, Prussian Minister for Public Welfare to Land Presidents, 17 September 1925, complaining about the insufficient training of medical students in obstetrics and gynaecology; see also the complaints of the doyen of German gynaecologists Georg Winter, in, 'Strittige Punkte', 1040; Hüssy, *Begutachtung und gerichtliche Beurteilung*, 8, reports many examples of 'horrifying mistakes' by doctors which 'demonstrate ignorance, lack of technical skill and gross negligence'.
120. Winter, 'Strittige Punkte', 104: warned that a manual curettage needed a deep anaesthetic but that many GPs did not use one because they had nobody trained at hand to do it. Either a second doctor, or, even better, a midwife should be called. It was quite wrong to use the help of an untrained 'wife' (clearly assuming doctors to be usually male). Not all doctors were patient and conscientious enough to perform D and C, see e.g. GSABD, Rep 84a, 17149.
121. Usborne, *Politics of the Body*, 187–89.
122. See the case of Dr Hope Bridges Adams Lehman discussed in Chapter 3.
123. E.g. GSABD, Rep 84a, 17149; 17156; Jahns, *Abtreibung in Duisburg*, 66–68; Inderheggen, *Abtreibung in M.-Gladbach*, 106–13; LAB Rep 58, 2349, midwife S. 1927–29 and 2064 homoeopath S., 1928. E.g. SHSAD, St.anw. Leipzig, 641, 663; GSABD, Rep 84a, 17122.
124. GSABD, Rep 84a, 17129; SHSAD, St.anw. Leipzig, 944.
125. GSABD, Rep 84a, 17109; cf. Jahns, *Abtreibung in Duisburg*, 67.
126. Jahns, *Abtreibung in Duisburg*, 67: the case of a miner's wife, whose four-year-old daughter told her playmates: 'My mummy does not need to carry any more babies in her tummy and your mummy does not either if my mummy wants it.'
127. BABL, 3001, 6233, vol. 2, Bl. 87–97; Heiser charged 20 RM, which was for syringing and supplying his own cream: LAB, Rep 58, 2453, vol. IX, 1928; Frau K. of Limburg also charged 20 to 30 Marks even at the height of inflation: GSABD, Rep 84a, 17109.
128. GSABD, Rep 84a, 17109.
129. By contrast, doctors tried for abortion also catered for middle-class women: e.g. LAB, Rep 58, 416, 2137–39, 2453, 2494; see also GSABD, Rep 84a, 17108, 17112, 17114 etc. The one notable exception was the chemist Heiser whose clients included women of all classes: LAB, Rep 58, 2453.

130. Jahns, *Abtreibung in Duisburg*, 63; 'Über die Mißstände auf dem Gebiete der Kurpfuscherei und Maßnahmen zu ihrer Beseitigung', *Veröffentlichung aus dem Gebiet der Medizinalverwaltung*, 15, 3, 34: amongst all lay practitioners in Berlin in 1926 most had previous occupations as artisans (275) and state officials were in second place (102).
131. See Chamberlain, *Old Wives' Tales*, 145-48.
132. E.g. F.E. Bilz, *Das neue Naturheilverfahren* (Dresden, many editions, here 1938).
133. Cf. Usborne, 'Women Doctors and Gender Identity'.
134. NRWHSAD, Reg.Dü, 38892, public prosecutor Dü, 10 December 1914; Inderheggen, *Abtreibung in M.-Gladbach*, 166.

Chapter 5 Notes

1. Max Marcuse, 'Zur Frage der Verbreitung und Methodik der willkürlichen Geburtenbeschränkung', e.g., 'as soon as the period was late, always jumped off tables and chairs and administered "deep" douches with soap water; "this has always led to *Kippen* in the 2nd month"' (case 25); 'since last *partum* no cohabitation. "Now my husband can go to other women; I don't want any more children"' (case 78); "I won't let my husband near me. He wants to throw me out for this but I don't mind" (case 98). See idem, *Der eheliche Präventivverkehr*.
2. E.g. Hagemann, *Frauenalltag und Männerpolitik*; cf. Hagemann, *Eine Frauensache. Alltagsleben und Geburtenpolitik 1919-1933* (Pfaffenweiler, 1991); Stefan Bajohr, *Lass dich nicht mit den Bengels ein! Sexualität, Geburtenregelung und Geschlechtsmoral im Braunschweiger Arbeitermilieu 1900 bis 1933* (Essen, 2001); cf. Kate Fisher, '"Didn't stop to think, I just didn't want another one": the Culture of Abortion in Interwar South Wales', in Franz X. Eder, Lesley A. Hall and Gert Hekma (eds), *Sexual Cultures in Europe. Themes in Sexuality* (Manchester, 1999) 213-55; idem, *Birth Control, Sex and Marriage in Britain*.
3. E.g., SAM, St.anw. LG Mü I, 1821a, trial against Freifrau v. l. R.; SAM, AG Mü 16535, criminal proceedings against Freifrau v. P.
4. E.g. SAM, St.anw. LG Mü, 1821a, medical expert Dr Blättner, 6.
5. Cf. Duden, Schlumbohm and Veit (eds), *Geschichte des Ungeborenen*, Foreword.
6. Sally Alexander, 'The Mysteries and Secrets of Women's Bodies', in Mica Nava and Alan O'Shea (eds), *Modern Times. Reflections on a Century of English Modernity* (London, 1996) 161-75, 175.
7. E.g. SHSAD, LG Leipzig, 593; LAK, 584.1, 707; NRWHSAD, Reg. Dü. 38892; HHSAW, Abt. 4653, 99; LAB, Rep 58, 2442, 2494, 416; SAM, St.anw. I, 834; ibid., St.anw. Traunstein, 15634 and 15701.
8. LAB, Rep 58, 2439, vol. I, Bl. 2.
9. Ibid., vol. 2, Bl. 175ff.; in this trial at least twenty-nine women were cited on whom Frau Spitzer had performed abortions, but this number is almost certainly too low, since more than forty women had entered their names in her two notebooks as clients.
10. I.e. the Netherlands, see de Blécourt, 'Cultures of Abortion in The Hague', 199; idem, *Het Amazonenleger*, 138; or in the U.S.A., Reagan, *When Abortion Was a Crime*, 114.
11. SAM, AG Mü 37110, Bl. 48, 4 February 1929.
12. See Schulte, *The Village in Court*, 13-16.
13. See Claudia Töngi, 'Gewalt gegen Schwangere vor dem urnerischen Strafgericht des 19. Jahrhunderts: Zur sozialen Bedeutung von Gewalt und Aggression', in Duden et al. (eds), *Geschichte des Ungeborenen*, 273-92, 277; Ulrike Gleixner, 'Geschlechterdifferenzen und die Faktizität des Fiktionalen. Zur Dekonstruktion frühneuzeitlicher Verhörprotokolle', *Werkstatt Geschichte*, 11 (1995), 65-70. Louise Jackson, 'The Child's Word in Court: Cases of Sexual Abuse in London, 1870-1914', in Margaret L. Arnot and Cornelie Usborne (eds), *Gender and Crime in Modern Europe* (London, 1999), 222-38.

14. This legal uncertainty caused Gustav Radbruch in 1922 to table his draft of a new penal code (*Entwurf eines Allgemeinen Deutschen Strafgesetzbuches*) which proposed impunity for the impossible attempt of terminating a pregnancy either when the means were inappropriate or because the woman was not pregnant. This draft was not accepted and §218 of 1926 contained the sentence: 'The attempt is punishable'. In other countries, e.g. the Netherlands, this was not the case after 1912; see de Blécourt, 'Cultures of Abortion in The Hague', 198.
15. Reagan, *When Abortion Was a Crime*, 114.
16. LAB, Rep 58, no. 2439, Bl. 21–24.
17. E.g. SAM, St.anw. Mü, 1821, medical expert opinion by Dr Blätter on H. Freifrau. v.l.R.
18. HHSAW, ABt. 463, 99 (9), Bl. 118.
19. GSABD, Rep 84a, no. 17107.
20. Ibid., Bl. 103.
21. E.g. Kathleen Canning, 'Feminist History after the Linguistic Turn: Historicizing Discourse and Experience', *Signs: Journal of Women in Culture and Society*, 21 (1994), 368–404, esp. 393ff.; idem, *Gender History in Practice*, 101ff.; Philipp Sarasin, 'Mapping the Body. Körpergeschichte zwischen Kosntruktivismus, Politik und "Erfahrung"', *Historische Anthropologie*, 7 (1999), 437–51; Lyndal Roper, 'Jenseits des linguisitic Turn', *Historische Anthropologie*, 7 (1999), 452–66.
22. Töngi, 'Gewalt gegen Schwangere', 278.
23. E.g. for a useful survey in English, Ute Frevert, *Women in German History* (Oxford, New York and Munich, 1989).
24. See Usborne, 'The New Woman and Generation Conflict'.
25. Duden, Schlumbohm and Veit, 'Vorwort', in idem (eds), *Geschichte des Ungeborenen*, 7.
26. Barbara Duden, 'Zwischen "wahrem Wissen" und Prophetie. Konzeptionen des Ungeborenen', in Duden et al., *Geschichte des Ungeborenen*, 11–13.
27. E.g. Labouvie, *Andere Umstände*; idem, *Beistand in Kindesnöten*; cf. Duden, *The Woman Beneath the Skin*; idem, *Der Frauenleib als öffentlicher Ort*; idem, 'Ein falsch Gewächs, ein unzeitig Wesen, gestocktes Blut'.
28. Michael Stolberg, 'Medical Popularization and the Patient in the Eighteenth Century', in Willem de Blécourt and Cornelie Usborne (eds), *Cultural Approaches to the History of Medicine. Mediating Medicine in Early Modern and Modern Europe* (Basingstoke, 2004), 89–107.
29. Schulte, *The Village in Court*, 14.
30. The concept of 'medicalization of society' has become of central importance in the social history of medicine since c.1980. Porter, for example, wrote of 'the widening provision of medical explanation, opinion, services and interventions; the infiltration of medicine into many spheres of life, from normal pregnancy and childbirth to alcohol and drugs related behaviour ... ', Roy Porter, *The Greatest Benefit to Mankind: A Medical History of Humanity from Antiquity to the Present* (London, 1997), 690.
31. Martin, *The Woman in the Body*, 5–11.
32. See Reagan, *When Abortion Was a Crime*, 6.
33. For an analysis of different layers of meaning in oral history, see Lutz Niethammer, 'Fragen – Antworten – Fragen. Methodische Erfahrungen und Erwägungen zur Oral History', in Lutz Niethammer and Alexander von Plato (eds), *'Wir kriegen andere Zeiten'. Auf der Suche nach der Erfahrung des Volkes in nachfaschistischen Ländern* (Berlin, 1985), 392–495; idem, 'Oral History', in Ilko-Sacha Kowalczuk (ed.), *Paradigmen deutscher Geschichtswissenschaft* (Berlin, 1994), 189–200.
34. SAM, AG Munich 16604, police statement, 4 February 1926.
35. Ibid., 10.45 a.m.
36. Ibid., 6 p.m.
37. Ibid., Bl. 36; the latter each received six months in prison.
38. SAM, AG 16595, police interview, 27 April 1925.
39. Ibid., Bl. 18–19.

40. Ibid., Bl. 40-42v.
41. Ibid., Frau S.
42. LAB, Rep 58, 2439, 1929-30, vol. 1, Bl. 15-17 and vol. 2, Bl. 119.
43. Ibid., vol. 1, Bl. 19-21.
44. Ibid., vol. 1, Bl. 51.
45. SAM, AG 16727, 1926.
46. E.g. LAB, Rep 58, 2439, vol. 2, recording clerk Haserrick; SAM St.anw., 15634, 1922; SAM, AG 37110, Bl. 51; SAM AG 16727, Bl. 8; HHSA, Schöff.ger. Limburg, Abt. 463, no. 99, 1924.
47. SAM, AG 16595, police interview, Bl. 65ff.
48. LAB, Rep 58, no. 2439, vol. 2, Bl. 190.
49. Idem, Bl. 195.
50. Ibid., Bl. 60, Elfriede W.; Bl. 69, Margarete H.
51. E.g., SAM, St.anw. 15701, Bl. 38, E.S., twenty-one years old.
52. SAM, AG Mü, 16727, p. 8, Karoline D.
53. See Cornelie Usborne, 'Rhetoric and Resistance: Rationalization of Reproduction in Weimar Germany', *Social Politics. International Studies in Gender, State, and Society*, special issue: Gender and Rationalization, 4 (1997), 65-89.
54. See Barndt, *Sentiment und Sachlichkeit*; Vibeke Rützou Petersen, *Women and Modernity in Weimar Germany: Reality and Representation in Popular Fiction* (New York and Oxford, 2001).
55. See Usborne, *Politics of the Body*, 98.
56. Winter, *Der künstliche Abort*, 3.
57. SHSAD, St.anw. Leipzig, 593, Bl. 1-4; ibid., 944, 1920: 'ihr Zeug sei seit 8 Tagen ausgeblieben'; ibid., 663, 1926.
58. SAM, AG 16727, 1926, Bl. 13Rs-14Rs.
59. Ibid., Bl. 2.
60. SAM, St.anw. 15701, 1934, Bl. 6.
61. Ibid., Bl. 6Rs, 7.
62. Ibid., Bl. 30-31.
63. LAB, Rep 58, 2439, vol. 2, Bl. 22, 22Rs.
64. Ibid., vol. 1, Bl. 82; HHSAW, Schöffengericht Limburg, 1924, Abt. 463, no. 99, Bl. 3, Bl. 95, Frau K.; SHSAD, St.anw. Leipzig, 663, 1926; ibid., 944, 1920.
65. E.g. SHSAD, St.anw. Leipzig, 663, 1926, case 1, 5, 9, 25.
66. SAM, St.anw. 15690, Bl. 24Rs.
67. SAM, AG 37110, Bl. 48Rs.
68. GSABD, Abt. I, Rep 84a, no. 17107, Bl. 14; SAM, St.anw. 15.634, Dr Hartmann, Bl. 45.
69. SAM, AG 16727, Bl. 1.
70. See Usborne, *Politics of the Body*, 111, 27.
71. E.g., LAB, Rep 58, 2439, vol. 1, Bl. 53, 55.
72. LAB Rep 58, 2439, Frau S. vol. 1, Bl. 53, Ehefrau Martha D.
73. Ibid., Bl. 55, Martha N.
74. LAB, Rep 58, 2439, vol. 1, Bl. 120, Oberstaatsanwalt bei d. Landgericht III, 11 February 1930.
75. SAM, Pol.Dir. 7214, files of the town council of Ansbach. The Munich police headquarters together with the equivalent body in Berlin were the leading authority for the combat of indecent literature.
76. See Usborne, *Politics of the Body*, 6-8.
77. See also advertisements in England and America, McLaren, *Birth Control*, 232-33; Brodie, *Contraception and Abortion in 19th-century America*, 180ff.
78. SAM, Pol.Dir. 7214, Schutzmannschaft d.Stadt Ansbach, 11 December 1924.
79. SAM, Pol.Dir. 7221.
80. SAM, Pol.Dir. 7231, *Deutsche Friseur Post*, no. 9, 1 May 1923; *Süddeutsche Wäschereizeitung*, no. 192/31, 29 November 1923.

Notes

81. SAM, Pol.Dir. 7249, n.d., a leaflet by 'Frau H. Rathjen, former district midwife, Sonderburg a. Alsen'.
82. See Willem de Blécourt, 'Hygienic Articles, Patent Medicines and Rubber Goods', in Marijke Gijswijt-Hofstra and Tilly Tansey (eds), *Biographies of Remedies. Drugs, Medicine and Contraception in Dutch and Anglo-American Healing Cultures* (Amsterdam and Atlanta, 2001), 183-202, 191-92; Knight, 'Women and Abortion in Victorian and Edwardian England', 61; McLaren, *Birth Control*, 232-41; Reagan, *When Abortion Was a Crime*, 44.
83. Cf. SAM, Pol.Dir., documentation of the *Landeszentralpolizeistelle zur Bekämpfung unzüchtiger Bilder und Schriften* at the police headquarters in Munich; §219 of the penal code of 1871 prescribed penal servitude of up to ten years for anybody who 'had provided for money the means for abortion or applied them on a pregnant woman who had aborted or killed her foetus'. Advertising for abortifacients was also punishable according to the pornography law of 1900, §184.3 of the penal code which prohibited advertising and display of 'objects intended for indecent use'. In 1915 military authorities prohibited advertising contraceptives and abortifacients and intensified police surveillance; see Usborne, *Politics of the Body*, 21.
84. SAM, Pol.Dir. 7214, Krim. Wachtmeister Hell, Hamburg, 15 November 1924.
85. Köhler, *Abtreibung in Gera*, 42, 34: newspaper advertisement of 1912: Sanitätshaus E. Velten.
86. See de Blécourt, *Het Amazonenleger*, 132; see Chapter 4 above and Usborne, 'Wise Women, Wise Men'.
87. SAM, Pol.Dir. 7221.
88. SAM, Pol.Dir. 7231, excerpts of the files of the *Gesundheitsamt* I 1668, 10 April 1921.
89. E.g. the Hamburg trial against twenty traders of a tea which was said to prevent harmlessly 'unpleasant consequences', SAM, Pol.Dir. 7175.
90. Cf. SAM, Pol.Dir. 7175, 7201, 7214, 7219, 7221, 7224, 7231, etc.
91. SAM, Pol.Dir. 7250.
92. E.g. SAM, AG 16727, 1926, Bl.1.
93. SAM, AG 37153, 1931; LAB, Rep 58, 2439, Handakten 1929, Bl. 16Rs; ibid., vol. 1, Bl. 34, 45.
94. Ibid., vol. 1, Bl. 26.
95. SAM, AG 37153, 1931, Bl. 5Rs.
96. GSAD, Abtl. I, Rep 84a, no. 17107, 1924.
97. SAM, Pol. Dir. 15658, 1926.
98. Marcuse, 'Zur Frage der Verbreitung', 775f.
99. Stolberg, 'Medical Popularization and the Patient', 101-02.
100. Reagan, *When Abortion Was a Crime*, 8-9.
101. Martin, *The Woman in the Body*, 45, 103, 107, 110.
102. HHSA, Schöff.ger. Limburg, Abt. 463, no. 99, vol. 3, Bl. 96, 97, 116.
103. GSABD, Abt. I, Rep 84a, no. 17107, the case of N., no p. no.
104. Ibid., case W.
105. Marcuse, 'Zur Frage der Verbreitung und Methodik'.
106. E.g. HHSA, Schöf.ger. Limburg, 1924, Abt. 463, no. 99, Bd. 3, Bl. 94, Frau Schm; LAB, Rep 58, 2439, Handakten 1929, Bl. 16Rs; SAM, St.anw. 15701, 1934, Bl. 31.
107. LAB, Rep 58, 2439, vol. 1, Bl. 53; SAD, 944 Landger. Leipzig, 1920, vol. III.
108. LAB, Rep 58, 2719, vol. 1, Bl. 1, 26, 53, 82; ibid., vol. 2, Emma E., Anna R. In Anglo-Saxon countries similar notions can be traced, such as 'caught' or fallen', see McLaren, *History of Contraception*, 230.
109. SAD, no. 593, 1919, Bl. 2.
110. LAB, Rep 58, 2719, vol. 1, Bl. 1-5.
111. E.g. SAM, St.anw. 15634, Bl. 93-4. See Reagan, *When Abortion Was a Crime*, 24; Knight, 'Women and Abortion in Victorian and Edwardian England'.
112. E.g. LAB, Rep 58, 2719 or HHSA, Schöff.ger. Limburg, Abt. 463, no. 99.

113. Cf. Leibrock-Plehn, 'Frühe Neuzeit', 75–81.
114. BABL, R 1501, 9347, Bl. 75; cf. Bergmann, *Die verhütete Sexualität*, 171f.
115. Usborne, *Politics of the Body*, 136–37; Ute Frevert, '"Fürsorgliche Belagerung": Hygienebewegung und Arbeiterfrauen im 19. und frühen 20. Jahrhundert', *Geschichte und Gesellschaft*, 11 (1985) 420–46.
116. See Usborne, 'Wise Women, Wise Men', 146–53.
117. HHSAW, Schöff.ger. Limburg, 1924, Abt. 463, no. 88, vol. 3, Bl. 109, 101.
118. LAB Rep 58, 2439, vol. Bl. 16v; SAM, Sta.anw. 15.634, Bl. 45: mentions 'kleine Blutklumpen' and a 'länglicher Fleischklumpen'.
119. SAM, AG Mü, 16510, 1925, Bl. 48Rs.
120. LAB, Rep 58, 2719, vol. 1, Bl. 26.
121. E.g. SAM, St.anw. 15.634, 1922, Dr H., interview by the invesitgating magistrate, 10 July 1922, p. 15.
122. LAB, Rep 58, 2442, Bl. 18–20RS.
123. Ibid., Bl. 21.
124. SAM, St.anw. 15690, Bl. 30–31. In German 'Abgang' can mean both expulsion or discharge and miscarriage.
125. SAM, St.anw., 15701, Bl. 5. This pragmatic and sober attitude by working-class women to their bodies' waste material is reminiscent of the infanticidal women at the turn of the century in rural Bavaria studied by Regina Schulte, 'Infanticide in Bavaria'.
126. HHSAW, Schöffenger. Limburg, 1924, Abt. 463, no. 99, vol. 3, Bl. 95, 109.
127. Usborne, *Politics of the Body*, 171, 190.
128. LAB, Rep 58, 2439, vol. 1, Bl. 19.
129. E.g., SAM, AG Mü, 16595, Bl. 34–35.
130. Ibid.; SHSAD, St.anw. Leipzig, 779, 1920; ibid., 656, 1922; ibid., 663, 1926; SAM, AG Mü, 16595, 1926; ibid., 16583, 1926; LAB, Rep 58, 2439; ibid., 2442, 1929–30; Jahns, *Abtreibung in Duisburg*, 64–65.
131. E.g. SAM, AG Mü, 16595, Bl. 34–35.
132. E.g. SAM, St.anw. 15634, 1922, cross-examination by the examining magistrate, 10 July 1922, 13.
133. E.g. LAB Rep 58, 2719, 1931–33, indictment, 12; HHSAW, Schöff.ger. Limburg, 1924, Abt. 463, no. 99, vol. 3, Bl. 96.
134. HHSAW, Schöffenger. Limburg, 1924, Abt. 463, no. 99, vol. 3, Bl. 95, 109.
135. See de Blécourt and Usborne, 'Women's Medicine, Women's Culture', 387, 390; to restore 'häusliches Glück' was indeed the promise often made in the advertisements of fortune-tellers in local newspapers to attract their customers.
136. Lüdtke, 'People Working', 90.

Chapter 6 Notes

1. HHSAW, St.anw. LG Limburg, Abt. 463, 99 (3), Bl. 113.
2. Ibid., Bl. 111.
3. Ibid., 99 (9), Bl. 20.
4. HHSAW, St.anw. LG Limburg, Abt. 463, 99 (9) Bl. 16.
5. McLaren, *Reproductive Rituals*, 90.
6. Helmuth Gensicke, *1200 Jahre (1235–1985) Oberbrechen* (Limburg, 1974), 19.
7. Helmuth Gensicke, *750 Jahre (1235–1985) Werschau. Aus der Geschichte von Werschau* (Werschau, 1985), 32.
8. HHSAW, St.anw. LG Limburg, Abt. 463, 99 (10), Bl. 65.
9. Karl Müller, *Unser Heimatbuch* (Neuss am Rhein, 1967), 70, 71, 80.
10. Gensicke, *750 Jahre Werschau*, 36; HHSAW, *Adressbuch Limburg*, 1928.

Notes

11. Anton Dommermuth, *Die landwirtschaftlichen Betriebsformen im Westerwald und im Limburger Becken in ihrer geographischen Bedingheit* (Frankfurt a.M., 1940), 55.
12. Erhard Grund, *Ohren. 1301-2001. Eine Ortsgeschichte* (Nordenstadt, 2001), 75.
13. Gensicke, *750 Jahre Werschau*, 33.
14. K.H.W. Schmidt, *Dabornaha. Die Geschichte eines Dorfes und seiner Landschaft* (Dauborn, 1984), 132, 205, 95-96, 133; see also Dommermuth, *Die landwirtschaftlichen Betriebsformen*, 57.
15. Müller, *Unser Heimatbuch*, 70, 71, 80.
16. Gensicke, *750 Jahre Werschau*, 36. But the address book for the village only listed twenty-seven farmers, HHSAW, *Adressbuch Limburg*, 1928.
17. Schmidt, *Dabornaha*, 158.
18. Müller, *Unser Heimatbuch*, 71.
19. Helmuth Gensicke & Egon Eichhorn, *Geschichte von Oberbrechen* (Brechen-Oberbrechen, 1975), 425.
20. Various books give conflicting dates: Müller, *Unser Heimatbuch*, 37 mentions 1877 but on p. 71 he talks of 1862; Gensicke and Eichhorn, *Geschichte von Oberbrechen*, 260 state that it opened in 1874.
21. Müller, *Unser Heimatbuch*, 37.
22. Ibid., 37; Fritz Geisthardt, *Wirtschaft in Mittelnassau. Hundert Jahre Industrie- und Handelskammer Limburg, 1864-1964* (Limburg, 1965), 63.
23. HHSAW, St.anw. LG Limburg, Abt. 463, 99 (4); Dietmar Petzina, Werner Abelshauser and A. Faust, *Sozialgeschichtliches Arbeitsbuch III., Materialien zur Statistik des Deutschen Reiches* (Munich, 1978), 99.
24. Wolfgang Hartke, 'Das Arbeits- und Wohnortsgebiet in Rhein-Mainischen Lebensraum', *Rhein-Mainische Forschungen*, 18 (1938), 14-15.
25. See Schulte, *The Village in Court*, 19.
26. Interview on 3 September 2001 with Frau W., daughter of a farmer who was involved in the Limburg trial.
27. HHSAW, St.anw. LG Limburg, Abt. 463, 99 (3), B1. 171.
28. Ibid., 99 (3), B1. 96, 17 August 1924.
29. Ibid., B1. 95, 102.
30. Ibid., 99 (3).
31. Ibid., B1. 188, 9 September 1924.
32. Ibid., B1. 97, 109.
33. Ibid., 99 (7), appeals.
34. Ibid., 99 (3), B1. 132Rs.
35. HHSAW, address book Limburg, 1928.
36. HHSAW, St.anw. LG Limburg, Abt. 463, 99 (3),
37. Ibid., B1. 129Rs-130.
38. The small village of Werschau alone mourned twelve dead soldiers, a huge loss for its 414 inhabitants, Gensicke, *750 Jahre Werschau*, 13. Kirberg with its 1,011 inhabitants lost fifty-one young men in the war, see Hugo Grün, *Kirberg, 1355-1955. Ein geschichtlicher Rückblick zur Erinnerung an die Stadtgründung und den Bau seiner Kirche* (Kirberg, 1955), 54. In Wolfenhausen (822 inh.) forty-four soldiers died, see Wolfgang Schopper, 'Erster Weltkrieg und Weimarer Republik', in Kreisausschuß des Landkreises Limburg-Weilburg et al., *Limburg-Weilburg. Beiträge zur Geschichte des Kreises* (Limburg an der Lahn, 1986), 455; Niederbrechen with 2,138 inhabitants lost seventy-two men in the war, see Müller, *Unser Heimatbuch*, 132.
39. Geisthardt, *Wirtschaft in Mittelnassau*, 88; Gensicke and Eichhorn, *Geschichte von Oberbrechen*, 262.
40. Schopper, 'Erster Weltkrieg', 457.
41. See Richard Bessel, *Germany After the First World War* (Oxford, 1993), 92-95.
42. Schopper, 'Erster Weltkrieg', 457, 468.

43. Cited in Gensicke, *750 Jahre Werschau*, 33.
44. HHSAW, St.anw. LG Limburg, Abt. 463, 99 (10), Bl. 70–74, 83.
45. Gensicke and Eichhorn, *Geschichte von Oberbrechen*, 262.
46. Cf. Ernst Langthaler and Reinhard Sieder (eds), *Über die Dörfer. Ländliche Lebenswelten in der Moderne* (Vienna, 2000), 24ff.
47. Wolfgang Kaschuba and Carola Lipp, *Dörfliches Überleben. Zur Geschichte materieller and sozialer Reproduktion ländlicher Gesellschaft im 19. und frühen 20. Jahrhundert* (Tübingen, 1982); cf. Langthaler and Sieder, *Über die Dörfer*, 19–20.
48. See Usborne, *Politics of the Body*, esp. 165ff.
49. HHSAW, St.anw. LG Limburg, Abt. 463, 99 (3), e.g. Bl. 124, Frau B. who had a douche after her period was delayed by only a few days.
50. Ibid., 99 (7), lawyer Dilllmann.
51. Ibid., 99 (3), Bl. 125, Emilie G.
52. Ibid., 99 (10), Bl. 48Rs, 49.
53. Ibid., 99 (10), Bl. 54, 54Rs.
54. Ibid., 99 (13), Pruss. Justice Min., 24 November 1926.
55. Ibid., 99 (7), letter 27 February 1925, Anna S.
56. Ibid., Frau Philipp Zeiger.
57. Ibid., Frau Heinrich Treib.
58. Ibid., Bl. 63, letter by lawyers Hilf and Fachinger, 17 February 1925.
59. Ibid., 99 (8), Bl. 32, 34.
60. Ibid., Bl. 38.
61. Ibid., letter 23 June 1925.
62. Ibid., 99 (14), appeal court decision.
63. Ibid., 99 (10), Bl. 57.
64. Ibid., Bl. 60.
65. Ibid., 99 (3), 101–102Rs.
66. Ibid., Bl. 168.
67. Ibid., Bl. 125.
68. Ibid., Bl. 169 and 99 (4), Bl. 13; 99 (6), Bl. 111.
69. Ibid., Bl. 130Rs, 99 (6), Bl. 112Rs.
70. Ibid., Bl. 169.
71. E.g. ibid., Bl.169–171, Frau Emil H., Frau Wihelm P., Frau Wilhelm C., Frau Wilhelm M., Wilhelm M.
72. Ibid., Bl. 127.
73. Ibid., Bl. 125–26.
74. Ibid., Bl. 109.
75. Ibid., Bl. 109, case 3, Blaser; case 6, Enkel.
76. Ibid., Bl. 168Rs.
77. Ibid., Bl. 96.
78. See de Blécourt, 'Cultures of Abortion in The Hague', 209.
79. HHSAW, St.anw. LG Limburg, Abt. 463, 99 (3), Bl. 132Rs, 133.
80. Ibid., Bl. 125.
81. Ibid., Bl. 132Rs, 133.
82. Ibid., Bl. 132, 167.
83. Ibid., Bl. 125.
84. On my recce in the area, in September 2001, this daughter, now in her late sixties, showed me round the village church and told me about the farms in existence during her childhood.
85. HHSAW, St.anw. LG Limburg, Abt. 463, 99 (3), Bl. 128–30.
86. Ibid., Bl. 95, 98.
87. Ibid., Bl. 127, 127Rs.
88. Ibid., Bl. 96.

89. Ibid., Bl. 93.
90. Ibid., 99 (9), Bl. 119.
91. Ibid., 99 (6), Bl. 113Rs.
92. Ibid., Bl. 101, in court December 1924.
93. Ibid., 99 (3), Bl. 188.
94. Ibid., Bl. 125, Frau G., Edmund B.
95. Ibid., 99 (6), Bl. 101, 10 December 24.
96. Ibid., 99 (3), Bl. 109, 20 August 1924; Bl. 188, 9 September 1924.
97. Ibid., 99 (6), Bl. 101.
98. Ibid., 99 (3), Bl. 109.
99. Ibid., case E., 20 August 1924.
100. Ibid., Bl. 188; the use of the word in German here is intriguing given that she was paid with 'Früchte' for having aborted a 'Frucht' (fruit).
101. E.g., ibid., Bl. 130Rs, 170.
102. Ibid., Bl. 201, 189.
103. Ibid., Bl. 124.
104. Ibid., Bl. 127.
105. Ibid., Bl. 127Rs, 167Rs, 170, 171, 190, 201.
106. Ibid., Bl. 127.
107. Ibid., Bl. 167Rs.
108. Ibid., 99 (1), letter received 5 May 1924.
109. Ibid., 99 (1), Bl. 19a, letter 28 May 1924; letter 17 May 1924; and Bl. 7, expert report, 23 May 1924.
110. Ibid., 99 (3), Bl. 93–94.
111. Ibid., Bl. 127, 127Rs.
112. Ibid., Bl. 130Rs–131.
113. Ibid., Bl. 129.
114. Ibid., 99 (9), Bl. 22.
115. Ibid., 99 (4), Bl. 46; the medical officer said: 'As far as her credibility goes, I would not judge this very highly. The statement about the rape of her employer seems confused and ambiguous, and should not be trusted.'
116. Ibid., Bl. 3, 7; 99 (9), 11.
117. Ibid., 99 (1), letters Anton Dillmann to the Amtsgericht at the Landgericht Limburg, Bl. 19a, 28 May 1924 and Bl. 25, 30 May 1924.
118. Ibid., Bl. 68, 29 July 1924.
119. Ibid., 99 (9), Bl. 118–21.
120. Ibid., 99 (10), 54.
121. GSABD, Rep. 84a, 17109, Bl. 52a.
122. Marcuse, 'Zur Frage der Verbreitung': at least twenty-four of the sixty-three women who practised contraception used coitus interruptus.

Chapter 7 Notes

1. E.g. for the experiential dimension of the body, Barbara Duden's groundbreaking *The Woman Beneath the Skin*; for a critique of a simplistic reading of the 'material body' see Judith Butler, *Bodies That Matter: On the Discursive Limits of 'Sex'* (London, 1993).
2. Kathleen Canning, *Gender History in Practice*, 172–73.
3. Canning, 'Der Körper der Staatsbürgerin als theoretisches und historisches Problem', in Beatrice Bowald, Alexandra Binnenkade, Sandra Büchel-Thalmeier and Monika Jacobs (eds), *KörperSinne: Körper im Spannungsfeld von Diskurs und Erfahrung* (Lucerne, 2002), 109–33; cf. Moira Gatens, *Imaginary Bodies: Ethics, Power, and Corporeality* (London, 1996).

Notes

4. Michel Foucault, *History of Sexuality: Vol. 1, An Introduction* (London, 1979), 105.
5. For mediation see Willem de Blécourt and Cornelie Usborne, 'Medicine, Mediation and Meaning', in idem (eds), *Cultural Approaches to the History of Medicine. Mediating Medicine in Early Modern and Modern Europe* (Basingstoke and New York, 2004), 1-10.
6. Jeffrey Weeks, *Making Sexual History* (Cambridge, 2000), 129.
7. Fisher, *Birth Control, Sex and Marriage*, 238-39.
8. *Lichtbild-Bühne*, 124, 24 May (1930); Manfred Georg, *Tempo*, 120, 24 May (1930).
9. Von Keitz, *Im Schatten des Gesetzes*, 176.
10. Krisztina Robert, '"All That is Best of the Modern Woman"? – Representations of Paramilitary Female War workers in British Popular Culture, 1914-1930s', in Jessica Meyer (ed.), *First World War and Popular Culture* (London, forthcoming).
11. Klaus Kreimeier, *Die Ufa-Story. Geschichte eines Filmkonzerns* (Munich, 1992), 122.
12. Von Keitz, *Im Schatten des Gesetzes*, 151.
13. Marcuse, 'Zur Frage der Verbreitung und Methodik', 753, 757-73, 775.
14. Marcuse, *Der eheliche Präventivverkehr*, e.g. cases 3, 6, 8, 166, 252.
15. Polano, 'Zur Frage der Geburtenbeschränkung', 569-72.
16. Marcuse, 'Zur Frage der Verbreitung', 754.
17. See Usborne, 'Body Biological to Body Politic'.
18. Fisher, *Birth Control, Sex and Marriage*, 238, 242.
19. Richard Hoggart, *The Uses of Literacy* (1957), cited in Cook, *The Long Sexual Revolution*, 128.
20. Marcuse, *Der eheliche Präventivverkehr*, 18, 19, 21-29, 32-33, 37, 39-40, 47-48 etc.
21. See Usborne, *Politics of the Body*, 2, 33; Jeffrey Weeks, *Sex, Politics and Society. The Regulation of Sexuality since 1800* (London and New York, 1981), 45.
22. See Sabine Kienitz, 'Body Damage: War Disability and Constructions of Masculinity in Weimar Germany', in Karen Hagemann and Stefanie Schüler-Springorum (eds), *Home/Front: The Military, War, and Gender in Twentieth-Century Germany* (Oxford, 2002), 181-204.
23. E.g., SAM, Sta.anw. Traunstein, 15690 and 15696; ibid., AG Mü, 37153.
24. See Linda Gordon, *Woman's Body, Woman's Right*, 412.
25. Cook, *The Long Sexual Revolution*, 243; cf. idem, 'Sex and the Doctors: the Medicalization of Sexuality as a Two-war Process in Early to Mid-Twentieth-century Britain', in de Blécourt and Usborne (eds), *Cultural Approaches*, 192-211.
26. Usborne, 'Women Doctors and Gender Identity'.
27. Julius Wolf, *Der Geburtenrückgang. Die Rationalisierung des Sexuallebens in unserer Zeit* (Jena, 1912); Felix Theilhaber, *Das sterile Berlin* (Berlin, 1913).
28. Marcuse, *Der eheliche Präventivverkehr*, 113.
29. Polano, 'Beitrag zur Frage der Geburtenbeschränkung', 574.
30. E.g., Rowe, *Representing Berlin*; Christiane Schönfeld (ed.), *Practicing Modernity. Female Creativity in the Weimar Republic* (Würzburg, 2006); Anthony McElligott (ed.), *The German Urban Experience 1900-1945. Modernity and Crisis* (London and New York, 2001).
31. Petersen, *Women and Modernity in Weimar Germany*.
32. Polano, 'Beitrag zur Frage der Geburtenbeschränkung', 573.
33. Marcuse, *Der eheliche Präventivverkehr*, 183-86.
34. Wolf, *Der Geburtenrückgang*; Paul Mombert, *Studien zur Bevölkerungsbewegung in Deutschland in den letzten Jahrzehnten mit besonderer Berücksichtigung der ehelichen Fruchtbarkeit* (Karlsruhe, 1907), 162; cf. Bergmann, *Die verhütete Sexualität*, 38ff.
35. Reinhard Spree, 'Der Geburtenrückgang in Deutschland vor 1939', *Demographische Informationen*, 3 (1984), 62.
36. See Chapter 1, note 4.
37. See Usborne, *Politics of the Body*, chap. 4.
38. Max Hirsch, *Fruchtabtreibung und Präventivverkehr*, 32f.
39. Polano, 'Beitrag zur Frage der Geburtenbeschränkung', 572.
40. Marcuse, 'Der eheliche Präventivverkehr', 383f.

41. See Usborne, *Politics of the Body*, 130-31.
42. Cf. Usborne, 'Rhetoric and Resistance'; Marcuse, *Der eheliche Präventivverkehr*, 110.
43. Hirsch, *Die Fruchtabtreibung*, 41.
44. Domansky, 'Militarization and Reproduction', 445, 459.
45. Canning, *Gender History in Practice*, 182.
46. See Usborne, 'Body Biological to Body Politic'.
47. BABL, NL Schreiber, no. 60, n.d.
48. BABL, R 1501, 9347, B1. 45.
49. See Usborne, 'The Christian Churches and the Regulation of Sexuality'; idem, *The Politics of the Body*, 71ff.
50. See Friedrich Wolf, 'Der Stuttgarter Prozeß um den §218', in J.W. Hauer, '§218. Eine sachliche Aussprache', *Der freie Dienst*, 1 (1931), 195-99; idem, *Sturm gegen den Paragraph 218. Unser Stuttgarter Prozeß* (Berlin, 1931); Else Kienle, *Frauen. Aus dem Tagebuch einer Ärztin* (Berlin, 1932).
51. Dr Käte Frankenthal, 'Question asked in the Prussian Diet', *Korrespondenz des Informationsbüros für Geburtenregelung*, 2 (1932), 4-9, 6.
52. Cf. other law theses: Jahns, *Abtreibung in Duisburg* (Düsseldorf, 1938); Krieger, 'Abtreibung in Freiburg'.
53. Inderheggen, *Abtreibung in Mönchen-Gladbach*, 19-20.
54. Inderheggen, *Abtreibung in M-Gladbach*, 131.
55. Exner cited in Inderheggen, *Abtreibung in Mönchen-Gladbach*, 131, 133-35: the study showed that 57.7 per cent of all cases which came to trial were punished with prison sentences of under three months and as many as 20.9 per cent with a fine; the most frequent (36.2 per cent) sentence for commercial abortion cases was gaol of one year and more, closely followed (31.4 per cent) by those of gaol terms between 3 and 12 months and, in third position, penal servitude (27.3 per cent), although the maximum penalty for this was penal servitude of 15 years.
56. Czarnowski, 'Women's Crimes, State Crimes', 238-39.
57. Ibid., 241.
58. LHAK, 605.2, 9965, LG Aurich, 8 June 1943.
59. Inderheggen, *Abtreibung in Mönchen-Gladbach*, 10-22: in 1937 the number of criminal investigations of suspected abortion cases went up from 97 in 1936 to 227.
60. Jahns, *Abtreibung in Duisburg*, 10.
61. Czarnowski, 'Women's Crimes, State Crimes', 247.
62. See Bock, *Zwangssterilisation*, 80ff.
63. Czarnowski, 'Women's Crimes, State Crimes', 241.
64. Ibid., 243f.
65. HSAK, 605.2, LG Trier, 13816, 22 October 1943, appeal by public prosecutor.
66. Jahns, *Abtreibung in Duisburg*, 40-42.
67. Krieger, 'Abtreibung in Freiburg i. Br.', 35-39.
68. Inderheggen, *Abtreibung in Mönchen-Gladbach*, 133, 145.
69. LHAK, 602.2, 10121; ibid., 10110, August 1942.
70. Inderheggen, *Abtreibung in Mönchen-Gladbach*, 145.
71. LHAK, 602.2, 2550, 1938.
72. LHAK, 605.2, Schwurgericht Trier, 7434, 1 October 1937.
73. Ibid., Landgericht Braunschweig, 89301, 1942.
74. Ibid., 3965, 22 March 1934.
75. Ibid., 6990, Schwurgericht Cologne, 16 March 1937.
76. Ibid., 7321, Schwurgericht Trier, 18 February 1937.
77. Czarnowski, 'Women's Crimes, State Crimes', 239, 242ff.
78. E.g., LHAK, 602.2, 9980, AG Cologne, October 1943; ibid., 10076 AG Gronau, September 1942; ibid., 10110, AG Wismar, August 1942; 605.2, 10311, AG Goslar, September 1942;

ibid., 10315, June 1941; 10376 AG Schwerin, September 1942; ibid., 605.2, 10495, June 1942.
79. HSAK, 605.2, 10439, LG Cologne, 11 May 1942.
80. E.g., HSAK, 605.2, 10495, 9 June 1942: a 24-year-old married woman whose husband had been drafted into the army in 1939 was said to have neglected her three young children during nightly meetings with several men.
81. Czarnowski, 'Women's Crimes, State Crimes', 247.
82. Quoted in Jahns, *Abtreibung in Duisburg*, 39.
83. LHAK, 605.2, Schwurgericht Koblenz, 4508, 31 October 1933.
84. LHAK, 605.2, Schwurgericht Trier, 2937, 1 February 1937.
85. BLHAP Pr.Br., Rep 3B, Fr.a.O., IMed, 281.
86. Harvey, 'Culture and Society in Weimar Germany', 282.
87. Helmut Lethen, *Cool Conduct: The Culture of Distance in Weimar Germany* (Berkeley, 2002); cf. Stephen Brockmann, 'Weimar Sexual Cynicism'.
88. Duden, *The Woman Beneath the Skin*.
89. Cf. Usborne, 'Rhetoric and Resistance'.

BIBLIOGRAPHY

A. Archive Materials

Archiv der Stiftung Deutsche Kinemathek Berlin
Zensurunterlagen
Blattsammlung
Originalfassungen der Filme

Brandenburgisches Landeshauptarchiv Potsdam (Sanssouci)
Polizeipräsidium Berlin Rep 30
Regierung Potsdam Rep 2A
Regierung Frankfurt a.O. Rep 3B
Landratsamt Cottbus Rep. 6B
Staatsanwaltschaft beim Landgericht Berlin Rep 12B
Staatsanwaltschaft beim Landgericht Cottbus
Staatsanwaltschaft beim Landgericht Frankfurt a.O.
Staatsanwaltschaft beim Landgericht Potsdam

Bundesarchiv Berlin (Lichterfelde)
Reichsgesundheitsamt R 86
Reichsministerium des Innern R 1501
Reichsjustizministerium R 3001
Institut für Sexualwissenschaft R 8069

Bundesarchiv-Filmarchiv Berlin
Zensurunterlagen
Reklamematerial
Originalfassungen der Filme

Geheimes Staatsarchiv Preussischer Kulturbesitz Berlin (Dahlem)
Preussisches Justizministerium Rep 84a

Hessisches Hauptstaatsarchiv Wiesbaden
Preußische Regierung Wiesbaden Abt 405
Preußisches Landratsamt Limburg a.d. Lahn Abt 411

Preußisches Landratsamt des Oberlahnkreises in Weilburg Abt 412
Abt 463, no. 99, vols 1-15, H. und A. K.

Historisches Archiv der Stadt Köln
Nachlaß des Reichskanzlers Wilhelm Marx

Landesarchiv Berlin
Generalstaatsanwaltschaft beim Landgericht II, Berlin Rep 58

Landeshauptarchiv Koblenz
Oberpräsidium der Rheinprovinz Best. 403
Bezirksregierung Koblenz Best. 441
Staatsanwaltschaft Koblenz Best. 584.1
Schwurgericht Köln Best. 605.2
Schwurgericht Trier Best. 605.2
Schwurgericht Trier Best. 605.2
Justizvollzugsanstalt Diez Best. 605.1
JVA Wittlich Best. 605.2

Nordrhein-Westfälisches Hauptstaatsarchiv Düsseldorf
Regierung Düsseldorf
Kreisarzt Düsseldorf
Landgericht Essen

Sächsisches Hauptstaatsarchiv Dresden
Kreishauptmannschaften Leipzig, Zwickau, Dresden
Ministerium der Auswärtigen Angelegenheiten, Medizinalwesen
Ministerium des Innern, Gesundheitswesen
Ministerium der Justiz
Nachrichtenstelle der Staatskanzlei
Staatsanwaltschaft beim Landgericht Leipzig
Zeitungsausschnittssammlung, Gesundheitswesen

Staatsarchiv München
Amtsgericht München AG
Gesundheitsämter
Landratsämter Aichach, Altötting, Dachau, Erding
Polizeidirektion München
Regierungsakten von Obberbayern
Staatsanwaltschaft beim Landgericht München
Staatsanwaltschaft beim Landgericht Traunstein

Stiftung Archiv der Akademie Der Künste Berlin
Erwin-Piscator-Center
Erich-Weinert-Archiv
Friedrich-Wolf-Archiv

Privatarchiv Dr Kurt Nemitz Bremen
Nachlaß Julius Moses

B. Filmography

Cyankali (§218) (1930), director: Hans Tintner; script: Hans Tintner based on the play *Cyankali*. §218 (1929) by Friedrich Wolf; producer: Atlantis-Film, Berlin; location: ASDKB.

Eine von uns (1932), director: Johannes Meyer; script: Irma von Cube, based on the novel *Gilgi – eine von uns* by Irmgard Keun (1931); producer: T.K. Filmproduktion; location: BAFA (incomplete).

Frauenarzt Dr Schäfer (1928), directors: Jakob and Luise Fleck; script: Jakob and Luise Fleck, producer: Hegewald-Film; location: missing.

Keimendes Leben (1918), part 2, director: Georg Jacobi; script: Dr Paul Meissner; producer: Produktions-Aktiengesellschaft 'Union' (PAGU); location: BAFA (fragment).

Kreuzzug des Weibes (1926), director: Martin Berger; script: Dosio Koffler, Martin Berger; producer: Arthur Ziem Internationale Film Exchange, Berlin; location: Deutsches Filminstitut, Frankfurt (video reconstructed by Ursula von Keitz).

Kuhle Wampe oder Wem gehört die Welt? (1932), director: Slatan Dudow; script: Bertolt Brecht, Ernst Ottwald, Slatan Dudow; producer: Prometheus Filmverleih und Vertrieb, Düsseldorf, Praesens-Film, Berlin, Tobis-Melofilm, Berlin (sound); location: ASDKB.

Madame Lu, die Frau für diskrete Beratung (1929), director: Franz Hofer; script: Franz Hofer; producer: Dr Lotte Dietrich, Filmproduktion und Vertrieb; location: BAFA.

Der Sittenrichter §218 (1929), director: Carl Heinz Wolff; script: Marie Louise Droop; producer: Albö-Film; location: missing.

C. Published Sources

Before 1945
Newspapers and journals (selected years)
Arbeiter-Illustrierte-Zeitung, 1930–33.
Die Ärztin. Monatsschrift des Bundes Deutscher Ärztinnen, 1931–33.
Der Film, Zeitschrift für die Gesamtinteressen der Kinematographie, Berlin, 1927ff.
Die Filmwoche. Die illustrierte Filmzeitschrift mit Phototeil, Berlin, 1926–33.
Film-Kurier. Theater Kunst, Varieté, Funk, Bild-Beilagen, kinotechnische Rundschau, Film-Musik, Tageszeitung, Berlin, 1918–33.
Der Kinematograph, Das älteste Film-Fachblatt, Düsseldorf, 1918–33.
Licht-Bild-Bühne. Die Fachzeitschrift der Filmindustrie, Berlin, 1918–33.
Medizinische Welt, 1930–33.
Reichsfilmblatt, Offizielles Organ des Verbandes der Lichtspiel Theater, Berlin, 1923–33.
Der Sozialistische Arzt. Vierteljahreszeitschrift des 'Vereins Sozialistischer Ärzte', 1926–31.

Books and journal articles

Adams, Hope Bridges, *Das Frauenbuch. Ein ärztlicher Ratgeber für die Frau in der Familie und bei Frauenkrankheiten* (Stuttgart, 1897).

Altenloh, Emilie, *Zur Soziologie des Kino: Die Kino-Unternehmung und die sozialen Schichten ihrer Besucher* (Jena, 1914; repr. Hamburg, 1977).

Bilz, F.E., *Das neue Naturheilverfahren* (Dresden, 1938).

Bornträger, Jean, 'Der Geburtenrückgang in Deutschland, seine Bewertung und Bekämpfung', *Veröffentlichungen aus dem Gebiete der Preußischen Medizinalverwaltung*, 1.13 (1912).

Braune, Rudolf, *Das Mädchen an der Orga Privat. Ein kleiner Roman aus Berlin* (Berlin, 1932).

Bredel, Willi, *Rosenhofstraße. Roman einer Arbeiterstraße* (Berlin, 1930).

Bumm, Ernst, 'Zur Frage des künstlichen Aborts', *Monatszeitschrift für Geburtshilfe und Gynäkologie* 43 (1916) 385-95.

———, 'Not und Fruchtabtreibung', *Münchener Medizinische Wochenschrift* 70, 1 February (1923) 468-72.

Credé [Hörder], Carl, *Volk in Not! Das Unheil des Abtreibungsparagraphen* (Dresden, 1927).

———, *Frauen in Not: §218* (Berlin, 1929).

———, *§218. Gequälte Menschen. Ein Schauspiel* (Berlin, 1930).

Deutscher Textilarbeiterverband (ed.), *Mein Arbeitstag, mein Wochenende. 150 Berichte von Textilarbeiterinnen* (Berlin, 1930).

Dührssen, Alfred, 'Die Reform des §218 (unter Berücksichtigung der Strafrechtsentwürfe von 1919 und 1925)', *Sexus*, IV (Leipzig, 1926) 48-121.

Ebermayer, Ludwig, *Arzt und Patient in der Rechtsprechung* (Berlin, 1924).

Ebstein, Erich (ed.), *Modernes Mittelalter. Eine Anklage auf Grund authentischen Materials von Dr. med. I. St., weiland Arzt in --burg* (Leipzig, 1921).

Fink, Lotte, 'Schwangerschaftsunterbrechung und Erfahrung aus Ehe- und Sexualberatung', *Die Ärztin*, 7 (1931) 70-74.

———, 'Die Tubensterilisation als Mittel der Geburtenregelung. Bericht über 375 Fälle der Ehe- und Sexualberatungsstelle Frankfurt a.M. (Mutterschutz)', *Medizinische Welt* (1931) 750-51.

Fraenkel, Ludwig, 'Physiologie der weiblichen Genitalorgane', in J. Halban and L. Seitz (eds), *Biologie und Pathologie des Weibes* (8 vols) (Berlin and Vienna, 1924-29) vol. I (1924) 517-634.

———, *Die Empfängnisverhütung, biologische Grundlage, Technik und Indikationen* (Stuttgart, 1932).

Franke, Ingeborg, 'Gilgi – Film, Roman und Wirklichkeit', *Der Weg der Frau* 3.2 (1932) 4-7.

Frankenthal, Käte, 'Fragen im Preußischen Landtag', *Korrespondenz des Informationsbüros für Geburtenregelung* 1 (1932) 4-9.

Grotjahn, Alfred (ed.), *Eine Kartothek zu §218: Ärztliche Berichte aus einer Kleinstadtpraxis über 426 künstliche Aborte in einem Jahr* (Berlin, 1932).

Grotjahn, Alfred and Gustav Radbruch, *Die Abtreibung der Leibesfrucht. Zwei Gutachten* (Berlin, 1921).

Hartke, Wolfgang, 'Das Arbeits- und Wohnortsgebiet in Rhein-Mainischen Lebensraum', *Rhein-Mainische Forschungen* 18 (1938) 14-15.

Himes, Norman, *A Medical History of Contraception* (London, 1936, repr. 1963).

Hirsch, Max, *Fruchtabtreibung und Präventivverkehr im Zusammenhang mit dem Geburtenrückgang* (Würzburg, 1914).
_____, *Die Fruchtabtreibung* (Stuttgart, 1921).
Höllein, Emil, *Gegen den Gebärzwang. Der Kampf um die bewußte Kleinhaltung der Familie* (Berlin, 1928).
Hüssy, Paul, *Begutachtung und gerichtliche Beurteilung von ärztlichen Kunstfehlern auf geburtshilflich-gynäkologischem Gebiete* (Stuttgart, 1935).
Inderheggen, Konstantin, *Das Delikt der Abtreibung im Landgerichtsbezirk Mönchen-Gladbach in der Zeit von 1908 bis 1938* (Jena, 1940).
Jahns, Helmuth, *Das Delikt der Abtreibung im Landgerichtsbezirk Duisburg in der Zeit von 1910-1935* (Düsseldorf, 1938).
Keun, Irmgard, *Gilgi - eine von uns* (Berlin, 1931).
Kienle, Else, *Frauen. Aus dem Tagebuch einer Ärztin* (Berlin, 1932).
Klauber, Leo, 'Die Abtreibung', in Ludwig Levy-Lenz (ed.), *Sexualkatastrophen. Bilder aus dem modernen Geschlechts- und Eheleben* (Leipzig, 1926).
_____, [article], *Der Sozialistische Arzt*, August (1928) 3.
Köhler, Wolfgang, *Das Delikt der Abtreibung im Bezirk des Landgerichts Gera in den Jahren 1896-1930* (Jena, 1935).
Krey, Franz, *Maria und der Paragraph. Ein Roman um §218* (Vienna, Berlin and Zürich, 1931).
Labhardt, Alf, 'Die Gefahren der künstlichen Eingriffe in das keimende Leben', *Das kommende Geschlecht, Zeitschrift für Familienpflege und geschlechtliche Volkserziehung auf biologischer und ethischer Grundlage* 1 (1921) 72-80.
Leideritz, Hans, *Die 'operationslose', indizierte Schwangerschafts-Unterbrechung* (Hamburg, 1932).
Levy-Lenz, Ludwig, *Wenn Frauen nicht gebären dürfen* (Berlin, 1928).
Liepmann, Wilhelm, *Die Abtreibung* (Berlin and Vienna, 1927).
Lönne, Friedrich, *Das Problem der Fruchtabtreibung vom medizinischen, juristischen und national-ökonomischen Standpunkt* (Berlin, 1924).
Lütgert, Wilhelm, 'Die Stellung der Evangelischen Kirche', in Arbeitsgemeinschaft für Volksgesundung e.V. (ed.) 'Paragraph 218. Sinn und Problematik der Abtreibungsparagraphen', *Schriften zur Volksgesundung* 17 (1931) 23-28.
Marcuse, Max, 'Zur Frage der Verbreitung und Methodik der willkürlichen Geburtenbeschränkung in Berliner Proletarierkreisen', *Sexualprobleme* 9 (1913) 752-80.
_____, *Der eheliche Präventivverkehr. Seine Verbreitung, Verursachung und Methodik. Dargestellt und beleuchtet an 300 Ehen. Ein Beitrag zur Symptomatik und Ätiologie der Geburtenbeschränkung* (Stuttgart, 1917).
_____, 'Der eheliche Präventivverkehr', in Max Marcuse (ed.), *Die Ehe. Ihre Physiologie, Psychologie, Hygiene und Eugenik. Ein biologisches Handbuch* (Berlin and Cologne, 1927) 379-99.
Mayer, Joseph, 'Katholische Sexualethik und Strafrechtsreform', *Mitteilungen des Reichsfrauenbeirats der Deutschen Zentrumspartei* 4 (1929) 1-11.
Mombert, Paul, *Studien zur Bevölkerungsbewegung in Deutschland in den letzten Jahrzehnten mit besonderer Berücksichtigung der ehelichen Fruchtbarkeit* (Karlsruhe, 1907).
Moses, Julius, 'Der Kampf um die Aufhebung des Abtreibungsparagraphen', *Biologische Heilkunst* 10 (1929) 933-35.

Polano, Oskar, 'Beitrag zur Frage der Geburtenbeschränkung', *Zeitschrift für Geburtshülfe und Gynäkologie*, 79 (1917) 567-78.
Radbruch, Gustav, 'Der künstliche Abort im geltenden und künftigen Strafrecht', *Monatsschrift des Bundes Deutscher Ärztinnen*, 4.
Stöcker, Helene, *Die Liebe und die Frauen* (Minden, 1906).
Theilhaber, Felix, *Das sterile Berlin* (Berlin, 1913).
Titmuss, R. and K., *Parents Revolt: A Study of the Declining Birth Rate in Acquisitive Societies* (London, 1942).
Toller, Ernst, *Masse Mensch* (Berlin, 1920).
Vollmann, Sigmund, *Die Fruchtabtreibung als Volkskrankheit. Gefahren, Ursachen, Bekämpfung* (Leipzig, 1925).
_____ , 'Die Bekämpfung der Abtreibungsseuche', *Ärztliches Vereinsblatt für Deutschland*, 52 (1925) 45.
Weil, Arthur (ed.), *Sexualreform und Sexualwissenschaft. Vorträge gehalten auf der 1. Internationalen Tagung für Sexualreform auf sexualwissenschaftlicher grundlage in Berlin* (Stuttgart, 1922).
Weinert, Erich, *Der Mahnruf* (Berlin, 1929).
Winter, Georg, *Der künstliche Abort, Indikationen, Methoden, Rechtspflege. Für den geburtshilflichen Praktiker* (Stuttgart, 1926).
_____ , 'Abtreibung oder künstlicher Abort?', *Medizinische Welt* 1 (1927) 52-54.
_____ , 'Strittige Punkte in der Behandlung des fieberhaften Aborts', *Medizinische Welt* 1 (1927) 1040-43.
Wolf, Friedrich, 'Der Stuttgarter Prozeß um den §218', in J.W. Hauer, '§218. Eine sachliche Aussprache', *Der freie Dienst* 1 (1931) 195-99.
_____ , *Sturm gegen den Paragraph 218. Unser Stuttgarter Prozeß* (Berlin, 1931).
_____ , *Dramen* (East Berlin, 1960).
Wolf, Julius, *Der Geburtenrückgang. Die Rationalisierung des Sexuallebens in unserer Zeit* (Jena, 1912).

After 1945

Books and journal articles

Alexander, Sally, 'The Mysteries and Secrets of Women's Bodies', in Mica Nava and Alan O'Shea (eds), *Modern Times. Reflections on a Century of English Modernity* (London, 1996) 161-75.
Ankum, Katharina von, 'Motherhood and the "New Woman". Vicki Baum's *stud.chem. Helene Willfüer* and Irmgard Keun's *Gilgi - eine von uns*', *Women in German Yearbook* 11 (1995) 171-88.
Arendt, Hans-Jürgen, 'Eine demokratische Massenbewegung unter der Führung der KPD im Frühjahr 1931. Die Volksaktion gegen den Paragraphen 218 und gegen die päpstliche Enzyklika Casti Connubi', *Zeitschrift für Geschichtswissenschaft*, 19 (1971) 213-23.
Arnot, Margaret L. and Cornelie Usborne (eds), *Gender and Crime in Modern Europe* (London, 1999).
Bajohr, Stefan, *Lass dich nicht mit den Bengels ein! Sexualität, Geburtenregelung und Geschlechtsmoral im Braunschweiger Arbeitermilieu 1900 bis 1933* (Essen, 2001).
Banks, J.A., *Prosperity and Parenthood: A Study of Family Planning among the Victorian Middle Class* (London, 1954).

Barndt, Kerstin, *Sentiment und Sachlichkeit. Der Roman der Neuen Frau in der Weimarer Republik* (Cologne, Weimar and Vienna, 2003).

Barrett, Michele, *Women's Oppression Today* (London, 1980).

Bergmann, Anna, *Die verhütete Sexualität. Die medizinische Bemächtigung des Lebens* (Berlin, 1998); (1st edn. *Die verhütete Sexualität. Die Anfänge der modernen Geburtenkontrolle* (Hamburg, 1992).

Bessel, Richard, *Germany After the First World War* (Oxford, 1993).

Bielefelder Graduiertenkolleg Sozialgeschichte (eds), *Körper macht Geschichte – Geschichte macht Körper* (Bielefeld, 1999).

Blécourt, Willem de, 'Time and the Anthropologist; or the Psychometry of Historiography', *Focaal, tijdschrift voor antropologie* 26/27 (1996) 17-24.

——, 'Cultures of Abortion in The Hague in the Early Twentieth Century', in Franz X. Eder, Lesley Hall and Gert Hekma (eds), *Sexual Cultures in Europe. Themes in Sexuality* (Manchester and New York, 1999) 195-212.

——, 'Illegale genezers en nep patienten. Over de aantrekkingskracht van unorthodoxe vormen van geneeskunde rond 1900', *Tijdschrift voor sociale geschiedenis* 25 (1999) 425-42.

——, *Het Amazonenleger. Irreguliere genezeressen in Nederland 1850-1930* (Amsterdam, 1999).

——, 'Prosecution and Popularity: the Case of the Dutch Sequah, 1891-1993', in John Woodward and Robert Jütte (eds), *Coping with Sickness. Medicine, Law and Human Rights – Historical Perspectives* (Sheffield, 2000) 75-90.

——, 'Hygienic Articles, Patent Medicines and Rubber Goods', in Marijke Gijswijt-Hofstra and Tilly Tansey (eds), *Biographies of Remedies. Drugs, Medicine and Contraception in Dutch and Anglo-American Healing Cultures* (Amsterdam and Atlanta, 2001) 183-202.

Blécourt, Willem de and Cornelie Usborne, 'Women's Medicine, Women's Culture: Abortion and Fortune-Telling in Early Twentieth-Century Germany and the Netherlands', *Medical History* 43 (1999) 376-92.

——, 'Medicine, Mediation and Meaning', in idem (eds), *Cultural Approaches to the History of Medicine. Mediating Medicine in Early Modern and Modern Europe* (Basingstoke and New York, 2004), 1-10.

Blécourt, Willem de and Cornelie Usborne (eds), *Alternative Medicine in Europe since 1800*, special issue *Medical History*, 43, 3 (1999).

——, *Cultural Approaches to the History of Medicine. Mediating Medicine in Early Modern and Modern Europe* (Basingstoke and New York, 2004).

Bleker, Johanna, 'Die ersten Ärztinnen und ihre Gesundheitsbücher für Frauen', in Eva Brinkschulte (ed.), *Weibliche Ärzte. Die Durchsetzung des Berufbildes in Deutschland* (Berlin 1993) 65-83.

Bock, Gisela, *Zwangssterilisation im Nationalsozialismus. Studien zur Rassenpolitik und Frauenpolitik* (Opladen, 1986).

Bock, Hans-Michael (ed.), *Cinegraph. Lexikon zum deutschsprachigen Film* (Munich, 1984).

Bodek, Richard, *Proletarian Performance in Weimar Berlin: Agitprop, Chorus, and Brecht* (Columbia, 1997).

Bothe, Detlef, *Neue Deutsche Heilkunde 1933-1945* (Husum, 1991).

Brinkschulte, Eva (ed.), *Weibliche Ärzte. Die Durchsetzung des Berufbildes in Deutschland* (Berlin 1993).
Brockmann, Stephen, 'Weimar Sexual Cynicism', in Thomas W. Kniesche and Stephen Brockmann (eds), *Dancing on the Volcano. Essays on the Culture of the Weimar Republic* (Columbia, 1994) 165–80.
Brodie, J. Farrell, *Contraception and Abortion in 19th-century America* (Ithaca and London, 1994).
Brookes, Barbara, 'The Illegal Operation. Abortion 1919–39', in London Feminist History Group (ed.), *The Sexual Dynamics of History* (London, 1983) 165–76.
――――, 'Women and Reproduction, 1860–1939', in Jane Lewis (ed.), *Labour and Love. Women's Experience of Home and Family, 1850–1940* (London, 1986) 149–71.
――――, *Abortion in England 1900–1967* (London, 1988).
Brooks, Peter, *The Melodramatic Imagination: Balzac, Henry James, Melodrama and the Mode of Excess* (New Haven, 1976).
Burke, Peter, 'Cultural History: Past, Present and Future', *Theoretische geschiedenis* 13 (1986) 187–96.
――――, *The Historical Anthroplogy of Early Modern Italy. Essays on Perception and Communication* (Cambridge, 1987).
Butler, Judith, *Bodies that Matter: On the Discursive Limits of 'Sex'* (London, 1993).
Canning, Kathleen, 'Feminist History after the Linguistic Turn: Historicizing Discourse and Experience', *Signs: Journal of Women in Culture and Society* 21 (1994) 368–404.
――――. 'Der Körper der Staatsbürgerin als theoretisches und historisches Problem', in Beatrice Bowald, Alexandra Binnenkade, Sandra Büchel-Thalmeier and Monika Jacobs (eds), *KörperSinne: Körper im Spannungsfeld von Diskurs und Erfahrung* (Lucerne, 2002) 109–33.
――――. *Gender History in Practice. Historical Perspectives on Bodies, Class and Citzenship* (Ithaca and London, 2006).
Chamberlain, Mary, *Old Wives Tales. Their History, Remedies and Spells* (London, 1981).
Cook, Hera, 'Sex and the Doctors: the Medicalization of Sexuality as a Two-war Process in Early to Mid-Twentieth-century Britain', in Willem de Blécourt and Cornelie Usborne, *Cultural Approaches to the History of Medicine. Mediating Medicine in Early Modern and Modern Europe* (Basingstoke and New York, 2004) 192–211.
――――, *The Long Sexual Revolution. English Women, Sex, and Contraception 1800–1975* (Oxford, 2004).
Crew, David, 'Alltagsgeschichte: A New Social History from Below?', *Central European History* 22 (1992) 394–407.
Czarnowski, Gabriele, 'Frauen als Mütter der "Rasse". Abtreibungsverfolgung und Zwangseingriff im Nationalsozialismus', in Gisela Staupe and Lisa Vieth (eds), *Unter allen Umständen. Zur Geschichte der Abtreibung* (Dresden and Berlin, 1993).
――――, 'Abortion as Political Conflict in the Unified Germany', *Parliamentary Affairs. A Journal of Comparative Politics*, 47 (1994) 252–67.
――――, 'Women's Crimes, State Crimes: Abortion in Nazi Germany', in Margaret L. Arnot and Cornelie Usborne (eds), *Gender and Crime in Modern Europe* (London, 1999) 238–56.
Dienel, Christiane, 'Das 20. Jahrhundert. Frauenbewegung, Klassenjustiz und das Recht auf Selbstbestimmung der Frau', in Robert Jütte (ed.), *Geschichte der Abtreibung von der Antike bis zur Gegenwart* (Munich, 1993) 140–68.

Dinges, Martin (ed.), *Medizinkritische Bewegungen im Deutschen Reich (ca. 1870–ca.1933)* (Stuttgart, 1996).
Dohrmann, Olaf, '"Kämpfer für eine Reform des §218", "Limonade" oder Gretchentragödie? *Cyankali* im sozialhistorischen und intermedialen Kontext', in Malte Hagener (ed.), *Geschlecht in Fesseln. Sexualität zwischen Aufklärung und Ausbeutung im Weimarer Kino 1918–1933* (Munich, 2000) 102–18.
Domansky, Elisabeth, 'Militarization and Reproduction in World War I Germany', in Geoff Eley (ed.), *Society, Culture, and State in Germany, 1870–1930* (Ann Arbor, 1996) 427–63.
Dommermuth, Anton, *Die landwirtschaftlichen Betriebsformen im Westerwald und im Limburger Becken in ihrer geographischen Bedingheit* (Frankfurt a.M., 1940).
Dove, Richard, *He was a German. A Biography of Ernst Toller* (London, 1990).
Duden, Barbara, '"Keine Nachsicht gegen das schöne Geschlecht." Wie sich Ärzte die Kontrolle über Gebärmütter aneigneten', in Susanne von Paczensky and Renate Sadrozinski (eds), *Paragraph 218*, (Reinbek, 1984) 114–33.
———, *The Woman Beneath the Skin. A Doctor's Patients in Eighteenth-Century Germany* (Cambridge, Mass.and London, 1991).
———, *Der Frauenleib als öffentlicher Ort. Vom Mißbrauch des Begriffs Leben* (Hamburg and Zurich, 1991).
———, *Der Griff nach dem ungeborenen Leben. Zur Subjektgenese des Embryos* (Pfaffenweiler, 1993).
———, *Disembodying Women. Perspectives of Pregnancy and the Unborn* (Harvard, 1993).
———, '"Ein falsch Gewächs, ein unzeitig Wesen, gestocktes Blut". Zur Geschichte von Wahrnehmung und Sichtweise der Leibesfrucht', in Gisela Staupe and Lisa Vieth (eds) *Unter anderen Umständen* (Dresden and Berlin, 1993) 27–35.
———, 'Zwischen "wahrem Wissen" und Prophetie. Konzeptionen des Ungeborenen', in Duden et al., *Geschichte des Ungeborenen. Zur Erfahrungs- und Wissenschaftsgeschichte der Schwangerschaft, 17. – 20. Jahrhundert* (Göttingen, 2002) 11–48.
Duden, Barbara, Jürgen Schlumbohm and Patrice Veit (eds), *Geschichte des Ungeborenen. Zur Erfahrungs- und Wissenschaftsgeschichte der Schwangerschaft, 17. – 20. Jahrhundert* (Göttingen, 2002).
Eder, Franz, *Kultur der Begierde. Eine Geschichte des Sexualität* (München, 2002).
Eisner, Lotte, *The Haunted Screen: Expressionism and the German Film and the Influence of Max Reinhardt* (Berkeley and Los Angeles, 1969).
Elsaesser, Thomas, *Weimar Cinema and After. Germany's Historical Imaginary* (London and New York, 2000).
Evans, Richard J., *Tales from the German Underworld* (New Haven and London, 1998).
Fisher, Kate, '"Didn't stop to think, I just didn't want another one": The Culture of Abortion in Interwar South Wales', in Franz X. Eder, Lesley A. Hall and Gert Hekma (eds) *Sexual Cultures in Europe. Themes in sexuality* (Manchester, 1999) 213–55.
———, *Birth Control, Sex and Marriage in Britain 1918–1960* (Oxford 2006).
Forbes, Jill, 'Retrospective: Kuhle Wampe oder wem gehört die Welt?', *Monthly Film Bulletin* 45 (July 1978) 146.
Foucault, Michel, *History of Sexuality: vol. 1, An Introduction* (London, 1979).

Frevert, Ute, '"Fürsorgliche Belagerung": Hygienebewegung und Arbeiterfrauen im 19. und frühen 20. Jahrhundert', *Geschichte und Gesellschaft* 11 (1985) 420-46.

———. *Women in German History* (Oxford, New York and Munich, 1989).

Führer, Karl Christian, 'Auf dem Weg zur Massenkultur? Kino und Rundfunk in der Weimarer Republik', *Historische Zeitschrift* 262 (1996) 739-82.

Gatens, Moira, *Imaginary Bodies: Ethics, Power, and Corporeality* (London, 1996).

Geisthardt, Fritz, *Wirtschaft in Mittelnassau. Hundert Jahre Industrie- und Handelskammer Limburg 1864-1964* (Limburg, 1965).

Gensicke, Helmuth, *1200 Jahre (1235-1985) Oberbrechen* (Limburg, 1974).

———, *750 Jahre (1235-1985) Werschau. Aus der Geschichte von Werschau* (Werschau, 1985).

Gensicke, Helmuth, and Egon Eichhorn, *Geschichte von Oberbrechen* (Brechen-Oberbrechen, 1975).

Gerhard-Teuscher, Ute, 'Frauenbewegung und §218', in Gisela Staupe and Lisa Vieth (eds), *Unter allen Umständen. Zur Geschichte der Abtreibung* (Dresden and Berlin, 1993) 104-13.

Gerhard, Ute (ed.) *Frauen in der Geschichte des Rechts. Von der frühren Neuzeit bis zur Gegenwart* (Munich, 1997).

Gilbert, Scott F. (ed.), *A Conceptual History of Modern Embryology* (Baltimore, 1991).

Gittings, Diana, *Fair Sex: Family Size and Structure 1900-1939* (London, 1982).

Gleixner, Ulrike, 'Geschlechterdifferenzen und die Faktizität des Fiktionalen. Zur Dekonstruktion frühneuzeitlicher Verhörprotokolle', *Werkstatt Geschichte* 11 (1995) 65-70.

Gordon, Linda, *Woman's Body, Woman's Right: A Social History of Birth Control in America* (Harmondsworth, 1977).

Grossmann, Atina, '"Satisfaction is Domestic Happiness": Mass Working-Class Sex Reform Organizations in the Weimar Republic', in Michael N. Dobkowski and Isidor Wallimann (eds), *Towards the Holocaust: The Social and Economic Collapse of the Weimar Republic* (Westport, Conn., 1983) 265-93.

———, 'The New Woman and the Rationalization of Sexuality in Weimar Germany', in Ann Snitow, Christine Stansell and Sharon Thompson (eds), *Powers of Desire: The Politics of Sexuality* (London, 1984) 190-211.

———, 'Berliner Ärztinnen und Volksgesundheit in der Weimarer Republik: Zwischen Sexualreform und Eugenik', in Christine Eifart and Susanne Rouette (eds), *Unter allen Umständen: Frauengeschichte in Berlin* (Berlin, 1986) 183-217.

———, *Reforming Sex. The German Movement for Birth Control and Abortion Reform 1920-1950* (New York and Oxford, 1995).

Grün, Hugo, *Kirberg, 1355-1955. Ein geschichtlicher Rückblick zur Erinnerung an die Stadtgründung und den Bau seiner Kirche* (Kirberg, 1955).

Grund, Erhard, *Ohren. 1301 - 2001. Eine Ortsgeschichte* (Nordenstadt, 2001).

Guttsman, W.L., *Workers' Culture in Weimar Germany. Between Tradition and Commitment* (New York, Oxford and Munich, 1990).

Hagemann, Karen, *Frauenalltag und Männerpolitik. Alltagsleben und gesellschaftliches Handeln von Arbeiterfrauen in der Weimarer Republik* (Bonn, 1990).

———, *Eine Frauensache. Alltagsleben und Geburtenpolitik 1919-1933* (Pfaffenweiler, 1991).

Hagemann, Karen and Stefanie Schüler-Springorum (eds), *Home/Front: The Military, War, and Gender in Twentieth-Century Germany* (Oxford, 2002).

Hagener, Malte (ed.), *Geschlecht in Fesseln. Sexualität zwischen Aufklärung und Ausbeutung im Weimarer Kino 1918-1933* (Munich, 2000).
Hansen, Miriam, *Babel and Babylon: Spectatorship in American Silent Film* (Cambridge, Mass., 1991).
Häntzschel, Hiltrud, *Irmgard Keun* (Reinbek, 2001).
Harsch, Donna, 'Society, the State, and Abortion in East Germany, 1950-1972', *The American Historical Review* 102 (1997) 53-84.
Harvey, Elizabeth, 'Culture and Society in Weimar Germany: the Impact of Modernism and Mass Culture', in Mary Fulbrook (ed.), *German History since 1800* (London, 1997) 279-97.
Haug, Alfred, *Die Reichsarbeitsgemeinschaft für eine Neue Deutsche Heilkunde (1935/36)* (Husum, 1985).
Herrmann, Bettina, 'Else Kienle (1900-1970) – Ein Ärztin im Mittelpunkt der Abtreibungsdebatte von 1931', in Eva Brinkschulte (ed.), *Weibliche Ärzte: Die Durchsetzung des Berufsbildes in Deutschland* (Berlin, 1993) 114-22.
Hopwood, Nick, 'Producing Development: The Anatomy of Human Embryos and the Norms of Wilhelm His', *Bulletin of the History of Medicine* 74 (2000) 29-79.
Huerkamp, Claudia, *Der Aufstieg der Ärzte im 19. Jahrhundert. Vom gelehrten Stand zum professionellen Experten: Das Beispiel Preußens* (Göttingen, 1985).
———, 'Medizinische Lebensreform im späten 19. Jahrhundert. Die Naturheilkundebewegung in Deutschland als Protest gegen die naturwissenschaftliche Universitätsmedizin', *Vierteljahresschrift für Sozial- und Wirtschaftsgeschichte* 73 (1986) 158-82.
Jackson, Louise, 'The Child's Word in Court: Cases of Sexual Abuse in London, 1870-1914', in Margaret L. Arnot and Cornelie Usborne (eds), *Gender and Crime in Modern Europe* (London, 1999) 222-38.
Jerouscheck, Günter, *Lebensschutz und Lebensbeginn. Kulturgeschichte des Abtreibungsverbot* (Stuttgart, 1989).
———, 'Zur Geschichte des Abtreibungsverbots', in Gisela Staupe and Lisa Vieth (eds), *Unter allen Umständen* (Dresden and Berlin, 1993) 11-26.
———, 'Die juristische Konstruktion des Abtreibungsverbot', in Ute Gerhard (ed.) *Frauen in der Geschichte des Rechts. Von der frühen Neuzeit bis zur Gegenwart* (Munich, 1997) 248-61.
Jochimsen, Luc, *Paragraph 218. Dokumentation eines hundertjährigen Elends* (Hamburg, 1971).
Jung, Ulli and Stephanie Roll, 'Women Enjoying Being Women. Some Observations on the Occasion of a Retrospective of Franz Hofer's Extant films in Saarbrücken', *Kintop. Jahrbuch zur Erforschung des frühen Films* 8 (1999) 159-68.
Jütte, Robert, *Geschichte der Alternativen Medizin. Von der Volksmedizin zu den unkonventionellen Therapien von heute* (Munich, 1996).
Jütte, Robert (ed.), *Geschichte der Abtreibung von der Antike bis zur Gegenwart* (Munich, 1993).
Kaes, Anton, 'The Debate About Cinema: Charting a Controversy (1909-1929)', *New German Critique* 40 (1987) 7-33.
———, 'Film in der Weimarer Republik', in Wolfgang Jacobsen, Anton Kaes and Hans Helmut Prinzler (eds), *Geschichte des Deutschen Films* (Stuttgart, 1993) 39-100.

Kaes, Anton, Martin Jay and Edward Dimendberg (eds), *The Weimar Republic Sourcebook* (Berkely, Los Angeles and Oxford, 1994).
Kaschuba, Wolfgang and Carola Lipp, *Dörfliches Überleben. Zur Geschichte materieller and sozialer Reproduktion ländlicher Gesellschaft im 19. und frühen 20. Jahrhundert* (Tübingen, 1982).
Keitz, Ursula von, *Im Schatten des Gesetzes. Schwangerschaftskonflikt und Reproduktion im deutschsprachigen Film 1918–1933* (Marburg, 2005).
—— . 'Sittenfilm zwischen Markt und Rechtspolitik. Martin Bergers *Kreuzzug des Weibes* (1926) und seine amerikanische Fassung *Unwelcome Children*', in Malte Hagener (ed.), *Geschlecht in Fesseln. Sexualität zwischen Aufklärung und Ausbeutung im Weimarer Kino 1918–1933* (Munich, 2000) 139–53.
Keller, Allan, *Scandalous Lady: The Life and Times of Madame Restell, New York's Most Notorius Abortionist* (New York, 1981).
Kienitz, Sabine, 'Body Damage: War Disability and Constructions of Masculinity in Weimar Germany', in Karen Hagemann and Stefanie Schüler-Springorum (eds), *Home/Front: The Military, War, and Gender in Twentieth-Century Germany* (Oxford, 2002) 181–204.
—— , 'Körper der Erinnerung. Kriegsinvalidät und Identitätspolitik im öffentlichen Raum in den 1920er Jahren', unpublished paper delivered at the Interdisciplinary Conference, University of Michigan, 'Rethinking Weimar', April 2002.
King, Lynda, *Best-Sellers By Design. Vicki Baum and the House of Ullstein* (Detroit, 1988).
Klasen, Eva-Maria, 'Die Diskussion über eine Krise der Medizin in Deutschland zwischen 1925 und 1935', unpubl. med. Diss. Mainz 1984.
Kniesche, Thomas W. and Stephen Brockmann (eds), *Dancing on the Volcano. Essays on the Culture of the Weimar Republic* (Columbia, 1994).
Knight, Patricia, 'Women and Abortion in Victorian and Edwardian England', *History Workshop Journal*, 4 (1977) 57–69.
Knodel, John E., *The Decline of Fertility in Germany, 1871–1939* (Princeton, NJ., 1974).
Kolb, Eberhard, *The Weimar Republic* (London, 1988).
Kosta, Barbara, 'Unruly Daughters and Modernity: Irmgard Keun's *Gilgi – eine von uns*', *The German Quaterly* 86 (1995) 271–86.
Kracauer, Siegfried, *From Caligari to Hitler. A Psychological History of the German Film* (Princeton, 1947, repr. 1974).
—— . *Das Ornament der Masse* (Frankfurt a.M., 1977).
Krauss, Marita, *Die Frau der Zukunft. Dr. Hope Bridges Adams Lehmann, 1855–1916, Ärztin und Reformerin* (Munich, 2002).
Kreimeier, Klaus, *Ufa-Story. Geschichte eines Filmkonzerns* (Munich, 1992).
Krieger, Werner, 'Erscheinungsformen und Strafzumessung bei der Abtreibung dargestellt an Hand von Gerichtsakten des Landgerichts und Amtsgerichts Freiburg im Breisgau aus den Jahren 1925–1951', unpubl. legal diss., Albert-Ludwig-University, (Freiburg i.Br., 1952).
Kulturamt der Landeshauptstadt Stuttgart, *Stuttgart in Dritten Reich, Friedrich Wolf. Die Jahre in Stuttgart, 1927–1933. Ein Beispiel* (Stuttgart, 1983).
Labisch, Alfons, *Homo Hygienicus. Gesundheit und Medizin in der Neuzeit* (Frankfurt and New York, 1992).
—— . 'From Traditional Individualism to Collective Professionalism: State, Patient, Compulsory Health Insurance, and the Panel Doctor Question in Gemany, 1883–1931', in Manfred Berg and Geoffrey Cocks (eds), *Medicine and Modernity.*

Public Health and Medical Care in Nineteenth- and Twentieth-Century Germany (Cambridge, 1997) 35-54.

Labouvie, Eva, *Andere Umstände. Eine Kulturgeschichte der Geburt* (Cologne, 1998).

———, *Beistand in Kindesnöten. Hebammen und weibliche Kultur auf dem Land (1550-1910)* (Frankfurt a.M., 1999).

Langthaler, Ernst and Reinhard Sieder (eds), *Über die Dörfer. Ländliche Lebenswelten in der Moderne* (Vienna, 2000).

Lehner, Karin, *Verpönte Eingriffe. Sozialdemokratische Reformbestrebungen zu den Abtreibungsbestimmungen in der Zwischenkriegszeit* (Vienna, 1989).

Leibrock-Plehn, Larissa, *Hexenkräuter oder Arznei. Die Abtreibungsmittel im 16. und 17. Jahrhundert* (Stuttgart, 1992).

———, 'Frühe Neuzeit. Hebammen, Kräutermedizin und weltliche Justiz', in Robert Jütte (ed.), *Geschichte der Abtreibung von der Antike bis zur Gegenwart* (Munich, 1993) 68-90.

Lethen, Helmut, *Cool Conduct: The Culture of Distance in Weimar Germany* (Berkeley, 2002).

Levi, Giovanni, 'On Microhistory', in Peter Burke (ed.), *New Perspectives on Historical Writing* (Cambridge, 1991) 93-113.

Lewis, Beth Irwin, '*Lustmord*: Inside the Windows of the Metropolis', in Katharina von Ankum (ed.), *Women in the Metropolis* (Berkeley, Los Angeles and London, 1997) 202-232.

Lindemann, Mary, *Health and Healing in Eighteenth-Century Germany* (Baltimore and London, 1996).

Lüdtke, Alf, 'Alltagsgeschichte: Aneignung und Akteure. Oder – es hat noch kaum begonnen!', *Werkstatt Geschichte* 17 (1997) 83-91.

———, 'People Working: Everyday-Life and German Fascism', *History Workshop Journal* 50 (2000) 75-92.

Lüdtke, Alf (ed.), *The History of Everyday Life. Reconstructing Historical Experiences and Ways of Life* (Princeton, 1995).

Martin, Emily, *The Woman in the Body. A Cultural Analysis of Reproduction* (Boston, Mass, 1987).

McCormick, Richard W., *Gender and Sexuality in Weimar Germany. Film, Literature and 'New Objectivity'* (New York, 2001).

McElligott, Anthony (ed.), *The German Urban Experience 1900-1945. Modernity and Crisis* (London and New York, 2001).

McGuire, Kristin, 'The *Neue Generation* of 1918/19: Helene Stöcker and Ideals of the Democratic Subject', unpublished paper delivered at the Interdisciplinary Conference, University of Michigan, 'Rethinking Weimar', April 2002.

McLaren, Angus, 'Women's Work and Regulation of Family Size: the Question of Abortion in the Nineteenth Century', *History Workshop Journal* 4 (1977) 70-81.

———, 'The Early Birth Control Movement: an Example of Medical Self-Help' in John Woodward and David Richards (eds), *Health Care and Popular Medicine in Nineteenth-Century England* (London, 1977) 89-194.

———, *Birth Control in Nineteenth-Century England* (New York, 1978).

———, *Reproductive Rituals: the Perception of Fertility in England from the Sixteenth Century to the Nineteenth Century* (London and New York, 1984).

———, *A History of Contraception from Antiquity to the Present Day* (Oxford, 1990).

Mohr, James, *Abortion in America* (New York and Oxford, 1978).

Moscucci, Ornella, *The Science of Woman: Gynaecology and Gender in England 1800-1929* (Cambridge, 1990).
Müller, Karl, *Unser Heimatbuch* (Neuss am Rhein, 1967).
Nead, Lynda, *Myths of Sexuality. Representations of Women in Victorian Britain* (Oxford, 1988).
Neumann, Robert P., 'Industrialization and Sexual Behaviour: Some Aspects of Working-Class Birth Control in Wilhelmine Germany', in Robert Bezucha (ed.), *Modern European Social History* (Lexington, Mass, 1972) 270-98.
Niedermayer, Albert, 'Schwangerschaft, Abortus, Geburt', *Handbuch der speziellen Pastoralmedizin*, III (Vienna, 1950).
Niethammer, Lutz, 'Fragen - Antworten - Fragen. Methodische Erfahrungen und Erwägungen zur Oral History', in Lutz Niethammer and Alexander von Plato (eds), *'Wir kriegen andere Zeiten'. Auf der Suche nach der Erfahrung des Volkes in nachfaschistischen Ländern* (Berlin, 1985) 392-445.
——, 'Oral History', in Ilko-Sacha Kowalczuk (ed.), *Paradigmen deutscher Geschichstwissenschaft* (Berlin 1994) 189-200.
Noonan Jr., John T. (ed.), *The Morality of Abortion: Legal and Historical Perspectives* (Cambridge, Mass., 1970).
Nye, Robert A., *Crime, Madness and Politics in Modern France. The Medical Concept of National Decline* (Princeton, 1984).
Oakley, Ann, 'Wisewoman and Medicine Man: Changes in the Management of Childbirth', in Juliet Mitchell and Ann Oakley (eds), *The Rights and Wrongs of Women* (London, 1976) 17-58.
O'Brien, Mary, *The Politics of Reproduction* (London, 1981).
Oertzen, Monika von, '"Nicht nur fort sollst du dich pflanzen, sondern hinauf": Die Ärztin und Sexualreformerin Anne-Marie Durand-Wever (1889-1970)', in Eva Brinkschulte (ed), *Weibliche Ärzte: Die Durchsetzung des Berufsbildes in Deutschland* (Berlin, 1993) 140-52.
Oliver, Martin (ed.), *Killing the Child Within* (London and New York, 2007).
Paczensky, Susanne von (ed.), *Wir sind keine Mörderinnen* (Reinbek, 1984).
Paczensky, Susanne von and Renate Sadrozinski (eds), *Die Neuen Moralisten. §218 - vom leichtfertigen Umgang mit einem Jahrhundertthema* (Reinbek, 1984).
——, *§218. Zu Lasten der Frauen* (Reinbek, 1988).
Petchesky, Rosalind Pollock, *Abortion and Woman's Choice* (London, 1986).
Petersen, Vibeke Rützou, *Women and Modernity in Weimar Germany. Reality and Representation in Popular Fiction* (New York, Oxford, 2001).
Petro, Patrice, *Joyless Street. Women and Melodramatic Representations in Weimar Germany* (Princeton, 1989).
Petzina, Dietmar, Werner Abelshauser and A. Faust, *Sozialgeschichtliches Arbeitsbuch III., Materialien zur Statistik des Deutschen Reiches* (Munich, 1978).
Peukert, Detlev J.K., *The Weimar Republic. The Crisis of Classical Modernity* (London, 1991).
Planert, Ute, *Antifeminismus im Kaiserreich. Diskurs, soziale Formation und politische Mentalität* (Göttingen, 1998).
——, 'Der dreifache Körper des Volkes: Sexualität, Biopolitik und die Wissenschaften vom Leben', *Geschichte und Gesellschaft* 26 (2000) 539-76.
Porter, Roy, *The Greatest Benefit to Mankind. A Medical History of Humanity from Antiquity to the Present* (London, 1997).
——, *Quacks, Fakers and Charlatans in English Medicine* (Stroud, 2000).

Reagan, Leslie, '"About to Meet Her Maker": Women, Doctors, Dying Declarations, and the State's Investigation of Abortion, Chicago, 1867-1940', *The Journal of American History* 77 (1991) 1240-64.

———, *When Abortion Was a Crime. Women, Medicine, and Law in the United States, 1867-1973* (Berkeley, 1997).

Reed, James, *From Private Vice to Public Virtue. The Birth Control Movement and American Society since 1830* (New York, 1978).

Reese, Dagmar, Eve Rosenhaft, Carola Sachse and Tilla Siegel (eds), *Rationale Beziehungen? Geschlechterverhältnisse im Rationalisierungsprozeß* (Frankfurt a.M., 1993).

Regin, Cornelia, *Selbsthilfe und Gesundheitspolitk. Die Naturheilbewegung im Kaiserreich (1889-1914)* (Stuttgart, 1995).

Robert, Krisztina, '"All That is Best of the Modern Woman"? - Representations of Paramilitary Female War Workers in British Popular Culture, 1914-1930', in Jessica Meyer (ed.), *First World War and Popular Culture* (London, forthcoming).

Roper, Lyndal, 'Jenseits des linguisitic turn', *Historische Anthropologie* 7 (1999) 452-66.

Rowbotham, Sheila, *A New World For Women. Stella Browne: Socialist Feminist* (London, 1977).

Rowe, Dorothy, *Representing Berlin. Sexuality and the City in Imperial and Weimar Germany* (Aldershot, 2003).

Ryter, Annemarie, 'Abtreibung in der Unterschicht zu Beginn des Jahrhunderts. Eine empirische Untersuchung von Strafgerichtsakten des Staatsarchivs Basel-Stadt', unpubl. M.A. dissertation (Lizentiatsarbeit), (University of Basle, 1983).

Sarasin, Philipp, 'Mapping the Body. Körpergeschichte zwischen Kosntruktivismus, Politik und "Erfahrung"', *Historische Anthropologie* 7 (1999) 437-51.

Sauerteig, Lutz, *Krankheit, Sexualität, Gesellschaft. Geschlechtskrankheiten und Gesundheitspolitik in Deutschland im 19. und 20. Jahrhundert* (Stuttgart, 1999).

Scheiterhöfen, Suzette von, *Termination and the Self. The Dialectics of Failed Motherhood* (London and Munich, 1984).

Schlumbohm, Jürgen, Barbara Duden, Jacques Gélis and Patrice Veit (eds), *Rituale der Geburt. Eine Kulturgeschichte* (Munich, 1998).

Schlüpmann, Heide, 'Kinosucht', *Frauen und Film* 33 (October 1982) 45-52.

———, 'Aufklärung als Subkultur. Madame Lu, Die Frau für diskrete Beratung', in Malte Hagener (ed.), *Geschlecht in Fesseln. Sexualität zwischen Aufklärung und Ausbeutung im Weimarer Kino 1918-1933* (Munich, 2000) 131-53.

Schmidt, K.H.W., *Dabornaha. Die Geschichte eines Dorfes und seiner Landschaft* (Dauborn, 1984).

Schneider, Petra, *Weg mit dem Paragraphen 218! Die Massenbewegung gegen das Abtreibungsverbot in der Weimarer Republik* (Berlin, 1975).

Schönfeld, Christiane (ed), *Practicing Modernity. Female Creativity in the Weimar Republic* (Würzburg, 2006).

Schopper, Wolfgang, 'Erster Weltkrieg und Weimarer Republik', in Kreisausschuß des Landkreises Limburg-Weilburg et al., *Limburg-Weilburg. Beiträge zur Geschichte des Kreises* (Limburg en der Lahn, 1986).

Schulte, Regina, 'Infanticide in Bavaria in the Nineteenth Century' in Hans Medick and David Sabean (eds), *Interest and Emotion. Essays on the Study of Family and Kinship* (Cambridge, 1984) 77-102.

―――, *Das Dorf im Verhör. Brandstifter, Kindsmörderinnen und Wilderer vor den Schranken des bürgerlichen Gerichts Oberbayern 1848–1910* (Reinbeck, 1989).
―――, *The Village in Court. Arson, Infanticide, and Poaching in the Court Records of Upper Bavaria, 1848–1910* (Cambridge, 1994).
Scott, Joan W., 'Experience', in Judith Butler and Joan W. Scott (eds), *Feminists Theorize the Political* (New York and London, 1992) 22–40.
Seidler, Eduard, 'Das 19. Jahrhundert. Zur Vorgeschichte des Paragraphen 218', in Robert Jütte (ed.), *Geschichte der Abtreibung* (Munich, 1993) 120–39.
Shorter, Edward, *A History of Women's Bodies* (London, 1982).
Smith-Rosenberg, Caroll, 'The Abortion Movement and the AMA, 1850–1880', in *Disorderly Conduct: Visions of Gender in Victorian America* (New York, 1985) 217–44.
Soden, Kristine von, 'Verwünschungen und Prophezeihungen. Die Befürwortung des §218 in der Weimarer Republik', in Susanne von Paczensky (ed.), *Wir sind keine Mörderinnen!* (Reinbek, 1984) 38–48.
―――, 'Auf der Suche nach den fortschrittlichen Ärzten', in Susanne von Pazensky and Renate Sadrozinski (eds), *Die neuen Moralisten* (Reinbeck, 1984) 127–37.
―――, 'Auf dem Weg zur "neuen Sexualmoral"', in Johanna Geyer-Kordesch and Annette Kuhn (eds), *Frauenkörper, Medizin, Sexualität* (Dusseldorf, 1986) 237–62.
―――, *Die Sexualberatungsstellen der Weimarer Republik, 1919–1933* (Berlin, 1988).
―――, '"§ 218 – streichen, nicht ändern!" Abtreibung und Geburtenregelung in der Weimarer Republik', in Gisela Staupe and Lisa Vieth (eds), *Unter anderen Umständen. Zur Geschichte der Abtreibung* (Dresden and Berlin, 1993) 36–51.
Spector, Scott, 'Was the Third Reich Movie-Made?', *American Historical Review* 106 (2001) 461–84.
Spree, Reinhard, *Soziale Ungleichheit vor Krankheit und Tod. Zur Sozialgeschichte des Gesundheitsbereichs im Deutschen Kaiserreich* (Göttingen, 1981).
―――, 'Der Geburtenrückgang in Deutschland vor 1939', *Demographische Informationen* (1984), 49–68.
―――, 'Kurpfuscherei-Bekämpfung und ihre soziale Funktionen während des 19. und 20. Jahrhunderts', in Alfons Labisch and Reinhard Spree (eds), *Medizinische Deutungsmacht im sozialen Wandel* (Bonn, 1989) 103–22.
Staupe, Gisela and Lisa Vieth (eds), *Unter anderen Umständen. Zur Geschichte der Abtreibung* (Dresden and Berlin, 1993).
Stolberg, Michael, 'Medical Popularization and the Patient in the Eighteenth Century', in Willem de Blécourt and Cornelie Usborne (eds), *Cultural Approaches to the History of Medicine. Mediating Medicine in Early Modern and Modern Europe* (Basingstoke, 2004) 89–107.
Stollberg, Gunnar, 'Die Naturheilvereine im Deutschen Kaiserreich', *Archiv für Sozialgeschichte* 28 (1988) 287–305.
Stürzbecher, Manfred, 'Die Bekämpfung des Geburtenrückganges und der Säuglingssterblichkeit im Spiegel der Reichstagsdebatten 1900–1930. Ein Beitrag zur Geschichte der Bevölkerungspolitik', unpubl. Ph.D. (Berlin, 1953).
Tatar, Maria, *Lustmord: Sexual Murder in Weimar Germany* (Princeton, 1995).
Tilly, Charles, *Big Structures, Large Processes, Huge Comparisons* (New York, 1984).
Töngi, Claudia, 'Gewalt gegen Schwangere vor dem urnerischen Strafgericht des 19. Jahrhunderts: Zur sozialen Bedeutung von Gewalt und Aggression', in Barbara Duden et al., (eds), *Geschichte des Ungeborenen. Zur Erfahrungs- und Wissenschaftsgeschichte des Schwangerschaft, 17.–20. Jahrhundert* (Göttingen, 2002) 273–92.

Usborne, Cornelie, 'Abtreibung: Mord, Therapie oder weibliches Selbstbestimmungsrecht? Der Paragraph 218 im medizinischen Diskurs der Weimarer Republik', in Johanna Geyer-Kordesch and Annette Kuhn (eds), *Frauenkörper, Medizin, Sexualität* (Düsseldorf, 1986) 192-236.

_____ , 'The Christian Churches and the Regulation of Sexuality in Weimar Germany', in Jim Obelkevich, Lyndal Roper and Raphael Samuel (eds), *Disciplines of Faith: Studies in Religion, Politics and Patriarchy* (London, 1987) 99-112.

_____ , *The Politics of the Body in Weimar Germany. Women's Reproductive Rights and Duties* (London and Ann Arbor, 1992).

_____ , *Frauenkörper – Volkskörper. Geburtenkontrolle und Bevölkerungspolitik in der Weimarer Republik* (Münster, 1994).

_____ , 'The New Woman and Generation Conflict: Perceptions of Young Women's Sexual Mores in the Weimar Republic', in Mark Roseman (ed.), *Generations in Conflict. Youth Revolt and Generation Formation in Germany 1770–1968* (Cambridge, 1995) 137-63.

_____ , 'Wise Women, Wise Men and Abortion in the Weimar Republic: Gender, Class and Medicine', in Lynn Abrams and Elizabeth Harvey (eds), *Gender Relations in German History. Power, Agency and Experience from the Sixteenth to the Twentieth Century* (London, 1996) 143-76.

_____ , 'Abortion for Sale! The Competition Between Quacks and Doctors in Weimar Germany', in Marijke Gijswijt-Hofstra, Hilary Marland and Hans de Waardt (eds), *Illness and Healing Alternatives in Western Europe* (London and New York, 1997) 183-204.

_____ , 'Rhetoric and Resistance: Rationalization of Reproduction in Weimar Germany', *Social Politics. International Studies in Gender, State, and Society* 4,1 (1997) 65-89.

_____ , 'Female Voices in Male Courtrooms – Abortion Trials in Weimar Germany', in John Woodward and Robert Jütte (eds), *Coping with Sickness. Medicine, Law and Human Rights – Historical Perspectives* (Sheffield 2000) 91-106.

_____ , 'Women Doctors and Gender Identity in Weimar Germany (1918-1933)', in Anne Hardy and Lawrence Conrad (eds), *Women and Modern Medicine* (Amsterdam, 2000) 109-126.

_____ , 'Heilanspruch und medizinische Kunstfehler. Abtreibungen durch Ärzte in der Weimarer Republik: offizielle Beurteilung und weibliche Erfahrung', *Medizin, Gesellschaft und Geschichte*, 19 (2001) 95-122.

_____ , '"Gestocktes Blut" oder "verfallen"? Widersprüchliche Redeweisen über unerwünschte Schwangerschaften und deren Abbruch zur Zeit der Weimarer Republik', in Duden, Schlumbohm and Veit (eds), *Geschichte des Ungeborenen* (Göttingen 2002) 293-326.

_____ , 'Body Biological to Body Politic: Women's Demands for Reproductive Self-Determination in World War I and Early Weimar Germany', in Geoff Eley and Jan Palmowski (eds), *Citizenship and National Identity in Twentieth Century Germany* (Palo Alto, forthcoming).

Walter, Franz, Viola Denecke and Cornelia Regin, *Sozialistische Gesundheits- und Lebensreformverbände* (Bonn, 1991).

Ward, Janet, 'The Artifice of Becoming (Weimar) Berlin', unpublished paper delivered at the Interdisciplinary Conference, University of Michigan, 'Rethinking Weimar', April 2002.

Weeks, Jeffrey, *Sex, Politics and Society. The Regulation of Sexuality since 1800* (London and New York, 1981).

―――, *Making Sexual History* (Cambridge, 2000).

Weindling, Paul, *Health, Race and German Politics Between National Unification and Nazism, 1870–1945* (Cambridge, 1989).

Welch, David, 'The Proletarian Cinema in the Weimar Republic', *Historical Journal of Film, Radio and Television* 1 (1981) 3–18.

Wolf, Emmi and Klaus Hammer (eds), *Cyankali von Friedrich Wolf. Eine Dokumentation* (Berlin and Weimar, 1978; repr. Stuttgart, 1983).

Wolff, Eberhard, '"Volksmedizin" – Abschied auf Raten. Vom definitorischen zum heuristischen Begriffsverständnis', *Zeitschrift für Volkskunde* 94 (1998) 233–57.

Woycke, James, *Birth Control in Germany 1871–1933* (London, 1988).

Zohn, Harry, (ed.), *Germany? Germany! The Kurt Tucholsky Reader* (London, 1990).

INDEX

Abortifacients, 37
   traffic with, 21
Aborting women,
   agency of, 16, 17, 131-8, 144-48, 160, 205
   experience of, 25, 90-93, 127-62
   language of, 20, 22, 25, 126-62
   representation of, 27, 57, 64, 108, 129
   social class of, 20, 34, 38, 51, 102, 108, 128, 157
   testimony of, 30, 127-62
   as victims, 16, 17, 39, 41, 50-51, 53, 55, 57, 59, 70, 89, 91, 108, 203, 205, 224
Abortion
   attitudes to,
      Churches', 155, 166
      in dominant discourse, 30, 62-63, 71-76, 88, 139, 181
      by grassroot, 14, 154-62, 180-81
      in popular culture, 53-54, 62
      women's, 15, 136-48, 154-62
   by region
      in Bavaria, 23, 139-42, 146
      in Berlin, 110-13, 115-16, 118, 120, 122, 130-35, 142-44, 147-48
      in Hesse, 25, 163-200
      in The Netherlands, 18, 110
      in Saxony, 21, 112-14, 121, 145
   commercial, 129, 210
      advertising, 24, 87, 109, 127, 129, 138, 151-4, 173, 217, 220
      by doctors, 68, 72, 77, 85-87
      illegality of, 5, 152-54, 217
      by lay abortionists, 4, 111-16, 163-200
      personal recommendations, 177-78
      traders of abortifacients, 4, 129, 151-54, 207, 20
   criminal,
      for accomplices, 136, 219-20
      amnesties, 222
      appeals, 182-84, 198
      for attempted abortion, 134, 150, 164, 219
      for doctors, 78, 80, 86
      for financial gain, 136, 194, 220, 222
      for lay abortionists, 78, 93, 103, 131, 164
      for midwives, 118-19
      penalty of, 130-36
      for simple abortion, 104, 132, 164
   estimates, 3, 10, 64, 117
   experience,
      and class, 20, 21, 65, 125, 128, 212-3
      in countryside, 165-66
      and marital status, 187-92
      and welfarism, 22, 53, 129
   fees,
      doctors', 81, 85-87, 124
      lay abortionists', 86, 124-25, 163, 179, 194-5
   grounds,
      eugenic, 35-36, 59, 215-18
      medical/therapeutic, 8, 35, 45, 65, 76, 78, 80, 82, 87, 215, 217
      after rape, 35-36, 54
      social, 35, 45, 82, 89, 215
      women's rights, 59, 215, 224
   historiography, 4, 8-22, 127
      campaigning literature, 10
      church historians, 9
      demographers, 9, 10
      feminist scholars, 10, 11, 13, 15
      gender historians, 201
      history from above, 14, 127
      history from below, 15, 28, 127
      social history of medicine, 10
      welfarism, 11
   law,
      British, 1967, ix
      Dakota, 2006, ix

Index

law, Germany,
  1871, 1, 4, 5, 44, 49, 103, 134
  1926, 5, 44, 45, 49, 66, 85, 103–4, 134, 165, 215
  1992, 6
  changing pattern of, 1871–1992, 4
  Enlightenment, 13
  Federal Republic of Germany, 1976, 4, 6
  German Democratic Republic of 1972, 4, 6
  Supreme Court Decree of 1927, 5, 45, 66, 78, 215
  Third Reich, 5, 217–18
methods,
  anaesthetics, 67–68, 83, 89–90, 124
  catheter, 101, 140
  curettage, 67, 71, 77, 81, 90, 123, 149
  doctors', 67, 75, 123–24
  douche, 100, 139–40, 147–49, 158, 163, 193, 196, 199
  lamenaria, 67, 77, 88, 123
  lay practitioners', 45, 47, 50, 88, 111–14, 123–24
  lysol, 111, 115, 124
  syringe (Mutterspritze), 99, 111, 118, 139, 142, 147, 154, 159, 167, 174, 185, 192–93, 195–96
  women's, 99, 217, 224
morbidity and mortality of,
  caused by doctors, 68–69, 74–79, 99
  caused by lay abortionists, 99, 115, 197
  caused by puerperal fever, 54
  statistics, 54, 59, 70
practice of, 14, 15, 23, 64–93, 215
  location, 176
  self-induced, 33, 43, 47, 90, 99–102, 139, 145, 209, 221
reform movement, 5, 9, 38, 45, 50–51, 53–54, 66, 72, 94, 207
  for women's rights, 10, 80, 82, 91–92, 215
Accomplices, 14, 20, 47, 90, 92, 102, 125, 163, 165, 219
Adams Lehmann, Hope Bridges, 79–85, 91–92, 210
Agitprop, 31, 49
Alltagsgeschichte, 17, 20
Altenloh, Emilie, 62–63
Alternative medicine, 21
Androgyny, 61
Antinatalism, 65

Back-steet abortionists, *see* Lay abortionists
Banks, J.A, 9
Baum, Vicki, 29, 40, 54, 57

Benjamin, Walter, 42
Berger, Martin, 31, 34–35, 47, 59
Bergmann, Anna, 13
Berlin, image of, 39, 224
Berliner Illustrirte Zeitung, 40
Beß, Jane, 54
Bewitchment, fear of, 131
Birth control,
  abortion as, 9, 57, 166, 180–81, 184, 224
  and class, 213
  danger of, 13
  and demographic change, 12, 175
  in historiography, 8, 16, 203
  knowledge of, 9, 199, 213
  as life-giving force, 12
  and modernization, 12
  positivism and, 12
  as social construct, 12
  traffic with, 21, 65, 193
  see also names of individual methods
Birth rate, decline of, 13, 64, 136, 170–72, 208, 213–15
Blackmail, 51, 112
Blécourt, Willem de, 18
Body,
  alternative perceptions of, 136–38, 148, 154–62
  control of, 181
  history of, 17, 19, 137–38, 201–2
Braune, Rudolf, 29
Brecht, Bertolt, 23, 28, 58, 63
Bredel, Willi, 29, 38
Brodie, Janet Farrell, 16
Brookes, Barbara, 11, 15, 20
Brooks, Peter, 61
Browne, Stella, 11
Bruckner, Ferdinand, 29
Bumm, Ernst, 76, 101
Bund deutscher Frauenvereine, 3
Bund für Mutterschutz, 3
Burke, Peter, 17
Busch, Ernst, 58

Canning, Kathleen, 19, 136, 201, 214
Caretaker, 33, 36–37, 56, 105, 110–11, 147
Catholic associations, 44
Catholic Church, 211, 215
  dogma on abortion, 7, 21
  Papal Encyclical, 1931, 3, 6
Catholics, 71, 80, 206
Censorship, 45, 55–56, 62, 204, 207
Centre Party, 5, 107
Cervical cap, 213–14
Chamberlain, Mary, 15
Child abandonment, 11

Index

Children born out of wedlock, 31, 193, 208, 221
Christ, Lena, 212
Church, 52-53
Cinema, industry, 29, 40
Coil, 213
Coitus interruptus, 12, 213, 223
Communication network, female, 174-78
Communists, 30, 51
Communist Party of Germany (KPD), 3, 26-27, 30, 44-45, 47, 51, 58, 72, 84
  propaganda, 216
  youth movement, 205
Compulsory abortion, 5
Consent, informed, 83-84
Contraception, *see* birth control
Cook, Hera, 15, 209
Credé, Carl, 28-29, 42, 48-50
Creutz, Walter, 31
Criminal courts,
  Amtsgericht, 21
  Landgericht, 21, 133
Criminal proceedings, 130-36
  gender prejudice, 135
Cultural anthropology, 17
Cultural history, 21
Cyankali. §*218*, 23, 26, 29, 37-39, 42-44, 46-47, 49-50, 53-54, 56, 105, 203-4, 210, 213
Czarnowski, Gabriele, 5, 6, 216-17, 224

Death penalty for abortion, 5
Degeneration, 35, 39, 64, 145
Delschaft, Maly, 31-33, 59
Demographic change, *see* Birthrate, decline of
Denunciation, 68, 71-72, 78, 81, 131-32, 139-40, 165, 195-98, 215
Depression, 3, 31, 40, 104
  abortion prevalence in, 3, 39, 104
  and eugenics, 13
Dix, Otto, 57
Döblin, Alfred, 28-29
Döderlein, Albert, 74-75, 78, 82-83
Domansky, Elisabeth, 13, 214
Droop, Marie Louise, 54-55
Duden, Barbara, 19, 137, 201, 224
Dudow, Slatan, 58
Dührssen, Alfred, 8, 70, 99

Ebermayer, Ludwig, 8, 97
Eine von uns, 40
Einstein, Albert, 29
Eisner, Lotte, 30
Eugenics, 65, 138
  and abortion decisions, 5, 13, 35, 54, 64, 84-85, 135, 204, 221
  and medical literature, 36
  policy of, 107, 216-18
Evans, Richard J., 18
Expressionism, 30, 39

Fallada, Hans, 29
Family,
  image of, 39, 41
  institution of, 62
Family planning, *see* Birth control
Feminine hygiene articles, 20
Feuchtwanger, Lion, 29
Film,
  industry, 29
  silent, 28-29
Fink, Lotte, 84-85
First World War, effects of, 65, 179, 214, 223
  on abortion law reform, 1
  on the family, 214
  on women's role, 136, 214
Fisher, Kate, 15, 20, 203, 205, 207
Fleck, Marie-Luise, 54
Foetus, 53, 129
  miscarried, 139-43, 147, 159
Forensic pathology, 68
Fortune-tellers, 22-23, 110-11, 130, 132, 150, 162, 207, 224
Foucault, Michel, 201-2
Frankenthal, Käte, 215
Frauenarzt Dr Schäfer, 54, 56
Frauennot - Frauenglück, 47

Gender,
  cooperation between, 20, 166-67, 186-87, 191-92, 207
  doctors', 65, 71, 79-85, 91
  identity, 57
  relations, 10-11, 20, 186, 292
  roles, 135-36, 145
  women's preference for female attendants, 109-110, 210
Generational relations, 11, 57, 208
German Medical Association, 34, 42, 96
Gilgi - eine von uns, 23, 29, 35-42, 54, 57, 59-61, 63, 125, 203-4, 213, 224
Gittings, Diana, 20
Gordon, Linda, 10-11, 13, 209
Gräfenberg ring, 214
Grossmann, Atina, 13, 17
Grosz, George, 57
Grotjahn, Alfred, 89, 215

Hansen, Miriam, 62,
Harbou, Thea von, 29

Harvey, Elizabeth, 224
Health insurance funds, 6, 37, 71–72, 81–82, 86, 98, 101, 129
  fraud of, 86
  law concerning, 96, 223
Helene Willfüer, see *Stud. chem. Helene Willfüer*
Himes, Norman, 9
Himmler, Heinrich, 217
Hippocratic oath, 8, 71
Hirsch, Max, 213–4
Hirschfeld, Magnus, 31, 108
Hirtsiefer, Heinrich, 107
History of crime, 28
Hodann, Max, 108
Hofer, Franz, 37
Hoggart, Richard, 207

Illegitimacy, *see* Children born out of wedlock
Imperial Germany,
  abortion bills, 1, 3
  attitudes to abortion, 4, 13, 31
  films, 31
Infanticide, 11, 223
Inflation, effects of, 179–80, 195, 199

Jacoby, Georg, 31, 204
Jerouschek, Günter, 13
Jochimsen, Luc, 9
Joyless Street, 57
Jütte, Robert, 97

Kaes, Anton, 60
Kästner, Erich, 28, 44
Keitz, Ursula von, 16, 36, 38, 56, 204
Kerr, Alfred, 50
Keun, Irmgard, 23, 29, 35–36, 38–42, 60–61
Kienle, Else, 40, 215
Klabund, 28
Klauber, Leo, 70, 72–73
Knight, Patricia, 15
Kollwitz, Käthe, 23, 39, 48–49
Kosta, Barbara, 39, 41
KPD, *see* Communist Party of Germany
Kracauer, Siegfried, 30, 34, 41, 62
Krauß, Werner, 31, 33, 36
Kreuzzug des Weibes, 23, 31–32, 34–35, 38–40, 42–43, 47, 50, 54, 59, 63, 105, 203–4, 210, 213
Krey, Franz, 23, 29, 38, 54
Kuhle Wampe oder Wem gehört die Welt?, 23, 58, 205
Kurierfreiheit, 24, 95–97

Lasker-Schüler, Else, 29
Lay abortionists, 102–5
  careers of, 24, 94, 111–22, 192–95
  class of, 117
  commercialism of, 4, 37–38, 47, 86–87, 102–5, 109
  danger of, 54, 97, 99, 160
  gender of, 105–111
  hostility to, 15, 16, 17, 26, 33, 36–37, 46–47, 53–55, 62, 70, 102–4, 109
  law concerning, 103–5
  popularity of, 24, 117, 125–26
  professionalism of, 14, 112–13, 119, 122, 192–93, 199
  representation of, 26, 31, 33, 36–38, 43, 46–47, 107–8, 140, 200
  safety record of, 25, 37–38, 43, 47, 112, 114–22, 164, 192–94
  training of, 111–12, 122, 193
Lethen, Helmuth, 224
Levi, Giovanni, 17
Levy-Lenz, Ludwig, 102
Lex-Nehrlinger, Alice, 54
Liedtke, Harry, 31, 33, 35
Ligori, Alfons von, 7
Lönne, Friedrich, 7, 8, 76
Lüdtke, Alf, 22, 162

McLaren, Angus, 8, 9, 14, 166
Madame Bäuerin, 212
Madame Lu, die Frau für diskrete Beratung, 37, 60, 150, 210, 213
Marcuse, Max, 127–28, 155, 199, 205–6, 208, 211–14, 224
Maria und der Paragraph, 23, 51, 54, 203, 213
Marriage,
  institution of, 57, 62
  trial, 57
Martin, Emily, 18, 138, 156
Mass culture, 27–29, 62
  critique of, 42
Medical Law of 1871, 70
Medical profession,
  abortion discourse, 59, 64, 70–71
  and abortion law reform, 4, 35, 54, 65–76, 94
  abortion policy of, 24, 87–90
  abortion practice, 14, 55, 65, 69, 74–79, 87–90, 223
  attitude to lay abortionists, 8, 24, 65–66, 70, 92–99
  and birth control, 65
  blunders, 66,
  commercial interests of, 72
  conservative members, 70

criticism of, 60
as expert witnesses, 67, 75, 78, 83
gynaecologists, 67, 69, 74, 76, 80, 86
hegemony of, 15, 66, 69-70, 211
influence on health policy, 64
judicial leniency towards, 78, 80, 93
malpractice or negligence, 67-69, 74-49
medicalization process, 23, 36, 62, 69, 96, 128, 137, 139-40, 143, 145, 160-61, 209
new medical findings, 7,
numbers of newly qualified members, 98
professionalization process, 22, 69, 94-96, 211
representation of, 31
right to terminate pregnancy, 65, 80, 82, 87
role of, 23, 96
socialist doctors, 65
status of, 24, 65, 92
training, 67, 74, 76, 93
women members, 65, 71, 79-85, 91, 210
women's encounter with, 16, 89, 91-93, 125
Mehring, Walter, 28
Melodrama, 61-62
Mensinga diaphragm, 213
Menstruation,
attitudes to, 88, 137, 156
obstructed/delayed, 129, 141, 144, 146, 148-52, 154. 157, 157, 159-60, 200, 207
restoration of, 134, 144, 146-47, 157, 193
Mental illness,
representation of, 33, 35-36
Microhistory, 17
Midwives, 24, 70, 78, 87, 89, 91, 105, 109, 111, 118-19, 121, 124, 140-41, 153, 158, 197, 209, 211, 217
hostility to, 81-82, 88
Misogyny, 57
Modernity, 22, 62
in art, 57
of Weimar Republic, 27, 39, 40-41, 128, 203, 212, 223
Mohr, James, 13
Montage, 59
Mosheim, Grete, 46
Motherhood,
ideology, 22, 137, 157
unmarried, 33, 35, 39-40, 54

National Socialist,
Germany, 5, 203, 216-23
ideology, 216

Nature therapy, 112-14
New Sobriety/Objectivity, 30, 53, 61
New Woman, 11, 35, 40-41, 57-59, 61-62, 145, 204, 211, 223-24
Nurses, 87

O'Brien, Mary, 13
Oswald, Richard, 31
§218. Gequälte Menschen, 42, 48-49

Patriarchy, 57, 60, 133, 204
Penal code, 34
reform of, 1, 66
Personal Data Protection, x
Petitions for legal reform, 1
Petro, Patrice, 40, 57, 61-62
Piscator, Erwin, 28, 43, 48-50
Planert, Ute, 13
Polano, Oskar, 205-6, 211-13, 224
Pollack Petchesky, Rosalind, 11, 13, 15
Popular culture, 20, 23, 24, 57, 63, 203-4, 224
abortion represented in, 4, 26-63, 137, 205, 210
women and, 30
Popular protest against §218, 1, 2-3, 27, 172-73, 87, 207
Population policy, 35-36, 41, 64-65
Pornography, 55
law, 56
Pregnancy, diagnosis of, 129, 134, 139-42, 149, 150, 155, 181
Proletarian women, see Women, working-class
Pronatalism, 22, 65, 138
Prostitution, 57
Protestant Church, 6, 7, 21, 166, 211, 215

Quack abortionists, see Lay abortionists
Quackery, 35, 94-95
campaign against, 94-99
German Society for the Repression of, 97
law, 95, 97
number of practitioners, 96-97

Rape, 35-36, 54-56, 59, 89, 190, 198, 204
Rationalization, 22
of sexuality, 144-45, 215, 223
Reagan, Leslie J., 16, 134, 156
Regin, Cornelia, 97
Rehfisch, Hans, 28
Reichslichtspielgesetz, 55
Religion, organized,
attitude to abortion, 3, 6, 7
response to abortion law, ix, 6
Religious differences, 21, 165, 206, 210-1

Index

Revenge, 132
Revolution 1918, effects on,
  abortion law reform, 1
  women's status, 71
Riese, Hertha, 85
Robert, Krisztina, 204
Roman Catholic Church, see Catholic Church
Rowbotham, Sheila, 10, 11, 13
Rural communities, 167–73, 212

Sauerbruch, Ferdinand, 74–75
Schlichter, Rudolf, 57
Schlüpmann, Heide, 60, 62
Schneider, Petra, 9
Schnitzler, Arthur, 29
Schreiber-Krieger, Adele, 214
Schulte, Regina, 18, 137
Second World War, effects on,
  abortion law, 5
  abortion numbers, 221
Seidler, Eduard, 5
Sexual abuse,
  of aborting women, 89, 116, 124
Sexual advice centres, 16, 85, 107, 213
Sexual enlightenment films, 45, 55
Sexually transmitted diseases, 97, 146, 149
  laws to combat, 149
Sex reform, 59, 105–9
  movement, 17, 34, 39, 41, 51, 85
Sexuality,
  extra-marital, 57
  history of, 202
  new freedom of, 62
  women's, 30, 39, 57–58, 60, 62, 162, 207, 209, 215
Shorter, Edward, 11, 12, 13
Sick funds, see Health insurance funds
Simmel, Georg, 42
Single motherhood, see motherhood, unmarried
Der Sittenrichter. §218. Eine wahre Begebenheit, 55
Smith-Rosenberg, Carroll, 3, 9, 12
Social Democratic Party (SPD), 28, 30–31, 40, 47, 58, 80
  press, 44
Socialists, 42, 52
  writers and artists, 23, 28, 42–53
Soden, Kristine von, 16
Spectators, female, 40–42, 62–63
Spree, Reinhard, 95
Sterilization, 81, 83–85, 89, 92, 116, 124, 210
  National Socialist laws, 218
Stöcker, Helene, 2, 108–9
Stolberg, Michael, 137, 156

Streitberg, Gisela von, 2
Stud. chem. Helene Willfüer, 29, 40, 54, 57, 59, 204, 213, 224
Suicide, 135
Sympathetic magic, 22, 130, 132, 162, 224

Thiele, Hertha, 58
Thomas, Wendelin, 72–73
Tintner, Hans, 45
Tissé, Eduard, 47
Toller, Ernst, 28–29
Tucholsky, Kurt, 28, 52

Veidt, Konrad, 31, 33

Weeks, Jeffrey, 202
Weindling, Paul, 13
Weinert, Erich, 23, 28, 51
Welfare state, 144
White-collar workers, female, 41–42, 51
Winter, Georg, 8, 123, 145
Wise women, see Lay abortionists
Wolf, Friedrich, 23, 26, 28–29, 37, 40, 42–45, 47, 50, 215
Women/s,
  affluent
    abortion practice of, 128, 185
    representation of, 38
  emancipation, 62, 224
  married
    abortion practice of, 57, 102, 165
  middle-class
    abortion practice of, 128, 157, 165, 213
    representation of, 26, 38–40, 57, 213
  movement,
    abortion activism of, 3, 6,
    in Federal Republic, 9, 10,
    radical feminists, 58
    in Weimar Republic, 1, 2, 9, 34, 53, 57
  role, 25, 208, 210
  unmarried,
    abortion practice of, 102, 135, 139, 165, 187
  working-class, 23, 203
    abortion practice of, 108, 125, 127–28, 139–48, 207
    representation of, 26, 30–31, 35–36, 38–43, 48–51, 57–58, 108
Working-class culture, 24, 27, 129, 131, 151
World League of Sexual Reform, 107–8
Woycke, James, 12, 13

Zille, Heinrich, 108
Zweig, Arnold, 29